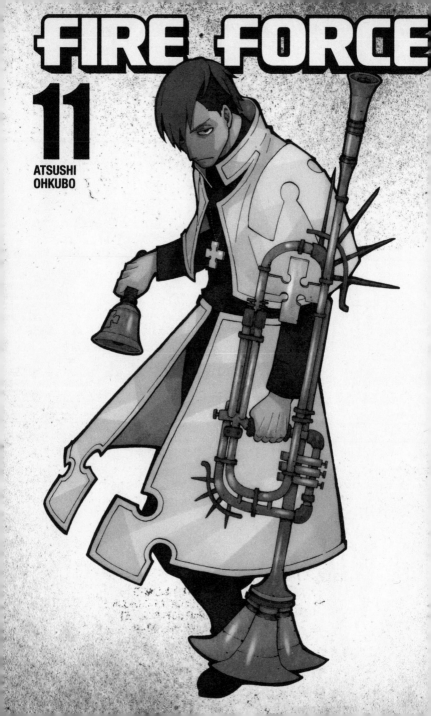

FIRE FORCE

11

ATSUSHI
OHKUBO

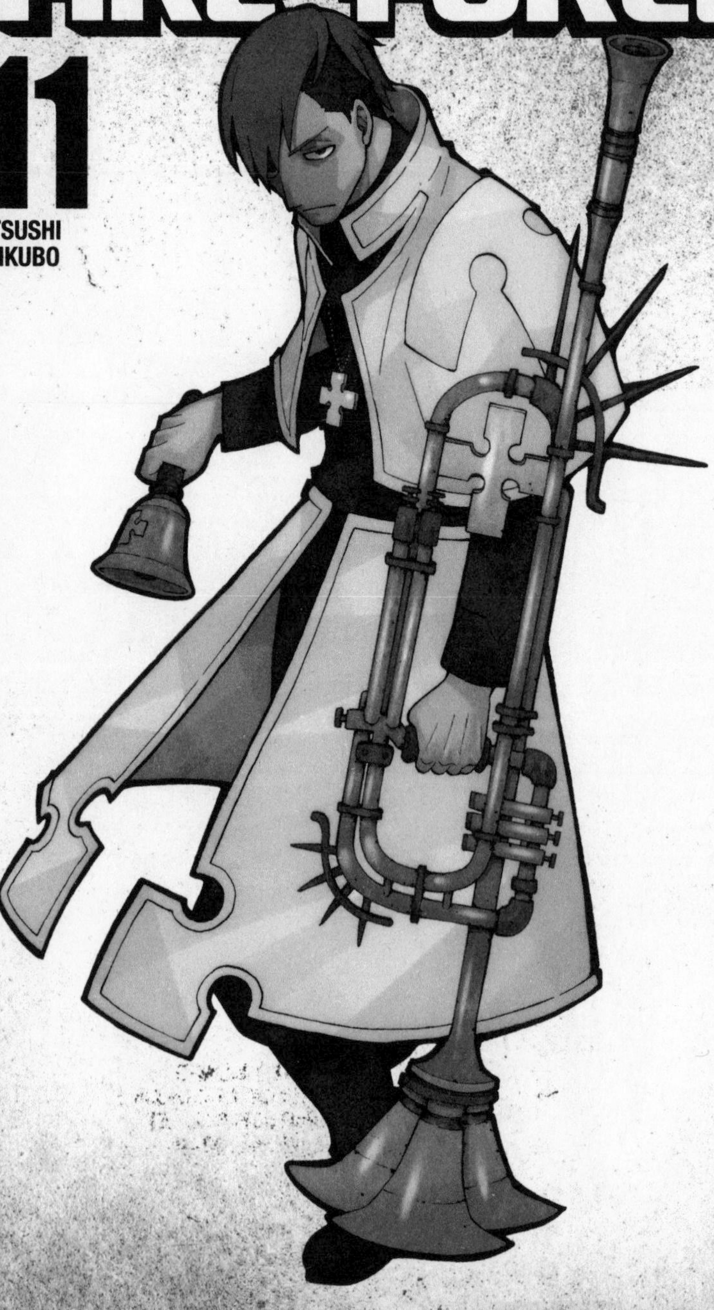

Ready Truth?

VOL.11

ATSUSHI OHKUBO

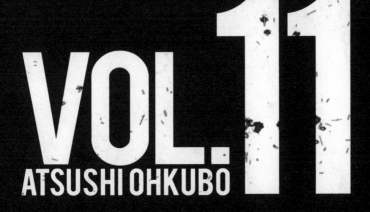

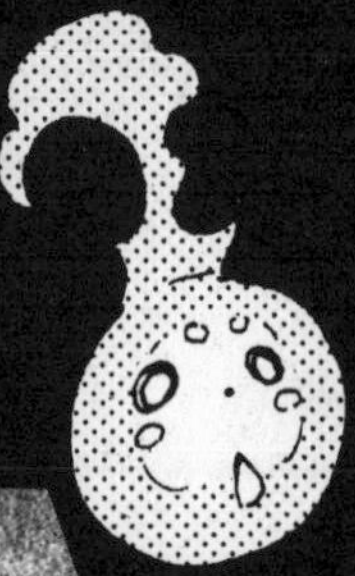

Are You
For The

FIRE
FORCE

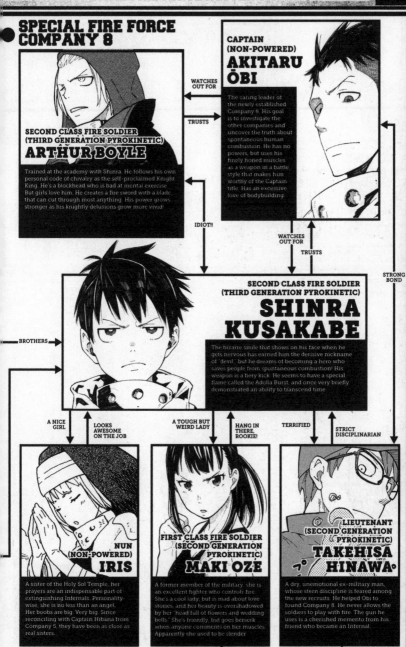

SPECIAL FIRE FORCE COMPANY 8

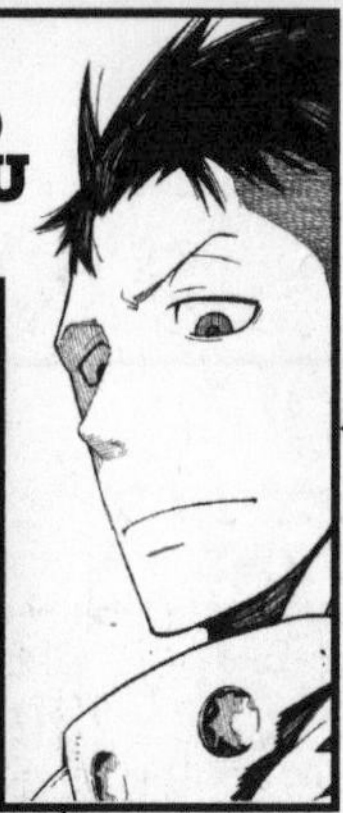

CAPTAIN
(NON-POWERED)
AKITARU ŌBI

The caring leader of the newly established Company 8. His goal is to investigate the other companies and uncover the truth about spontaneous human combustion. He has no powers, but uses his finely honed muscles as a weapon in a battle style that makes him worthy of the Captain title. Has an excessive love of bodybuilding.

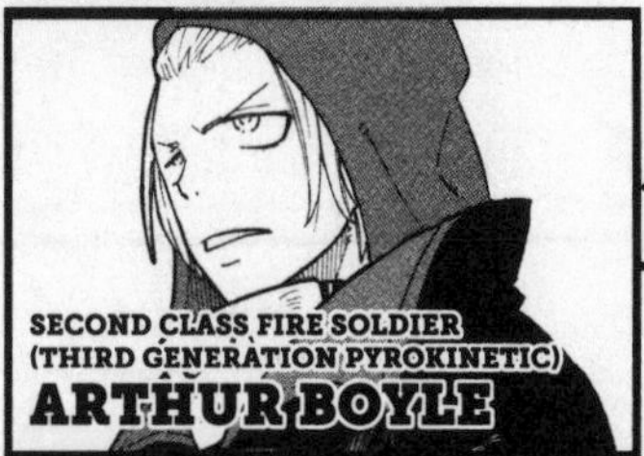

SECOND CLASS FIRE SOLDIER
(THIRD GENERATION PYROKINETIC)
ARTHUR BOYLE

Trained at the academy with Shinra. He follows his own personal code of chivalry as the self-proclaimed Knight King. He's a blockhead who is bad at mental exercise But girls love him. He creates a fire sword with a blade that can cut through most anything. His power grows stronger as his knightly delusions grow more vivid!

WATCHES OUT FOR

TRUSTS

IDIOT!!

WATCHES OUT FOR

TRUSTS

STRONG BOND

BROTHERS

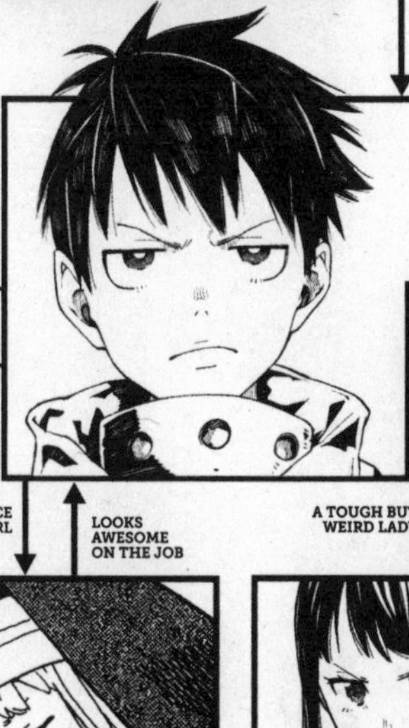

SECOND CLASS FIRE SOLDIER
(THIRD GENERATION PYROKINETIC)
SHINRA KUSAKABE

The bizarre smile that shows on his face when he gets nervous has earned him the derisive nickname of "devil," but he dreams of becoming a hero who saves people from spontaneous combustion! His weapon is a fiery kick. He seems to have a special flame called the Adolla Burst, and once very briefly demonstrated an ability to transcend time.

A NICE GIRL

LOOKS AWESOME ON THE JOB

A TOUGH BUT WEIRD LADY

HANG IN THERE, ROOKIE!

TERRIFIED

STRICT DISCIPLINARIAN

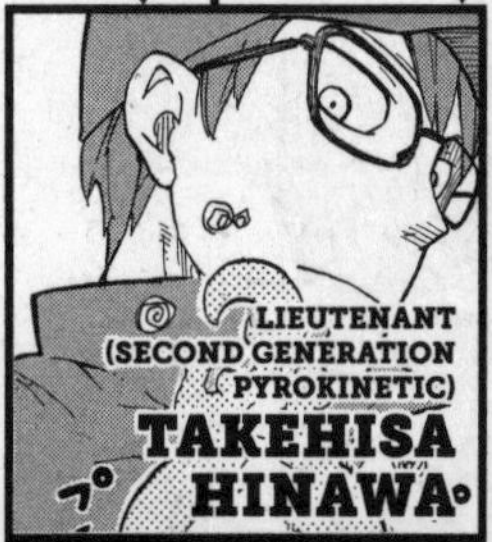

LIEUTENANT
(SECOND GENERATION PYROKINETIC)
TAKEHISA HINAWA

A dry, unemotional ex-military man, whose stern discipline is feared among the new recruits. He helped Obi to found Company 8. He never allows the soldiers to play with fire. The gun he uses is a cherished memento from his friend who became an Internal.

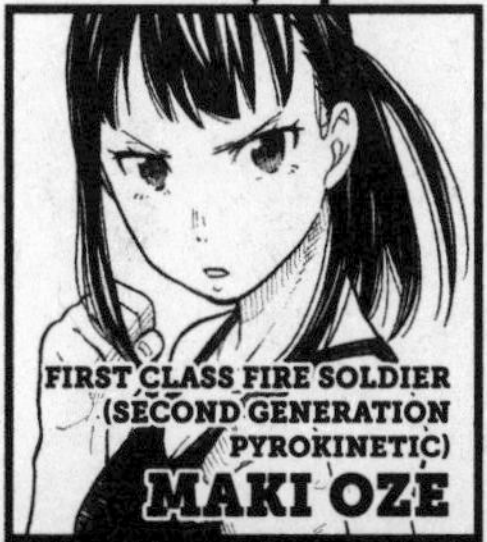

FIRST CLASS FIRE SOLDIER
(SECOND GENERATION PYROKINETIC)
MAKI OZE

A former member of the military, she is an excellent fighter who controls fire. She's a cool lady, but is mad about love stories, and her beauty is overshadowed by her "head full of flowers and wedding bells." She's friendly, but goes berserk when anyone comments on her muscles. Apparently she used to be slender.

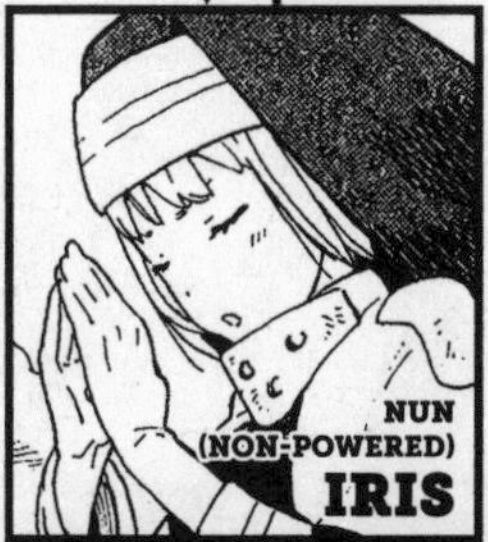

NUN
(NON-POWERED)
IRIS

A sister of the Holy Sol Temple, her prayers are an indispensable part of extinguishing Infernals. Personality-wise, she is no less than an angel. Her boobs are big. Very big. Since reconciling with Captain Hibana from Company 5, they have been as close as real sisters.

THE GIRLS' CLUB

RESPECTS

SPECIAL FIRE FORCE COMPANY 1

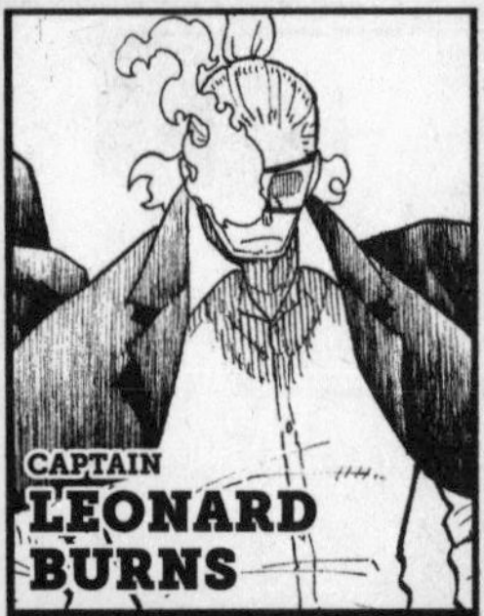
CAPTAIN
LEONARD BURNS

A fire soldier who ran to the scene of the fire that took Shinra's family when he was young. He commands the elite Company 1, and has overwhelming skill. He holds some kind of secret...?

FOLLOWERS OF THE EVANGELIST

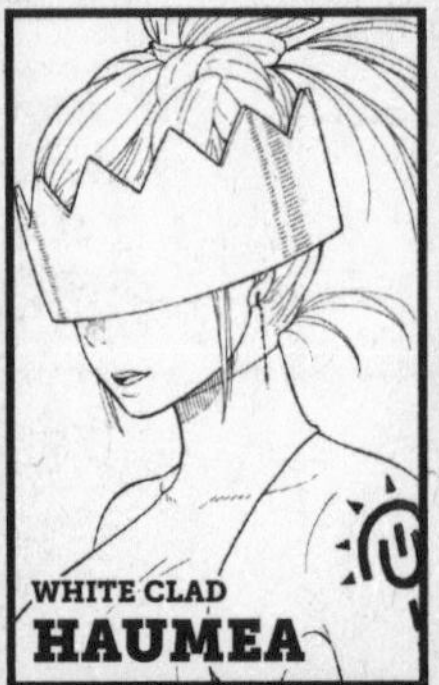
WHITE CLAD
HAUMEA

One of the Evangelist's white-clad combatants. After Shō begins to open his heart to Shinra, she neutralizes the knight commander with a power still shrouded in mystery and takes him back to the Evangelist.

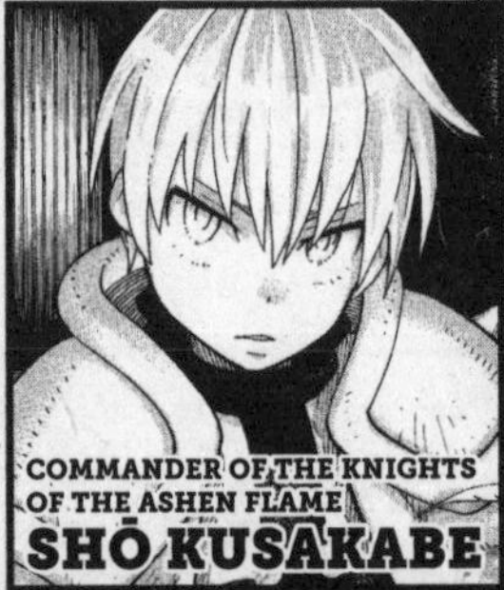
COMMANDER OF THE KNIGHTS OF THE ASHEN FLAME
SHŌ KUSAKABE

Shinra's long-lost brother, the commander of an order of knights that works for the Evangelist. He has the astounding ability to stop time for all but himself! Through a direct confrontation with Shinra, the two begin to regain their brotherly bond, but Haumea intervenes.

SPECIAL FIRE FORCE COMPANY 6

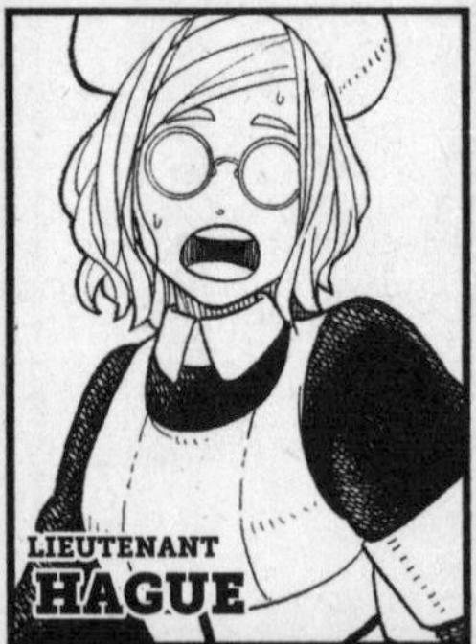
LIEUTENANT
HAGUE

A soldier at Special Fire Hospital 6, where Shinra was taken for emergency treatment after his fight with Shō. She has a mild-mannered personality, and her catchphrase is "Shock!!"

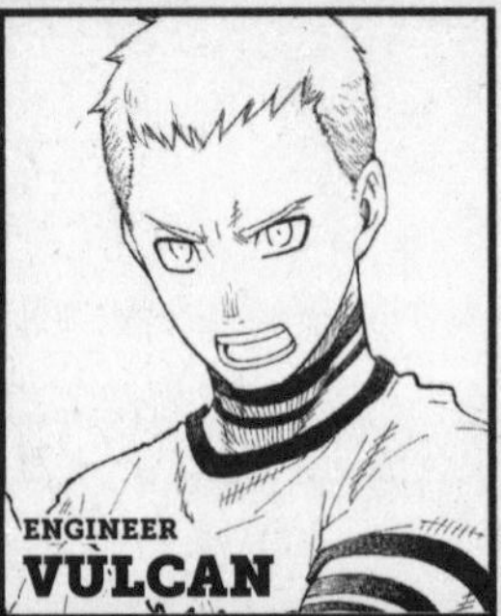
ENGINEER
VULCAN

The greatest engineer of the day, renowned as the God of Fire and the Forge. He originally hated the Fire Force, but he sympathized with Ōbi's and Shinra's ideals and agreed to join Company 8 as their engineer. His dream is to revive the world's extinct animals!

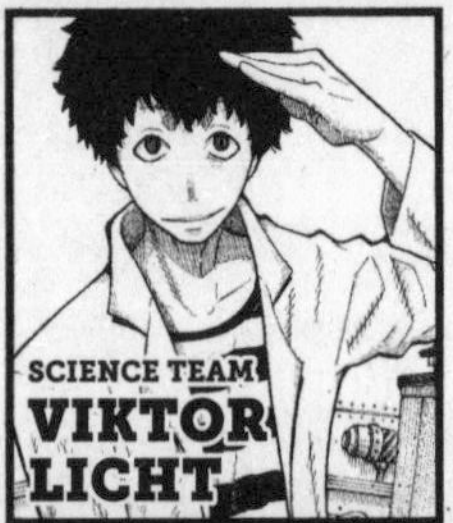
SCIENCE TEAM
VIKTOR LICHT

A morally ambiguous man deployed from Haijima Industries to fill the vacancy in Company 8's science department. Apparently a genius.

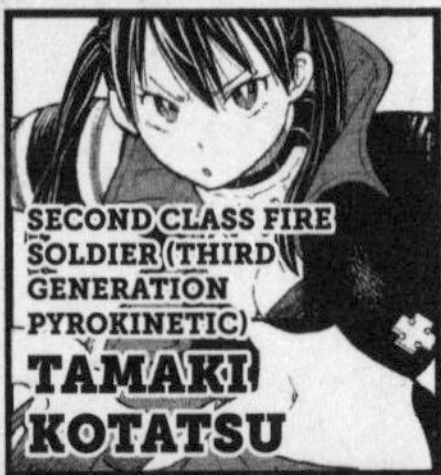
SECOND CLASS FIRE SOLDIER (THIRD GENERATION PYROKINETIC)
TAMAKI KOTATSU

Originally a rookie member of Company 1, she was caught up in the treasonous plot of her superior officer Hoshimiya, and is currently being disciplined under Company 8's watch. A tough girl with an unfortunate "lucky lecher lure" condition, she nevertheless has a pure heart.

SUMMARY...

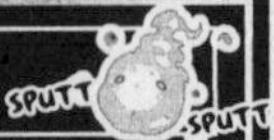
SPUTT
SPUTT

Shinra fights for his life after his touching reunion with Shō results in a possibly fatal injury. He is taken to Special Fire Hospital 6, a facility that specializes in treating pyrokinetics, and his life is saved. When he wakes from his coma, who should appear before Shinra but Captain Burns of Special Fire Force Company 1. He says he has come to discuss the fire that took Shinra's family 12 years ago, but what is he really after...?!

FIRE FORCE 11
CONTENTS

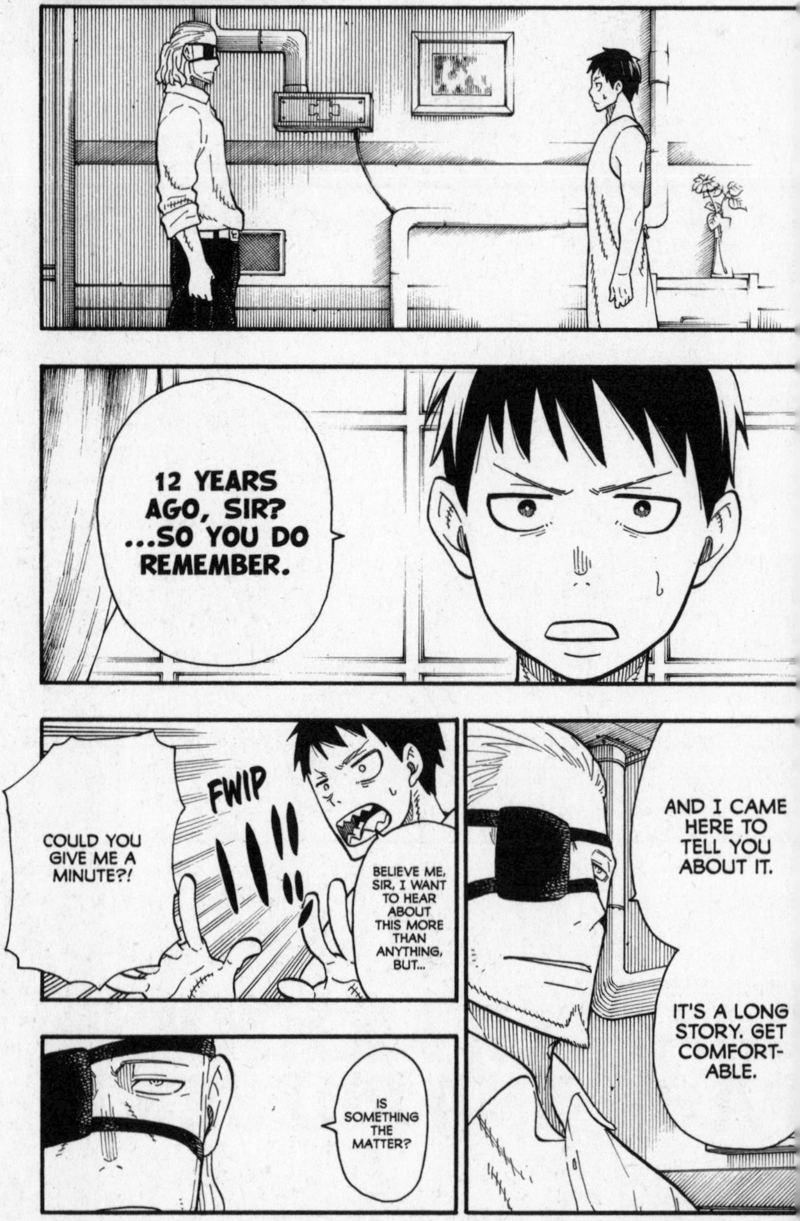
12 YEARS AGO, SIR? ...SO YOU DO REMEMBER.
AND I CAME HERE TO TELL YOU ABOUT IT.
IT'S A LONG STORY. GET COMFORTABLE.
BELIEVE ME, SIR, I WANT TO HEAR ABOUT THIS MORE THAN ANYTHING, BUT...
FWIP
COULD YOU GIVE ME A MINUTE?!
IS SOMETHING THE MATTER?

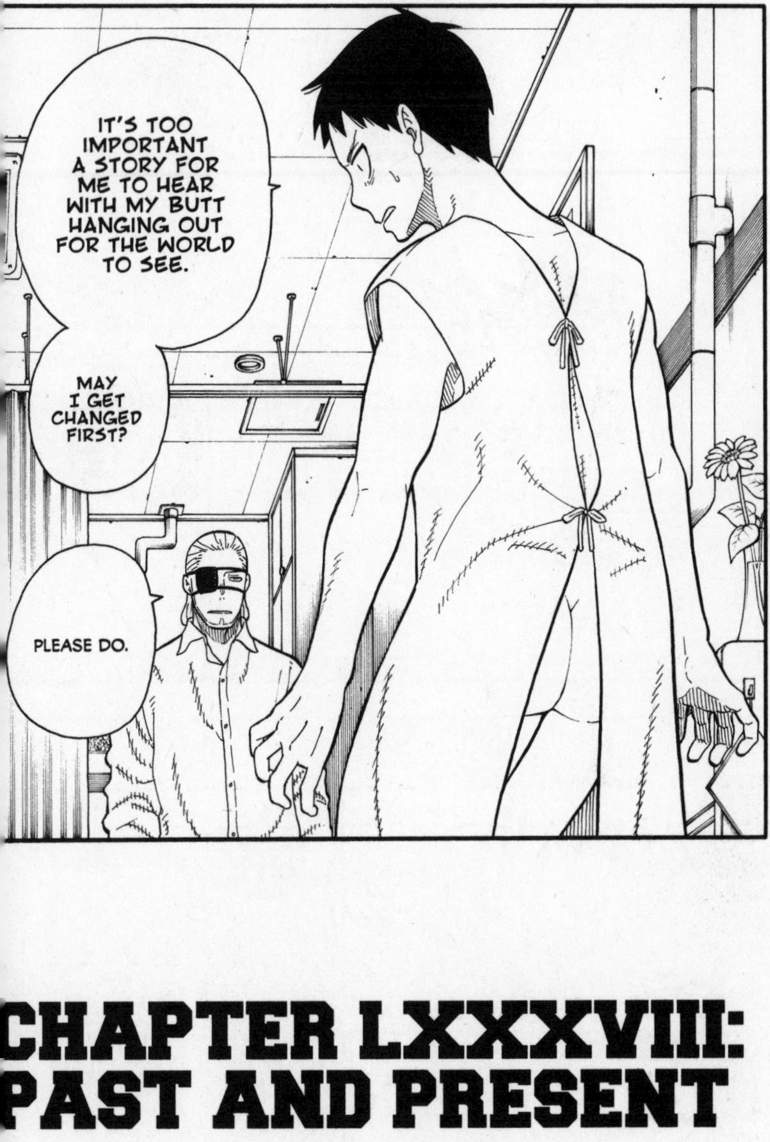
IT'S TOO IMPORTANT A STORY FOR ME TO HEAR WITH MY BUTT HANGING OUT FOR THE WORLD TO SEE.
MAY I GET CHANGED FIRST?
PLEASE DO.

CHAPTER LXXXVIII: PAST AND PRESENT

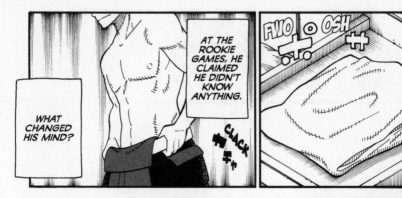

FWOOSH
AT THE ROOKIE GAMES, HE CLAIMED HE DIDN'T KNOW ANYTHING.
CLACK
WHAT CHANGED HIS MIND?
!
NO STITCHES OR ANYTHING. IT ALREADY LOOKS LIKE AN OLD SCAR.
I SAW THE COMPANY 6 CREST OUTSIDE THE WINDOW... SO I GUESS THEY'RE THE ONES THAT FIXED ME UP.
FIRE FO
6
TOKYO

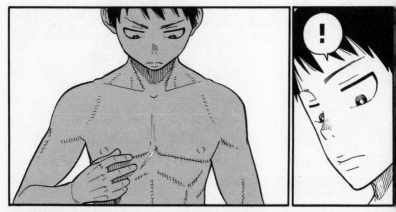

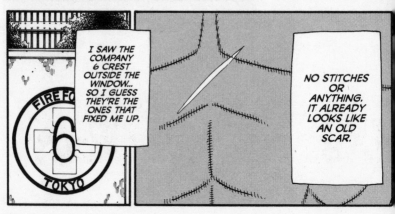

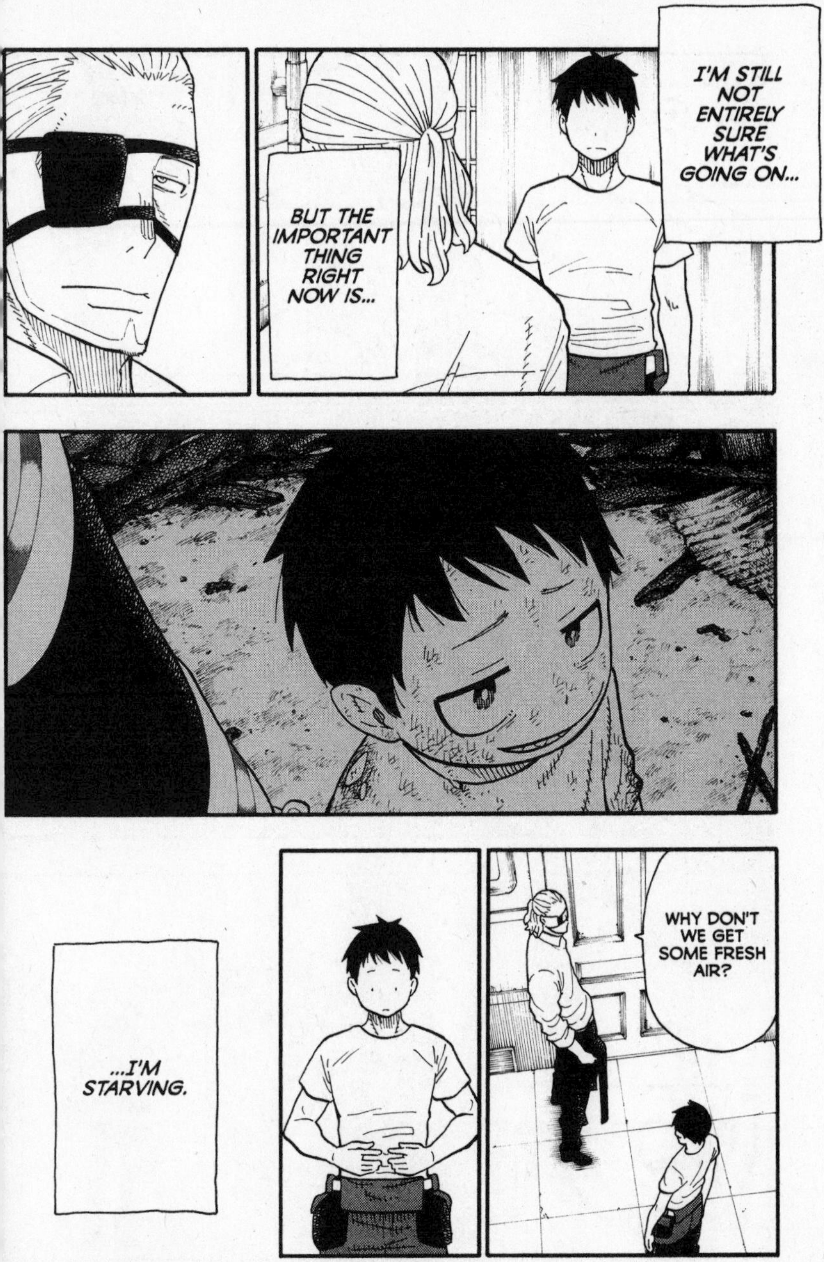
I'M STILL NOT ENTIRELY SURE WHAT'S GOING ON...
BUT THE IMPORTANT THING RIGHT NOW IS...
WHY DON'T WE GET SOME FRESH AIR?
...I'M STARVING.

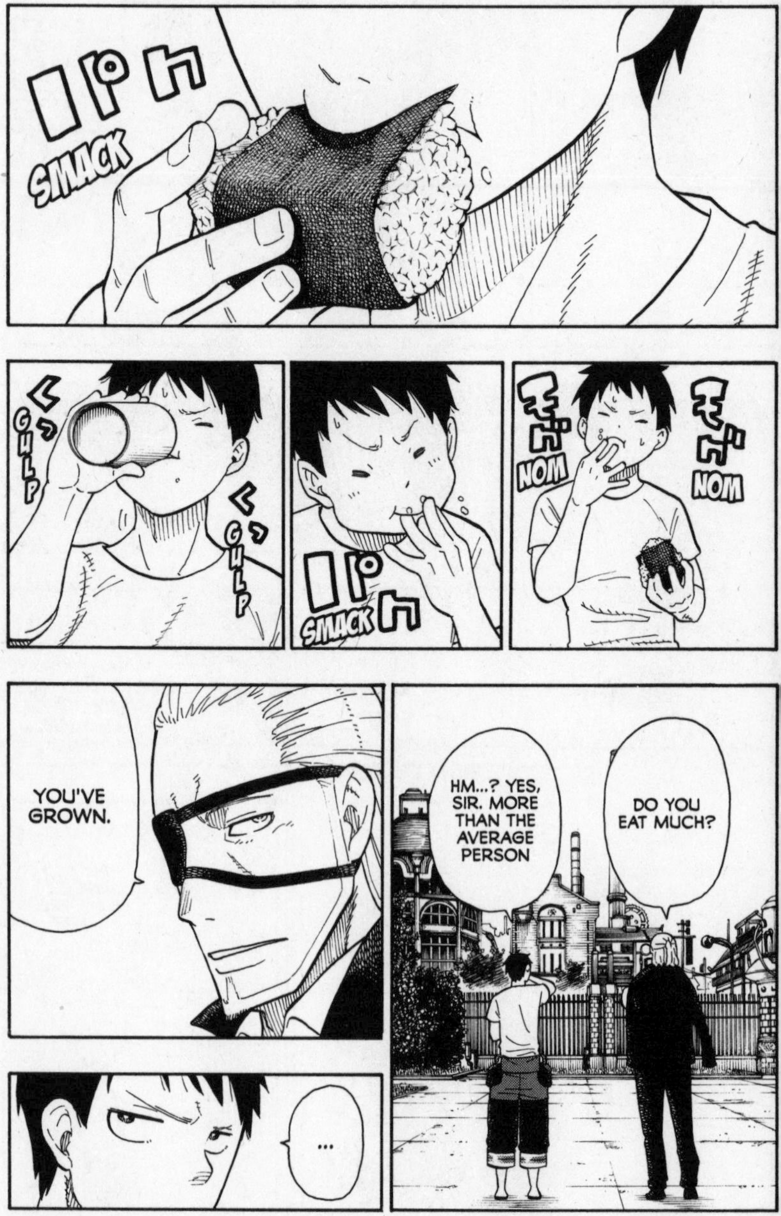
SMACK
NOM
NOM
SMACK
GULP
GULP
DO YOU EAT MUCH?
HM...? YES, SIR. MORE THAN THE AVERAGE PERSON
YOU'VE GROWN.
...

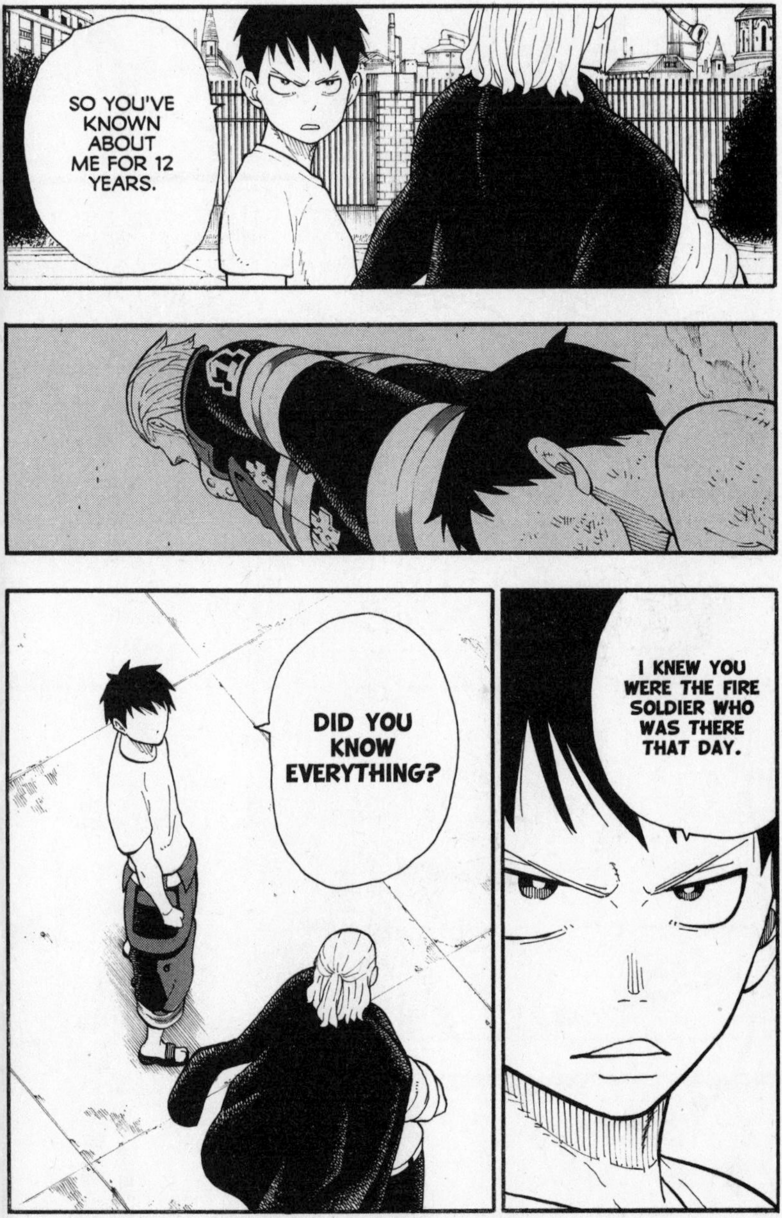
SO YOU'VE KNOWN ABOUT ME FOR 12 YEARS.
I KNEW YOU WERE THE FIRE SOLDIER WHO WAS THERE THAT DAY.
DID YOU KNOW EVERYTHING?

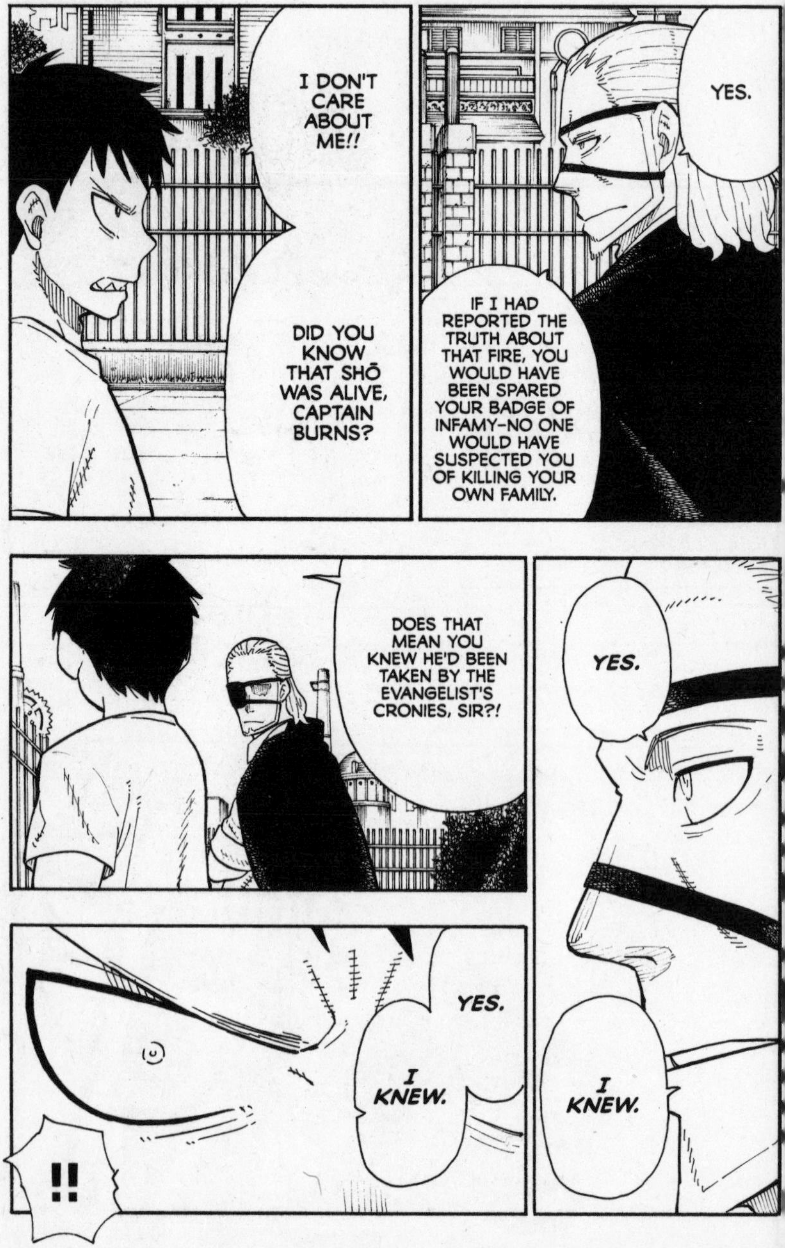
YES.
IF I HAD REPORTED THE TRUTH ABOUT THAT FIRE, YOU WOULD HAVE BEEN SPARED YOUR BADGE OF INFAMY–NO ONE WOULD HAVE SUSPECTED YOU OF KILLING YOUR OWN FAMILY.
I DON'T CARE ABOUT ME!!
DID YOU KNOW THAT SHŌ WAS ALIVE, CAPTAIN BURNS?
YES.
I KNEW.
DOES THAT MEAN YOU KNEW HE'D BEEN TAKEN BY THE EVANGELIST'S CRONIES, SIR?!
YES.
I KNEW.
!!

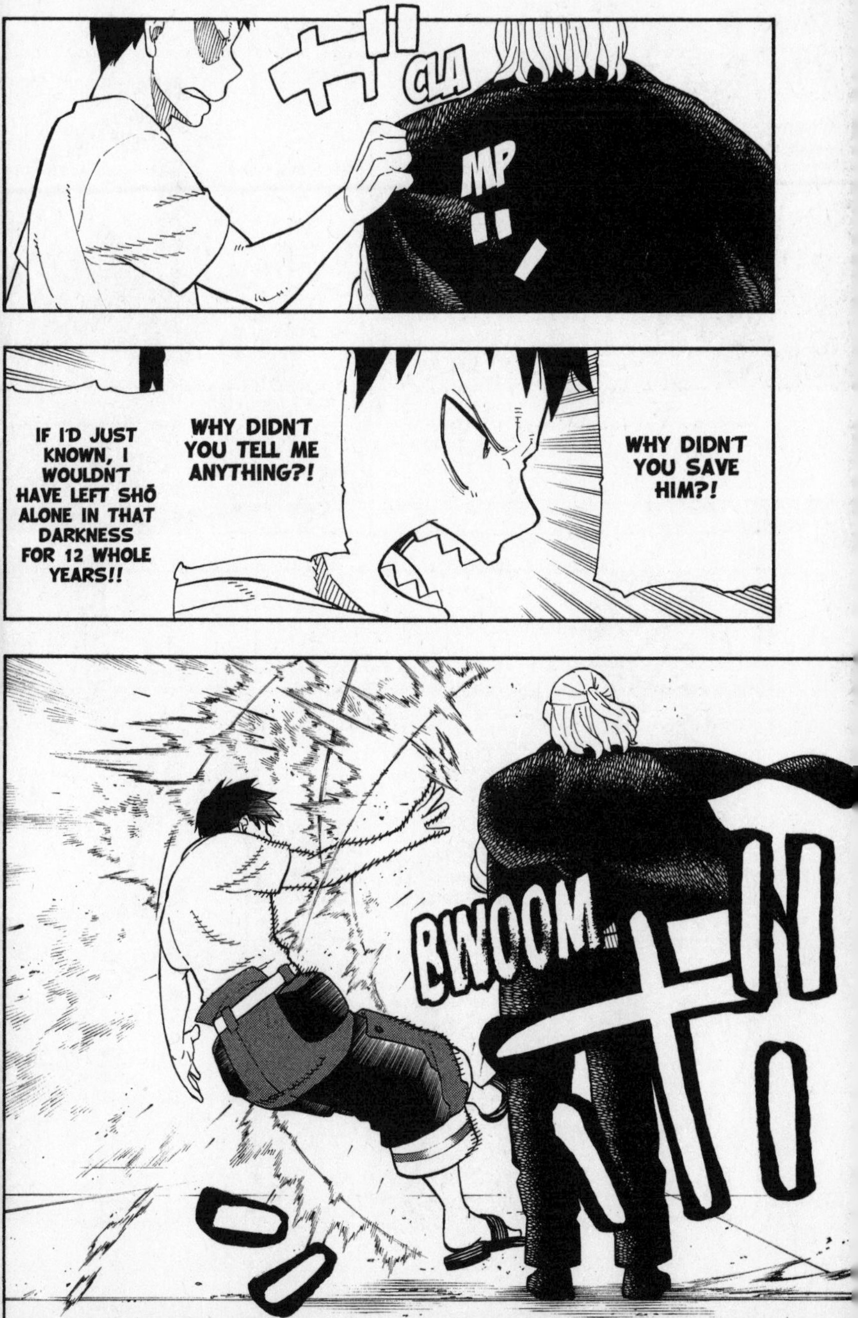
CLA
MP
WHY DIDN'T YOU SAVE HIM?!
WHY DIDN'T YOU TELL ME ANYTHING?!
IF I'D JUST KNOWN, I WOULDN'T HAVE LEFT SHŌ ALONE IN THAT DARKNESS FOR 12 WHOLE YEARS!!
BWOOM...

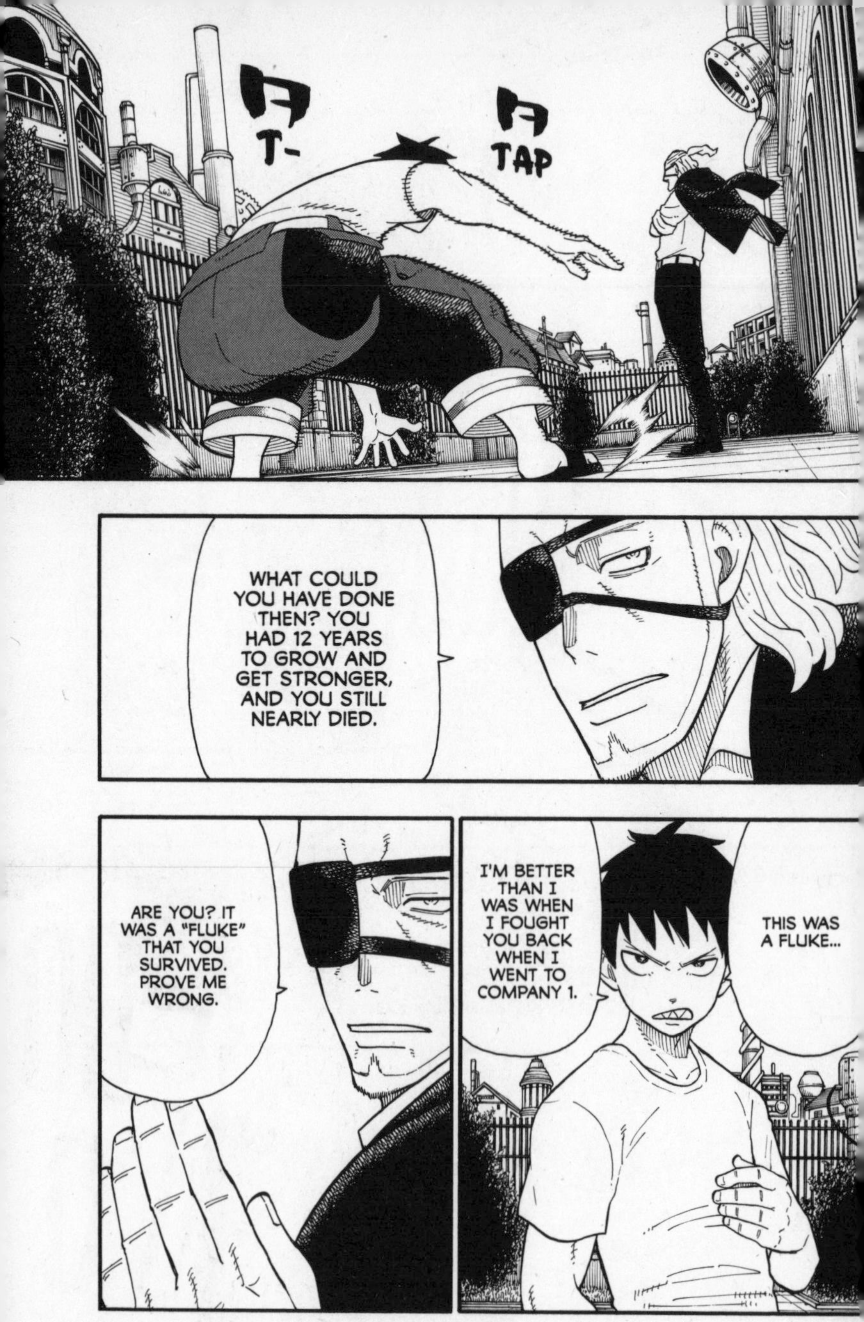
T- TAP
WHAT COULD YOU HAVE DONE THEN? YOU HAD 12 YEARS TO GROW AND GET STRONGER, AND YOU STILL NEARLY DIED.
THIS WAS A FLUKE...
I'M BETTER THAN I WAS WHEN I FOUGHT YOU BACK WHEN I WENT TO COMPANY 1.
ARE YOU? IT WAS A "FLUKE" THAT YOU SURVIVED. PROVE ME WRONG.

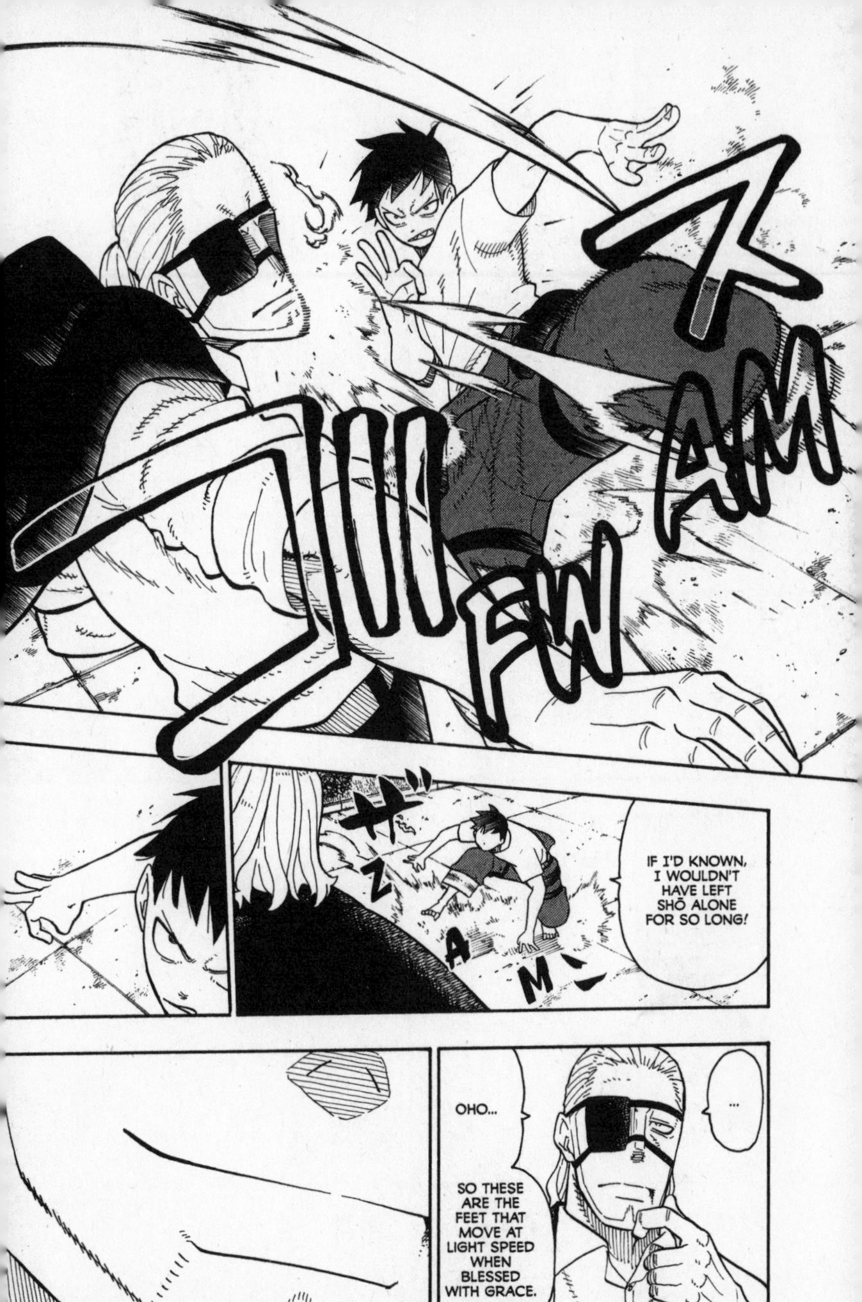
FWAM
IF I'D KNOWN, I WOULDN'T HAVE LEFT SHŌ ALONE FOR SO LONG!
...
OHO...
SO THESE ARE THE FEET THAT MOVE AT LIGHT SPEED WHEN BLESSED WITH GRACE.

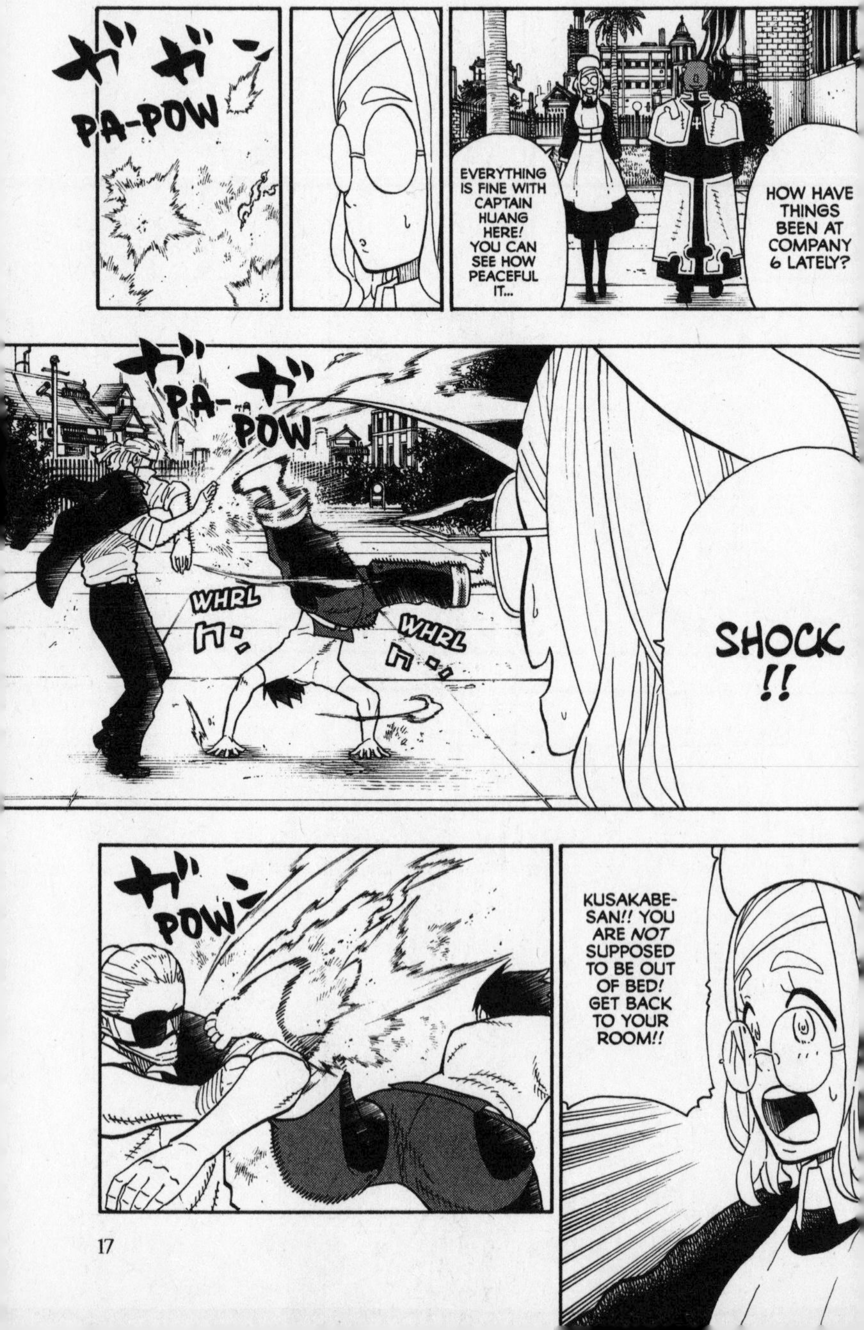
HOW HAVE THINGS BEEN AT COMPANY 6 LATELY?
EVERYTHING IS FINE WITH CAPTAIN HUANG HERE! YOU CAN SEE HOW PEACEFUL IT...
PA-POW
SHOCK!!
PA-POW
WHRL
WHRL
KUSAKABE-SAN!! YOU ARE *NOT* SUPPOSED TO BE OUT OF BED! GET BACK TO YOUR ROOM!!
POW

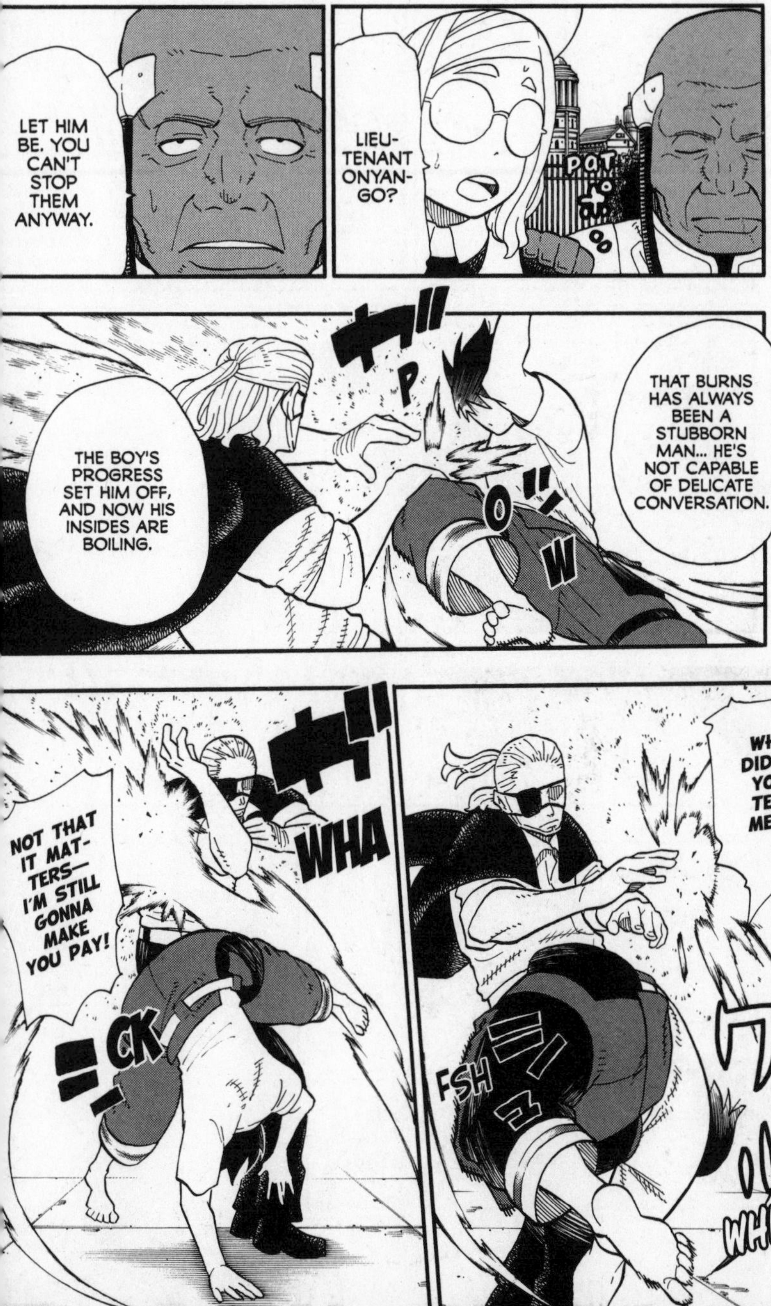
LIEU-TENANT ONYAN-GO?
pat
LET HIM BE. YOU CAN'T STOP THEM ANYWAY.
THAT BURNS HAS ALWAYS BEEN A STUBBORN MAN... HE'S NOT CAPABLE OF DELICATE CONVERSATION.
P
W
THE BOY'S PROGRESS SET HIM OFF, AND NOW HIS INSIDES ARE BOILING.
WHY DIDN'T YOU TELL ME?!
WHIRL
FSH
WHA
NOT THAT IT MAT-TERS— I'M STILL GONNA MAKE YOU PAY!
CK

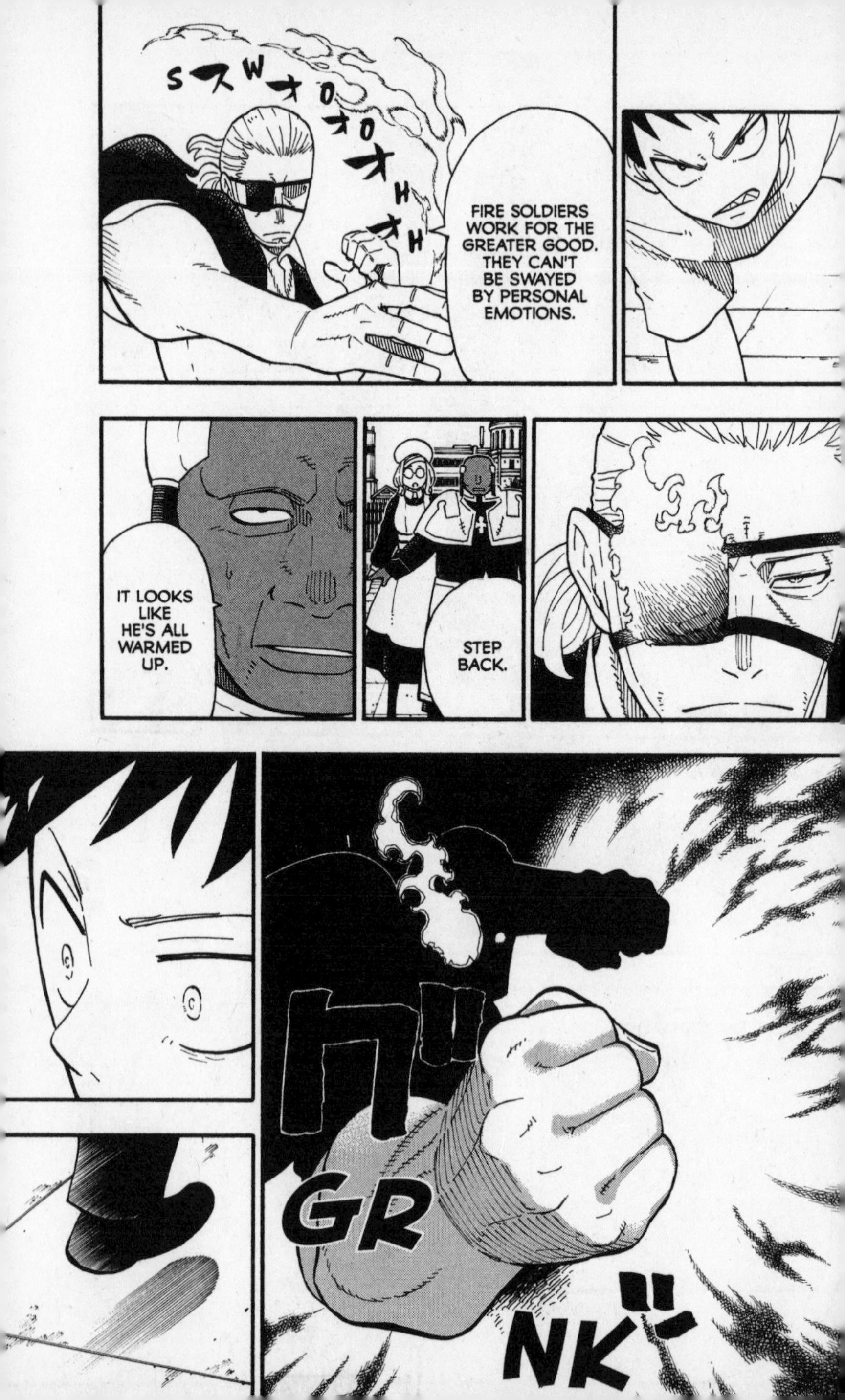
FIRE SOLDIERS WORK FOR THE GREATER GOOD. THEY CAN'T BE SWAYED BY PERSONAL EMOTIONS.
SWOOHH
STEP BACK.
IT LOOKS LIKE HE'S ALL WARMED UP.
GR
NK

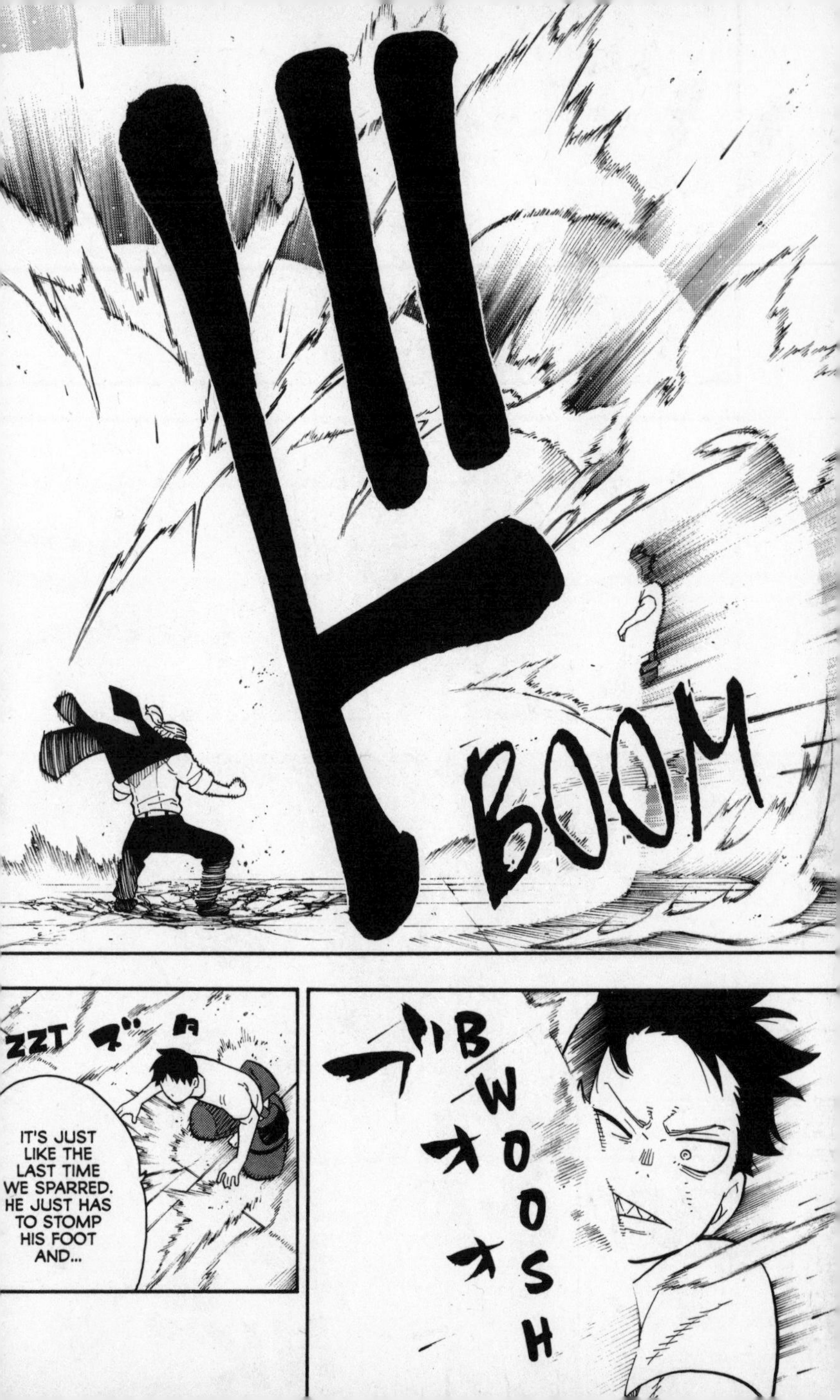
ド
BOOM
ブォォ
BWOOSH
ZZT
IT'S JUST LIKE THE LAST TIME WE SPARRED. HE JUST HAS TO STOMP HIS FOOT AND...

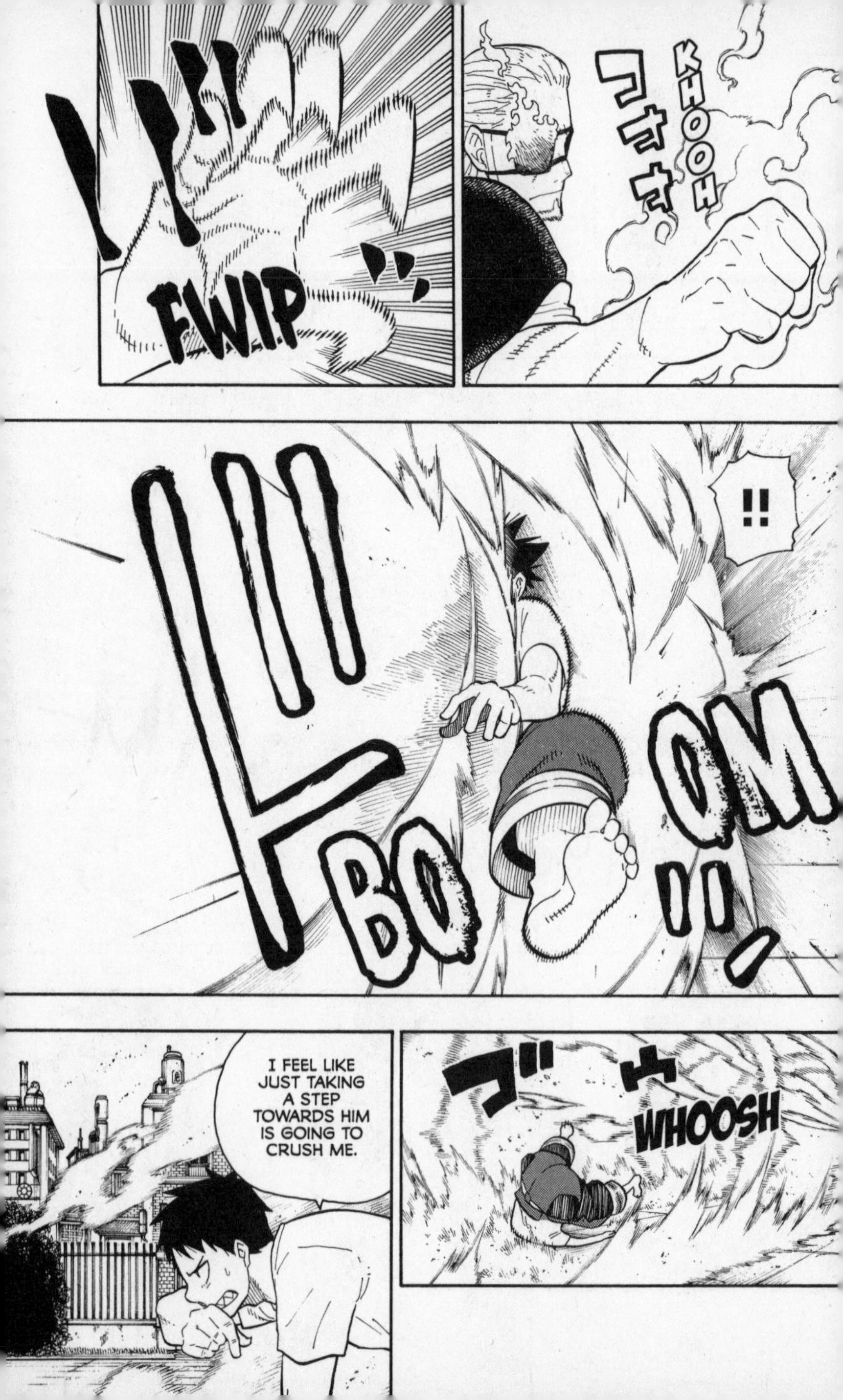

KHOOOH
FWIP
!!
BOOM!!
WHOOSH
I FEEL LIKE JUST TAKING A STEP TOWARDS HIM IS GOING TO CRUSH ME.

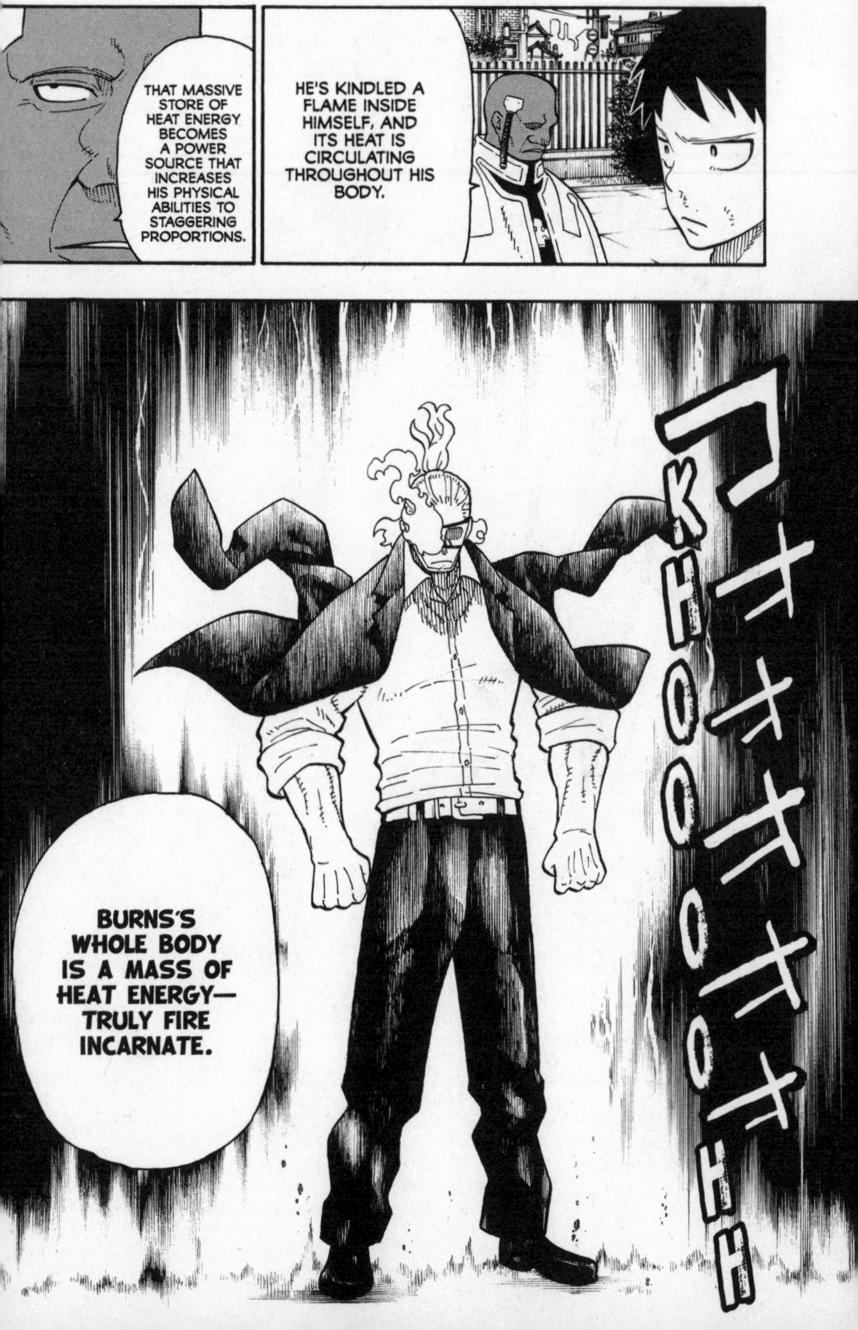
HE'S KINDLED A FLAME INSIDE HIMSELF, AND ITS HEAT IS CIRCULATING THROUGHOUT HIS BODY.
THAT MASSIVE STORE OF HEAT ENERGY BECOMES A POWER SOURCE THAT INCREASES HIS PHYSICAL ABILITIES TO STAGGERING PROPORTIONS.
KHOOOOHH
BURNS'S WHOLE BODY IS A MASS OF HEAT ENERGY—TRULY FIRE INCARNATE.

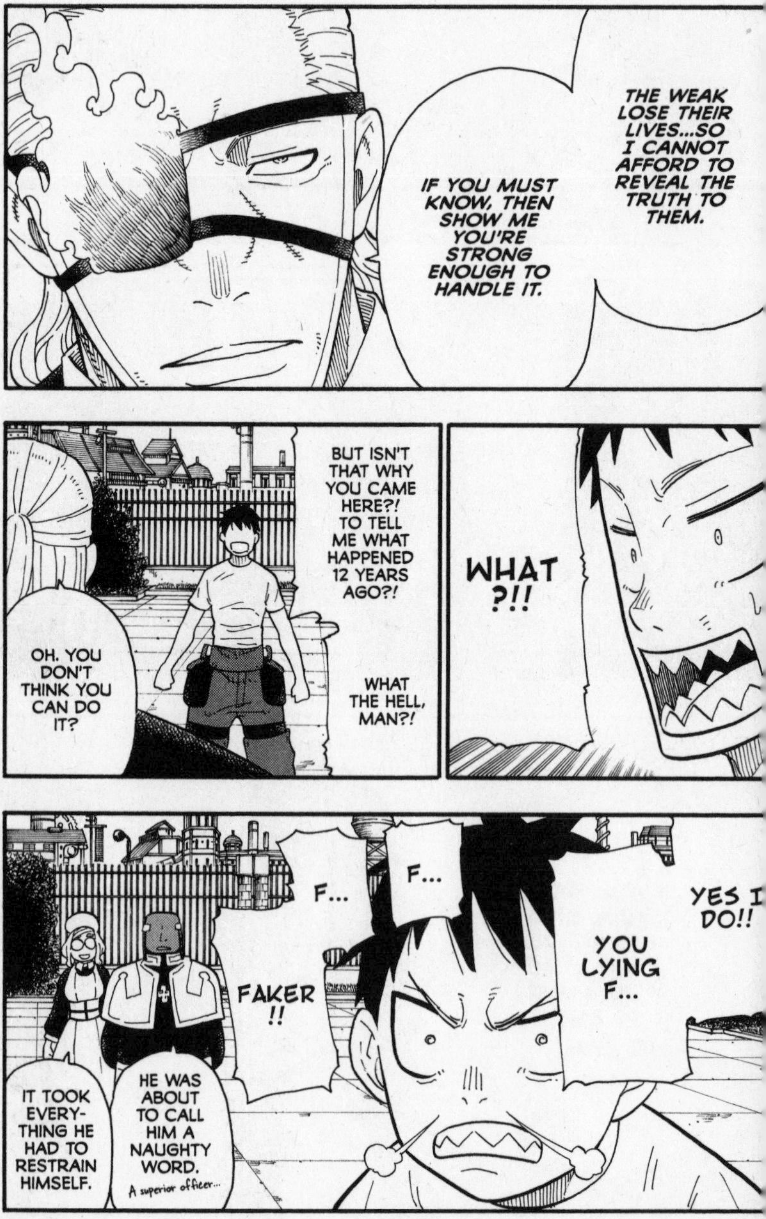
THE WEAK LOSE THEIR LIVES...SO I CANNOT AFFORD TO REVEAL THE TRUTH TO THEM.
IF YOU MUST KNOW, THEN SHOW ME YOU'RE STRONG ENOUGH TO HANDLE IT.
WHAT ?!!
BUT ISN'T THAT WHY YOU CAME HERE?! TO TELL ME WHAT HAPPENED 12 YEARS AGO?!
WHAT THE HELL, MAN?!
OH. YOU DON'T THINK YOU CAN DO IT?
YES I DO!!
YOU LYING F...
F...
F...
FAKER !!
HE WAS ABOUT TO CALL HIM A NAUGHTY WORD.
A superior officer...
IT TOOK EVERY-THING HE HAD TO RESTRAIN HIMSELF.

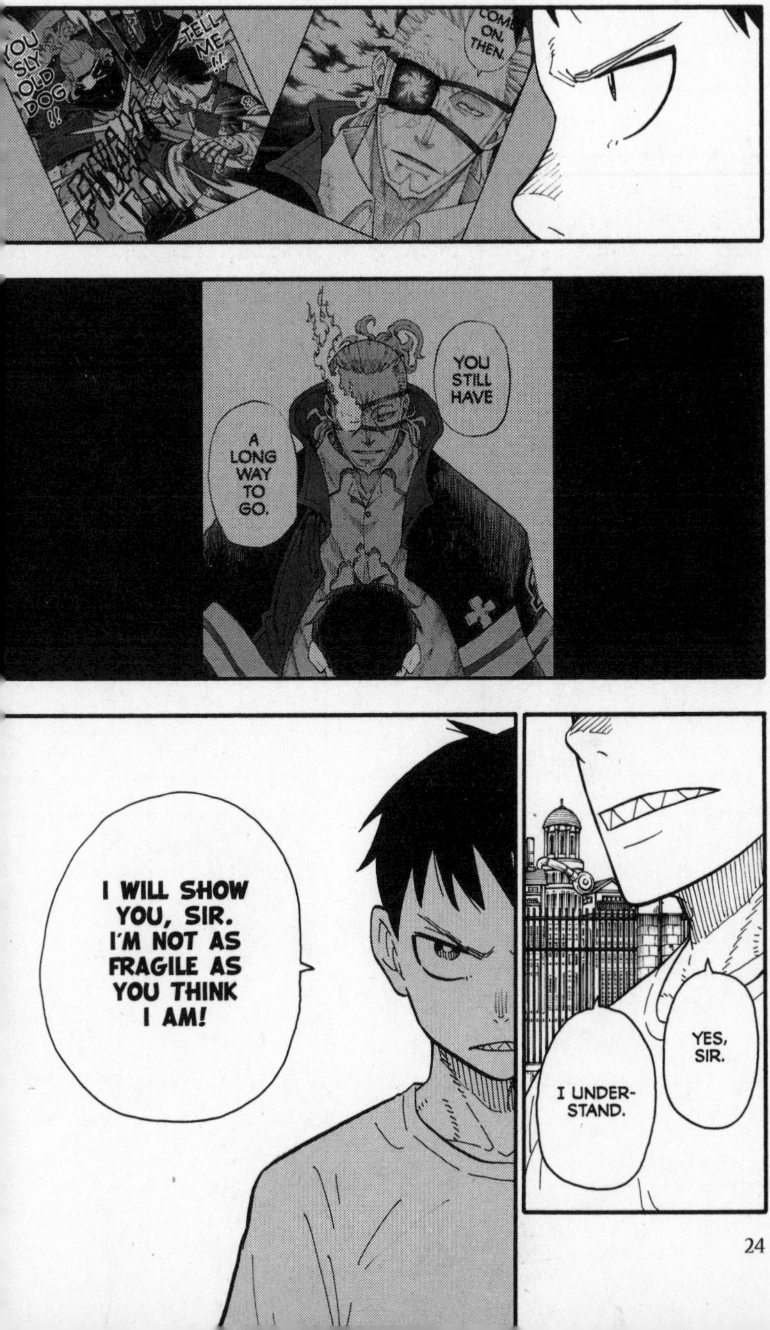
COME ON, THEN.
TELL ME!!
YOU SLY OLD DOG!!
YOU STILL HAVE
A LONG WAY TO GO.
YES, SIR.
I UNDER-STAND.
I WILL SHOW YOU, SIR. I'M NOT AS FRAGILE AS YOU THINK I AM!

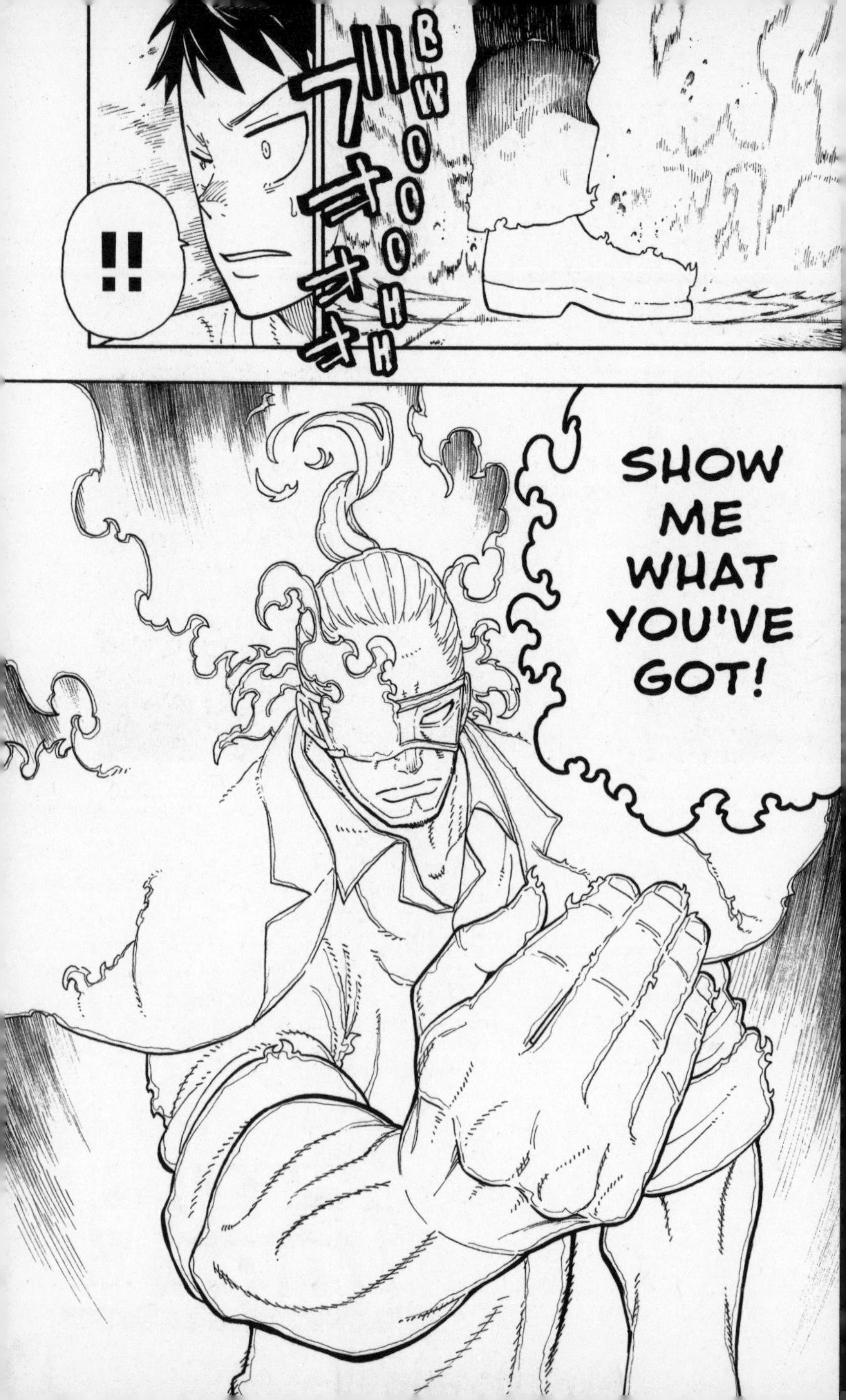
BWOOOHH
!!
SHOW ME WHAT YOU'VE GOT!

FIRE FORCE

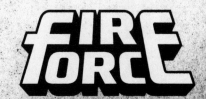

CHAPTER LXXXIX: FIERY PAST

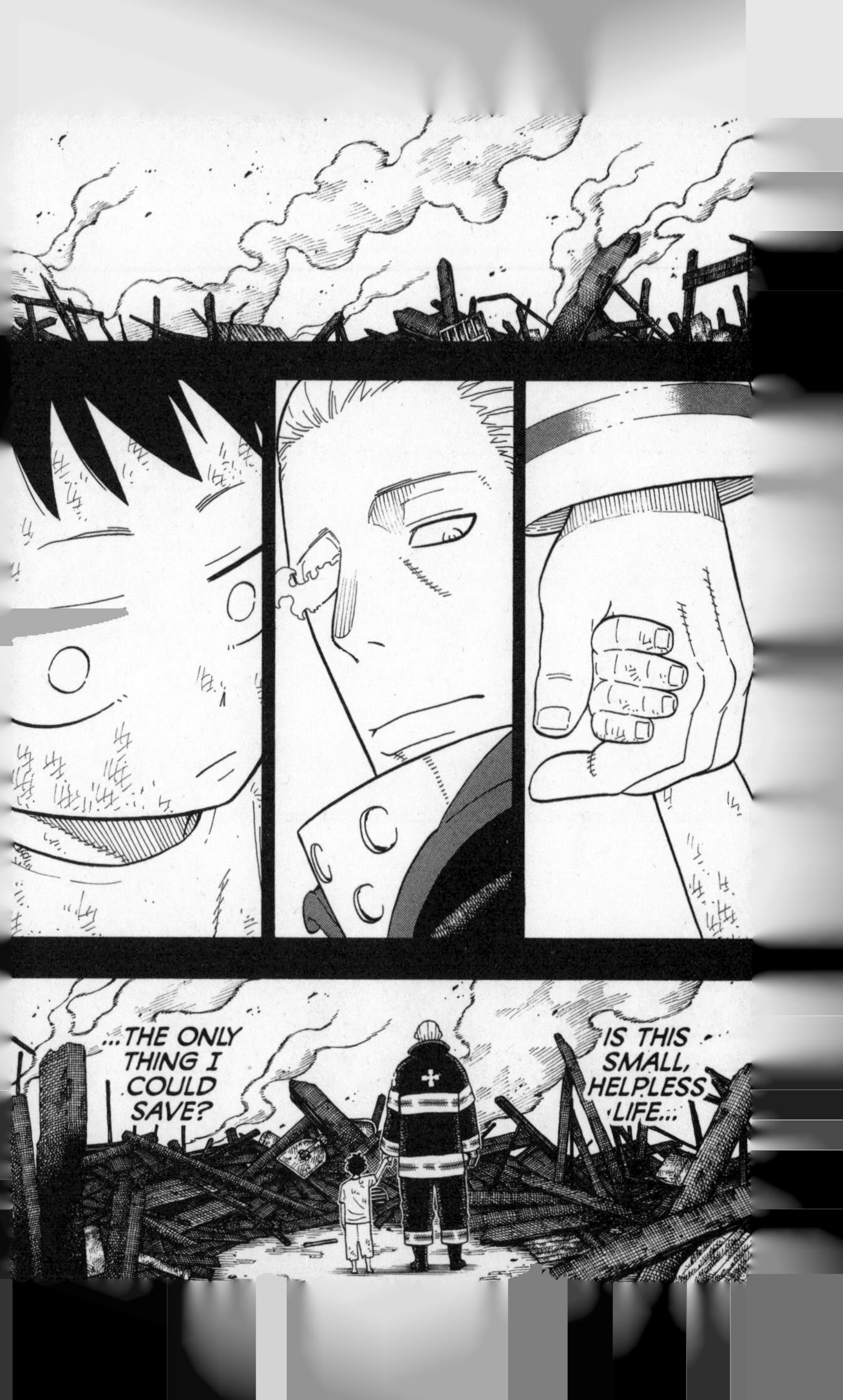
IS THIS SMALL, HELPLESS LIFE...
...THE ONLY THING I COULD SAVE?

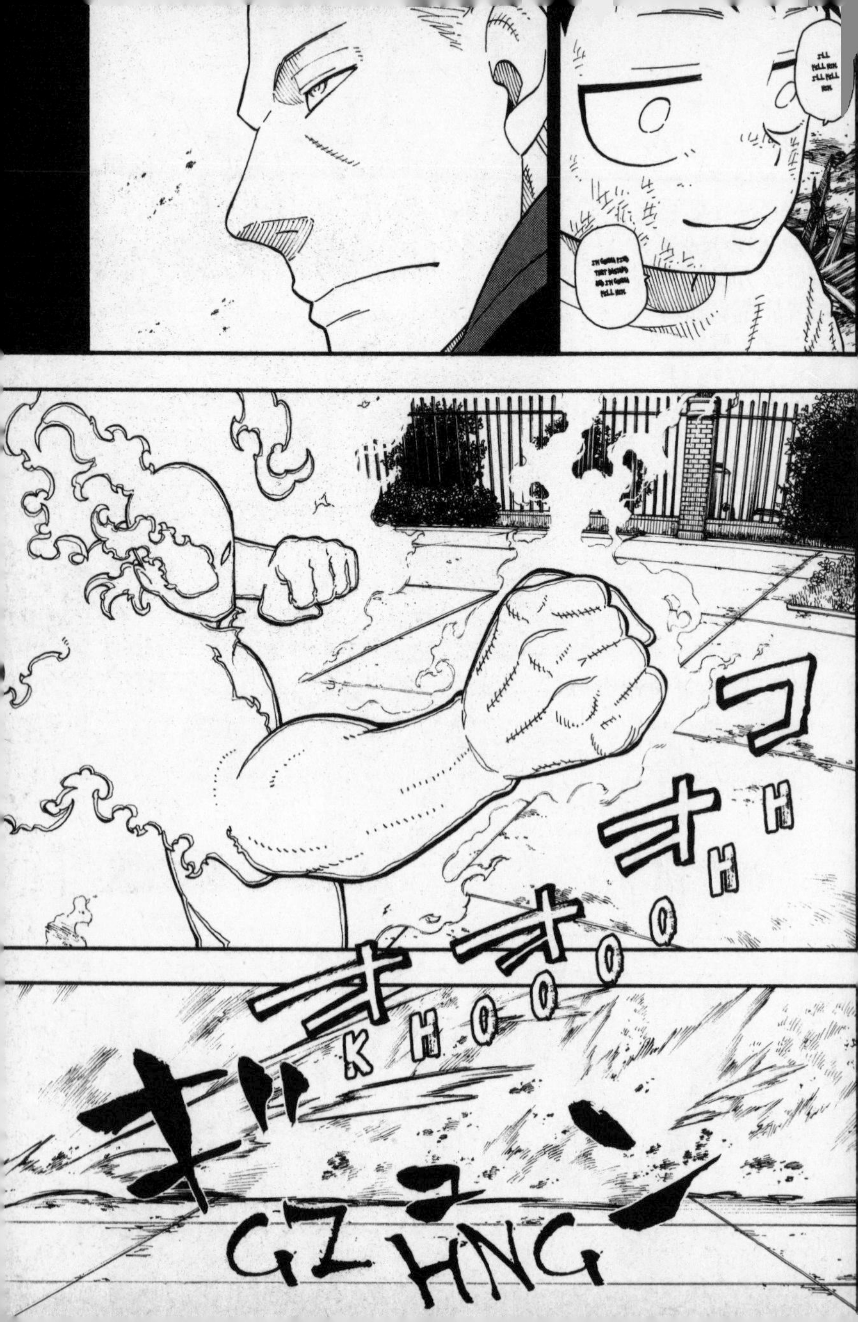
I'LL KILL HIM. I'LL KILL HIM.
I'M GONNA FIND THAT BASTARD AND I'M GONNA KILL HIM.
KHOOOOHH
GZ HNG

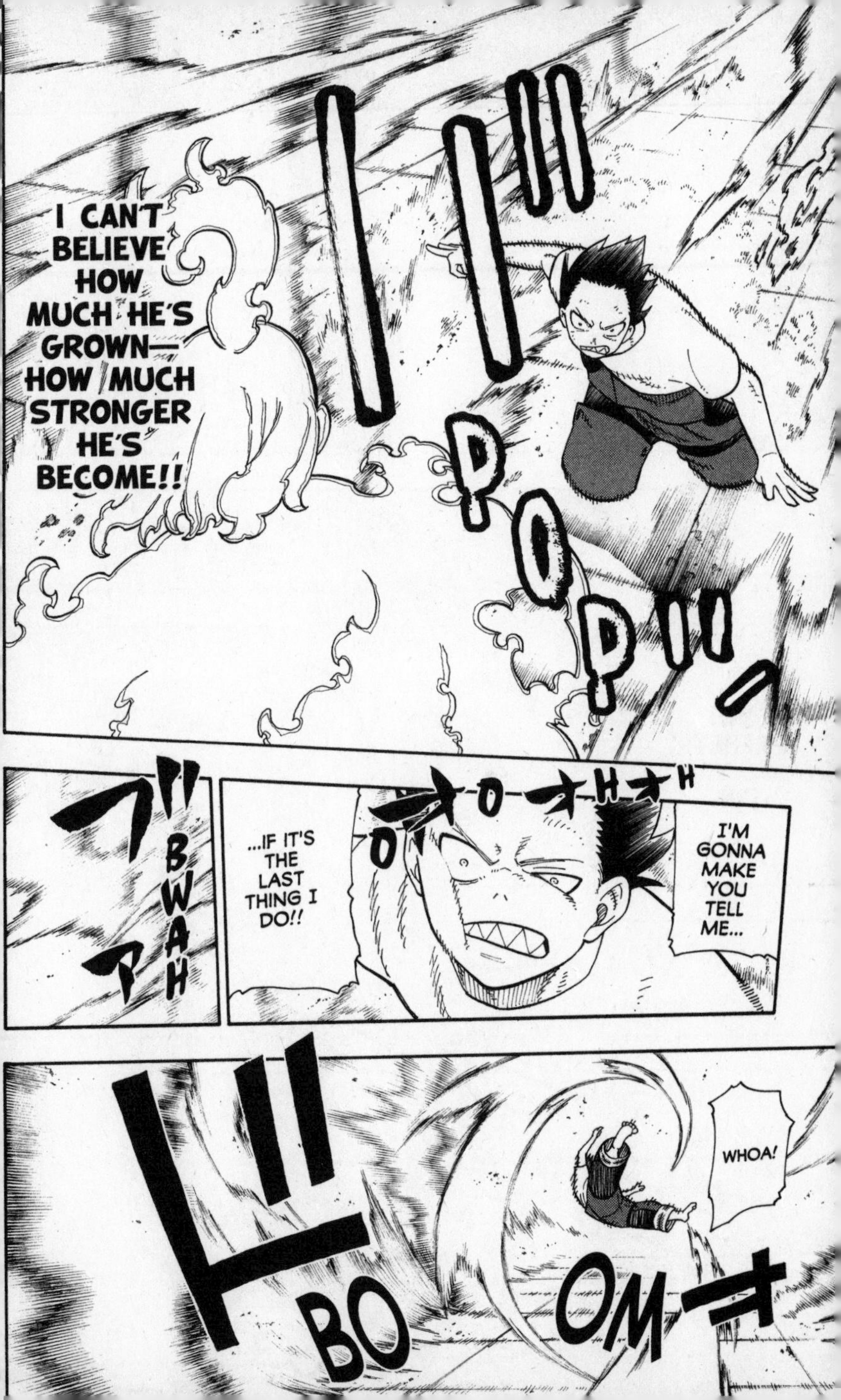
I CAN'T BELIEVE HOW MUCH HE'S GROWN—HOW MUCH STRONGER HE'S BECOME!!
POP!!
I'M GONNA MAKE YOU TELL ME...
...IF IT'S THE LAST THING I DO!!
BWAH
WHOA!
BOOM

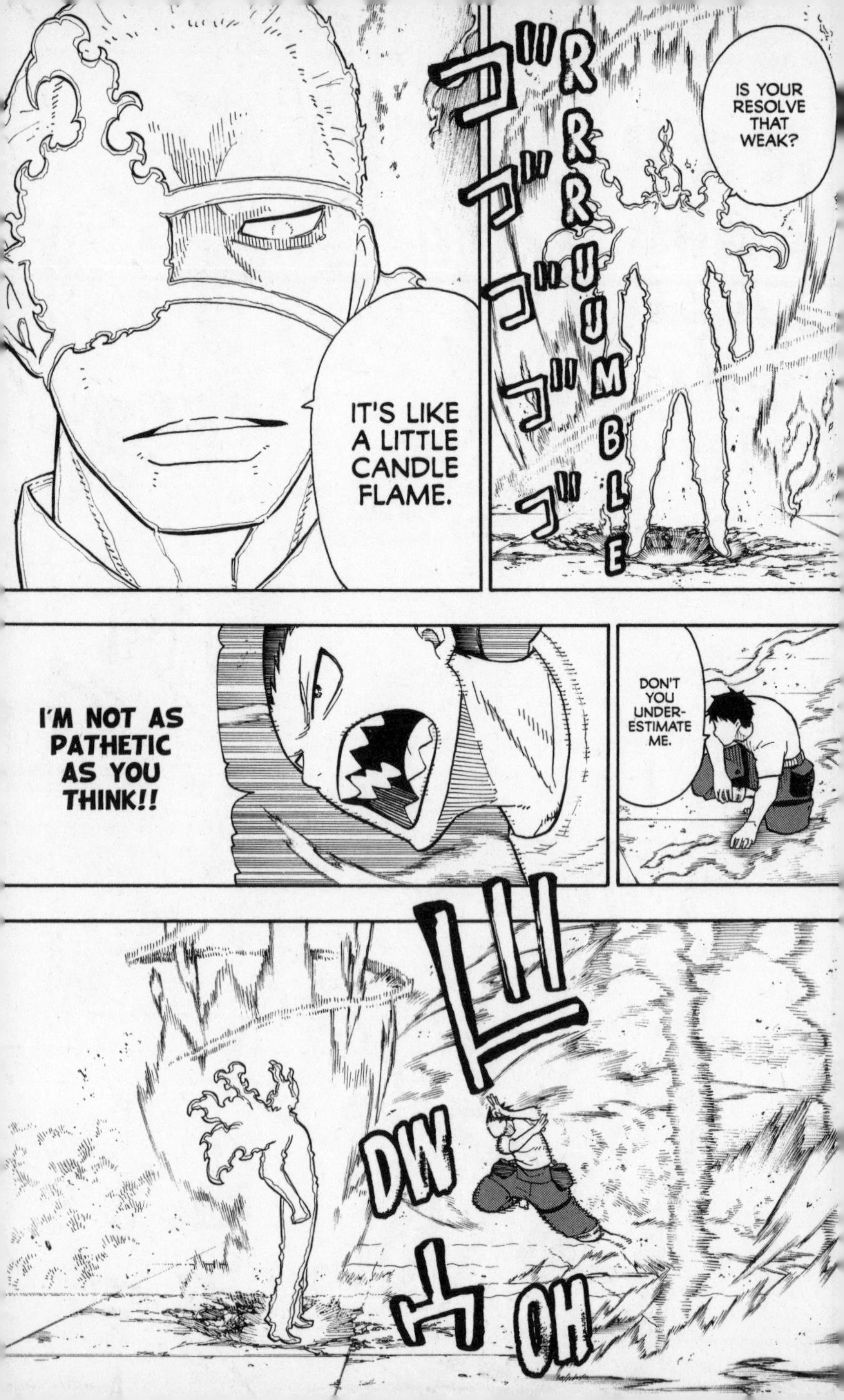

IS YOUR RESOLVE THAT WEAK?
RRRUMBLE
IT'S LIKE A LITTLE CANDLE FLAME.
DON'T YOU UNDER-ESTIMATE ME.
I'M NOT AS PATHETIC AS YOU THINK!!
DW
OH

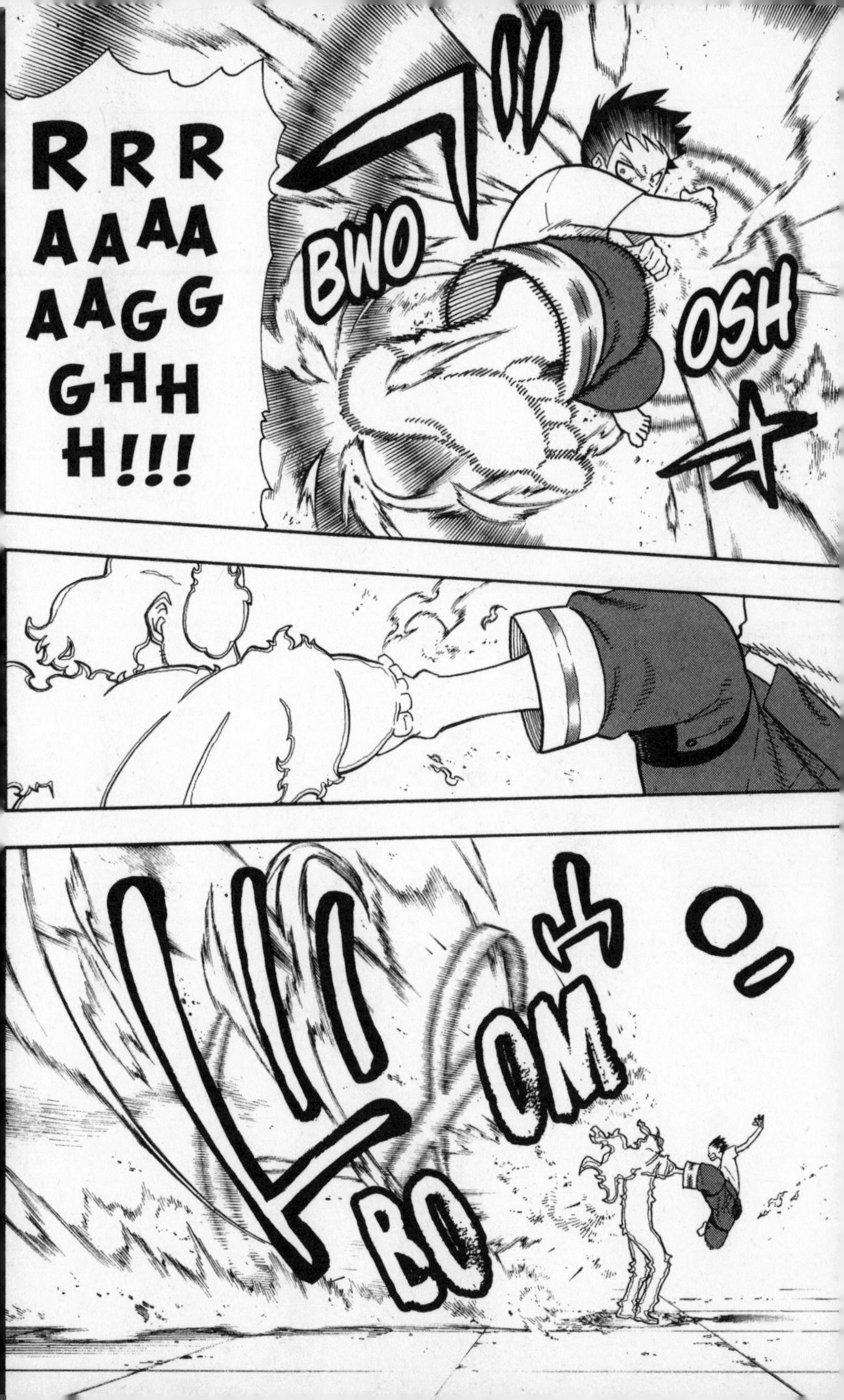
BWOOSH
RRRAAAAAAGGGHHH!!!
BOOM

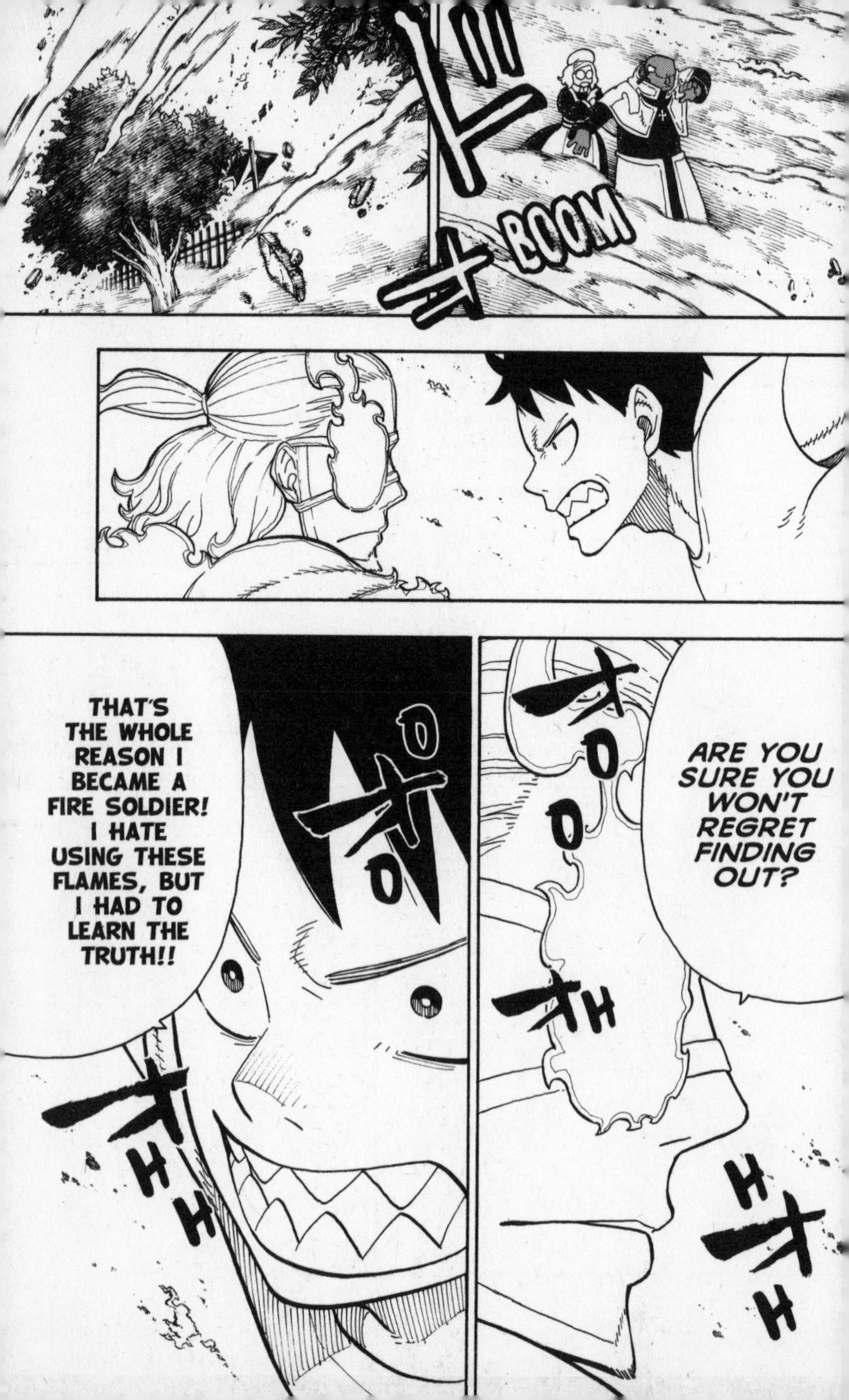
BOOM
ARE YOU SURE YOU WON'T REGRET FINDING OUT?
THAT'S THE WHOLE REASON I BECAME A FIRE SOLDIER! I HATE USING THESE FLAMES, BUT I HAD TO LEARN THE TRUTH!!

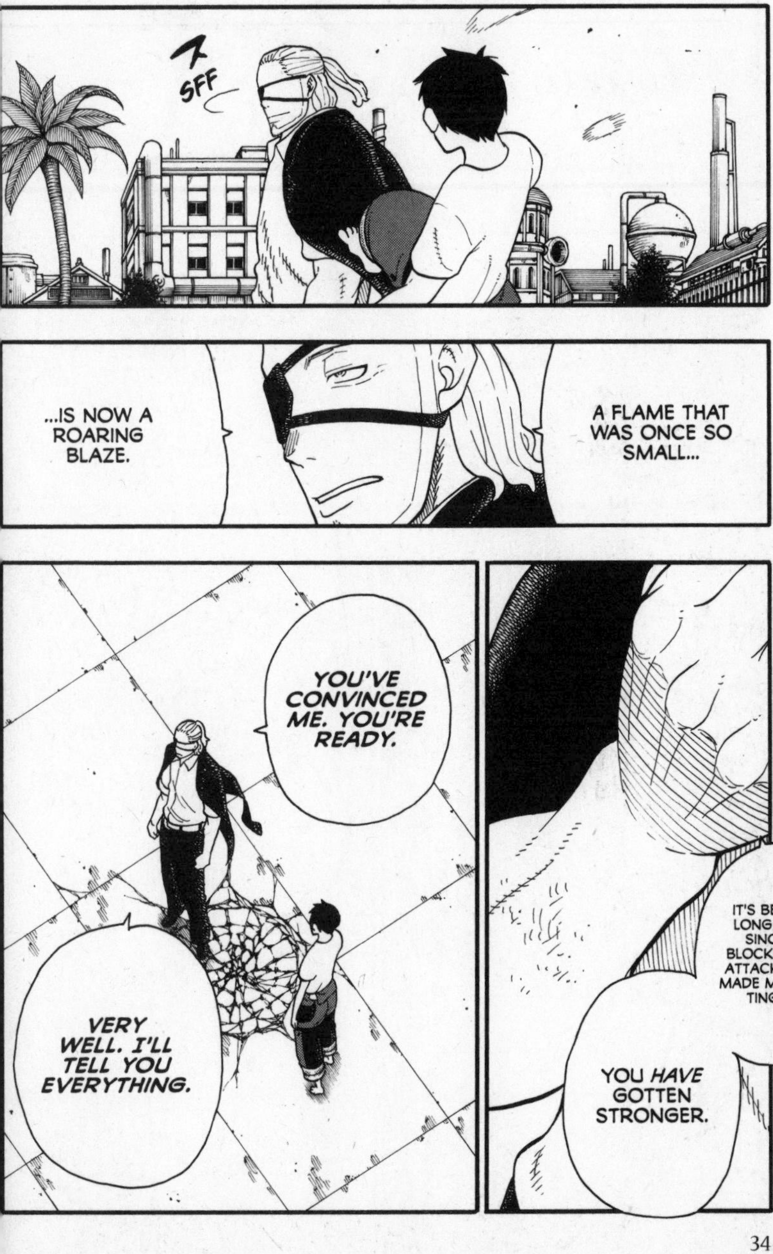
ス
SFF
A FLAME THAT WAS ONCE SO SMALL...
...IS NOW A ROARING BLAZE.
IT'S BEEN A LONG TIME SINCE I BLOCKED AN ATTACK THAT MADE MY ARM TINGLE.
YOU *HAVE* GOTTEN STRONGER.
YOU'VE CONVINCED ME. YOU'RE READY.
VERY WELL. I'LL TELL YOU EVERYTHING.

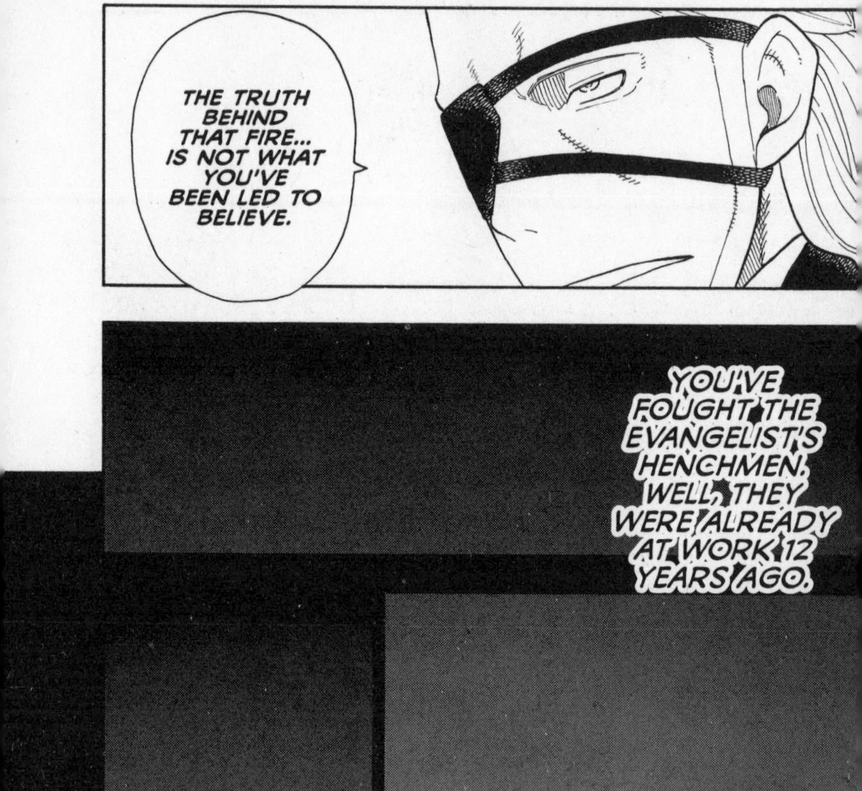
THE TRUTH BEHIND THAT FIRE... IS NOT WHAT YOU'VE BEEN LED TO BELIEVE.
YOU'VE FOUGHT THE EVANGELIST'S HENCHMEN. WELL, THEY WERE ALREADY AT WORK 12 YEARS AGO.

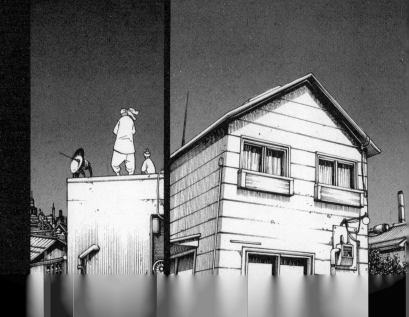

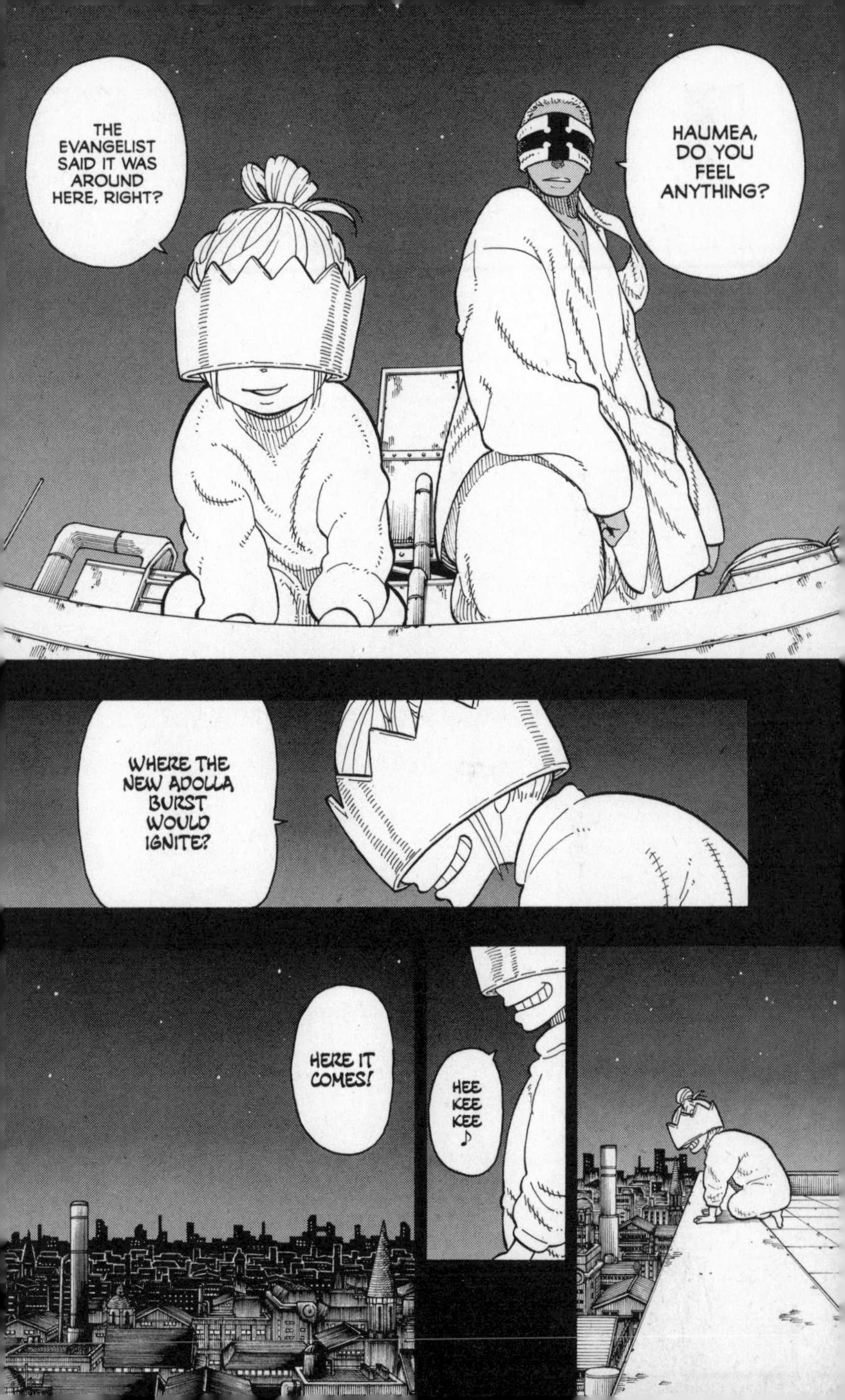
HAUMEA, DO YOU FEEL ANYTHING?
THE EVANGELIST SAID IT WAS AROUND HERE, RIGHT?
WHERE THE NEW ADOLLA BURST WOULD IGNITE?
HEE KEE KEE ♪
HERE IT COMES!

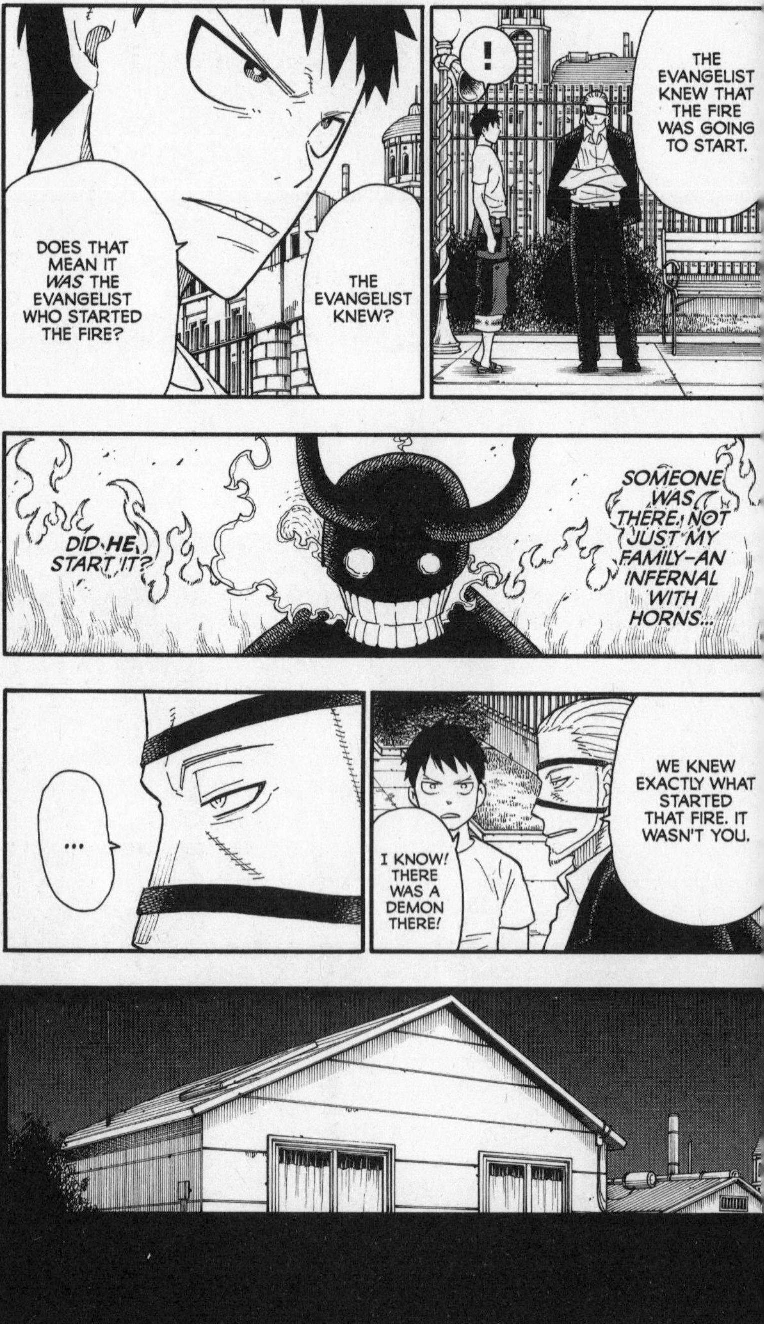
!
THE EVANGELIST KNEW THAT THE FIRE WAS GOING TO START.
THE EVANGELIST KNEW?
DOES THAT MEAN IT *WAS* THE EVANGELIST WHO STARTED THE FIRE?
SOMEONE WAS THERE. NOT JUST MY FAMILY—AN INFERNAL WITH HORNS...
DID HE START IT?
WE KNEW EXACTLY WHAT STARTED THAT FIRE. IT WASN'T YOU.
I KNOW! THERE WAS A DEMON THERE!
...

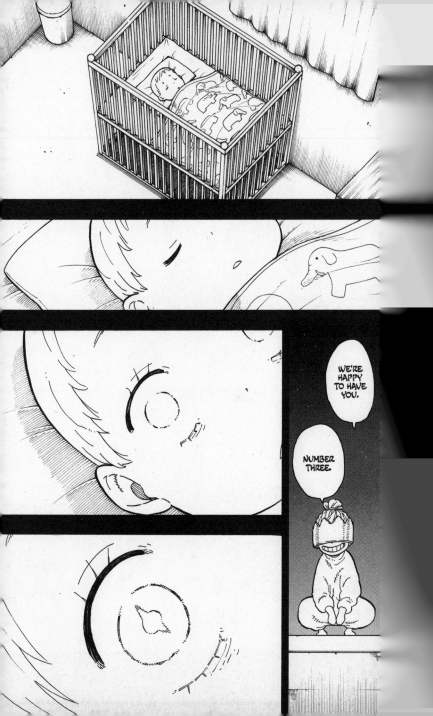

WE'RE HAPPY TO HAVE YOU.

NUMBER THREE.

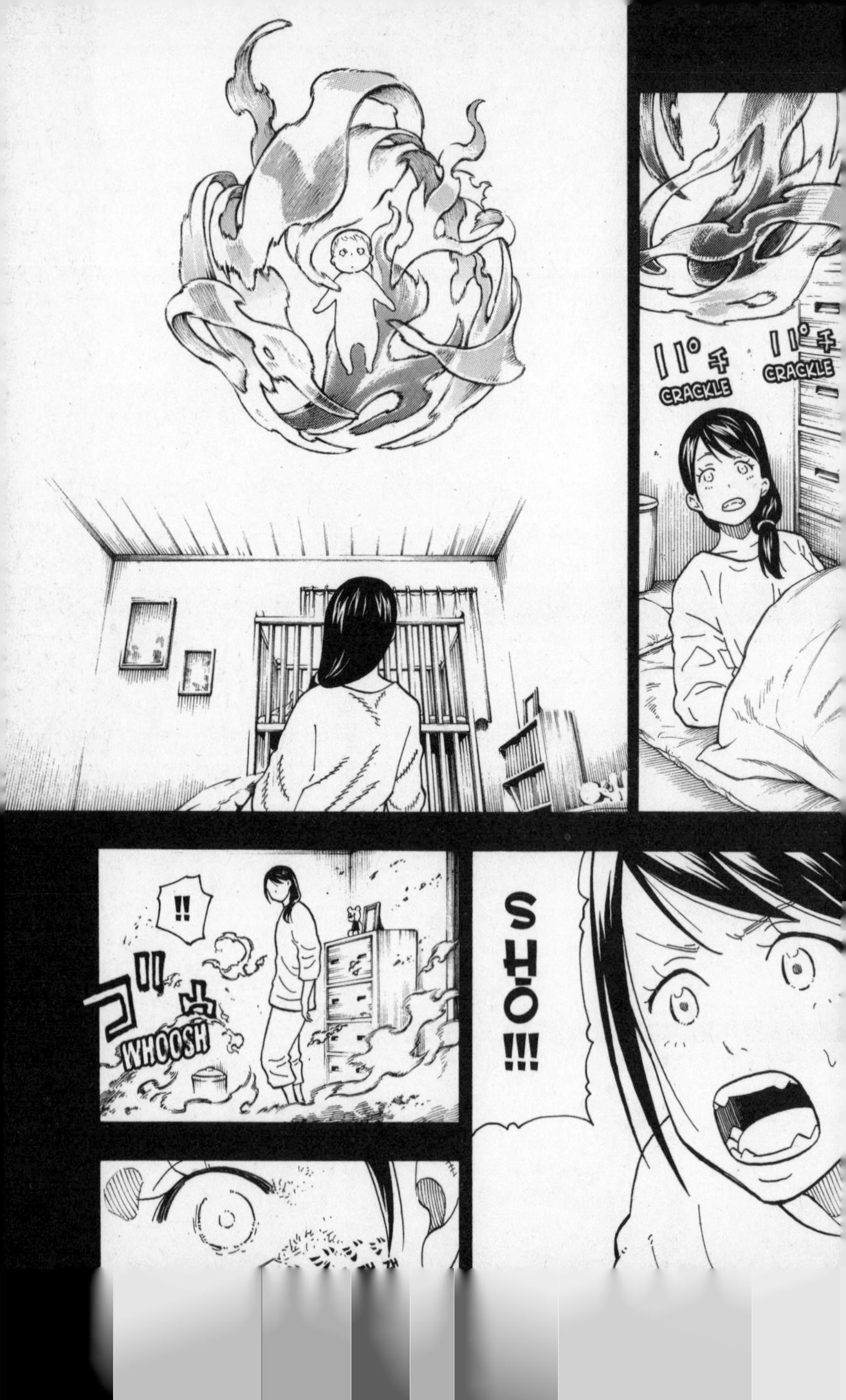
CRACKLE
CRACKLE
SHO!!!
!!
WHOOSH

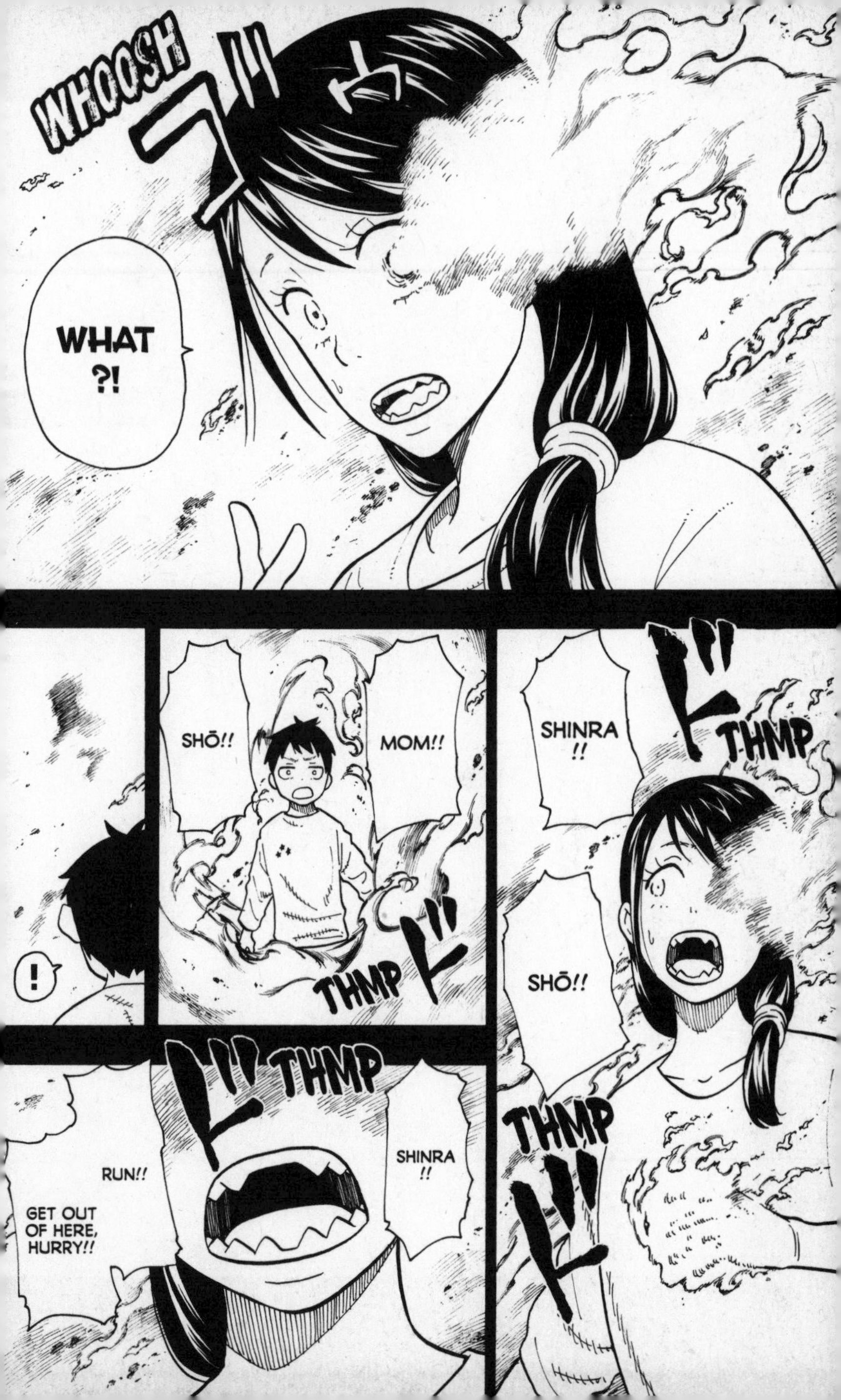
WHOOSH
WHAT ?!
SHINRA !!
THMP
SHŌ!!
THMP
MOM!!
SHŌ!!
THMP
!
THMP
SHINRA !!
RUN!!
GET OUT OF HERE, HURRY!!

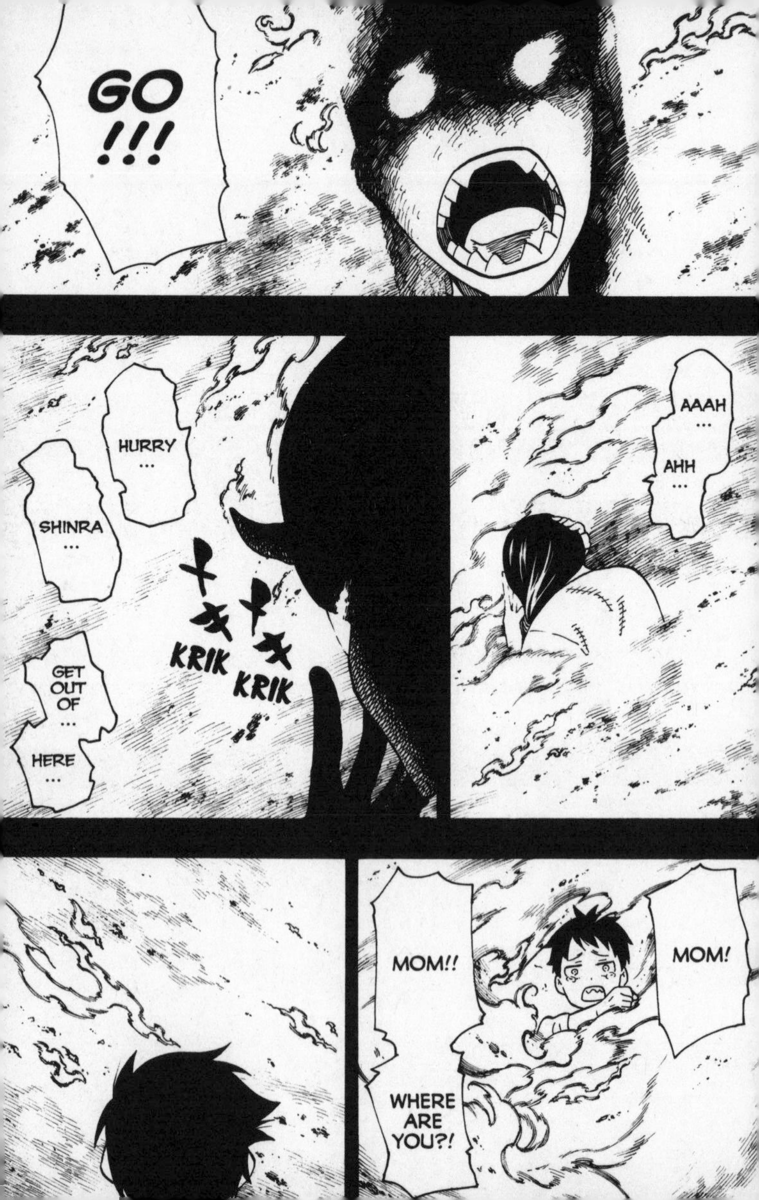
GO!!!
AAAH... AHH...
HURRY...
SHINRA...
KRIK KRIK
GET OUT OF... HERE...
MOM!
MOM!!
WHERE ARE YOU?!

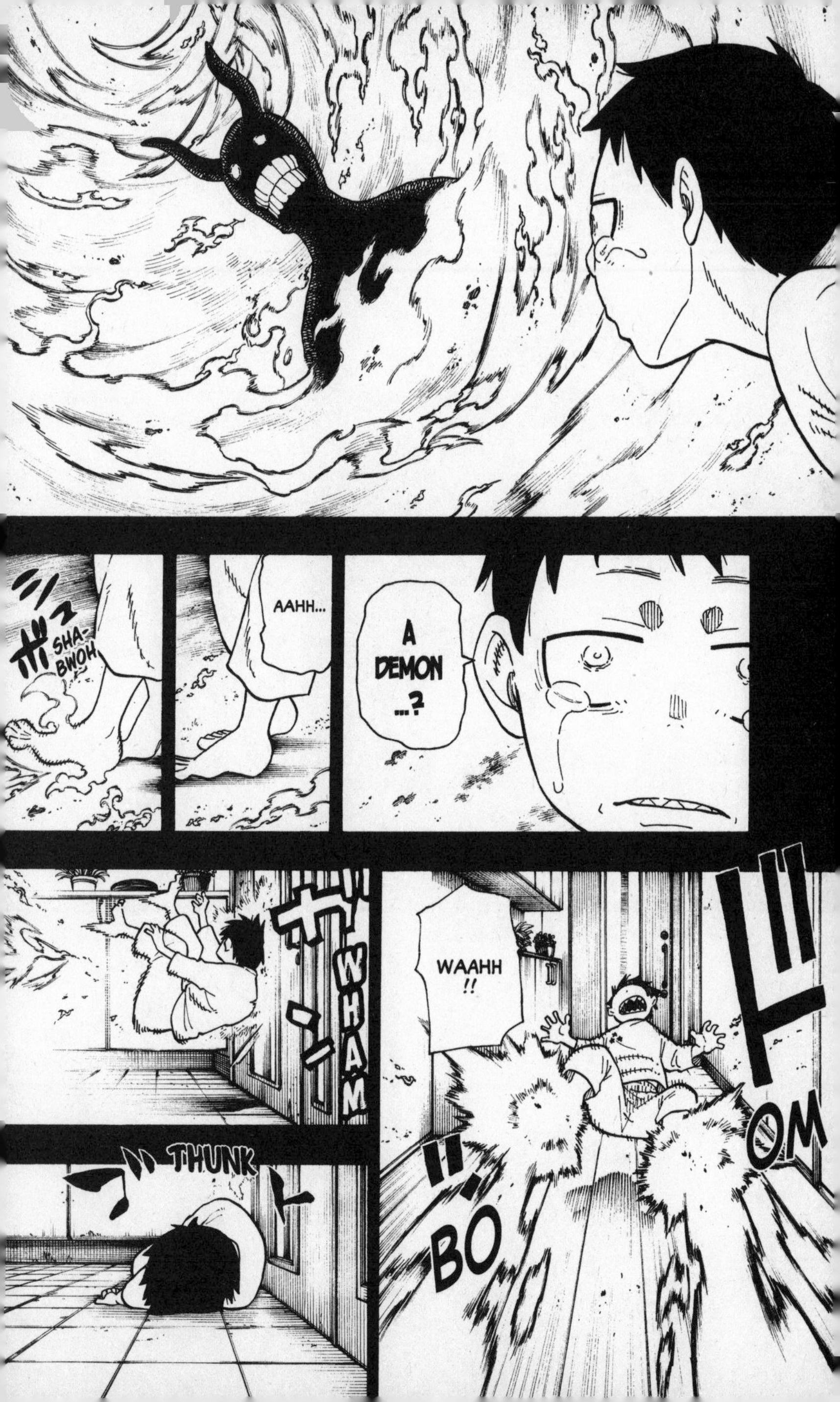

A DEMON ...?
AAHH...
SHA-BWOH
WAAHH !!
BOOM
WHAM
THUNK

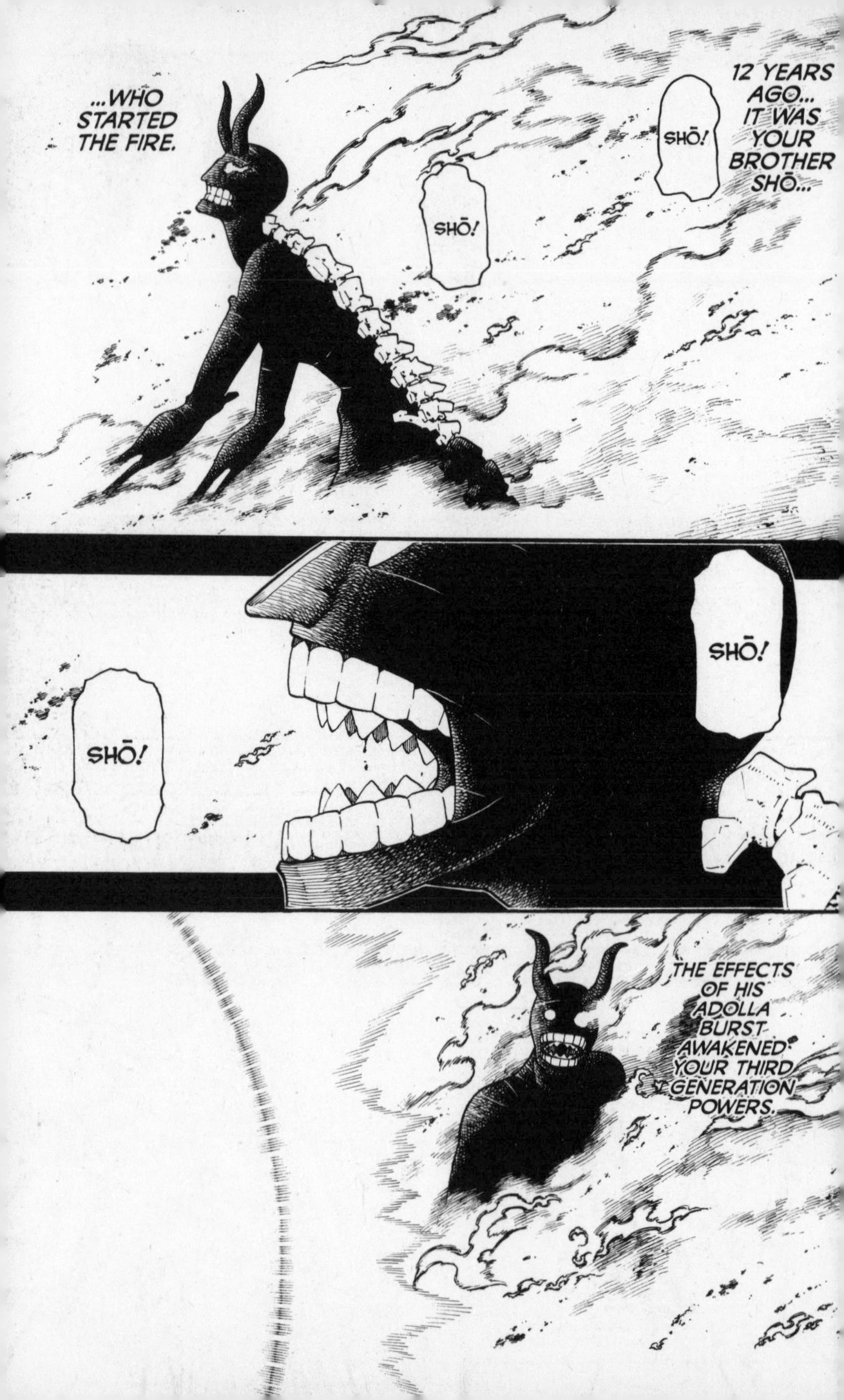
12 YEARS AGO... IT WAS YOUR BROTHER SHŌ...
SHŌ!
SHŌ!
...WHO STARTED THE FIRE.
SHŌ!
SHŌ!
THE EFFECTS OF HIS ADOLLA BURST AWAKENED YOUR THIRD GENERATION POWERS.

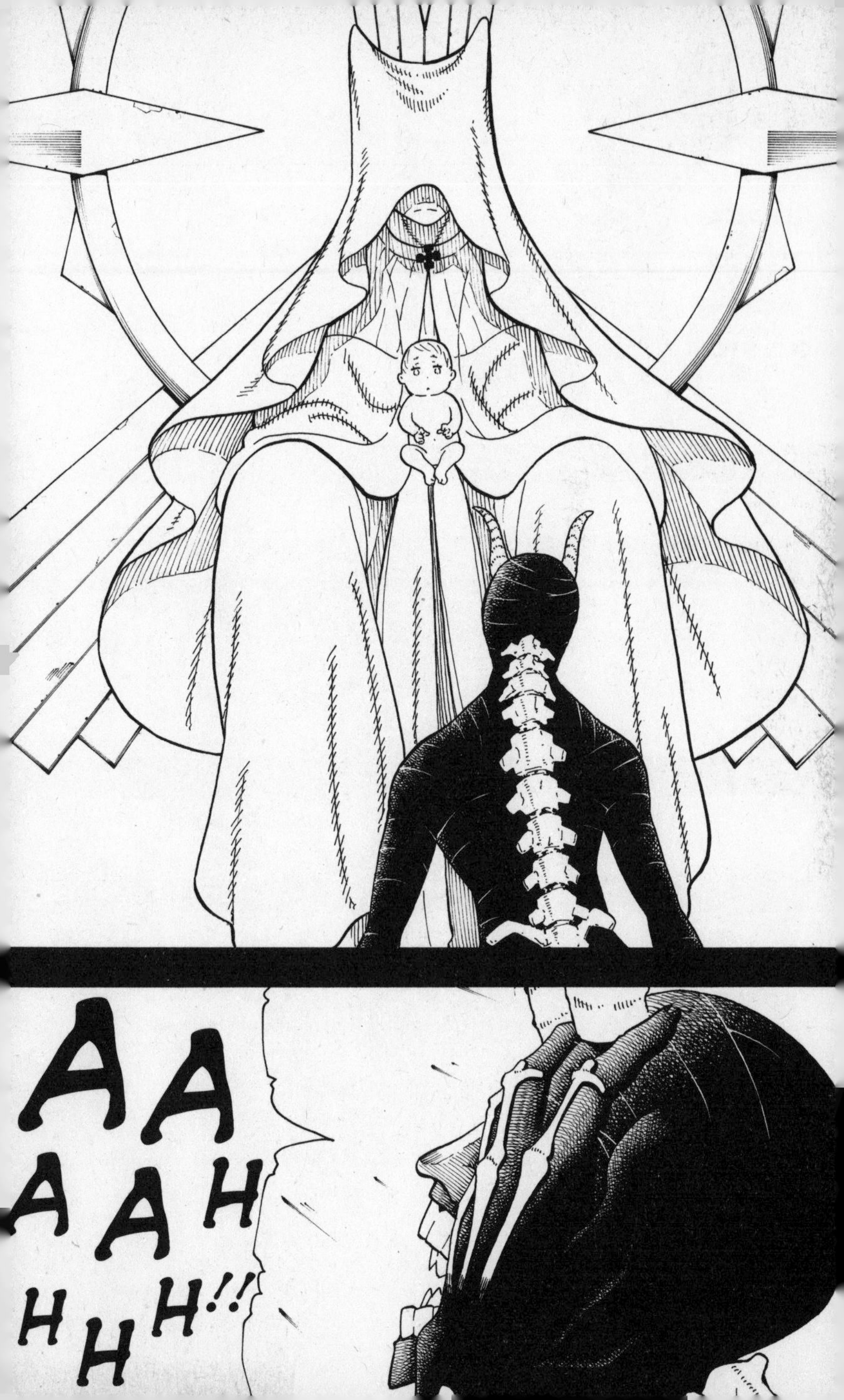
AAAAHHHH!!

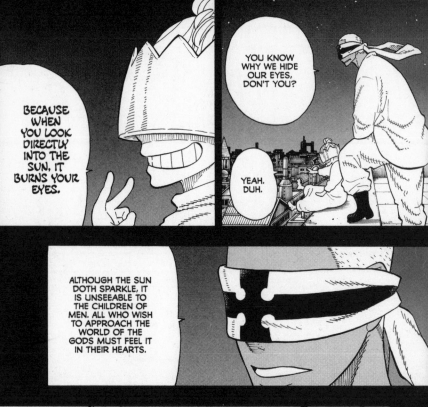

YOU KNOW WHY WE HIDE OUR EYES, DON'T YOU?

BECAUSE WHEN YOU LOOK DIRECTLY INTO THE SUN, IT BURNS YOUR EYES.

YEAH. DUH.

ALTHOUGH THE SUN DOTH SPARKLE, IT IS UNSEEABLE TO THE CHILDREN OF MEN. ALL WHO WISH TO APPROACH THE WORLD OF THE GODS MUST FEEL IT IN THEIR HEARTS.

THE HORNED INFERNAL YOU CLAIM YOU SAW...

GRK.

GRK

GR-GRK

GRK

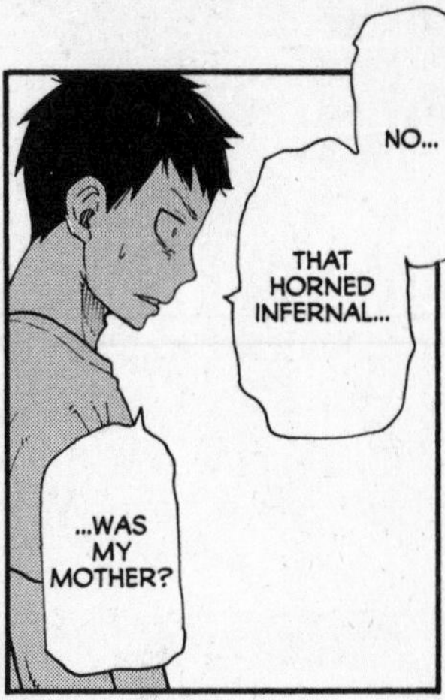
NO...
THAT HORNED INFERNAL...
...WAS MY MOTHER?
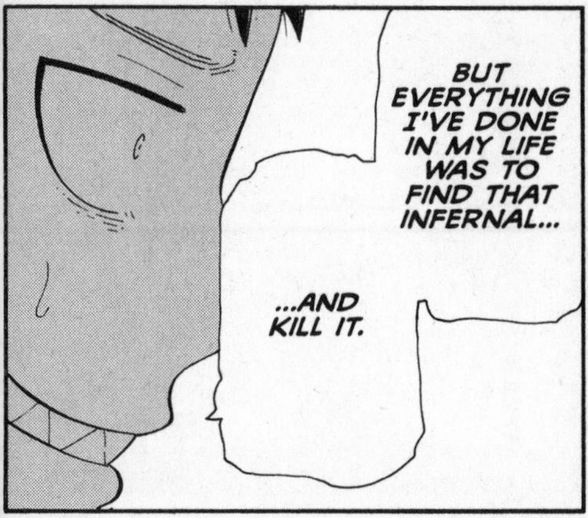
BUT EVERYTHING I'VE DONE IN MY LIFE WAS TO FIND THAT INFERNAL...
...AND KILL IT.
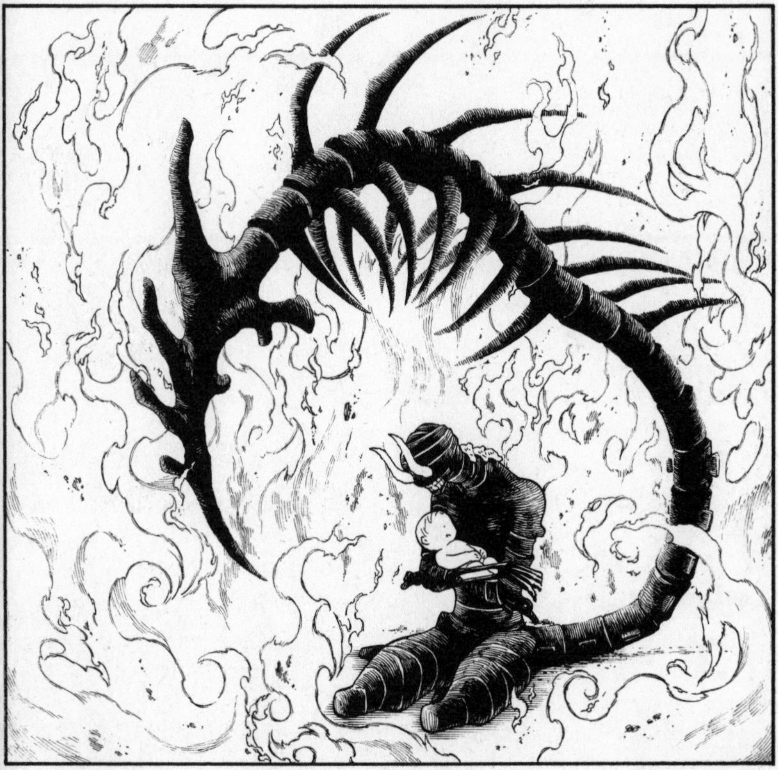

CHAPTER XC: AT TRAGEDY'S END

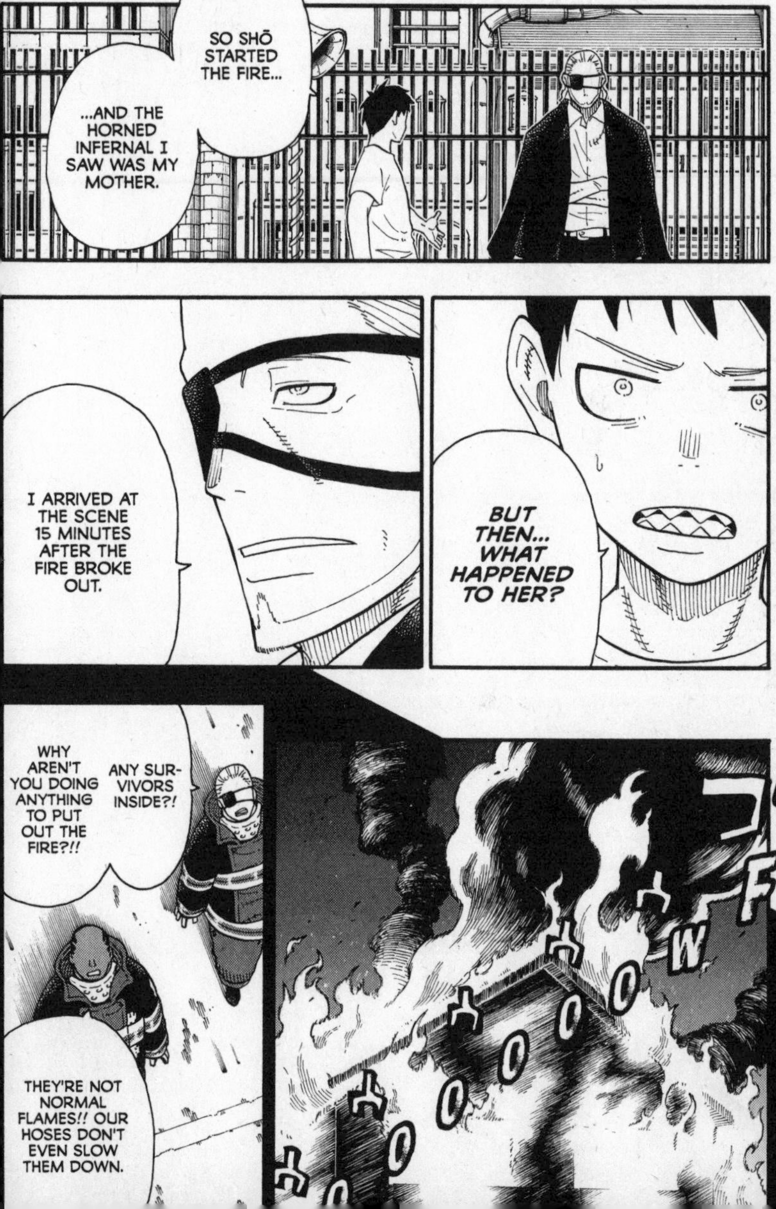
SO SHŌ STARTED THE FIRE...
...AND THE HORNED INFERNAL I SAW WAS MY MOTHER.
BUT THEN... WHAT HAPPENED TO HER?
I ARRIVED AT THE SCENE 15 MINUTES AFTER THE FIRE BROKE OUT.
FWOOOOOOOO
ANY SURVIVORS INSIDE?!
WHY AREN'T YOU DOING ANYTHING TO PUT OUT THE FIRE?!!
THEY'RE NOT NORMAL FLAMES!! OUR HOSES DON'T EVEN SLOW THEM DOWN.

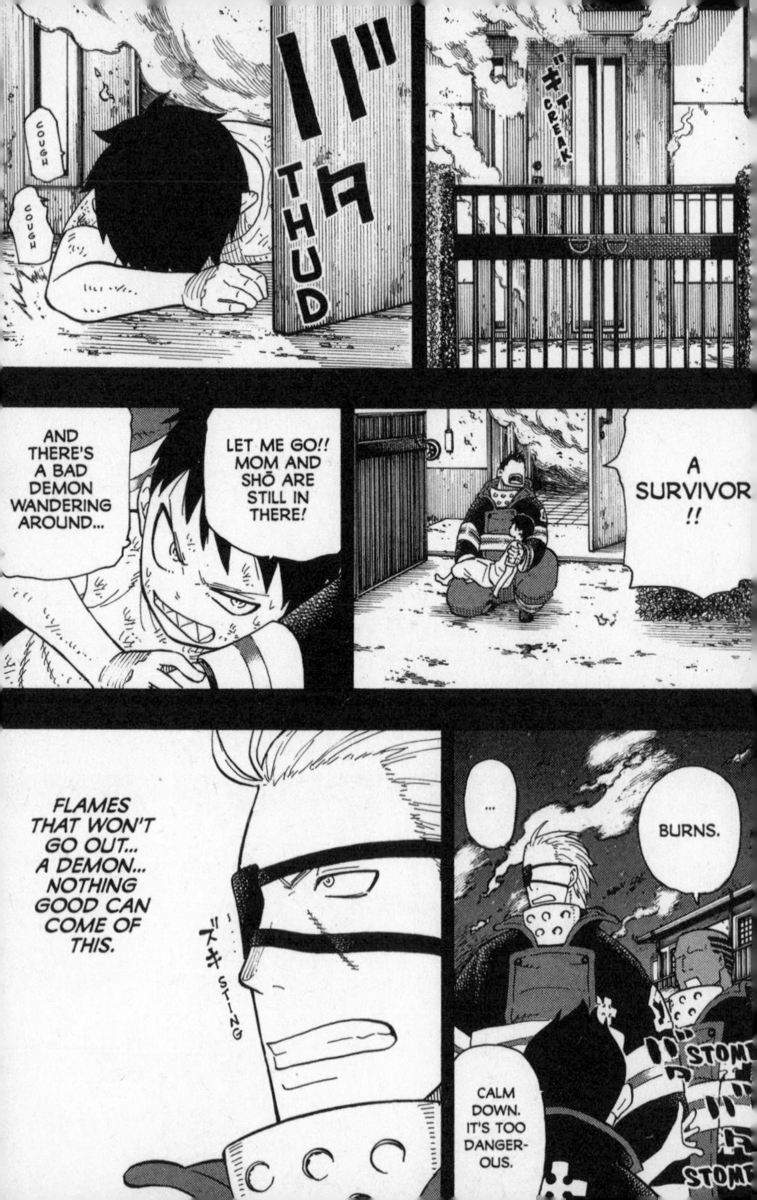
CREAK
THUD
COUGH
COUGH
A SURVIVOR!!
LET ME GO!! MOM AND SHŌ ARE STILL IN THERE!
AND THERE'S A BAD DEMON WANDERING AROUND...
BURNS.
...
CALM DOWN. IT'S TOO DANGER-OUS.
STING
FLAMES THAT WON'T GO OUT... A DEMON... NOTHING GOOD CAN COME OF THIS.

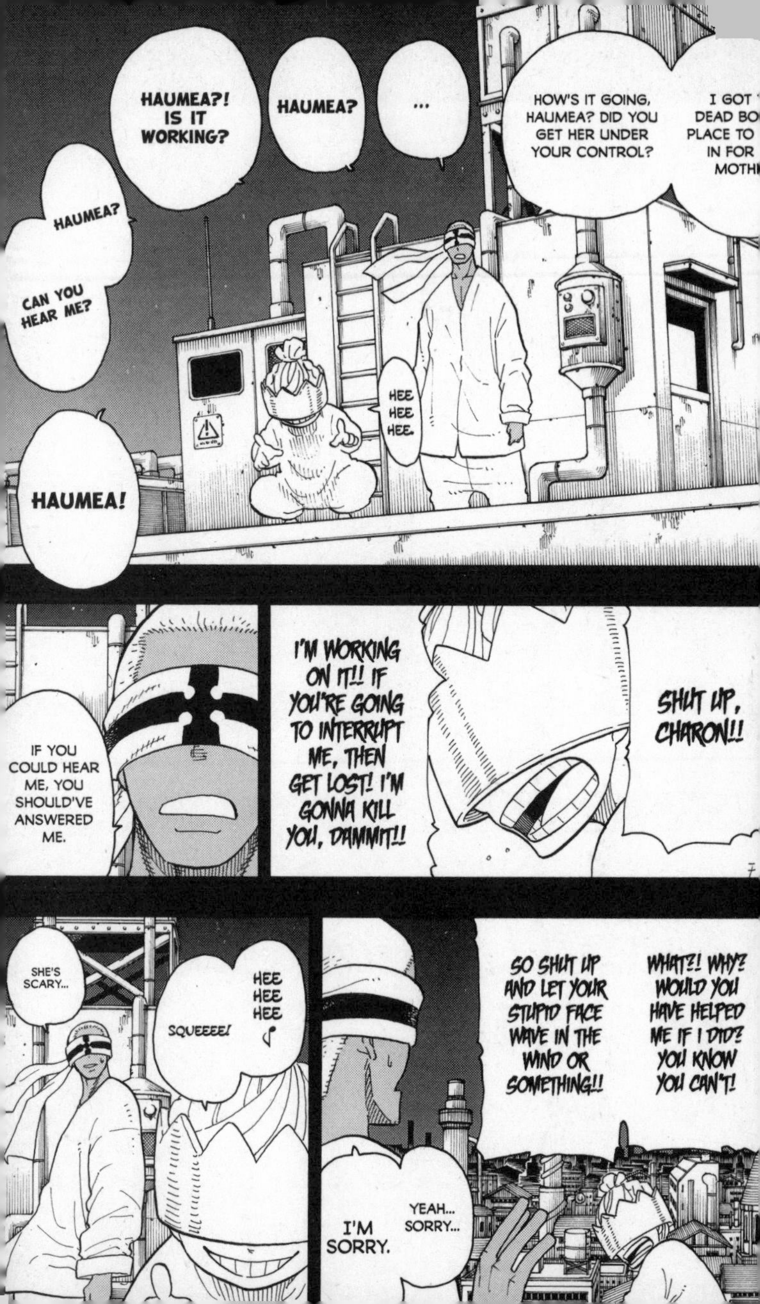
HOW'S IT GOING, HAUMEA? DID YOU GET HER UNDER YOUR CONTROL?
...
HAUMEA?
HAUMEA?! IS IT WORKING?
HAUMEA?
CAN YOU HEAR ME?
HEE HEE HEE.
HAUMEA!
SHUT UP, CHARON!!
I'M WORKING ON IT!! IF YOU'RE GOING TO INTERRUPT ME, THEN GET LOST! I'M GONNA KILL YOU, DAMMIT!!
IF YOU COULD HEAR ME, YOU SHOULD'VE ANSWERED ME.
WHAT?! WHY? WOULD YOU HAVE HELPED ME IF I DID? YOU KNOW YOU CAN'T!
SO SHUT UP AND LET YOUR STUPID FACE WAVE IN THE WIND OR SOMETHING!!
YEAH... SORRY...
I'M SORRY.
HEE HEE HEE ♪
SQUEEEE!
SHE'S SCARY...

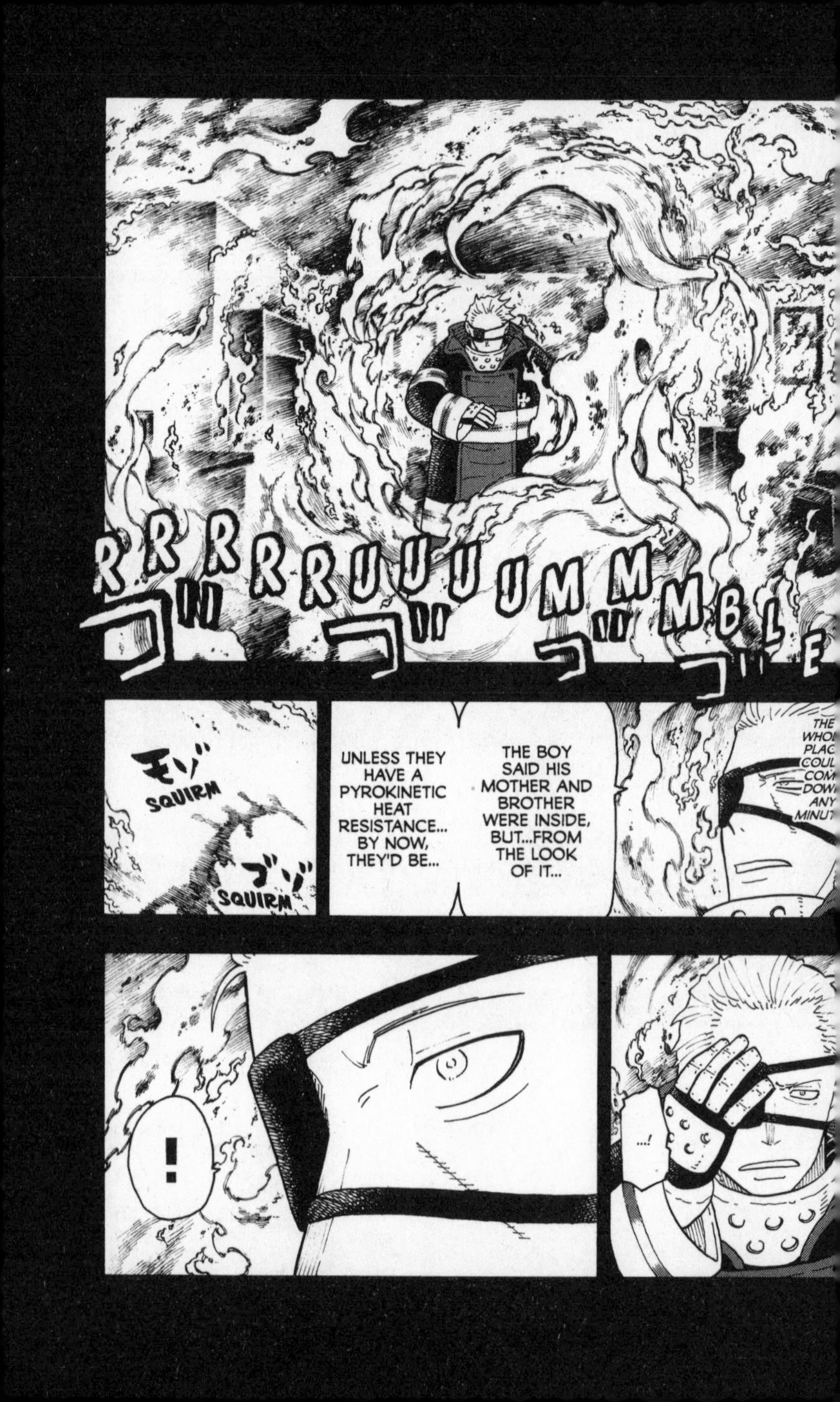
RRRRRUUUUMMMBLE
THE WHOL PLAC COUL COM DOW ANY MINUT
THE BOY SAID HIS MOTHER AND BROTHER WERE INSIDE, BUT...FROM THE LOOK OF IT...
UNLESS THEY HAVE A PYROKINETIC HEAT RESISTANCE... BY NOW, THEY'D BE...
SQUIRM
SQUIRM
...!
!

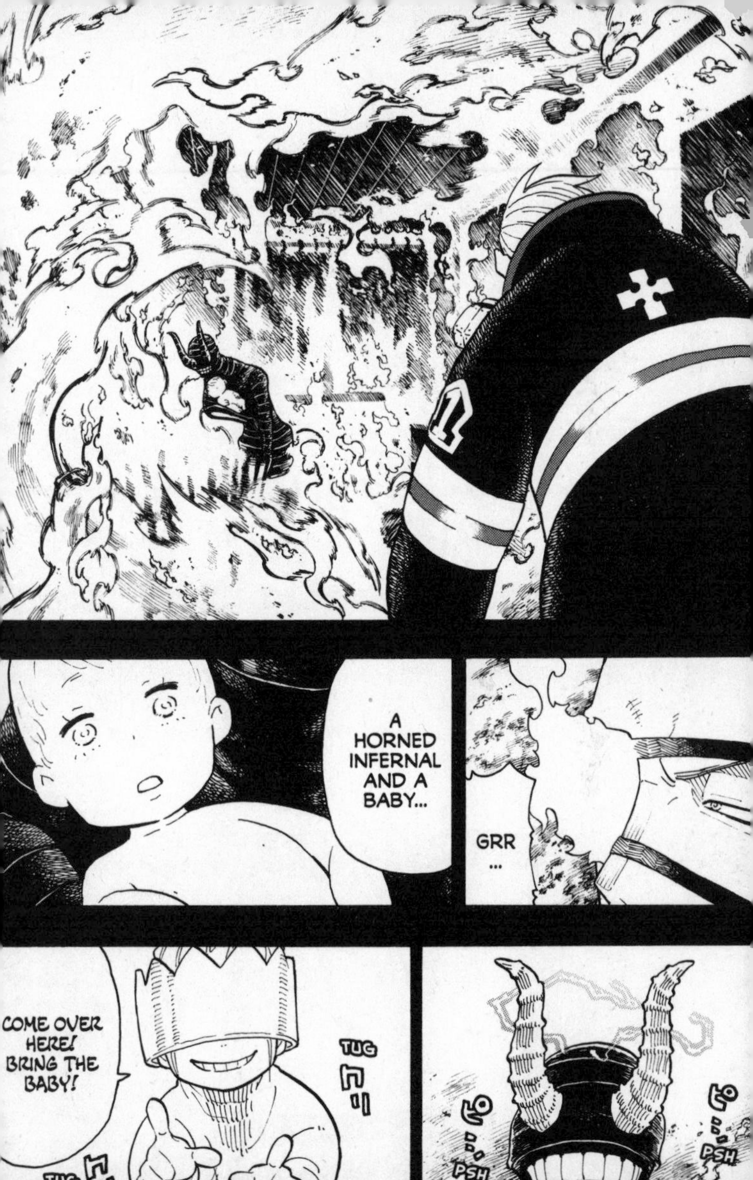
GRR
...
A HORNED INFERNAL AND A BABY...
PSH
PSH
COME OVER HERE! BRING THE BABY!
TUG
TUG

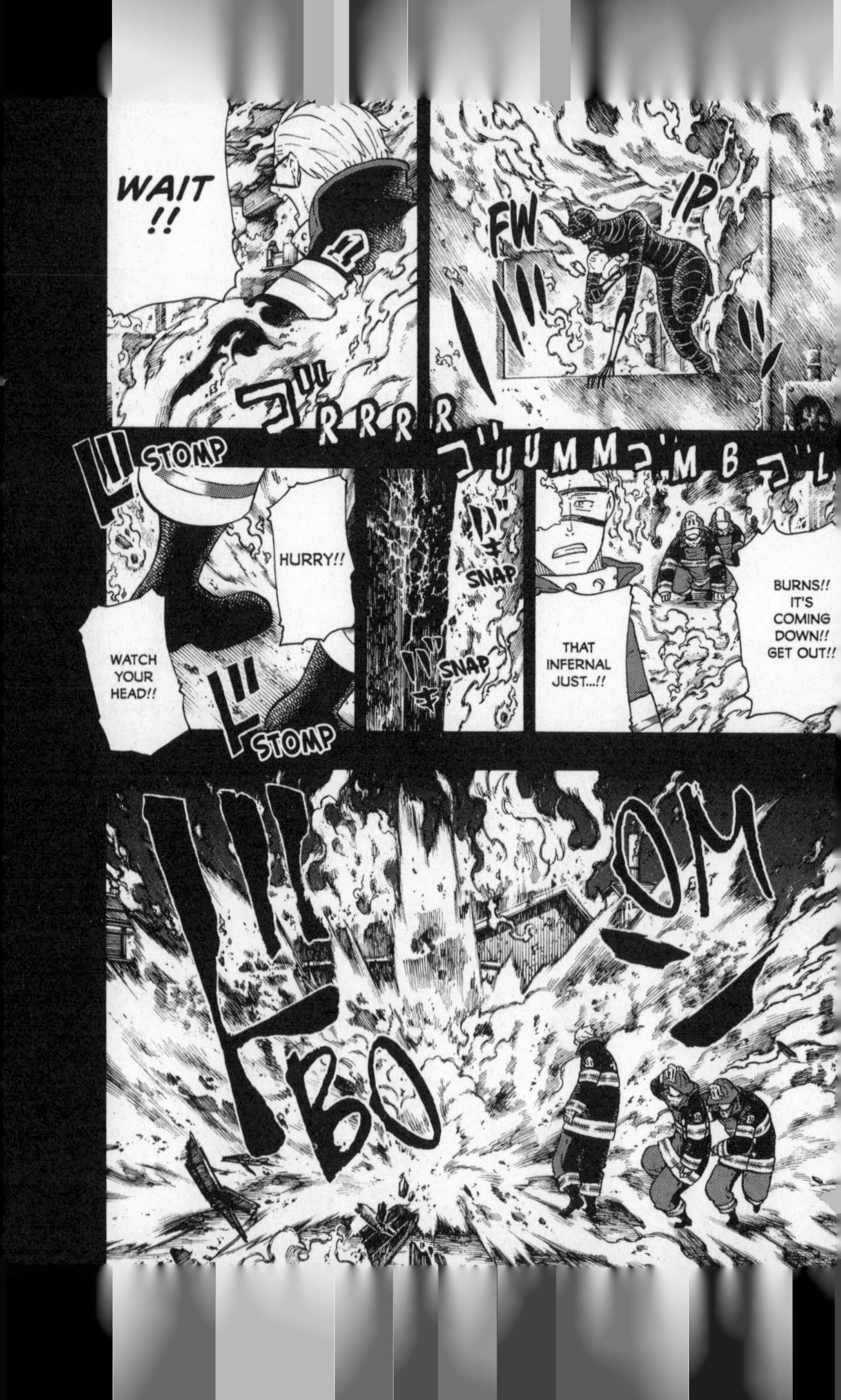

FW
IP
WAIT!!
RRRR
UMMM
MBL
BURNS!! IT'S COMING DOWN!! GET OUT!!
THAT INFERNAL JUST...!!
SNAP
SNAP
HURRY!!
STOMP
WATCH YOUR HEAD!!
STOMP
BO
OM

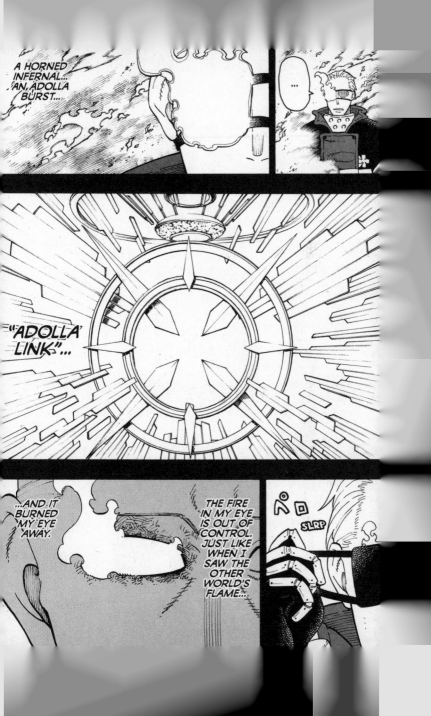

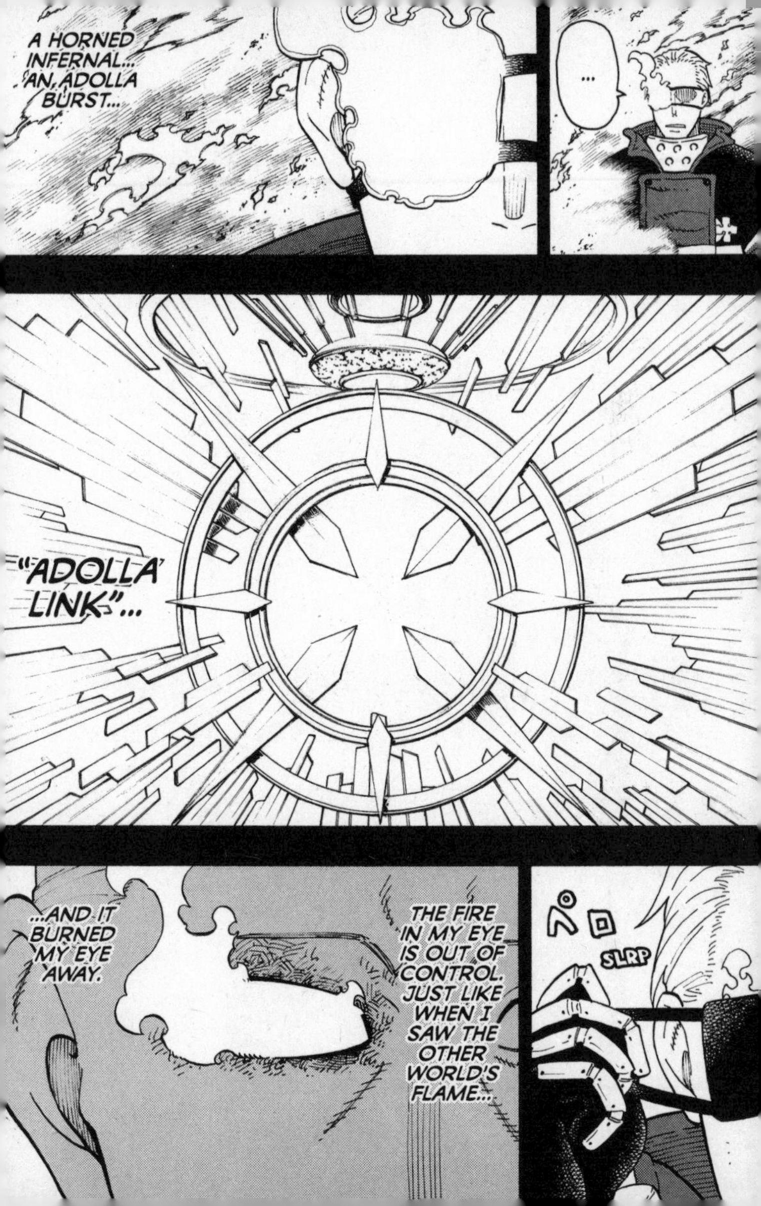
...
A HORNED INFERNAL... AN ADOLLA BURST...
"ADOLLA LINK"...
ペロ
SLRP
THE FIRE IN MY EYE IS OUT OF CONTROL. JUST LIKE WHEN I SAW THE OTHER WORLD'S FLAME...
...AND IT BURNED MY EYE AWAY.

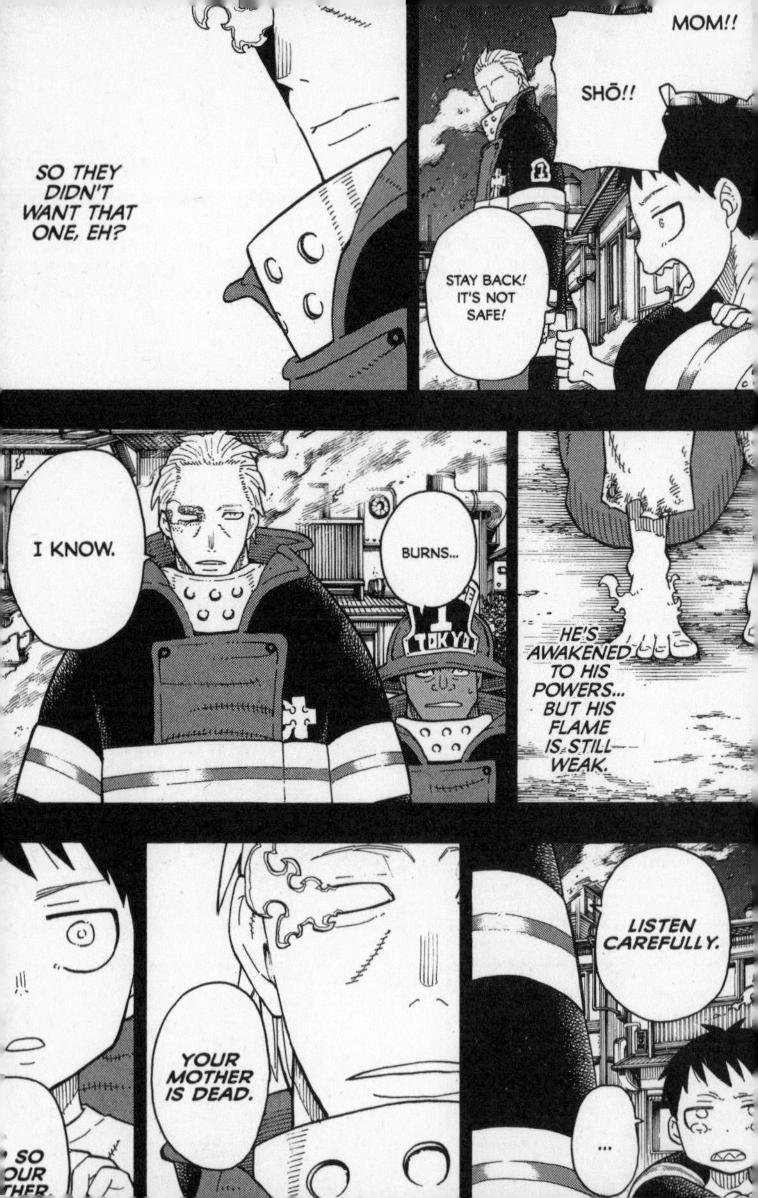
MOM!!
SHŌ!!
STAY BACK! IT'S NOT SAFE!
SO THEY DIDN'T WANT THAT ONE, EH?
HE'S AWAKENED TO HIS POWERS... BUT HIS FLAME IS STILL WEAK.
BURNS...
I KNOW.
LISTEN CAREFULLY.
...
YOUR MOTHER IS DEAD.
!!

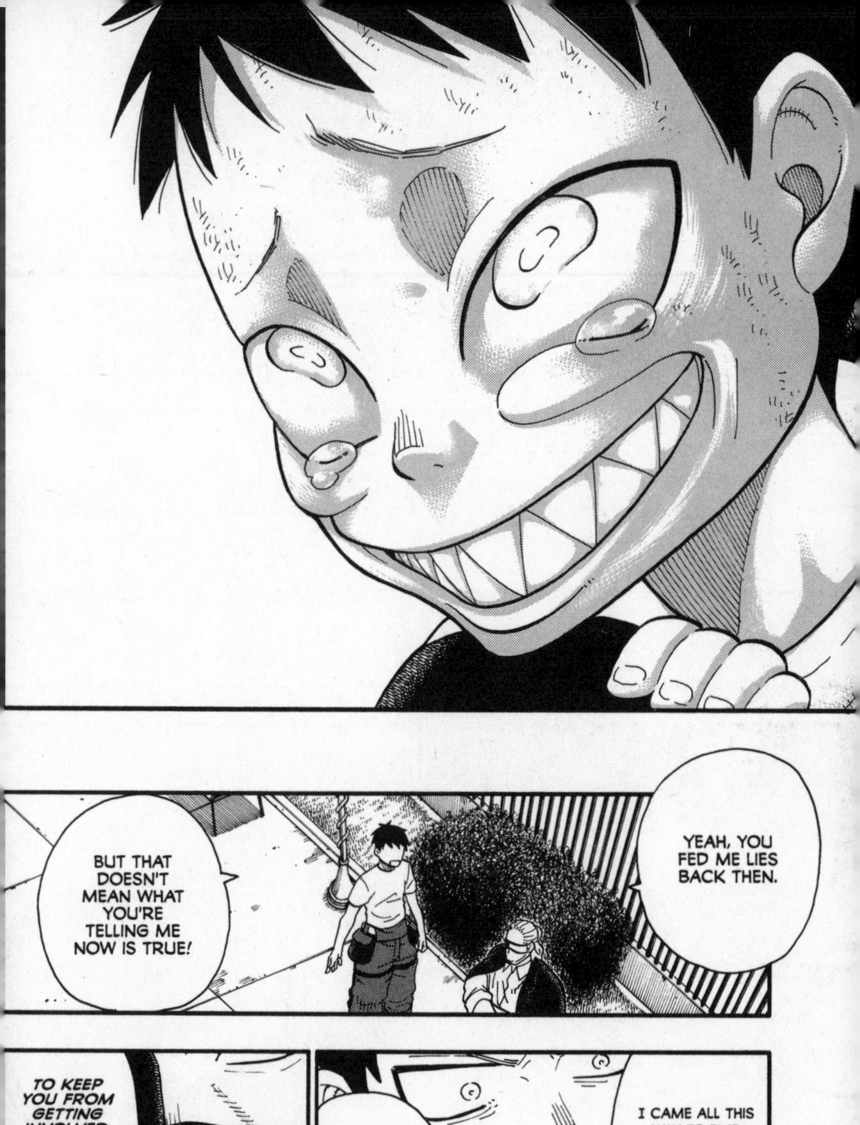
YEAH, YOU FED ME LIES BACK THEN.
BUT THAT DOESN'T MEAN WHAT YOU'RE TELLING ME NOW IS TRUE!
I CAME ALL THIS WAY TO FIND THAT DEMON... AND YOU WANT ME TO BELIEVE IT WAS MY MOTHER?
WHY WOULD YOU LIE TO ME?
TO KEEP YOU FROM GETTING INVOLVED. I KNEW THEY MIGHT EVENTUALLY COME AFTER YOU, TOO.

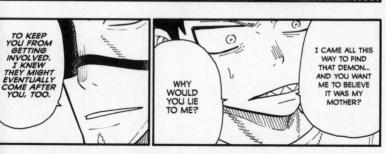

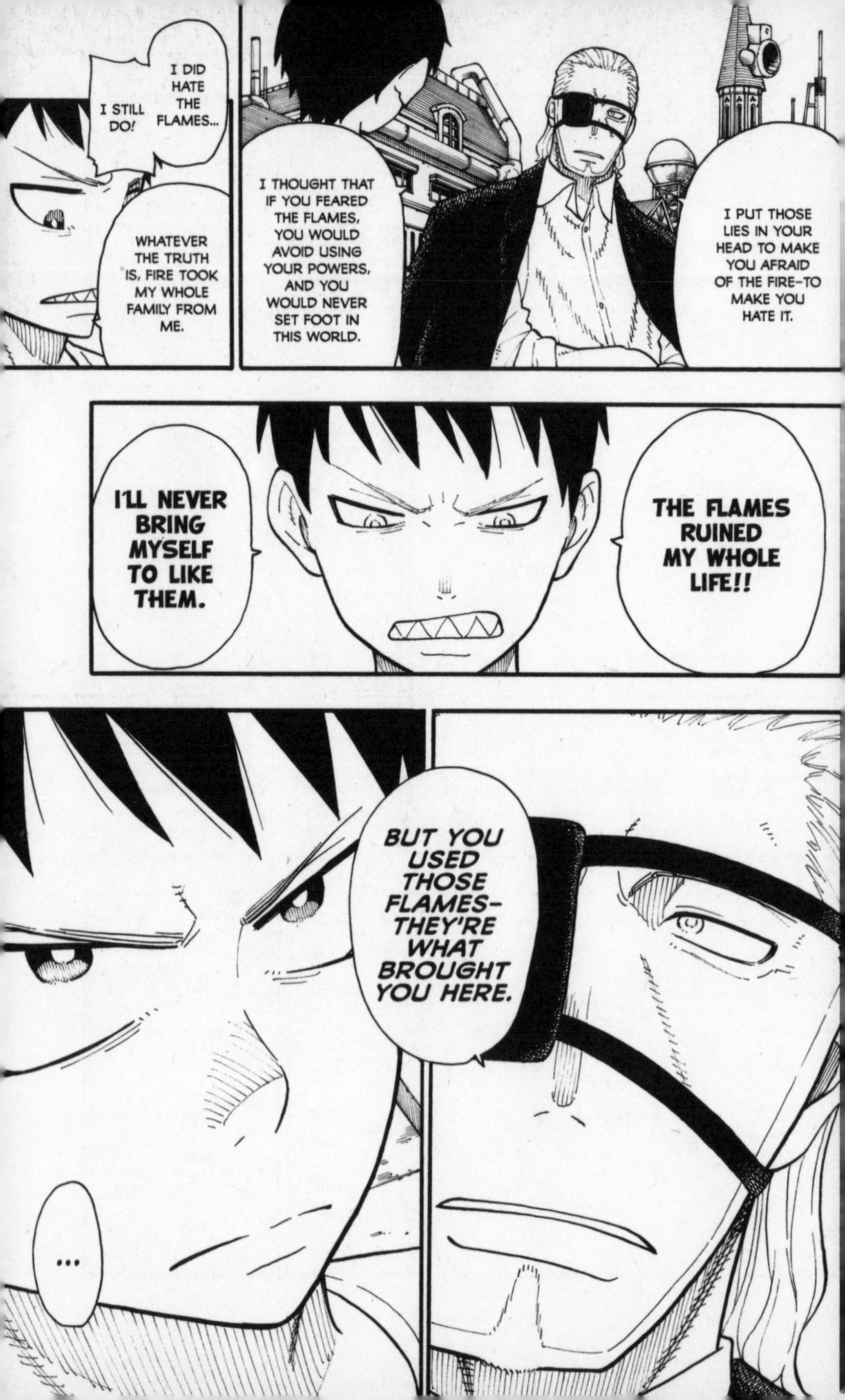
I PUT THOSE LIES IN YOUR HEAD TO MAKE YOU AFRAID OF THE FIRE—TO MAKE YOU HATE IT.
I THOUGHT THAT IF YOU FEARED THE FLAMES, YOU WOULD AVOID USING YOUR POWERS, AND YOU WOULD NEVER SET FOOT IN THIS WORLD.
I DID HATE THE FLAMES...
I STILL DO!
WHATEVER THE TRUTH IS, FIRE TOOK MY WHOLE FAMILY FROM ME.
THE FLAMES RUINED MY WHOLE LIFE!!
I'LL NEVER BRING MYSELF TO LIKE THEM.
BUT YOU USED THOSE FLAMES—THEY'RE WHAT BROUGHT YOU HERE.
...

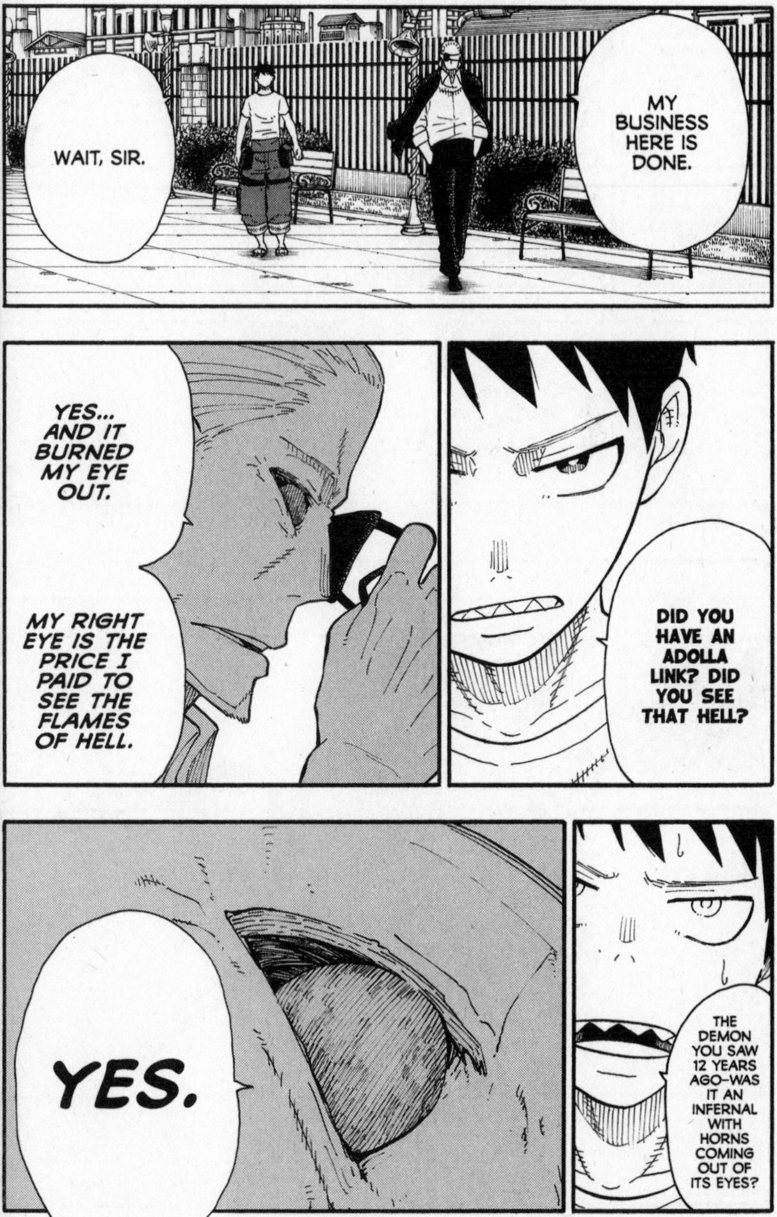
MY BUSINESS HERE IS DONE.
WAIT, SIR.
DID YOU HAVE AN ADOLLA LINK? DID YOU SEE THAT HELL?
YES... AND IT BURNED MY EYE OUT.
MY RIGHT EYE IS THE PRICE I PAID TO SEE THE FLAMES OF HELL.
THE DEMON YOU SAW 12 YEARS AGO—WAS IT AN INFERNAL WITH HORNS COMING OUT OF ITS EYES?
YES.

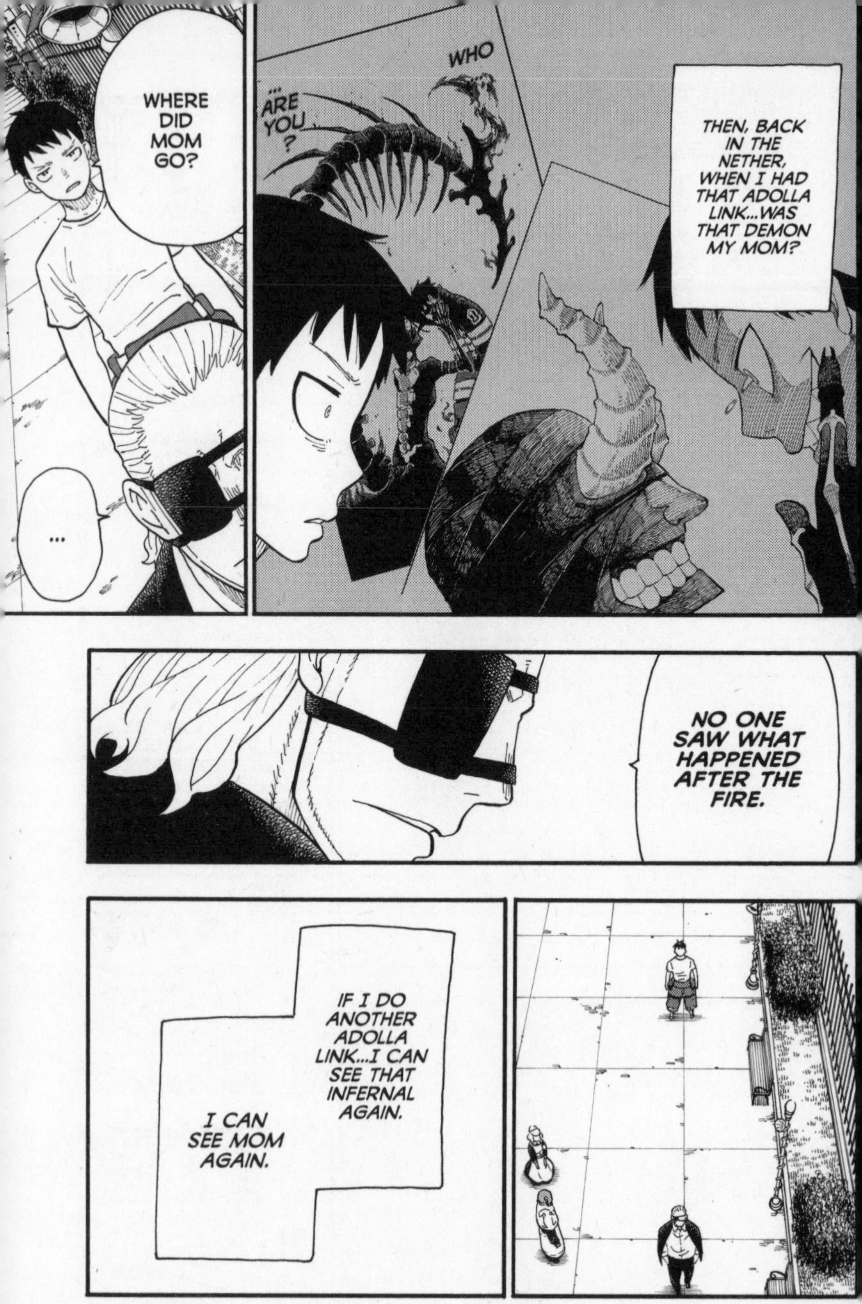
THEN, BACK IN THE NETHER, WHEN I HAD THAT ADOLLA LINK...WAS THAT DEMON MY MOM?
WHO ...ARE YOU?
WHERE DID MOM GO?
...
NO ONE SAW WHAT HAPPENED AFTER THE FIRE.
IF I DO ANOTHER ADOLLA LINK...I CAN SEE THAT INFERNAL AGAIN.
I CAN SEE MOM AGAIN.

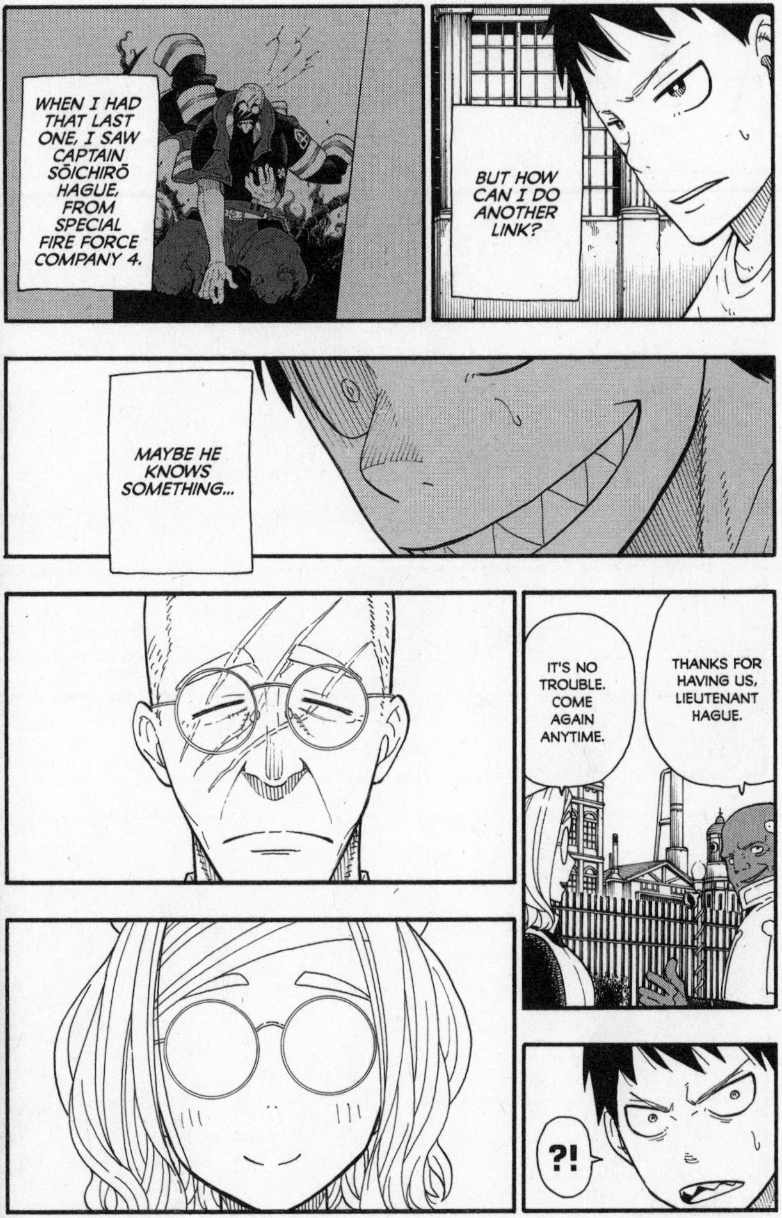
BUT HOW CAN I DO ANOTHER LINK?
WHEN I HAD THAT LAST ONE, I SAW CAPTAIN SŌICHIRŌ HAGUE, FROM SPECIAL FIRE FORCE COMPANY 4.
MAYBE HE KNOWS SOMETHING...
THANKS FOR HAVING US, LIEUTENANT HAGUE.
IT'S NO TROUBLE. COME AGAIN ANYTIME.
?!

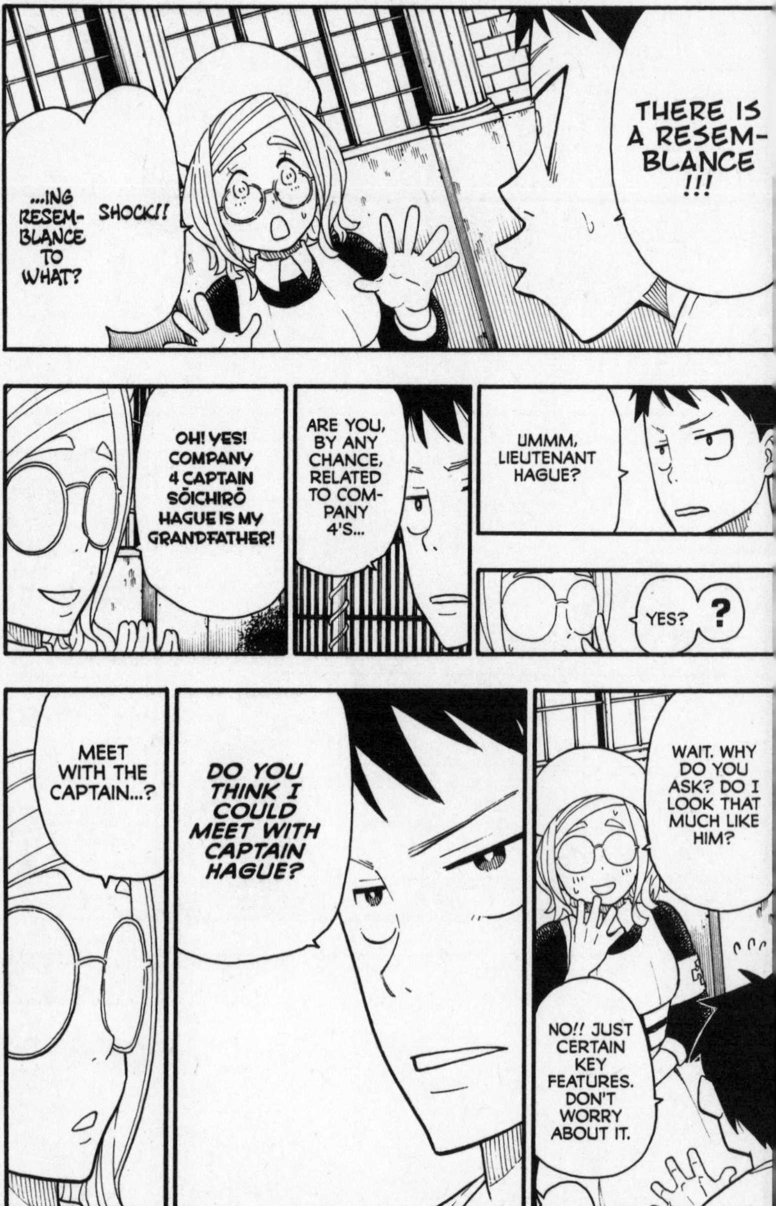
THERE IS A RESEMBLANCE !!!
SHOCK!!
...ING RESEMBLANCE TO WHAT?
UMMM, LIEUTENANT HAGUE?
YES?
?
ARE YOU, BY ANY CHANCE, RELATED TO COMPANY 4'S...
OH! YES! COMPANY 4 CAPTAIN SŌICHIRŌ HAGUE IS MY GRANDFATHER!
WAIT. WHY DO YOU ASK? DO I LOOK THAT MUCH LIKE HIM?
NO!! JUST CERTAIN KEY FEATURES. DON'T WORRY ABOUT IT.
DON'T WORRY?
DO YOU THINK I COULD MEET WITH CAPTAIN HAGUE?
MEET WITH THE CAPTAIN...?

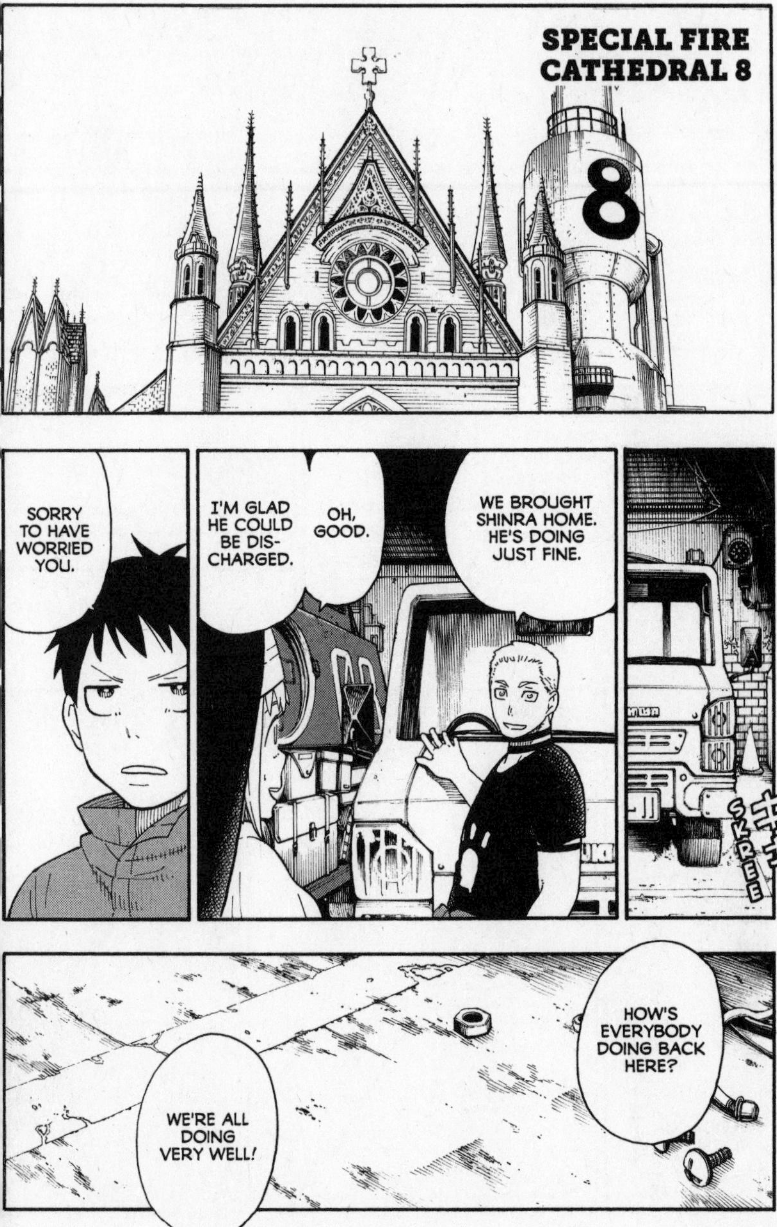
SPECIAL FIRE CATHEDRAL 8
SKREE
WE BROUGHT SHINRA HOME. HE'S DOING JUST FINE.
OH, GOOD.
I'M GLAD HE COULD BE DISCHARGED.
SORRY TO HAVE WORRIED YOU.
HOW'S EVERYBODY DOING BACK HERE?
WE'RE ALL DOING VERY WELL!

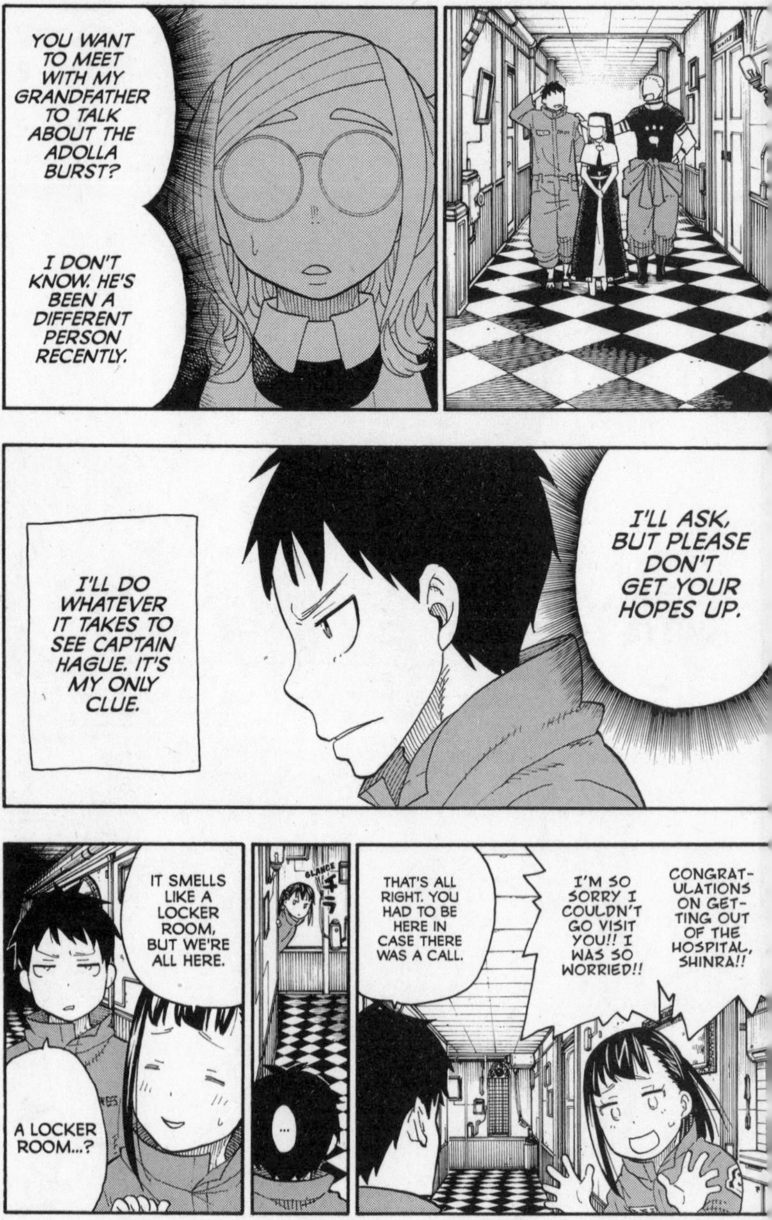
YOU WANT TO MEET WITH MY GRANDFATHER TO TALK ABOUT THE ADOLLA BURST?
I DON'T KNOW. HE'S BEEN A DIFFERENT PERSON RECENTLY.
I'LL ASK, BUT PLEASE DON'T GET YOUR HOPES UP.
I'LL DO WHATEVER IT TAKES TO SEE CAPTAIN HAGUE. IT'S MY ONLY CLUE.
CONGRATULATIONS ON GETTING OUT OF THE HOSPITAL, SHINRA!!
I'M SO SORRY I COULDN'T GO VISIT YOU!! I WAS SO WORRIED!!
THAT'S ALL RIGHT. YOU HAD TO BE HERE IN CASE THERE WAS A CALL.
GLANCE
...
IT SMELLS LIKE A LOCKER ROOM, BUT WE'RE ALL HERE.
A LOCKER ROOM...?

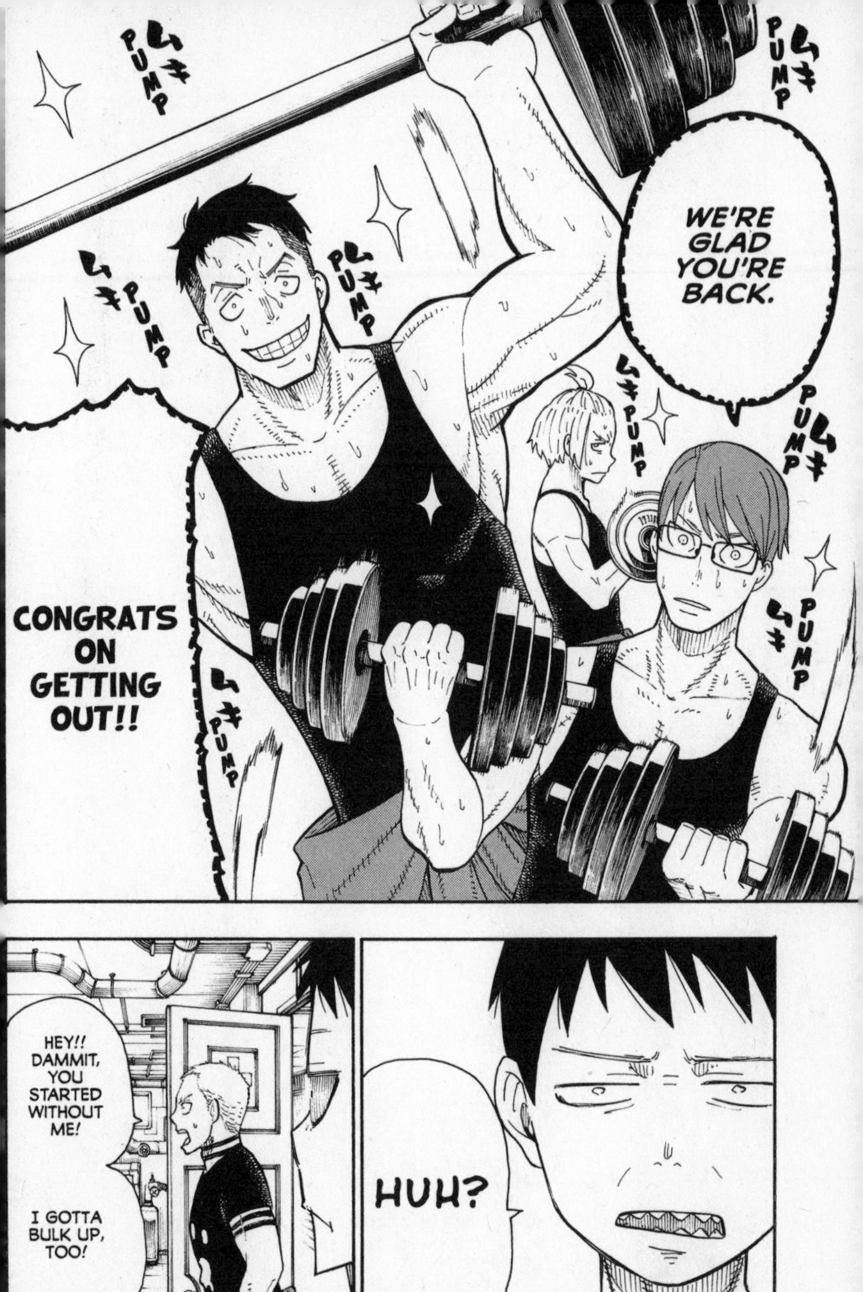
ムキ PUMP
WE'RE GLAD YOU'RE BACK.
ムキ PUMP
ムキ PUMP
ムキ PUMP
ムキ PUMP
ムキ PUMP
ムキ PUMP
CONGRATS ON GETTING OUT!!
ムキ PUMP
HUH?
HEY!! DAMMIT, YOU STARTED WITHOUT ME!
I GOTTA BULK UP, TOO!

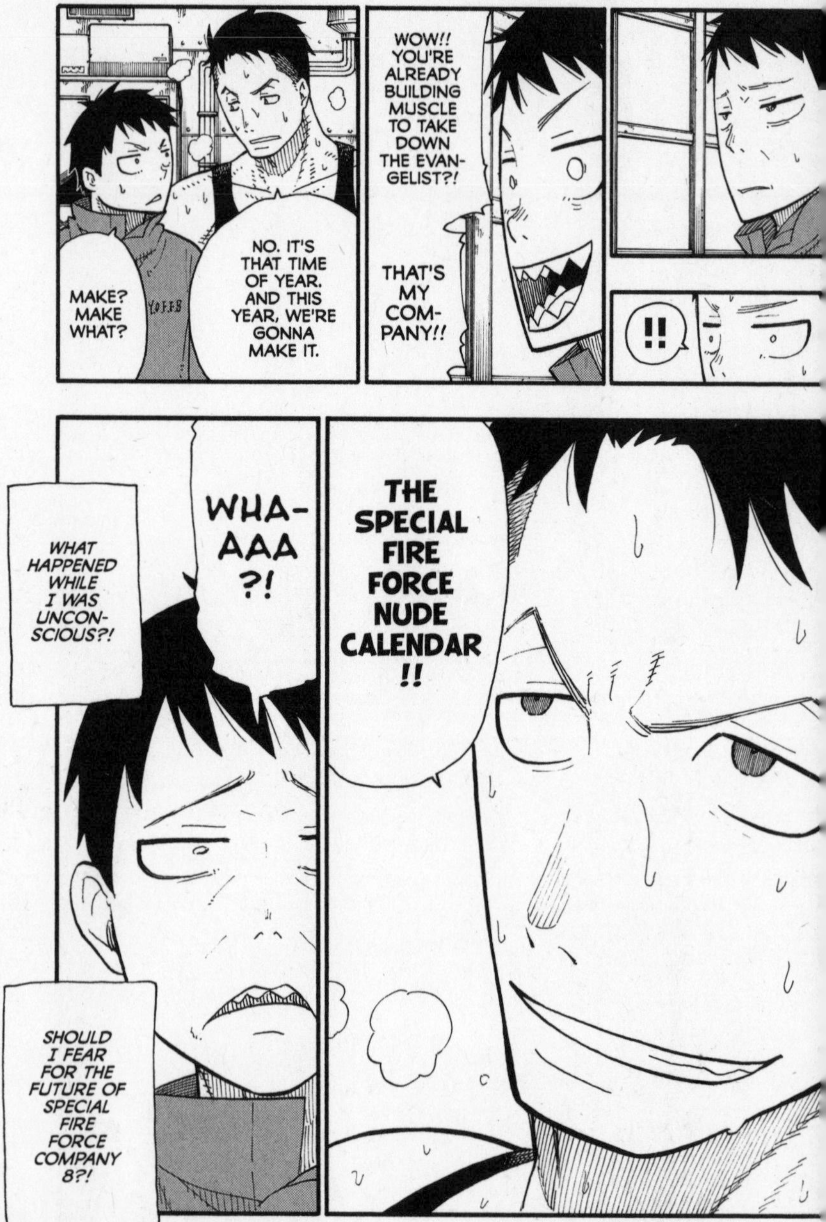
!!
WOW!! YOU'RE ALREADY BUILDING MUSCLE TO TAKE DOWN THE EVANGELIST?!
THAT'S MY COMPANY!!
NO. IT'S THAT TIME OF YEAR. AND THIS YEAR, WE'RE GONNA MAKE IT.
MAKE? MAKE WHAT?
THE SPECIAL FIRE FORCE NUDE CALENDAR!!
WHA-AAA?!
WHAT HAPPENED WHILE I WAS UNCONSCIOUS?!
SHOULD I FEAR FOR THE FUTURE OF SPECIAL FIRE FORCE COMPANY 8?!

FIRE FORCE

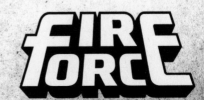

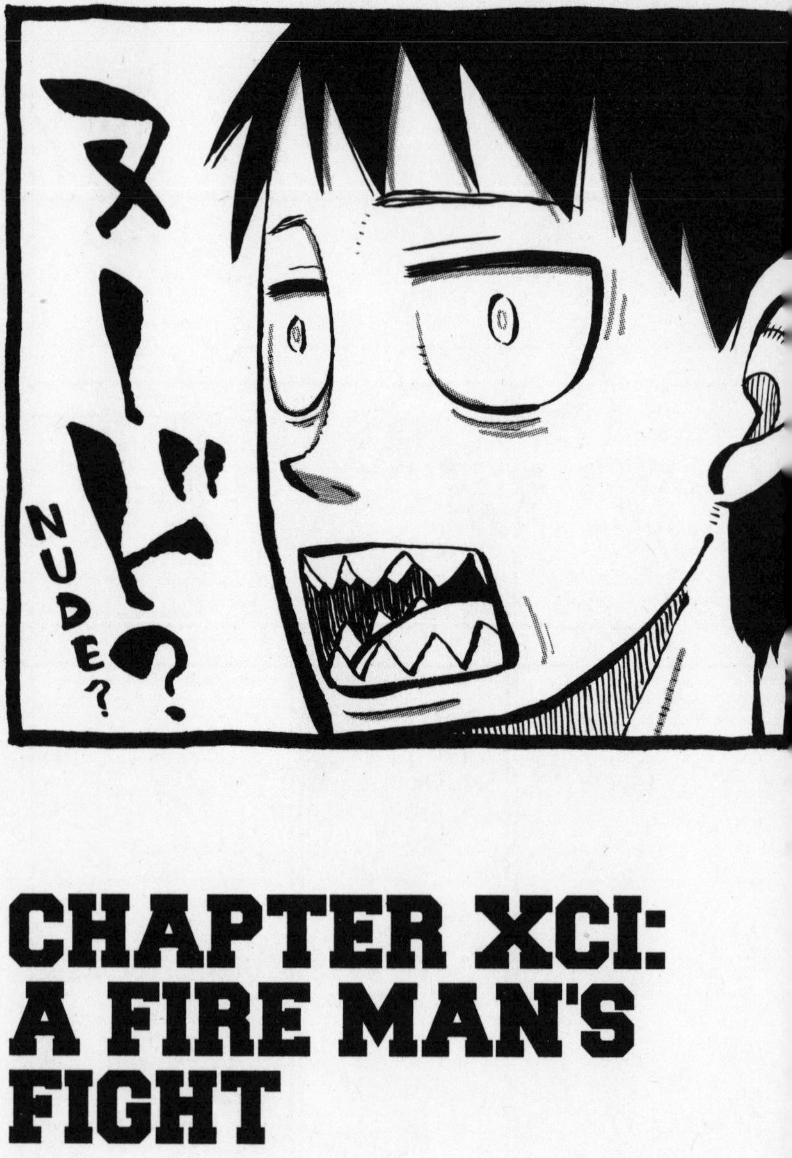
ヌード？
NUDE?

CHAPTER XCI: A FIRE MAN'S FIGHT

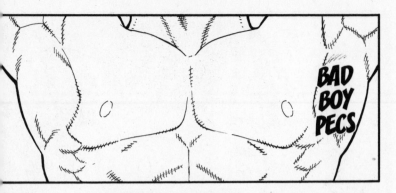

BAD BOY PECS
UH...
THE SPECIAL FIRE FORCE NUDE CALENDAR... SIR?
ASSERTIVE ABS
YES, THE NUDE CALEN- DAR.
SHY DORSALS

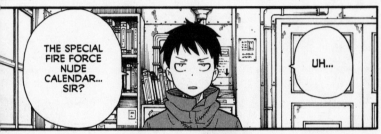

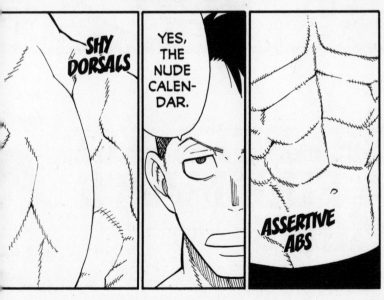

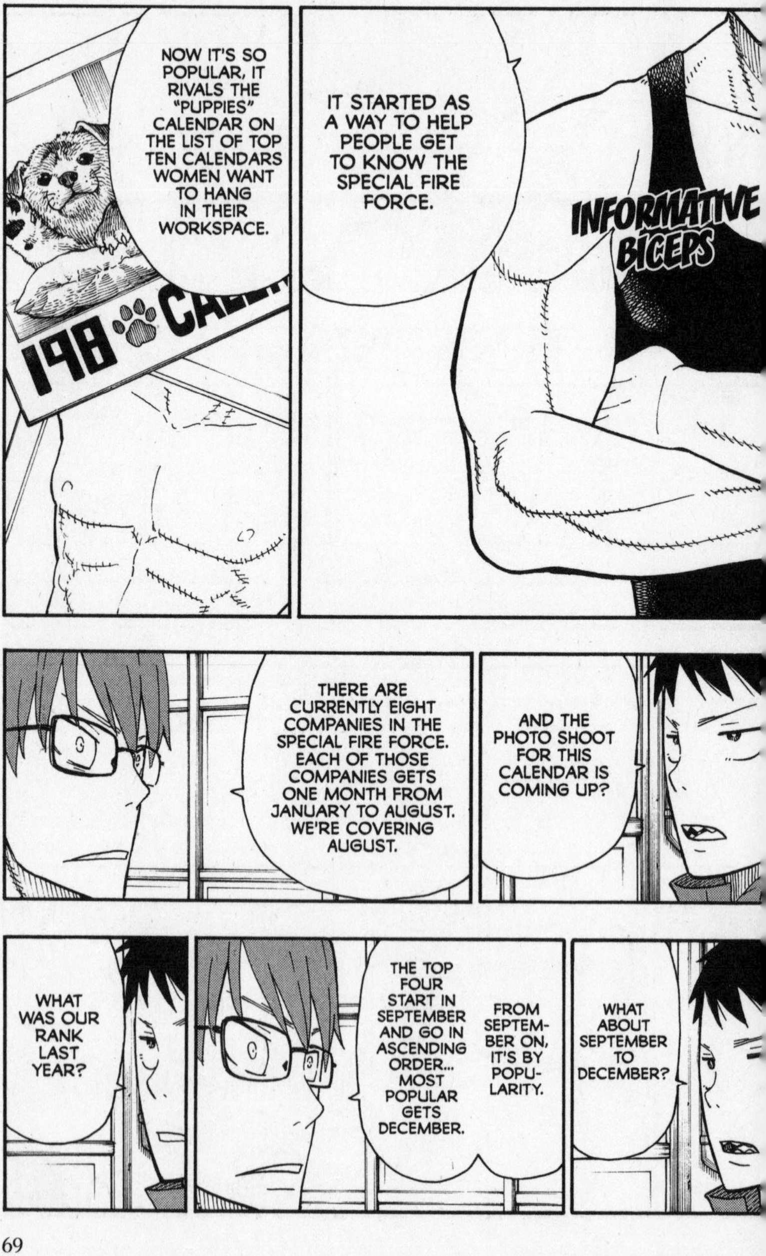
IT STARTED AS A WAY TO HELP PEOPLE GET TO KNOW THE SPECIAL FIRE FORCE.
INFORMATIVE BICEPS
NOW IT'S SO POPULAR, IT RIVALS THE "PUPPIES" CALENDAR ON THE LIST OF TOP TEN CALENDARS WOMEN WANT TO HANG IN THEIR WORKSPACE.
198
AND THE PHOTO SHOOT FOR THIS CALENDAR IS COMING UP?
THERE ARE CURRENTLY EIGHT COMPANIES IN THE SPECIAL FIRE FORCE. EACH OF THOSE COMPANIES GETS ONE MONTH FROM JANUARY TO AUGUST. WE'RE COVERING AUGUST.
WHAT ABOUT SEPTEMBER TO DECEMBER?
FROM SEPTEMBER ON, IT'S BY POPULARITY.
THE TOP FOUR START IN SEPTEMBER AND GO IN ASCENDING ORDER... MOST POPULAR GETS DECEMBER.
WHAT WAS OUR RANK LAST YEAR?

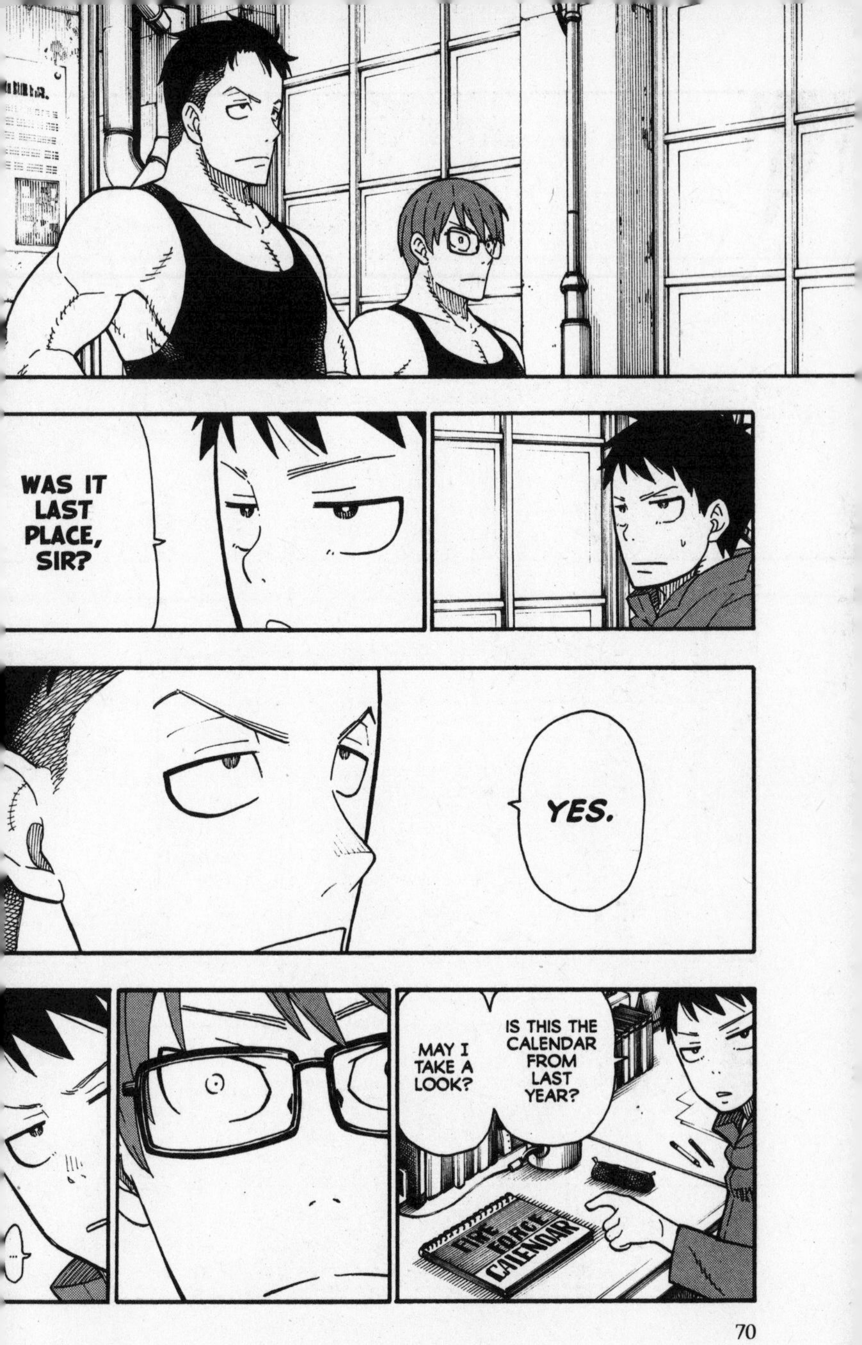
WAS IT LAST PLACE, SIR?
YES.
IS THIS THE CALENDAR FROM LAST YEAR?
MAY I TAKE A LOOK?
FIRE FORCE CALENDAR
...

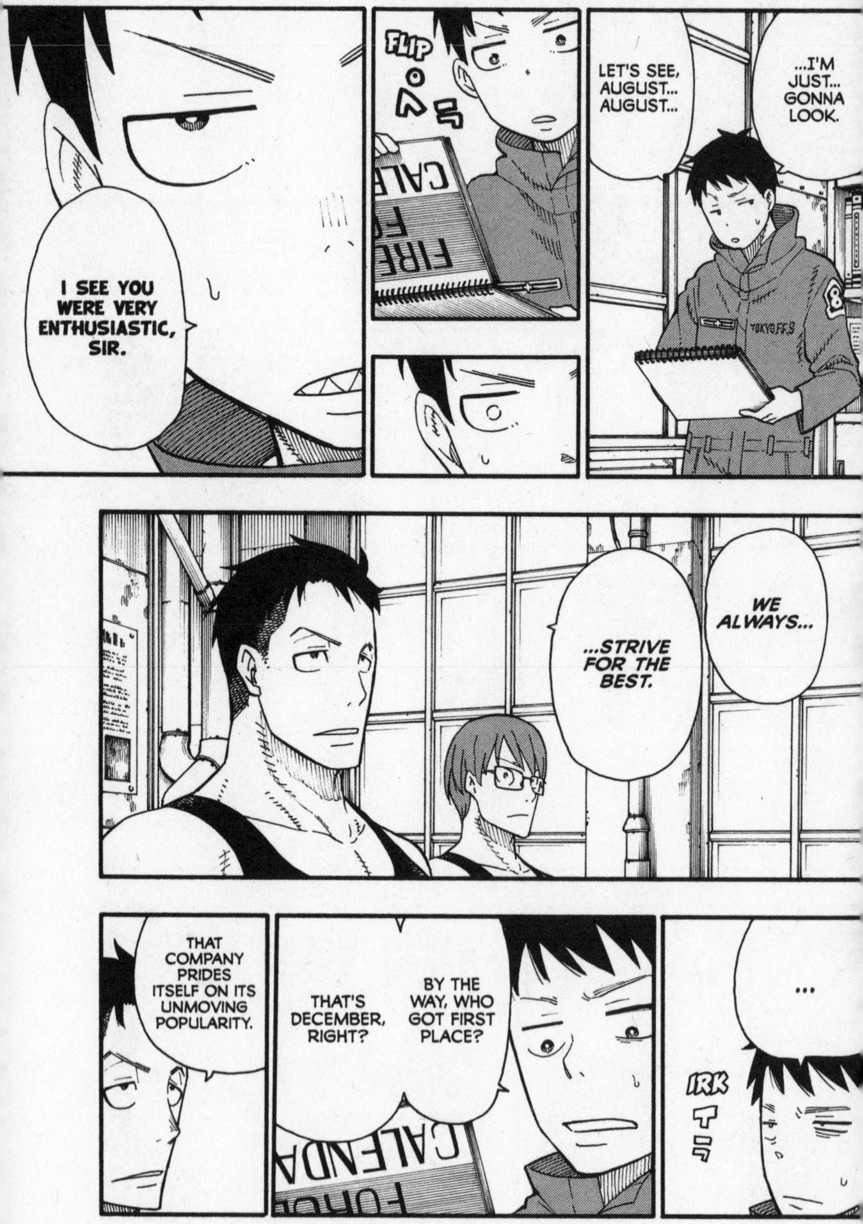
...I'M JUST... GONNA LOOK.
LET'S SEE, AUGUST... AUGUST...
FLIP
I SEE YOU WERE VERY ENTHUSIASTIC, SIR.
WE ALWAYS...
...STRIVE FOR THE BEST.
...
IRK
BY THE WAY, WHO GOT FIRST PLACE?
THAT'S DECEMBER, RIGHT?
THAT COMPANY PRIDES ITSELF ON ITS UNMOVING POPULARITY.

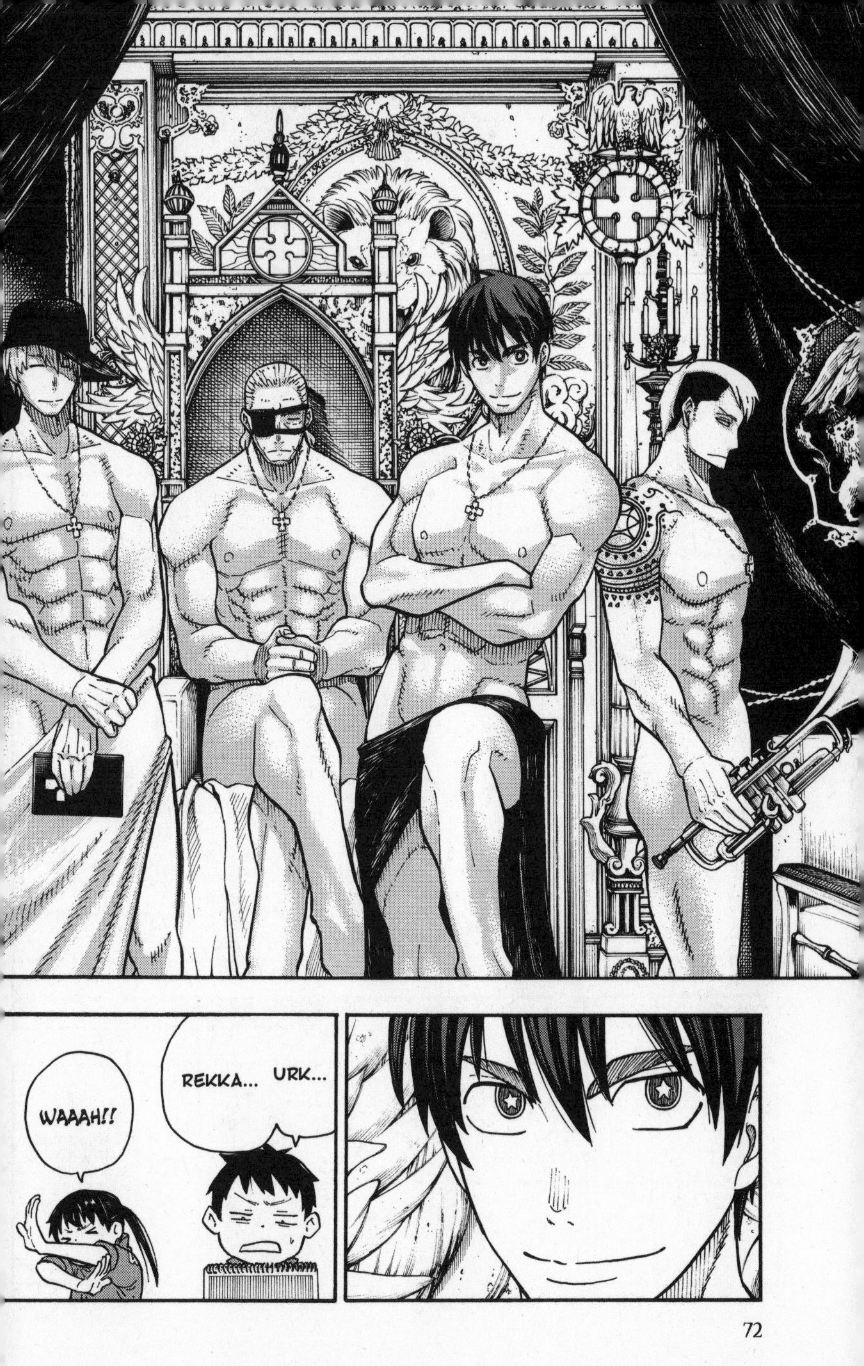
REKKA... URK...
WAAAH!!

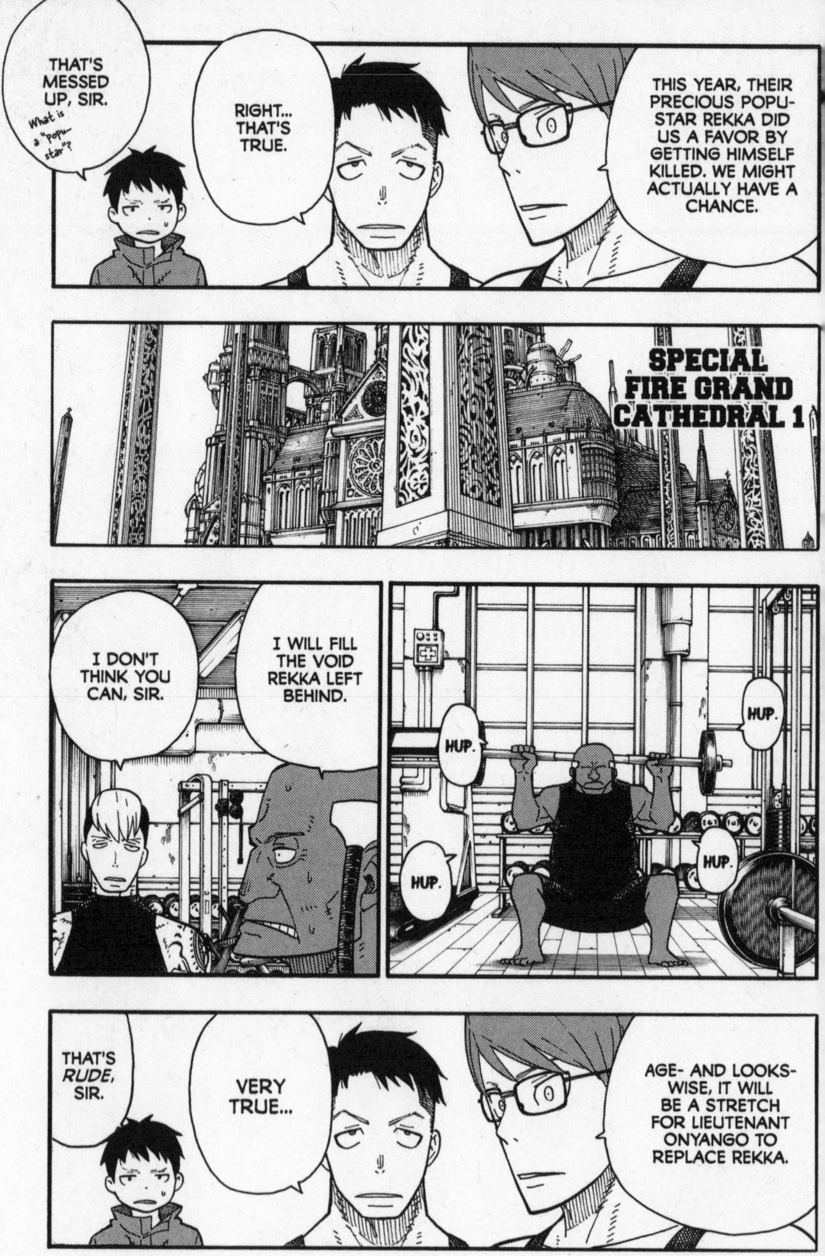

THIS YEAR, THEIR PRECIOUS POPU-STAR REKKA DID US A FAVOR BY GETTING HIMSELF KILLED. WE MIGHT ACTUALLY HAVE A CHANCE.
RIGHT... THAT'S TRUE.
THAT'S MESSED UP, SIR.
What is a "popu-star"?
SPECIAL FIRE GRAND CATHEDRAL 1
HUP.
HUP.
HUP.
HUP.
I WILL FILL THE VOID REKKA LEFT BEHIND.
I DON'T THINK YOU CAN, SIR.
AGE- AND LOOKS-WISE, IT WILL BE A STRETCH FOR LIEUTENANT ONYANGO TO REPLACE REKKA.
VERY TRUE...
THAT'S *RUDE*, SIR.

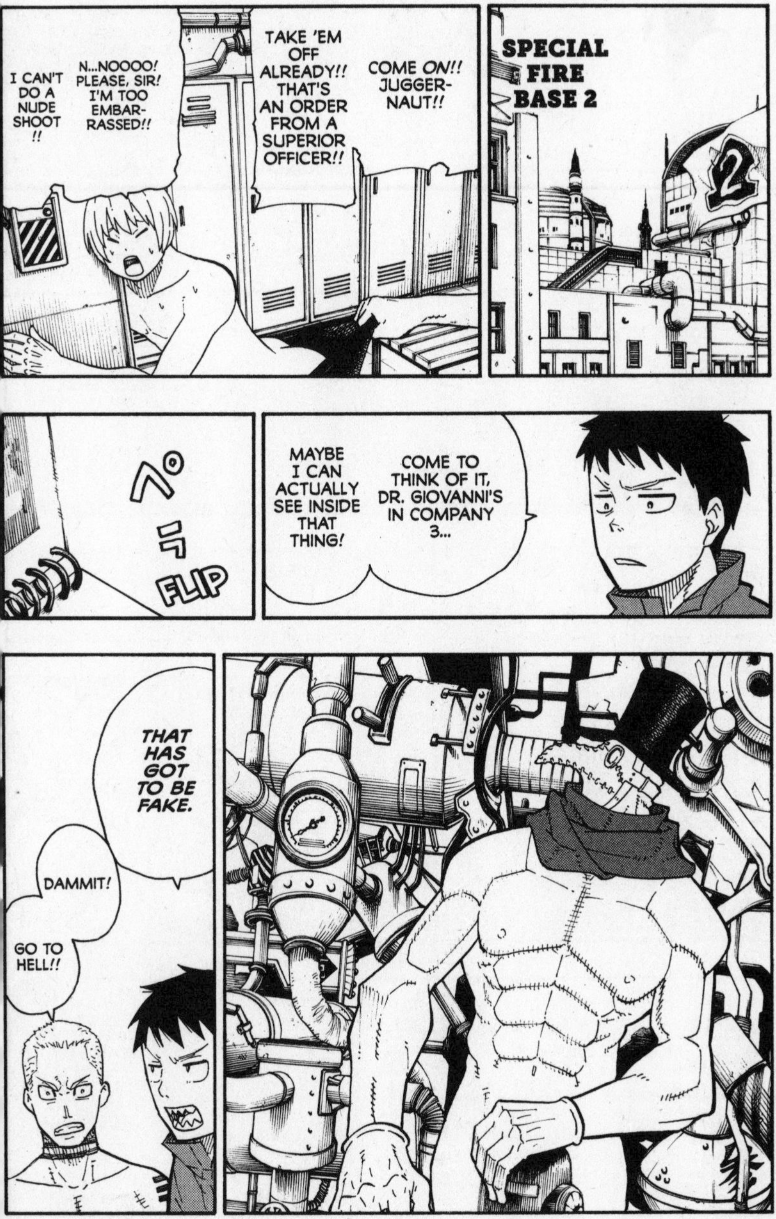
SPECIAL FIRE BASE 2
COME ON!! JUGGERNAUT!!
TAKE 'EM OFF ALREADY!! THAT'S AN ORDER FROM A SUPERIOR OFFICER!!
N...NOOOO! PLEASE, SIR! I'M TOO EMBARRASSED!!
I CAN'T DO A NUDE SHOOT!!
COME TO THINK OF IT, DR. GIOVANNI'S IN COMPANY 3...
MAYBE I CAN ACTUALLY SEE INSIDE THAT THING!
へら
FLIP
THAT HAS GOT TO BE FAKE.
DAMMIT!
GO TO HELL!!

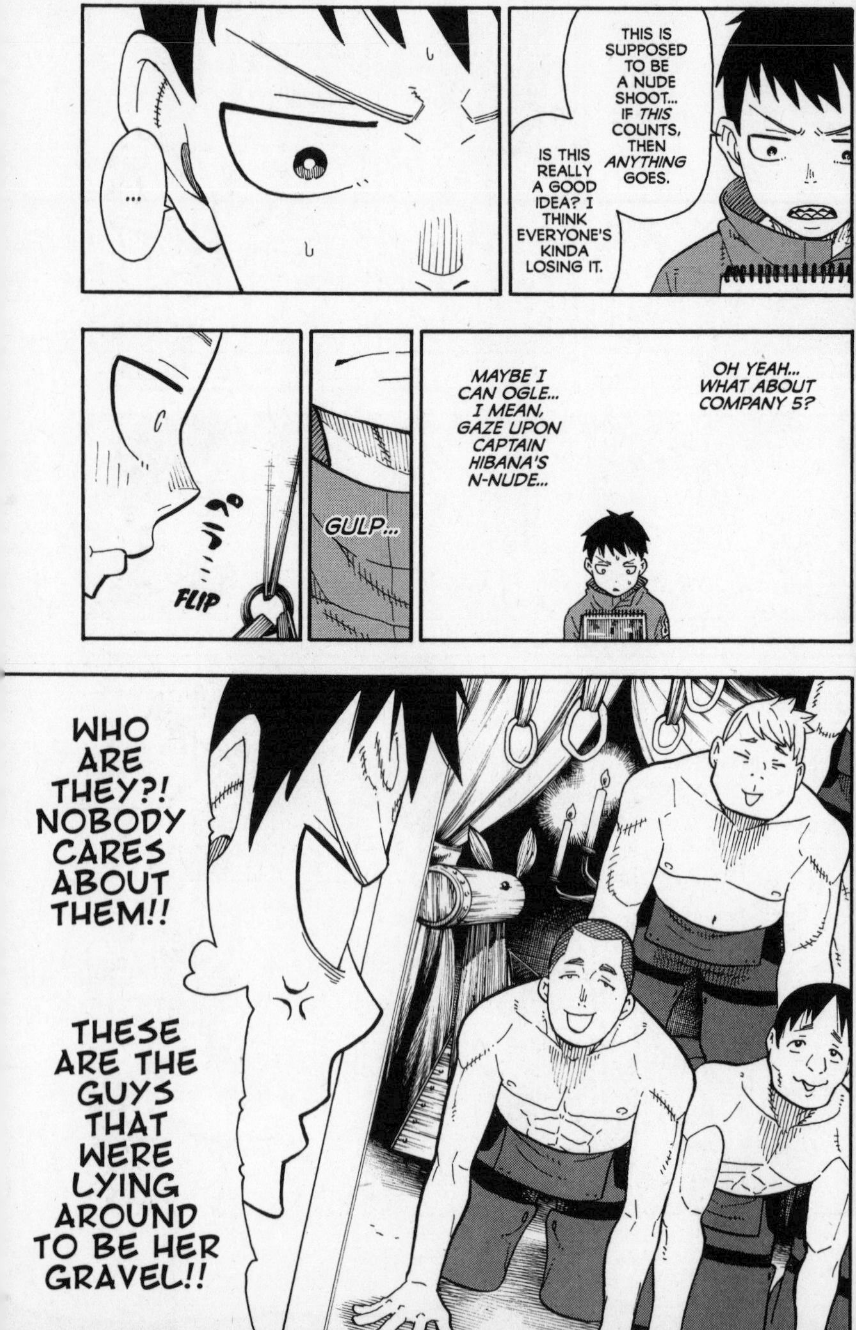
THIS IS SUPPOSED TO BE A NUDE SHOOT... IF *THIS* COUNTS, THEN *ANYTHING* GOES.
IS THIS REALLY A GOOD IDEA? I THINK EVERYONE'S KINDA LOSING IT.
...
OH YEAH... WHAT ABOUT COMPANY 5?
MAYBE I CAN OGLE... I MEAN, GAZE UPON CAPTAIN HIBANA'S N-NUDE...
GULP...
FLIP
WHO ARE THEY?! NOBODY CARES ABOUT THEM!!
THESE ARE THE GUYS THAT WERE LYING AROUND TO BE HER GRAVEL!!

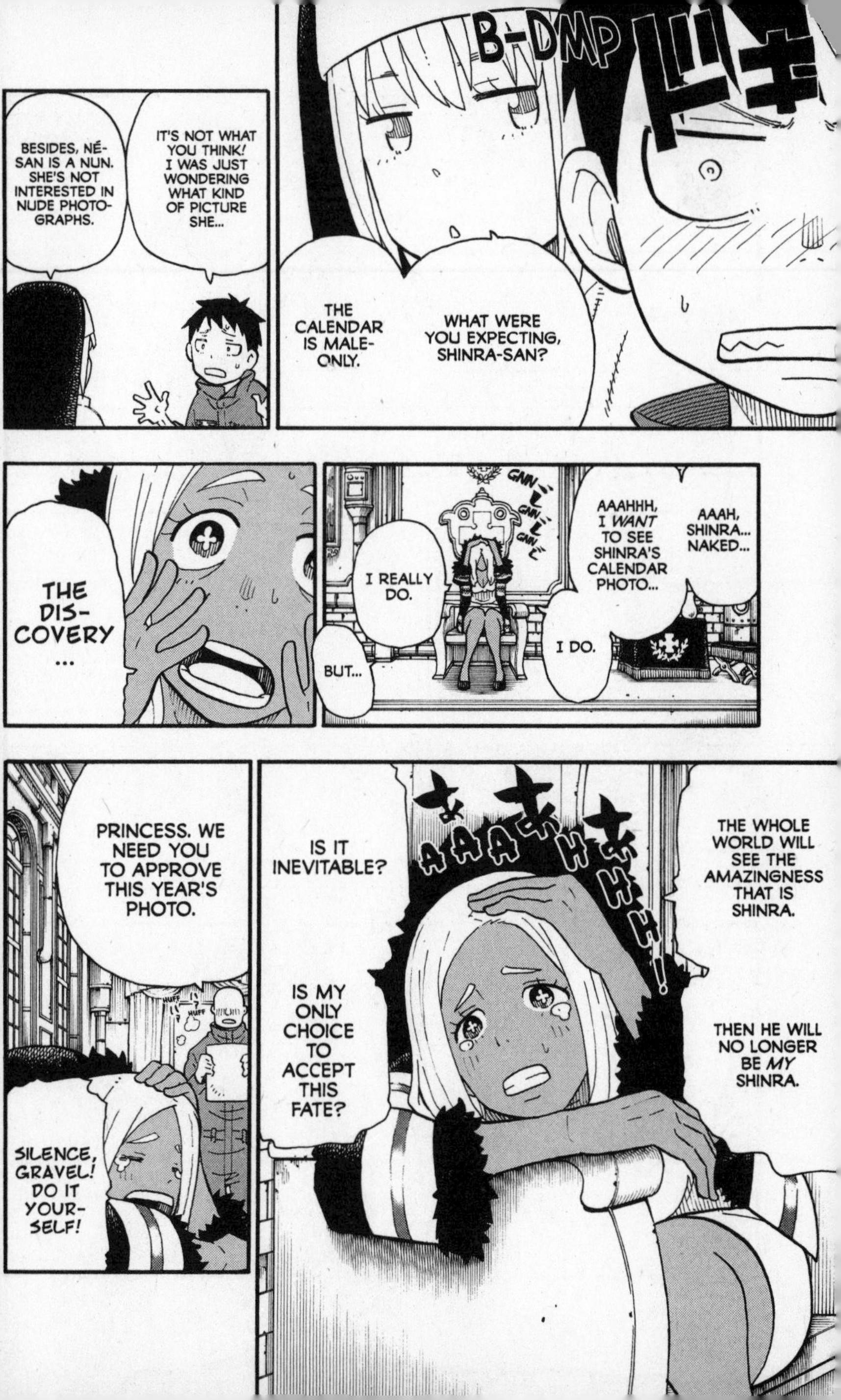
B-DMP
ドキッ
WHAT WERE YOU EXPECTING, SHINRA-SAN?
THE CALENDAR IS MALE-ONLY.
IT'S NOT WHAT YOU THINK! I WAS JUST WONDERING WHAT KIND OF PICTURE SHE...
BESIDES, NÉ-SAN IS A NUN. SHE'S NOT INTERESTED IN NUDE PHOTO-GRAPHS.
AAAH, SHINRA... NAKED...
AAAHHH, I *WANT* TO SEE SHINRA'S CALENDAR PHOTO...
I DO.
GAN GAN GAN
I REALLY DO.
BUT...
THE DIS-COVERY ...
THE WHOLE WORLD WILL SEE THE AMAZINGNESS THAT IS SHINRA.
AAAAHHHHHH!
IS IT INEVITABLE?
THEN HE WILL NO LONGER BE *MY* SHINRA.
IS MY ONLY CHOICE TO ACCEPT THIS FATE?
PRINCESS. WE NEED YOU TO APPROVE THIS YEAR'S PHOTO.
HUFF HUFF
SILENCE, GRAVEL! DO IT YOURSELF!

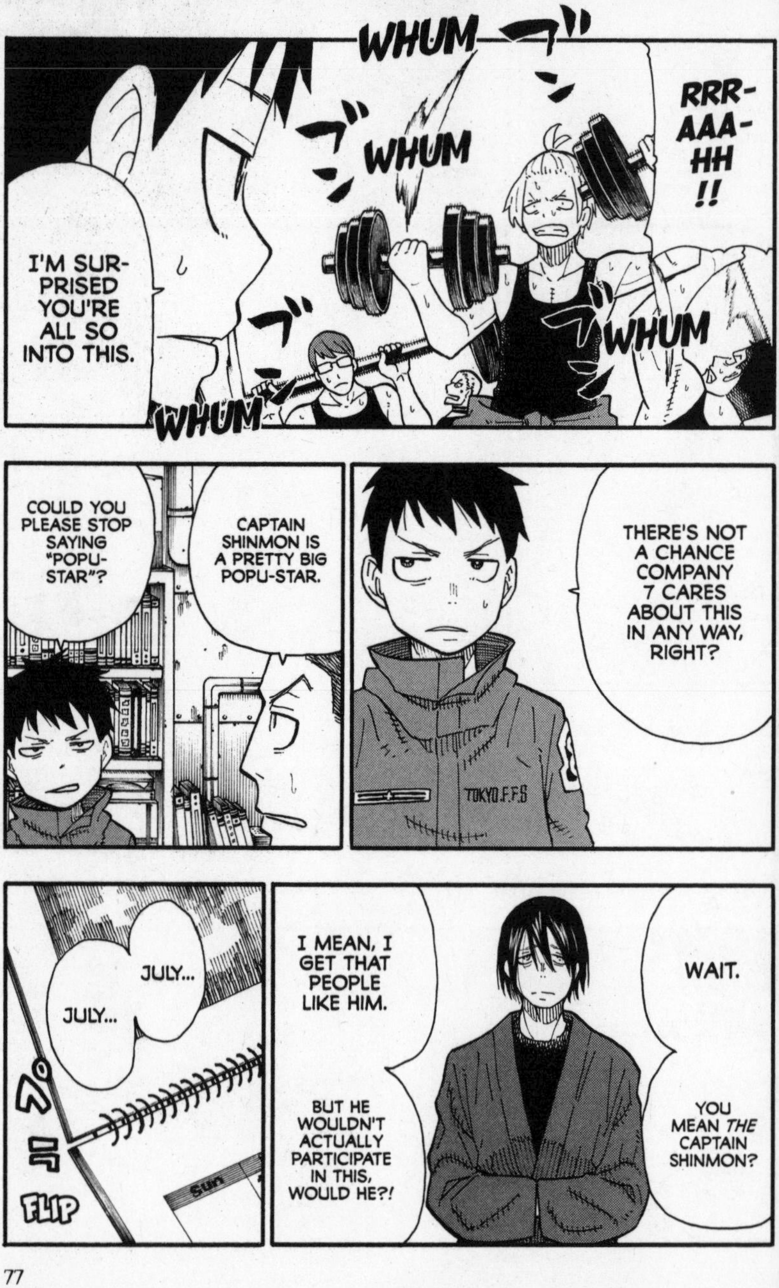
RRR-AAA-HH!!
WHUM
ブン
WHUM
ブン
WHUM
ブン
I'M SURPRISED YOU'RE ALL SO INTO THIS.
WHUM
THERE'S NOT A CHANCE COMPANY 7 CARES ABOUT THIS IN ANY WAY, RIGHT?
TOKYO F.F.S
CAPTAIN SHINMON IS A PRETTY BIG POPU-STAR.
COULD YOU PLEASE STOP SAYING "POPU-STAR"?
WAIT.
YOU MEAN *THE* CAPTAIN SHINMON?
I MEAN, I GET THAT PEOPLE LIKE HIM.
BUT HE WOULDN'T ACTUALLY PARTICIPATE IN THIS, WOULD HE?!
JULY...
JULY...
FLIP
Sun

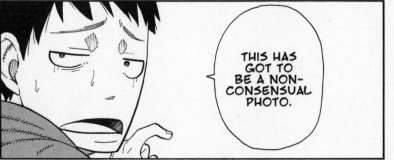

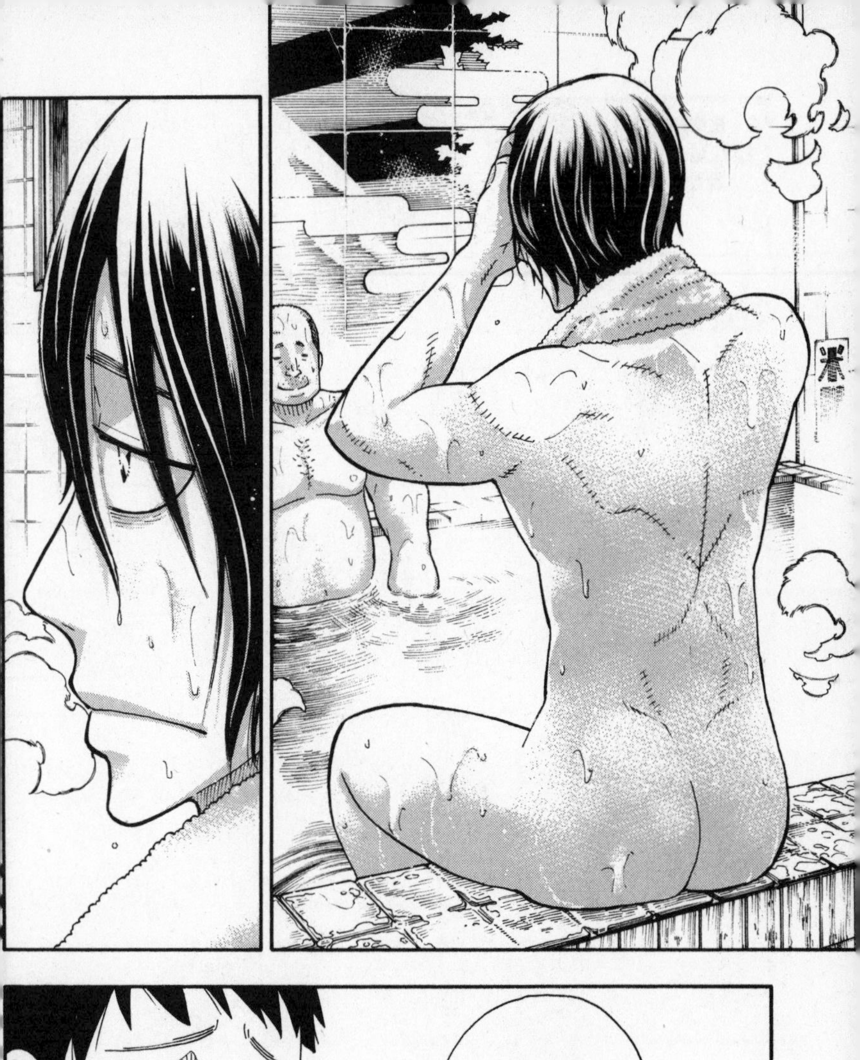
THIS HAS GOT TO BE A NON-CONSENSUAL PHOTO.

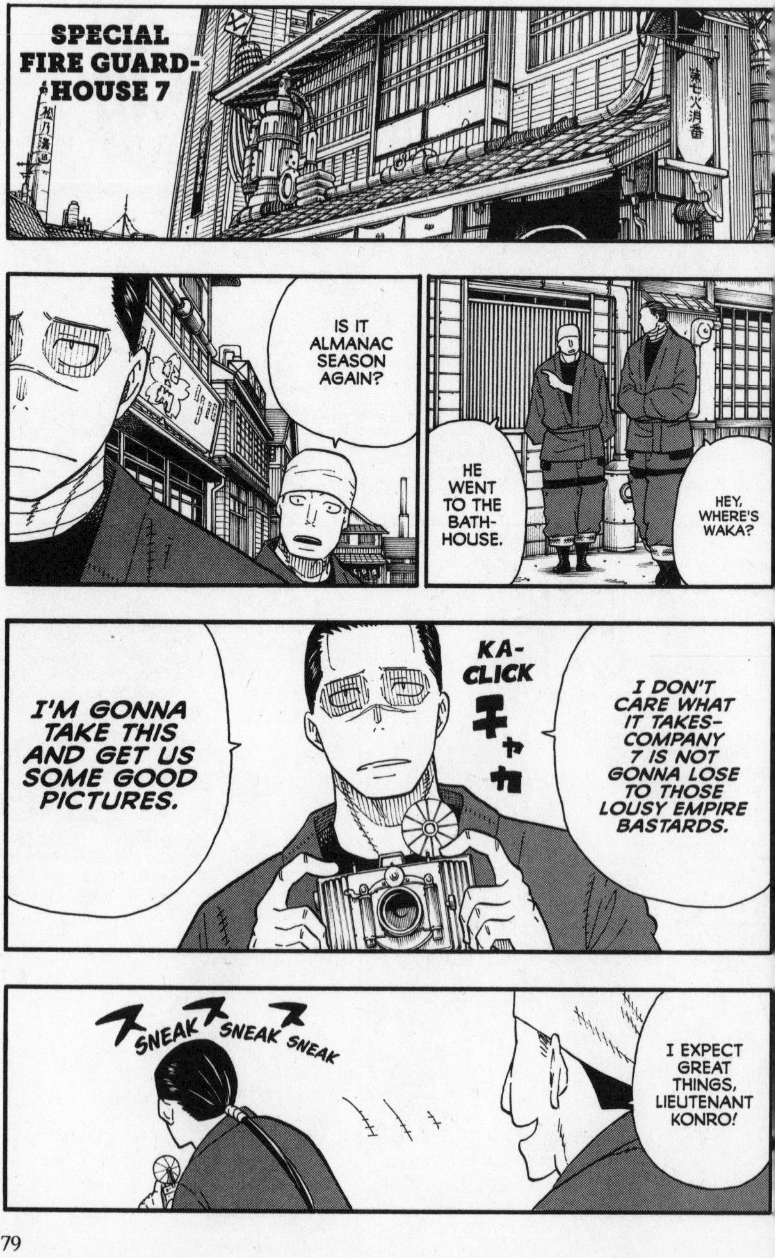
SPECIAL FIRE GUARD-HOUSE 7
HEY, WHERE'S WAKA?
HE WENT TO THE BATH-HOUSE.
IS IT ALMANAC SEASON AGAIN?
I DON'T CARE WHAT IT TAKES- COMPANY 7 IS NOT GONNA LOSE TO THOSE LOUSY EMPIRE BASTARDS.
KA-CLICK
チャカ
I'M GONNA TAKE THIS AND GET US SOME GOOD PICTURES.
I EXPECT GREAT THINGS, LIEUTENANT KONRO!
SNEAK SNEAK SNEAK

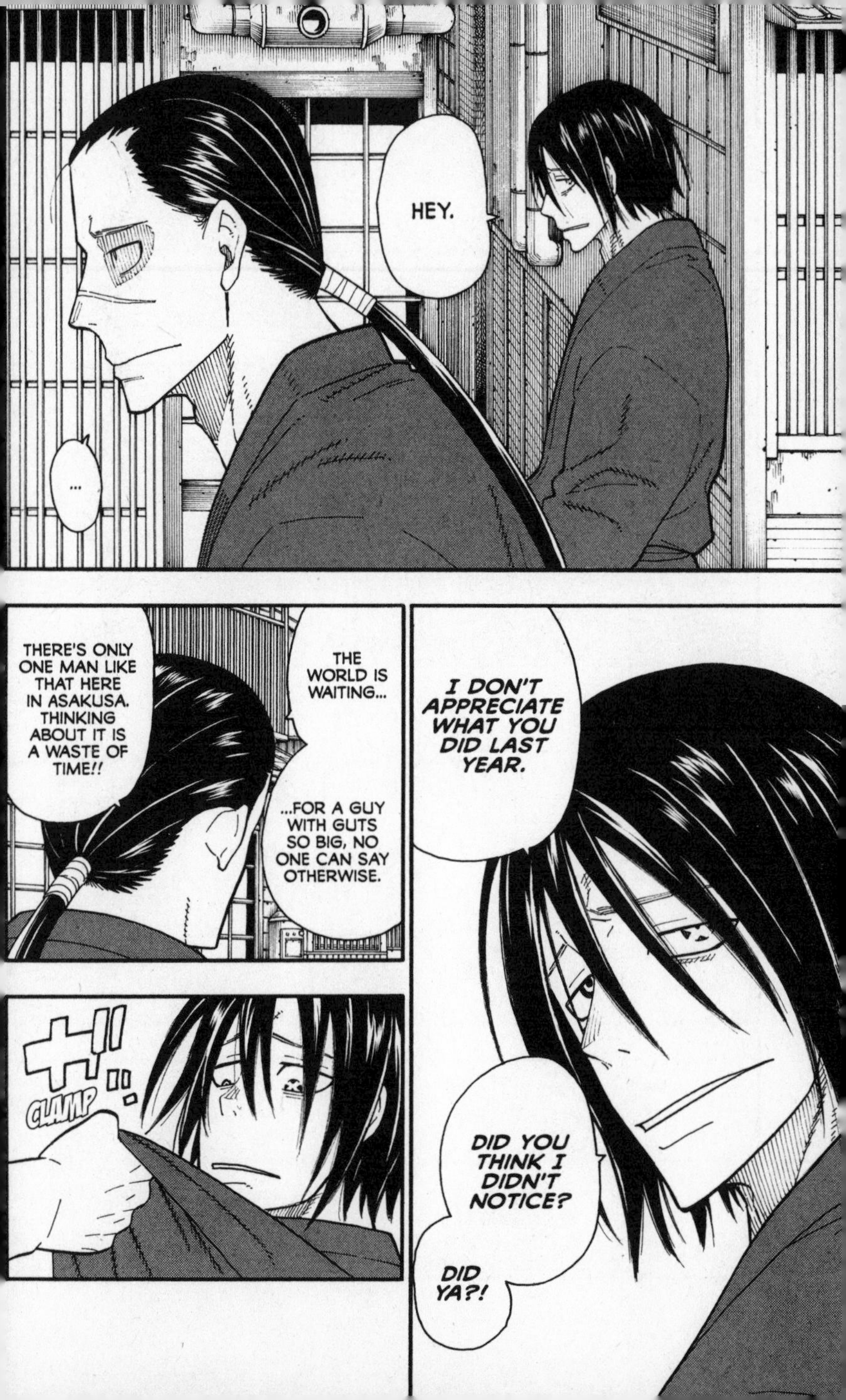
HEY.
...
I DON'T APPRECIATE WHAT YOU DID LAST YEAR.
DID YOU THINK I DIDN'T NOTICE?
DID YA?!
THE WORLD IS WAITING...
...FOR A GUY WITH GUTS SO BIG, NO ONE CAN SAY OTHERWISE.
THERE'S ONLY ONE MAN LIKE THAT HERE IN ASAKUSA. THINKING ABOUT IT IS A WASTE OF TIME!!
CLAMP

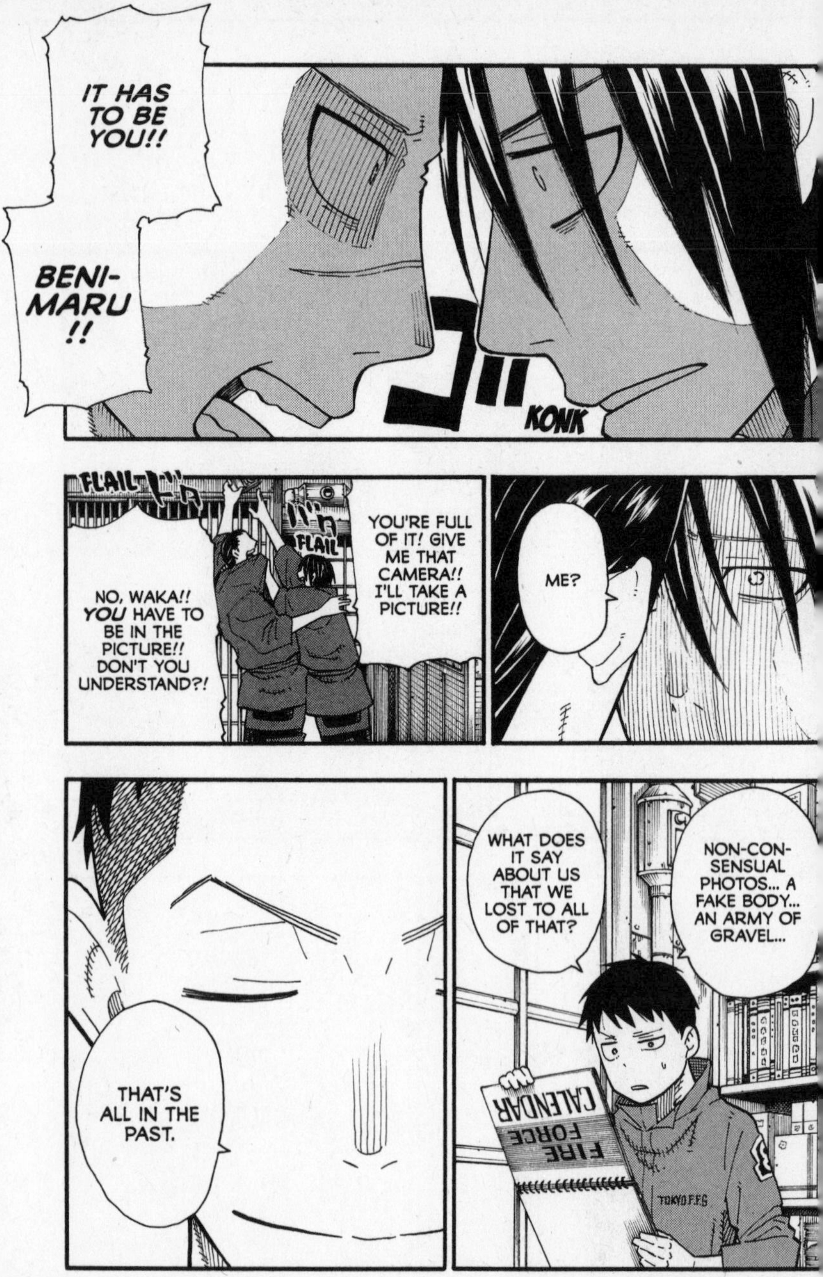

IT HAS TO BE YOU!!
BENI-MARU!!
KONK
ME?
FLAIL
FLAIL
YOU'RE FULL OF IT! GIVE ME THAT CAMERA!! I'LL TAKE A PICTURE!!
NO, WAKA!! *YOU* HAVE TO BE IN THE PICTURE!! DON'T YOU UNDERSTAND?!
NON-CON-SENSUAL PHOTOS... A FAKE BODY... AN ARMY OF GRAVEL...
WHAT DOES IT SAY ABOUT US THAT WE LOST TO ALL OF THAT?
FIRE FORCE CALENDAR
TOKYO F.F.G
THAT'S ALL IN THE PAST.

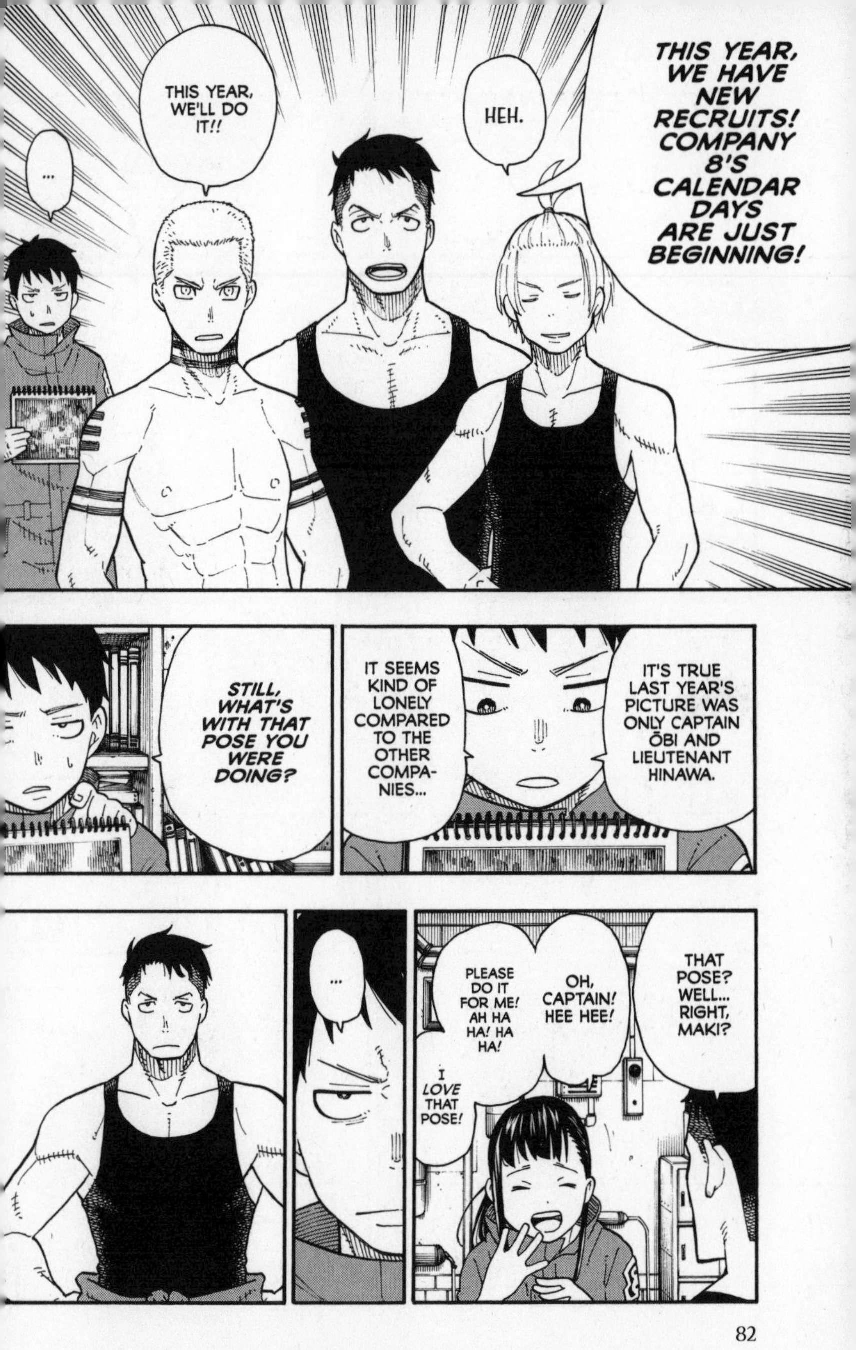
THIS YEAR, WE HAVE NEW RECRUITS! COMPANY 8'S CALENDAR DAYS ARE JUST BEGINNING!
HEH.
THIS YEAR, WE'LL DO IT!!
...
IT'S TRUE LAST YEAR'S PICTURE WAS ONLY CAPTAIN ŌBI AND LIEUTENANT HINAWA.
IT SEEMS KIND OF LONELY COMPARED TO THE OTHER COMPANIES...
STILL, WHAT'S WITH THAT POSE YOU WERE DOING?
THAT POSE? WELL... RIGHT, MAKI?
OH, CAPTAIN! HEE HEE!
PLEASE DO IT FOR ME! AH HA HA! HA HA!
I *LOVE* THAT POSE!
...

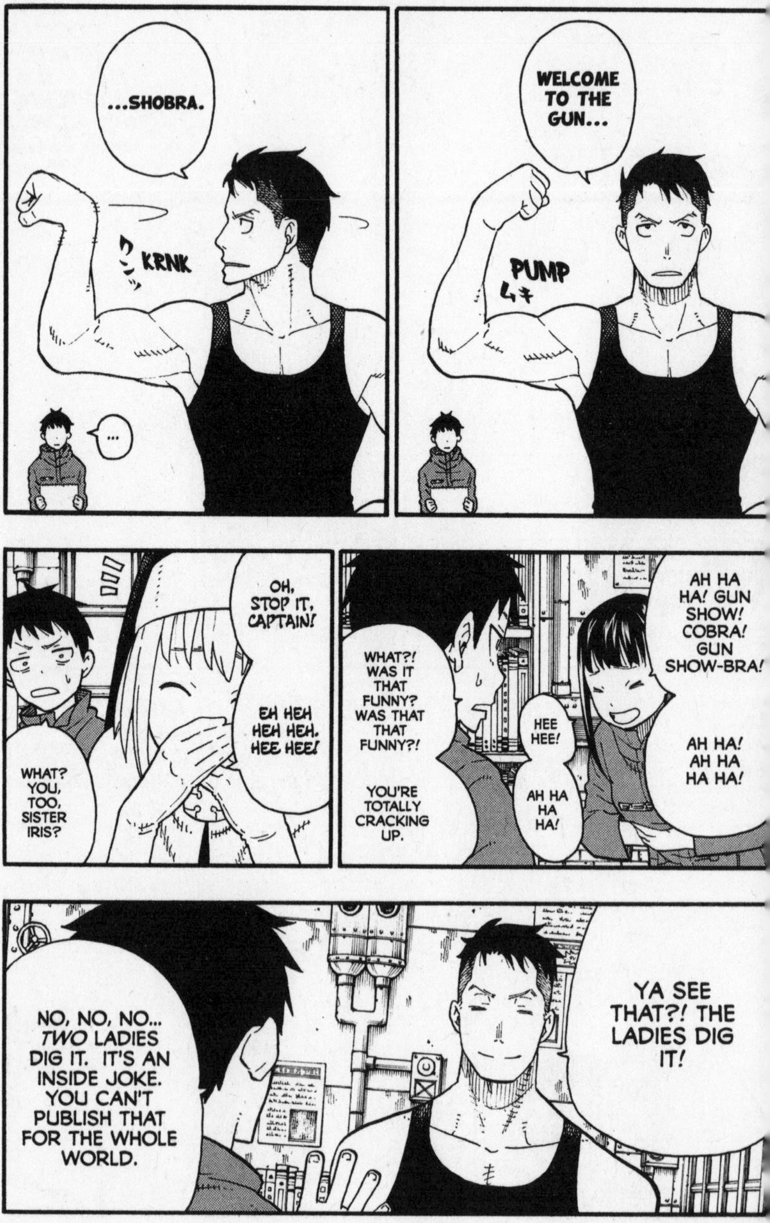

WELCOME TO THE GUN...
PUMP
ムキ
...SHOBRA.
KRNK
...
AH HA HA! GUN SHOW! COBRA! GUN SHOW-BRA!
AH HA! AH HA HA HA!
WHAT?! WAS IT THAT FUNNY? WAS THAT FUNNY?!
HEE HEE!
AH HA HA HA!
YOU'RE TOTALLY CRACKING UP.
OH, STOP IT, CAPTAIN!
EH HEH HEH HEH. HEE HEE!
WHAT? YOU, TOO, SISTER IRIS?
YA SEE THAT?! THE LADIES DIG IT!
NO, NO, NO... *TWO* LADIES DIG IT. IT'S AN INSIDE JOKE. YOU CAN'T PUBLISH THAT FOR THE WHOLE WORLD.

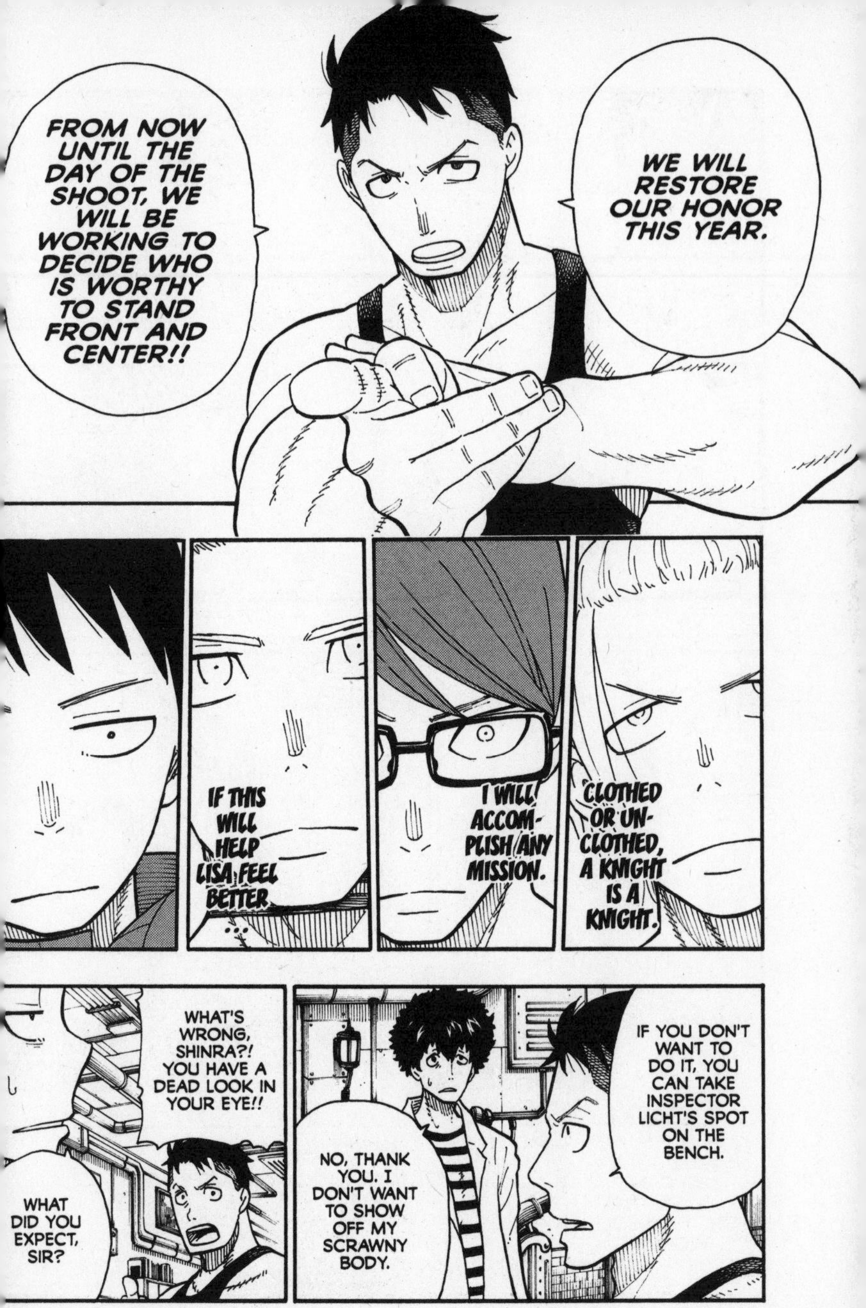
WE WILL RESTORE OUR HONOR THIS YEAR.
FROM NOW UNTIL THE DAY OF THE SHOOT, WE WILL BE WORKING TO DECIDE WHO IS WORTHY TO STAND FRONT AND CENTER!!
CLOTHED OR UN-CLOTHED, A KNIGHT IS A KNIGHT.
I WILL ACCOM-PLISH ANY MISSION.
IF THIS WILL HELP LISA FEEL BETTER ...
IF YOU DON'T WANT TO DO IT, YOU CAN TAKE INSPECTOR LICHT'S SPOT ON THE BENCH.
NO, THANK YOU. I DON'T WANT TO SHOW OFF MY SCRAWNY BODY.
WHAT'S WRONG, SHINRA?! YOU HAVE A DEAD LOOK IN YOUR EYE!!
WHAT DID YOU EXPECT, SIR?

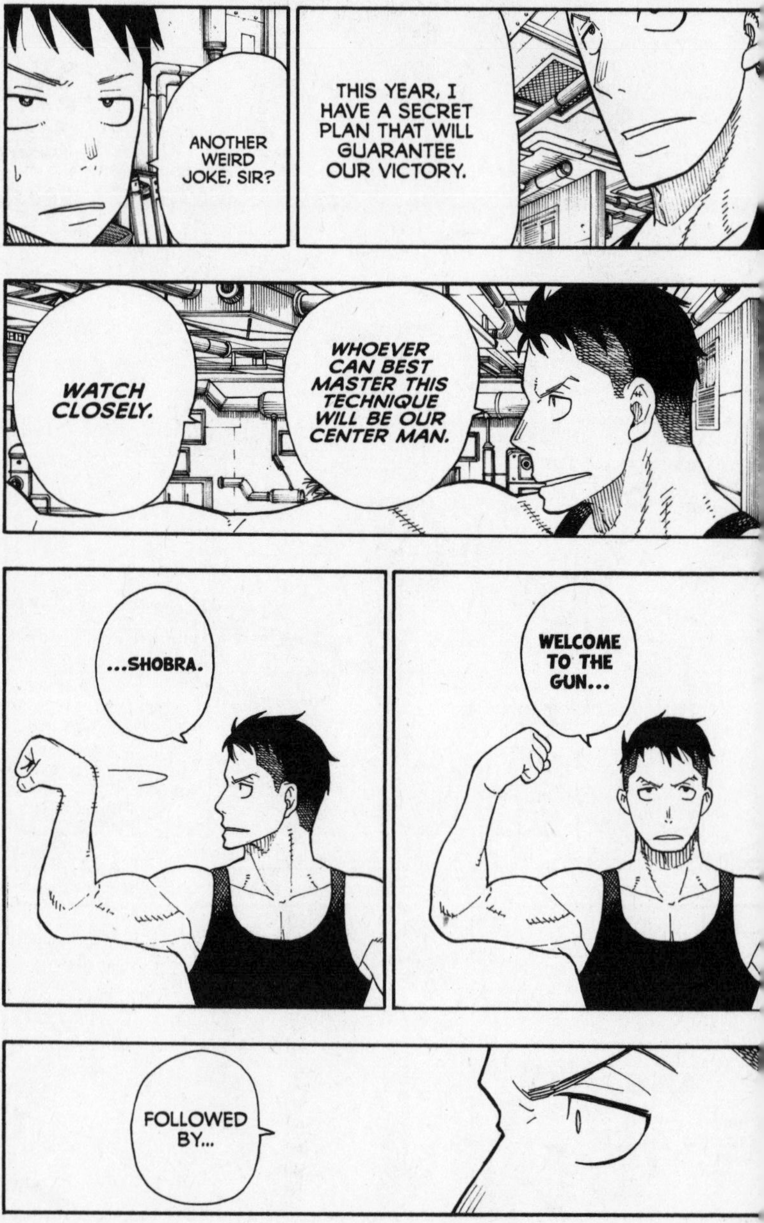
THIS YEAR, I HAVE A SECRET PLAN THAT WILL GUARANTEE OUR VICTORY.
ANOTHER WEIRD JOKE, SIR?
WHOEVER CAN BEST MASTER THIS TECHNIQUE WILL BE OUR CENTER MAN.
WATCH CLOSELY.
WELCOME TO THE GUN...
...SHOBRA.
FOLLOWED BY...

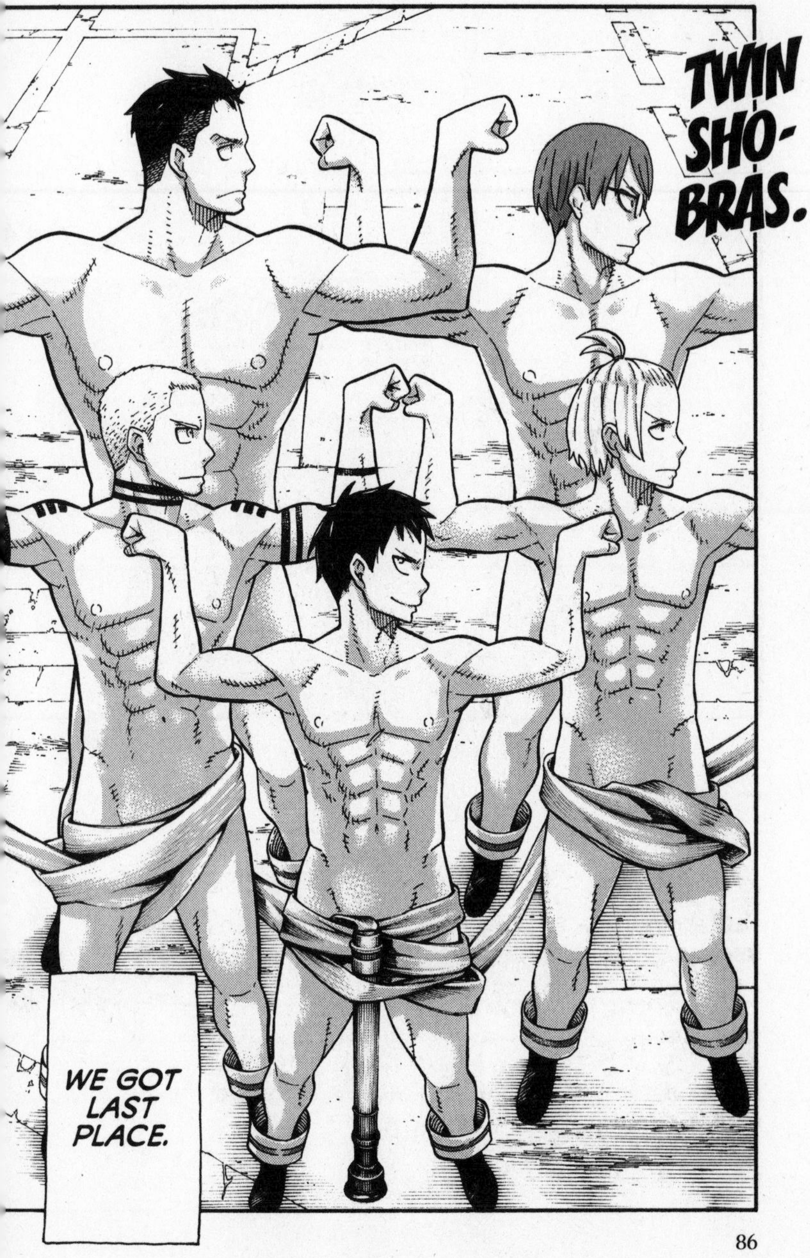
TWIN SHO-BRAS.
WE GOT LAST PLACE.

CHAPTER XCII: THE LIEUTENANT REMODELING PROJECT

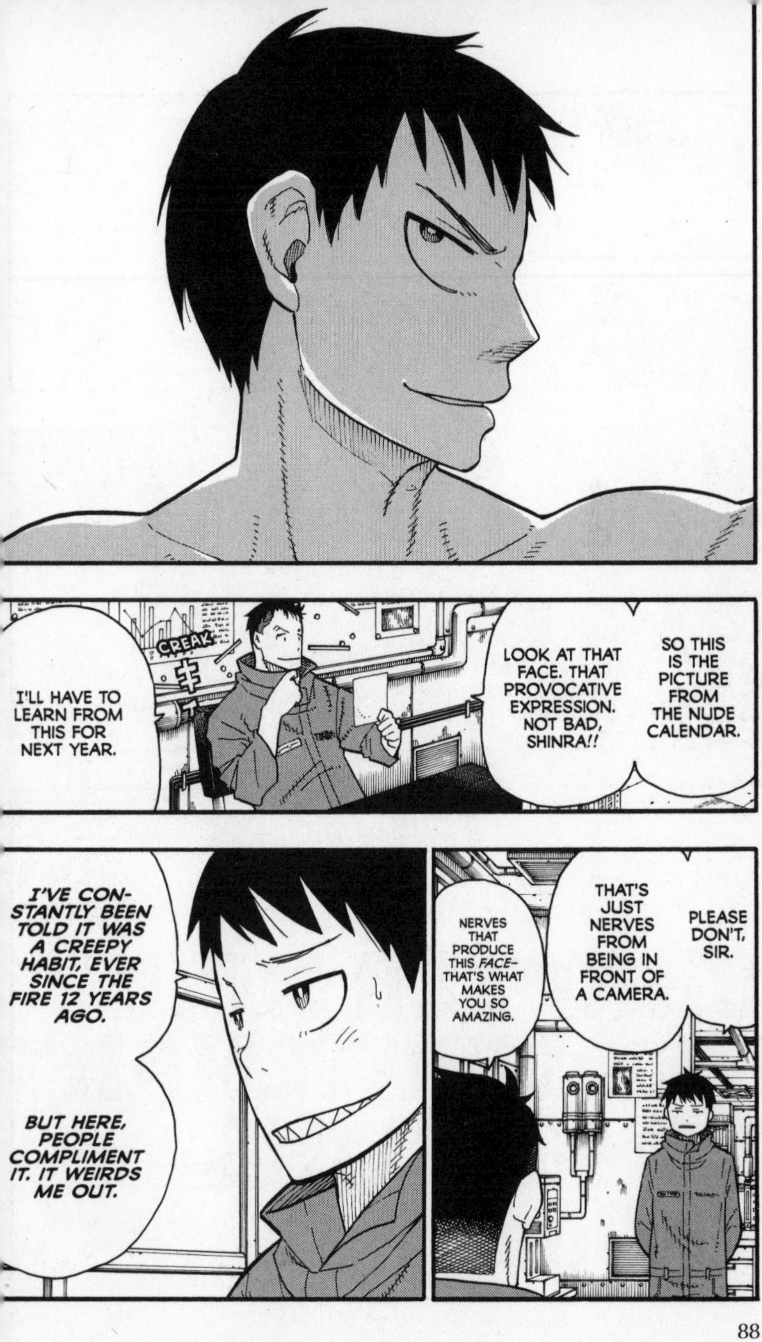
SO THIS IS THE PICTURE FROM THE NUDE CALENDAR.
LOOK AT THAT FACE. THAT PROVOCATIVE EXPRESSION. NOT BAD, SHINRA!!
CREAK
I'LL HAVE TO LEARN FROM THIS FOR NEXT YEAR.
PLEASE DON'T, SIR.
THAT'S JUST NERVES FROM BEING IN FRONT OF A CAMERA.
NERVES THAT PRODUCE THIS *FACE*—THAT'S WHAT MAKES YOU SO AMAZING.
I'VE CONSTANTLY BEEN TOLD IT WAS A CREEPY HABIT, EVER SINCE THE FIRE 12 YEARS AGO.
BUT HERE, PEOPLE COMPLIMENT IT. IT WEIRDS ME OUT.

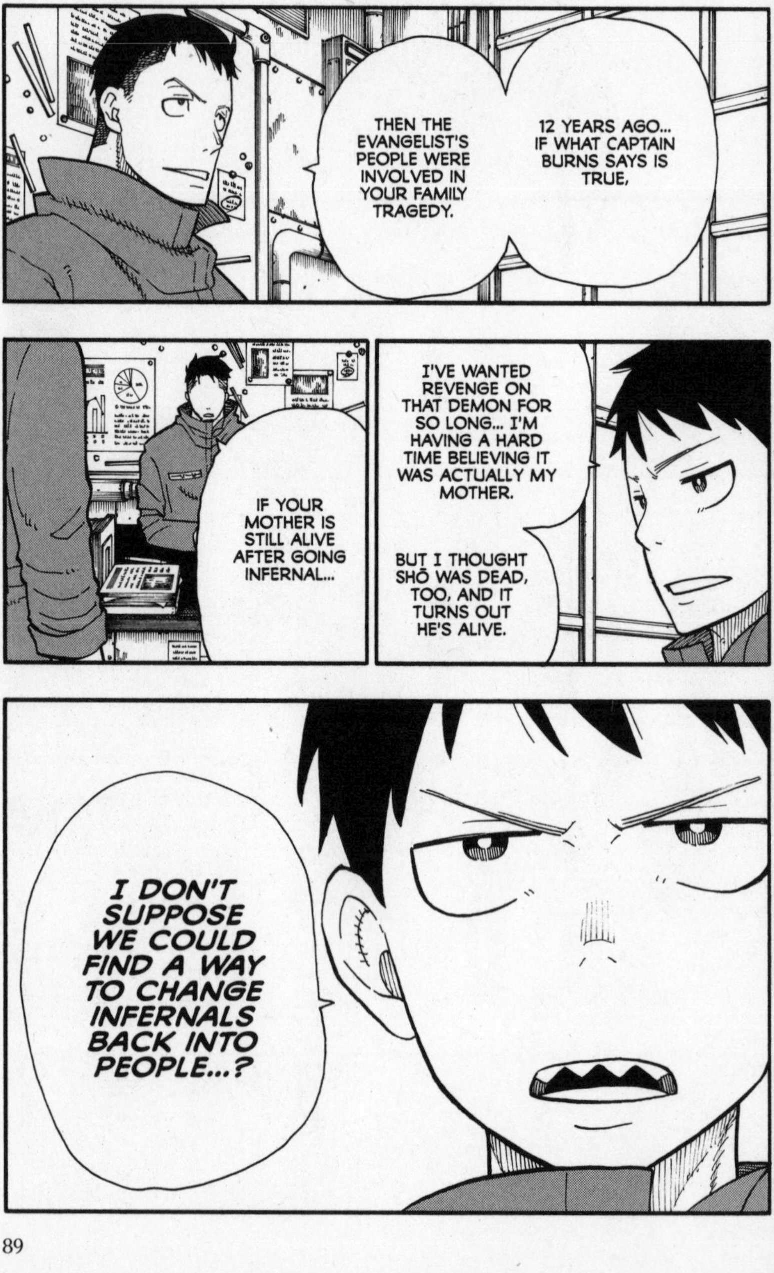
12 YEARS AGO... IF WHAT CAPTAIN BURNS SAYS IS TRUE,
THEN THE EVANGELIST'S PEOPLE WERE INVOLVED IN YOUR FAMILY TRAGEDY.
I'VE WANTED REVENGE ON THAT DEMON FOR SO LONG... I'M HAVING A HARD TIME BELIEVING IT WAS ACTUALLY MY MOTHER.
BUT I THOUGHT SHŌ WAS DEAD, TOO, AND IT TURNS OUT HE'S ALIVE.
IF YOUR MOTHER IS STILL ALIVE AFTER GOING INFERNAL...
I DON'T SUPPOSE WE COULD FIND A WAY TO CHANGE INFERNALS BACK INTO PEOPLE...?

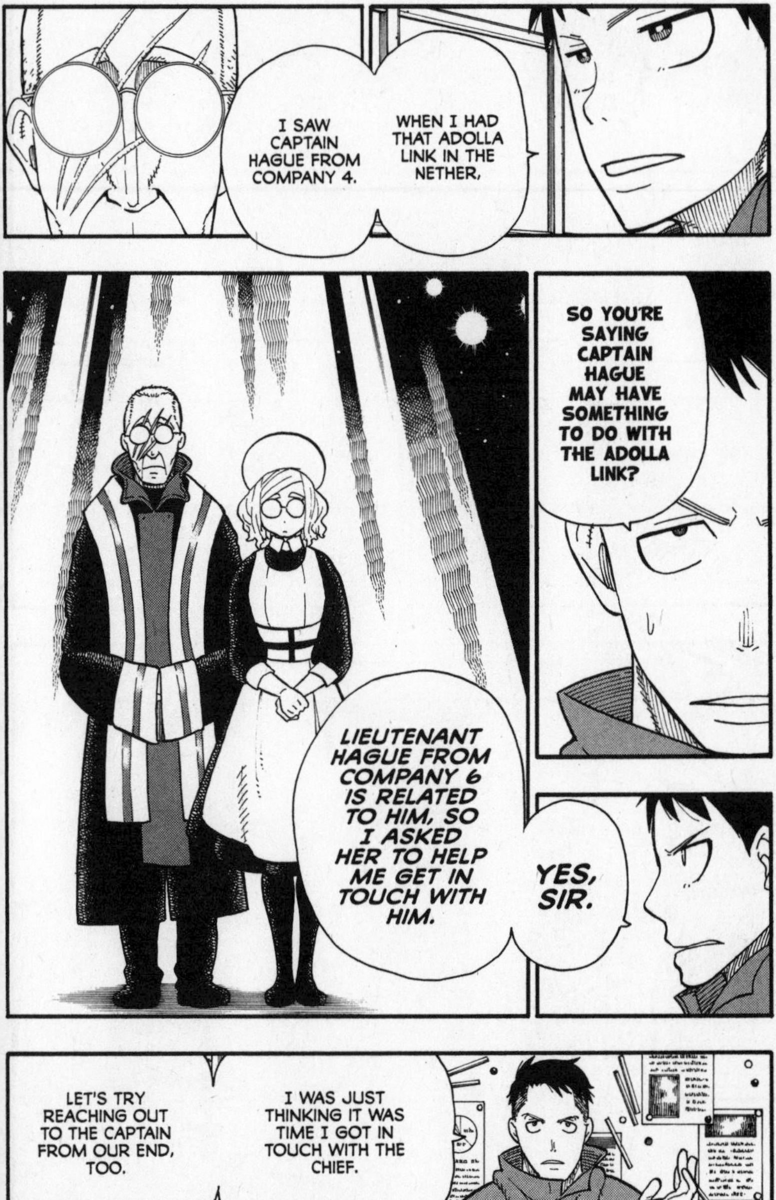
WHEN I HAD THAT ADOLLA LINK IN THE NETHER,
I SAW CAPTAIN HAGUE FROM COMPANY 4.
SO YOU'RE SAYING CAPTAIN HAGUE MAY HAVE SOMETHING TO DO WITH THE ADOLLA LINK?
YES, SIR.
LIEUTENANT HAGUE FROM COMPANY 6 IS RELATED TO HIM, SO I ASKED HER TO HELP ME GET IN TOUCH WITH HIM.
I WAS JUST THINKING IT WAS TIME I GOT IN TOUCH WITH THE CHIEF.
LET'S TRY REACHING OUT TO THE CAPTAIN FROM OUR END, TOO.

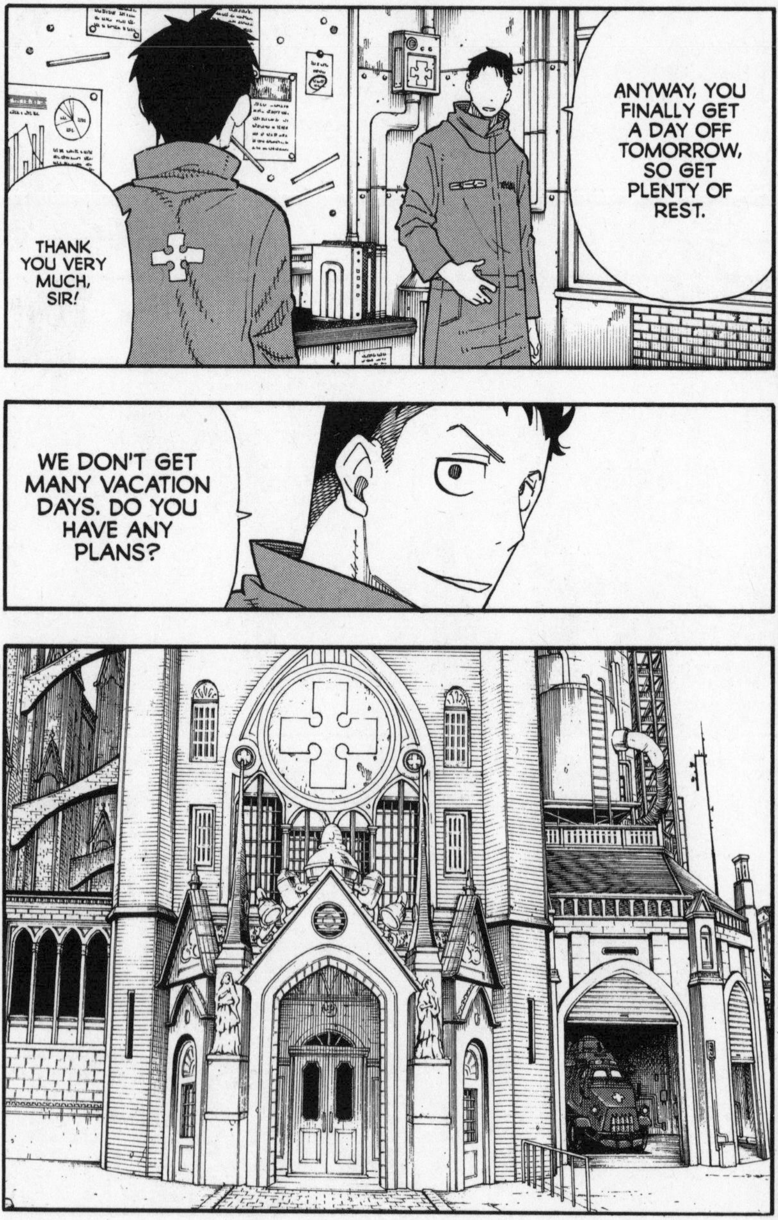
ANYWAY, YOU FINALLY GET A DAY OFF TOMORROW, SO GET PLENTY OF REST.
THANK YOU VERY MUCH, SIR!
WE DON'T GET MANY VACATION DAYS. DO YOU HAVE ANY PLANS?

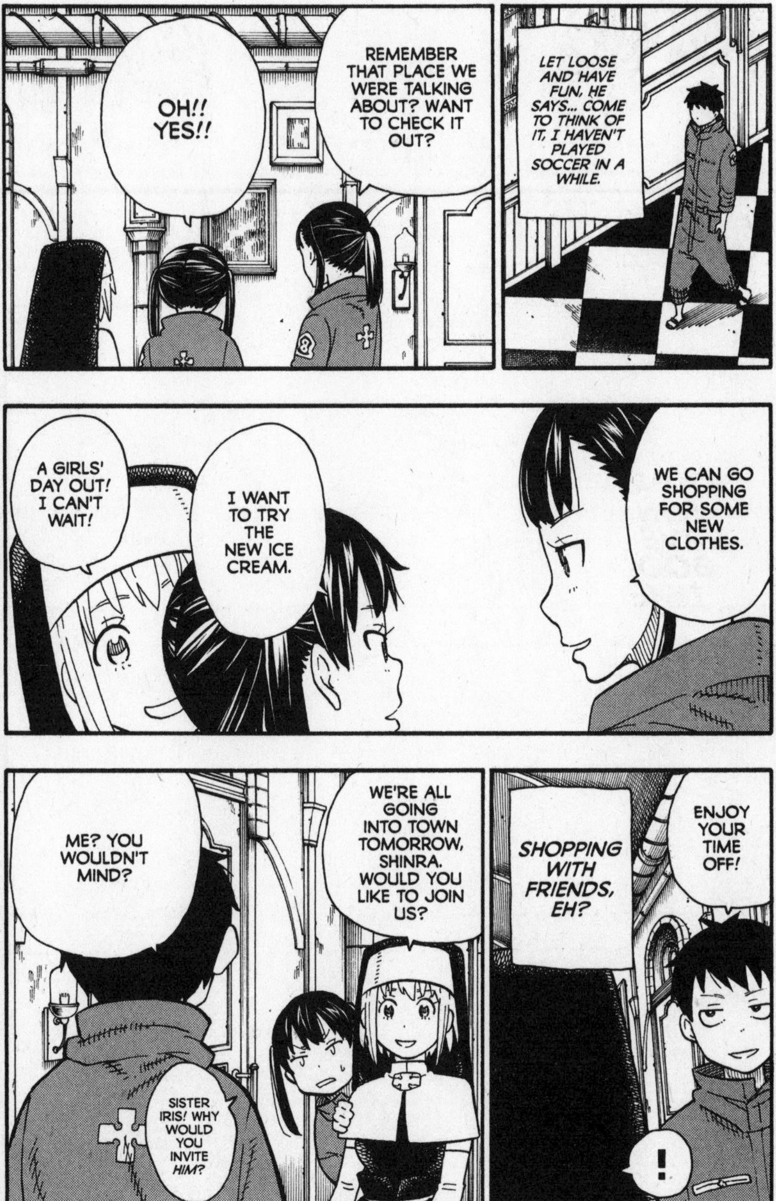
LET LOOSE AND HAVE FUN, HE SAYS... COME TO THINK OF IT, I HAVEN'T PLAYED SOCCER IN A WHILE.
REMEMBER THAT PLACE WE WERE TALKING ABOUT? WANT TO CHECK IT OUT?
OH!! YES!!
WE CAN GO SHOPPING FOR SOME NEW CLOTHES.
I WANT TO TRY THE NEW ICE CREAM.
A GIRLS' DAY OUT! I CAN'T WAIT!
ENJOY YOUR TIME OFF!
SHOPPING WITH FRIENDS, EH?
!
WE'RE ALL GOING INTO TOWN TOMORROW, SHINRA. WOULD YOU LIKE TO JOIN US?
ME? YOU WOULDN'T MIND?
SISTER IRIS! WHY WOULD YOU INVITE HIM?

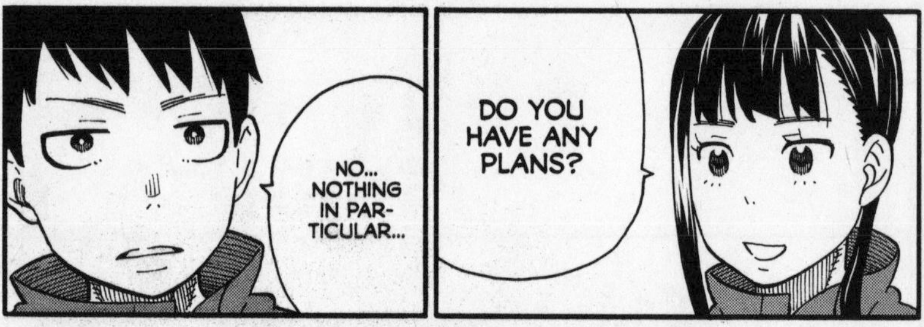
DO YOU HAVE ANY PLANS?
NO... NOTHING IN PAR-TICULAR...

Hat: Don't Cry Bypass

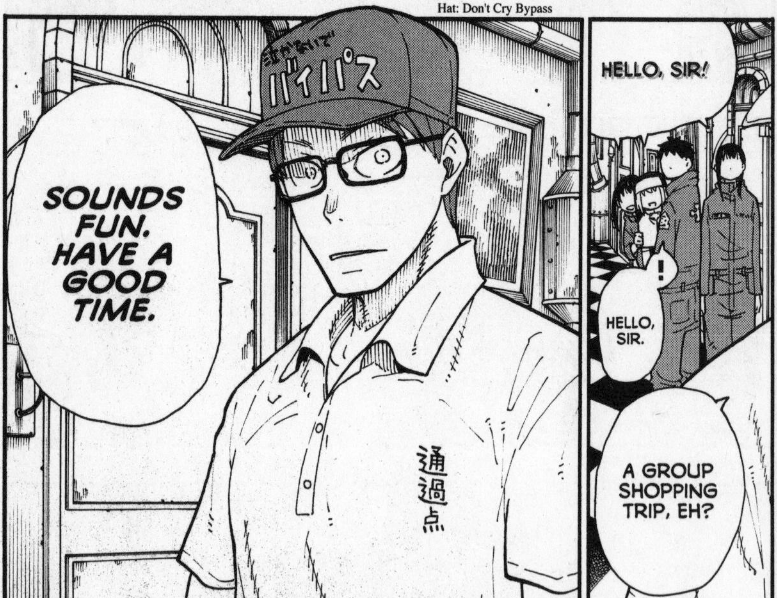
HELLO, SIR!
!
HELLO, SIR.
A GROUP SHOPPING TRIP, EH?
泣かないで
バイパス
SOUNDS FUN. HAVE A GOOD TIME.
通過点

Shirt: Checkpoint

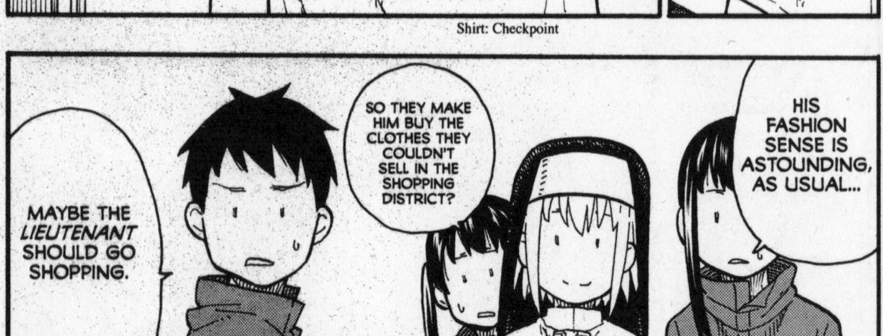
HIS FASHION SENSE IS ASTOUNDING, AS USUAL...
SO THEY MAKE HIM BUY THE CLOTHES THEY COULDN'T SELL IN THE SHOPPING DISTRICT?
MAYBE THE *LIEUTENANT* SHOULD GO SHOPPING.

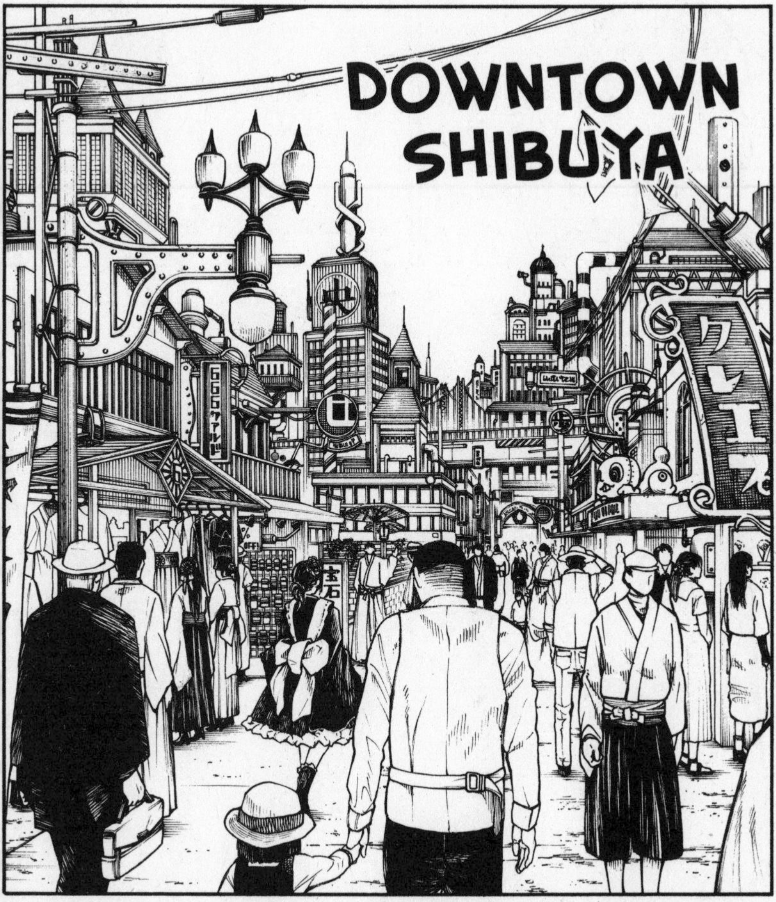
DOWNTOWN
SHIBUYA
宝石
OFF

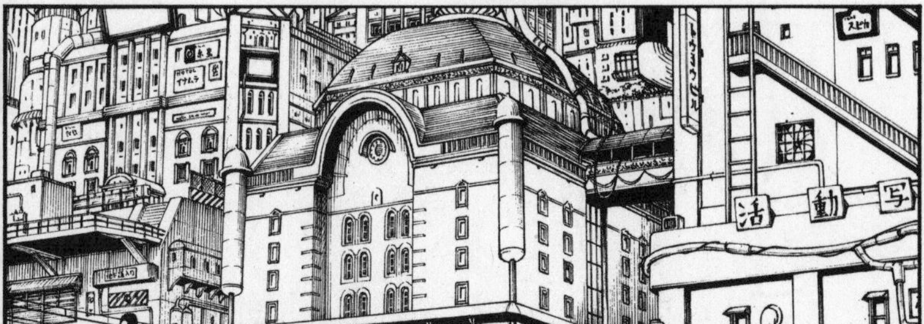
活 動 写

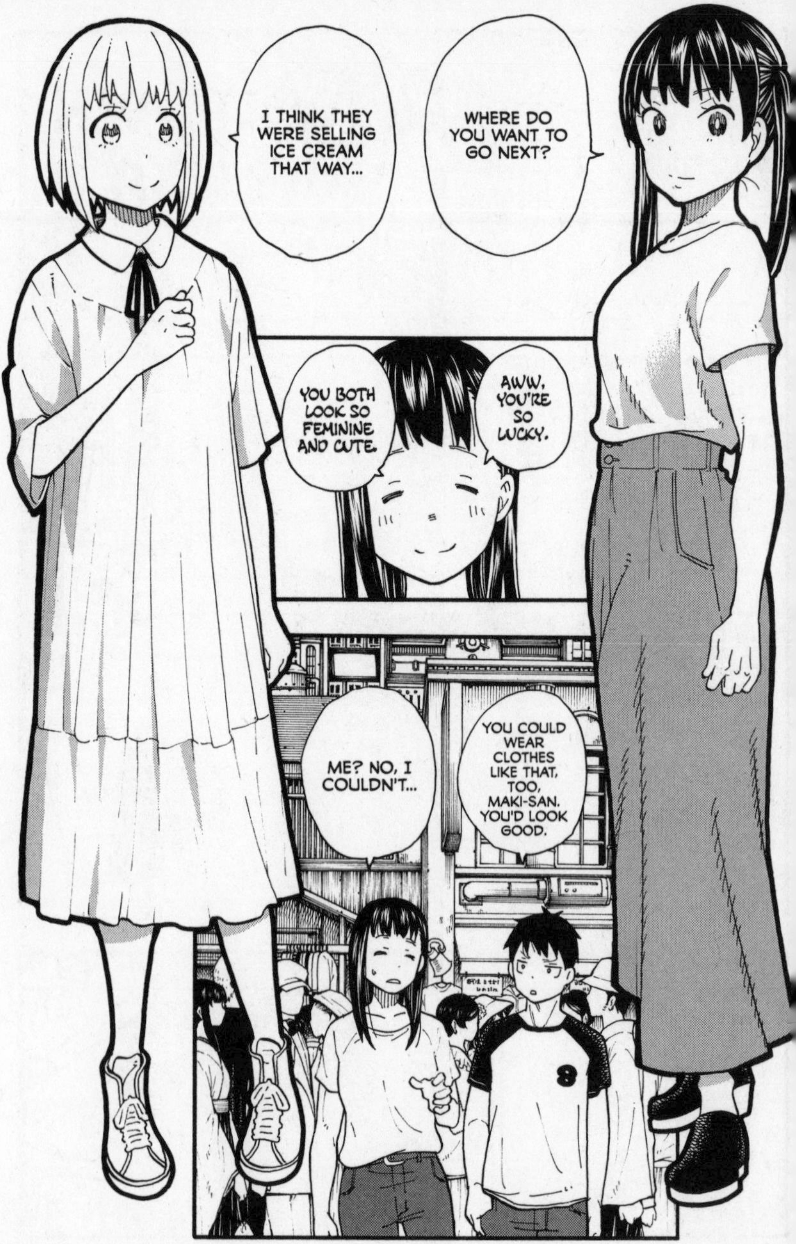
WHERE DO YOU WANT TO GO NEXT?
I THINK THEY WERE SELLING ICE CREAM THAT WAY...
AWW, YOU'RE SO LUCKY.
YOU BOTH LOOK SO FEMININE AND CUTE.
YOU COULD WEAR CLOTHES LIKE THAT, TOO, MAKI-SAN. YOU'D LOOK GOOD.
ME? NO, I COULDN'T...

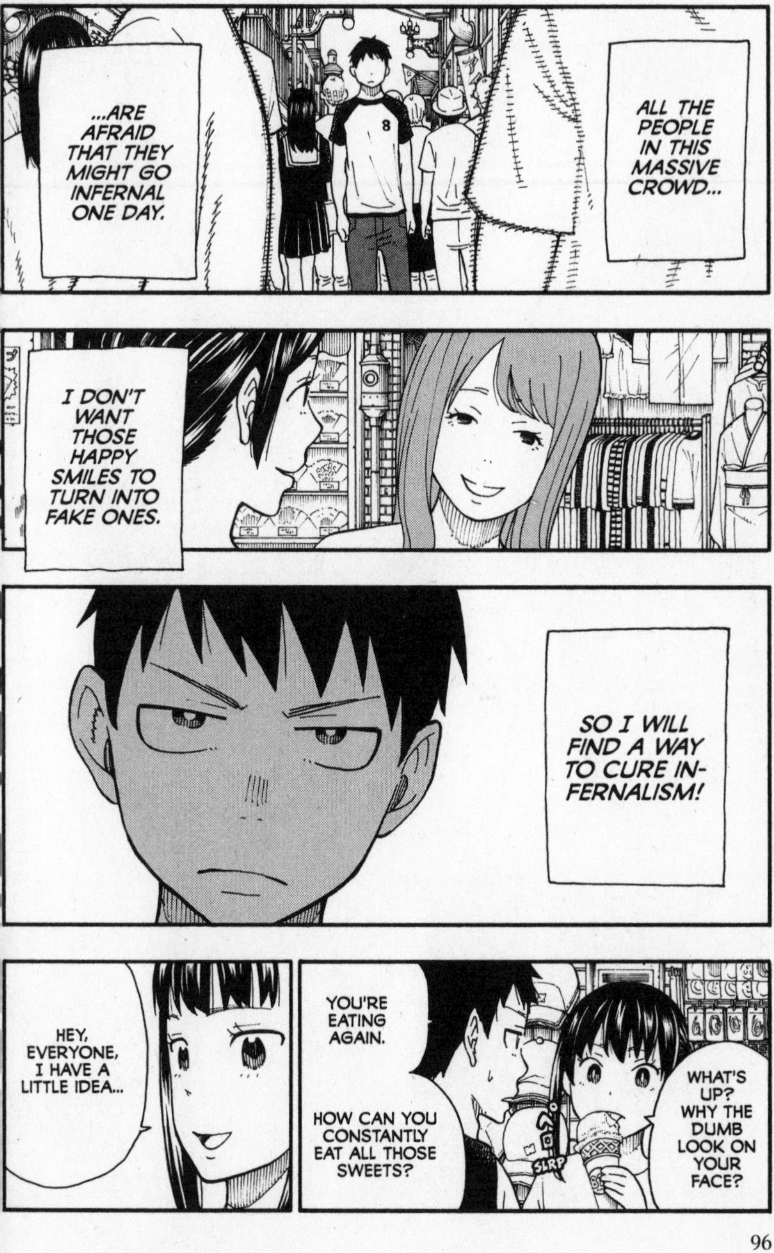
ALL THE PEOPLE IN THIS MASSIVE CROWD...
...ARE AFRAID THAT THEY MIGHT GO INFERNAL ONE DAY.
I DON'T WANT THOSE HAPPY SMILES TO TURN INTO FAKE ONES.
SO I WILL FIND A WAY TO CURE IN-FERNALISM!
WHAT'S UP? WHY THE DUMB LOOK ON YOUR FACE?
SLRP
YOU'RE EATING AGAIN.
HOW CAN YOU CONSTANTLY EAT ALL THOSE SWEETS?
HEY, EVERYONE, I HAVE A LITTLE IDEA...

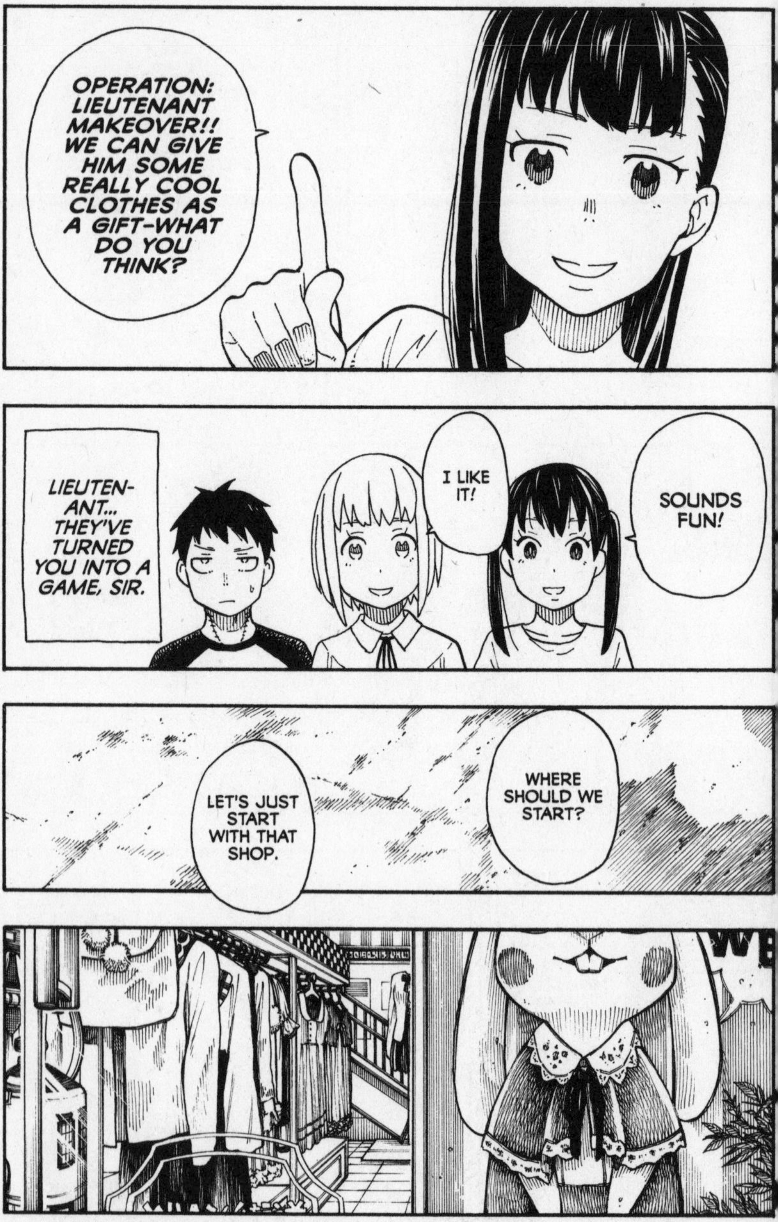
OPERATION: LIEUTENANT MAKEOVER!! WE CAN GIVE HIM SOME REALLY COOL CLOTHES AS A GIFT–WHAT DO YOU THINK?
SOUNDS FUN!
I LIKE IT!
LIEUTEN-ANT... THEY'VE TURNED YOU INTO A GAME, SIR.
WHERE SHOULD WE START?
LET'S JUST START WITH THAT SHOP.

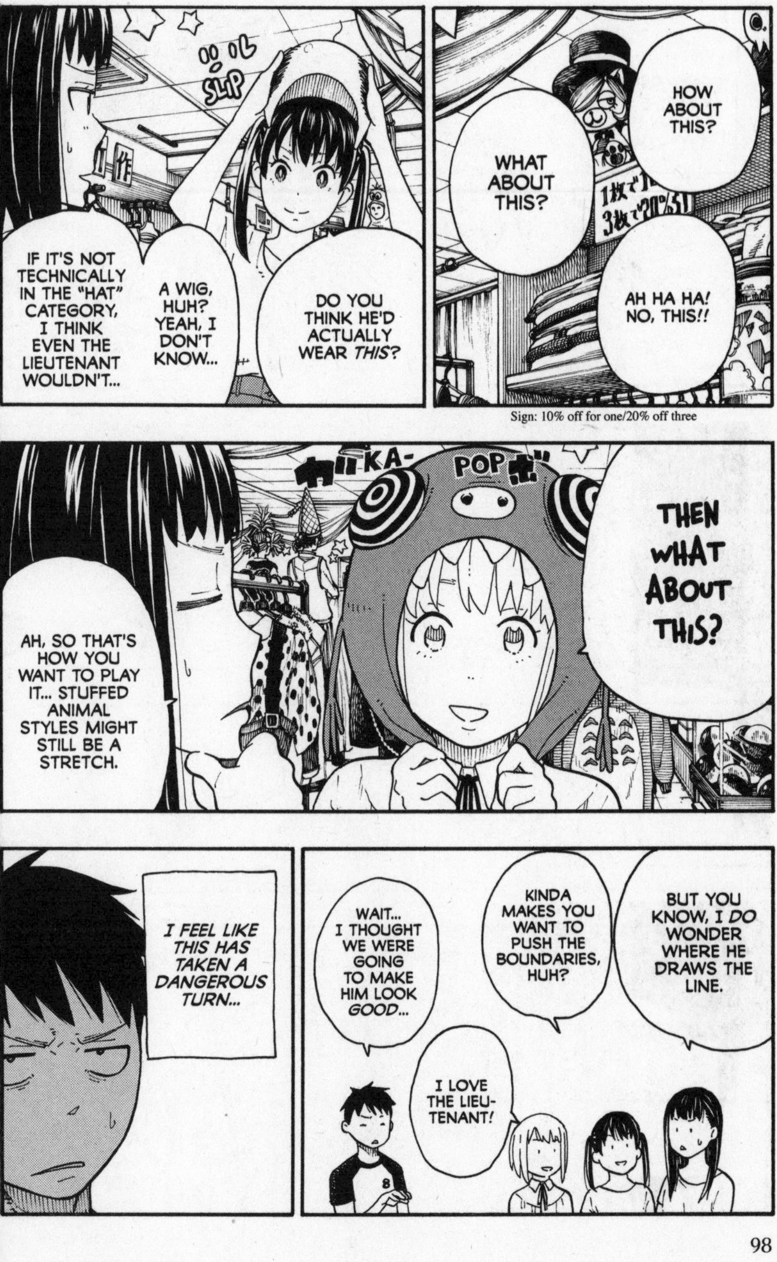
HOW ABOUT THIS?
WHAT ABOUT THIS?
AH HA HA! NO, THIS!!
SLIP
DO YOU THINK HE'D ACTUALLY WEAR *THIS*?
A WIG, HUH? YEAH, I DON'T KNOW...
IF IT'S NOT TECHNICALLY IN THE "HAT" CATEGORY, I THINK EVEN THE LIEUTENANT WOULDN'T...
THEN WHAT ABOUT THIS?
KA-POP
AH, SO THAT'S HOW YOU WANT TO PLAY IT... STUFFED ANIMAL STYLES MIGHT STILL BE A STRETCH.
BUT YOU KNOW, I *DO* WONDER WHERE HE DRAWS THE LINE.
KINDA MAKES YOU WANT TO PUSH THE BOUNDARIES, HUH?
WAIT... I THOUGHT WE WERE GOING TO MAKE HIM LOOK *GOOD*...
I LOVE THE LIEUTENANT!
I FEEL LIKE THIS HAS TAKEN A DANGEROUS TURN...

Sign: 10% off for one/20% off three

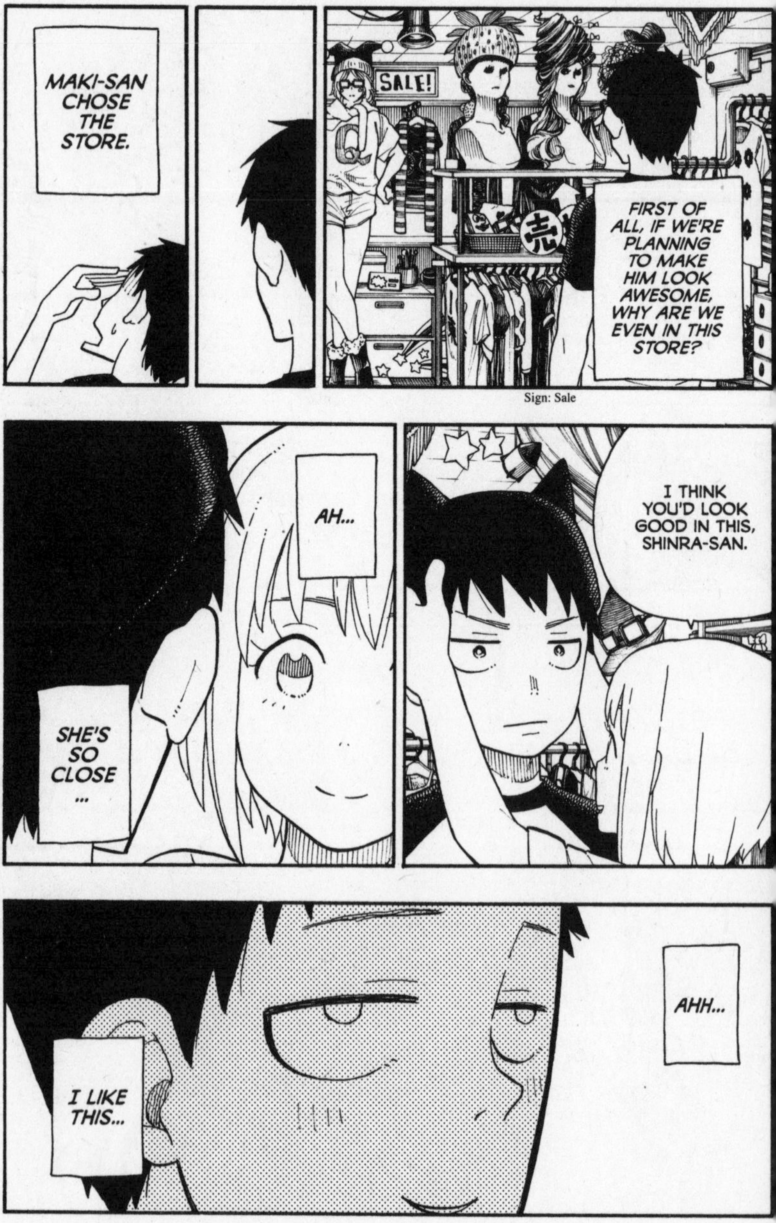
SALE!
FIRST OF ALL, IF WE'RE PLANNING TO MAKE HIM LOOK AWESOME, WHY ARE WE EVEN IN THIS STORE?
MAKI-SAN CHOSE THE STORE.
I THINK YOU'D LOOK GOOD IN THIS, SHINRA-SAN.
AH...
SHE'S SO CLOSE ...
AHH...
I LIKE THIS...

Sign: Sale

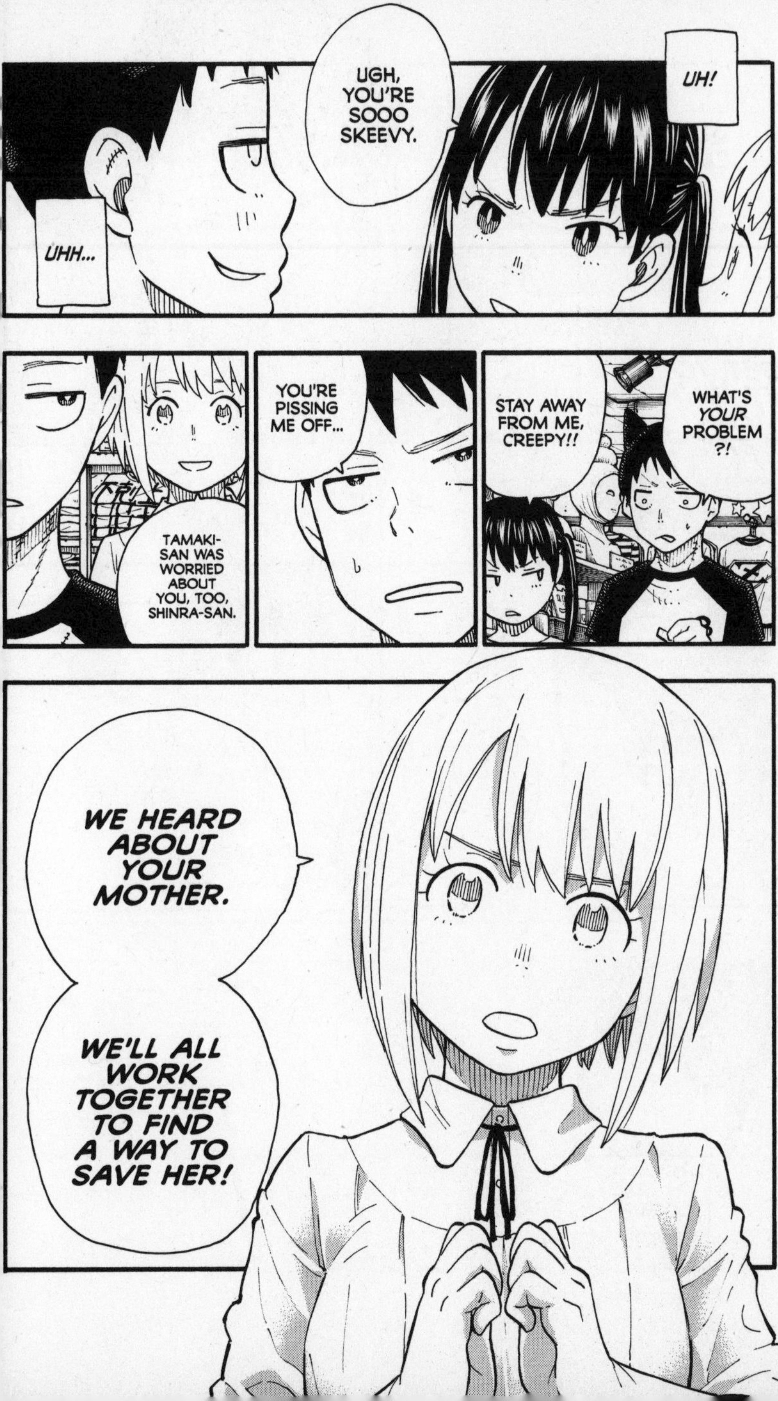
UH!
UGH, YOU'RE SOOO SKEEVY.
UHH...
WHAT'S YOUR PROBLEM ?!
STAY AWAY FROM ME, CREEPY!!
YOU'RE PISSING ME OFF...
TAMAKI-SAN WAS WORRIED ABOUT YOU, TOO, SHINRA-SAN.
WE HEARD ABOUT YOUR MOTHER.
WE'LL ALL WORK TOGETHER TO FIND A WAY TO SAVE HER!

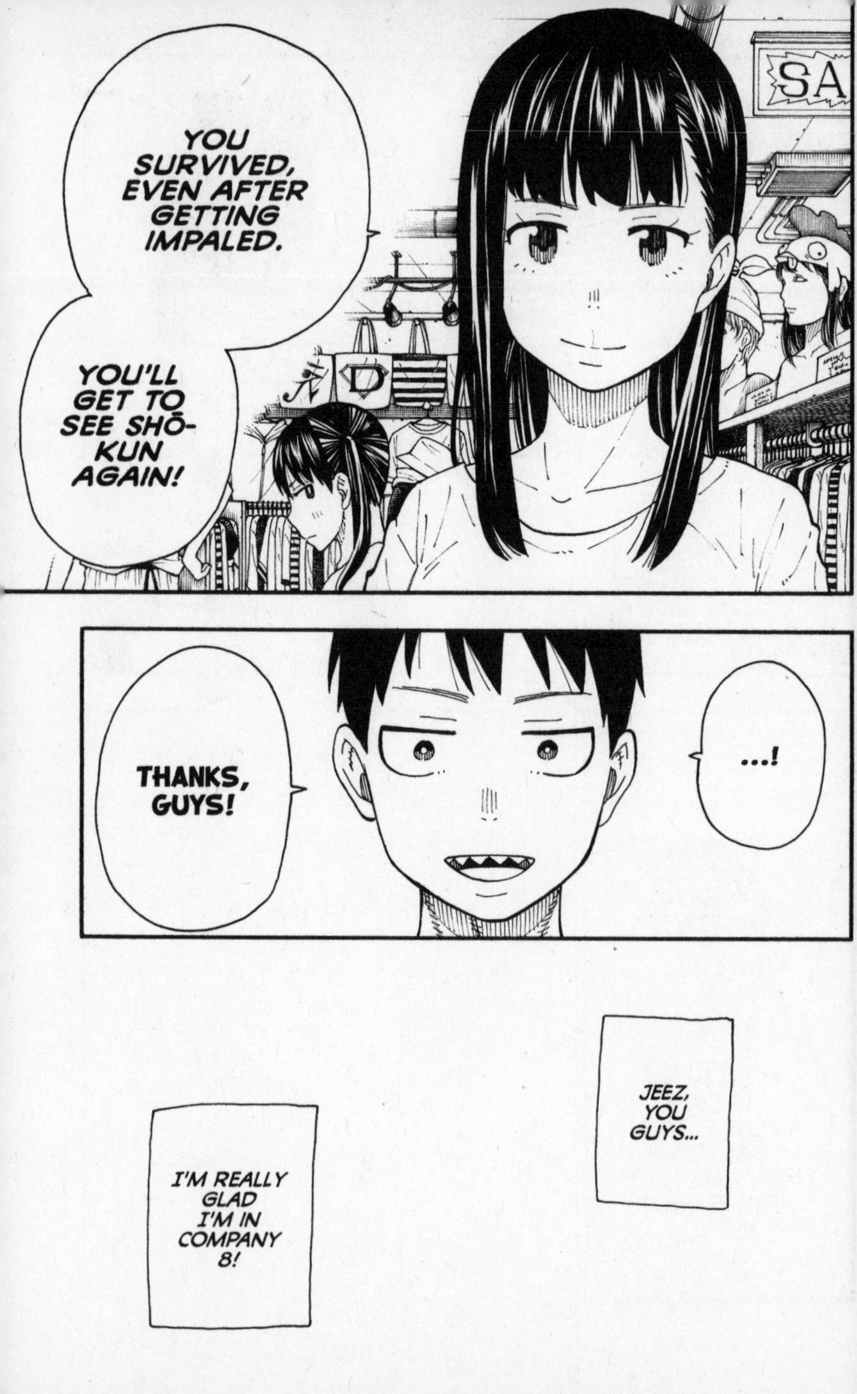
YOU SURVIVED, EVEN AFTER GETTING IMPALED.
YOU'LL GET TO SEE SHŌ-KUN AGAIN!
...!
THANKS, GUYS!
JEEZ, YOU GUYS...
I'M REALLY GLAD I'M IN COMPANY 8!

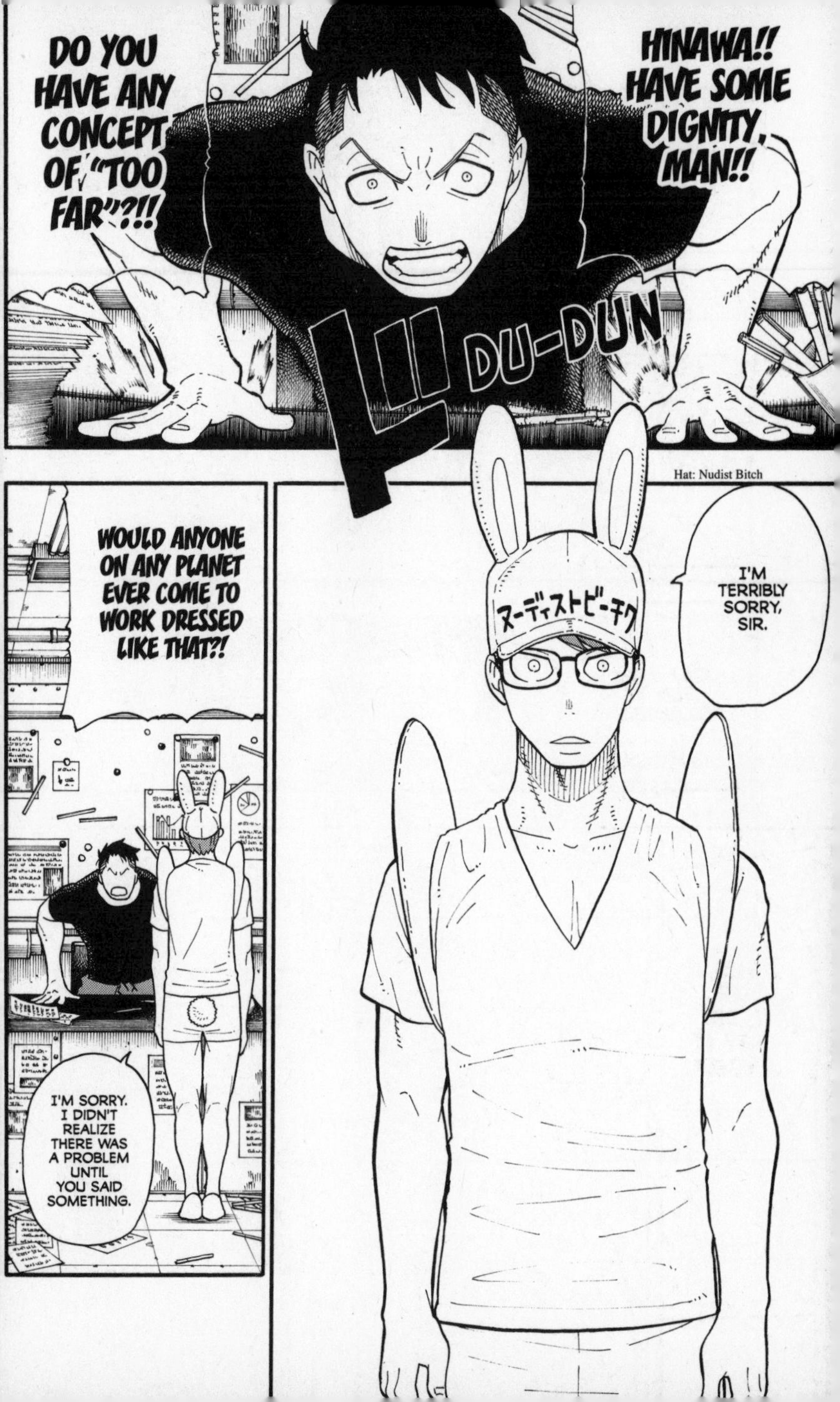
HINAWA!! HAVE SOME DIGNITY, MAN!!
DO YOU HAVE ANY CONCEPT OF "TOO FAR"?!!
DU-DUN
Hat: Nudist Bitch
ヌーディストビーチク
I'M TERRIBLY SORRY, SIR.
WOULD ANYONE ON ANY PLANET EVER COME TO WORK DRESSED LIKE THAT?!
I'M SORRY. I DIDN'T REALIZE THERE WAS A PROBLEM UNTIL YOU SAID SOMETHING.

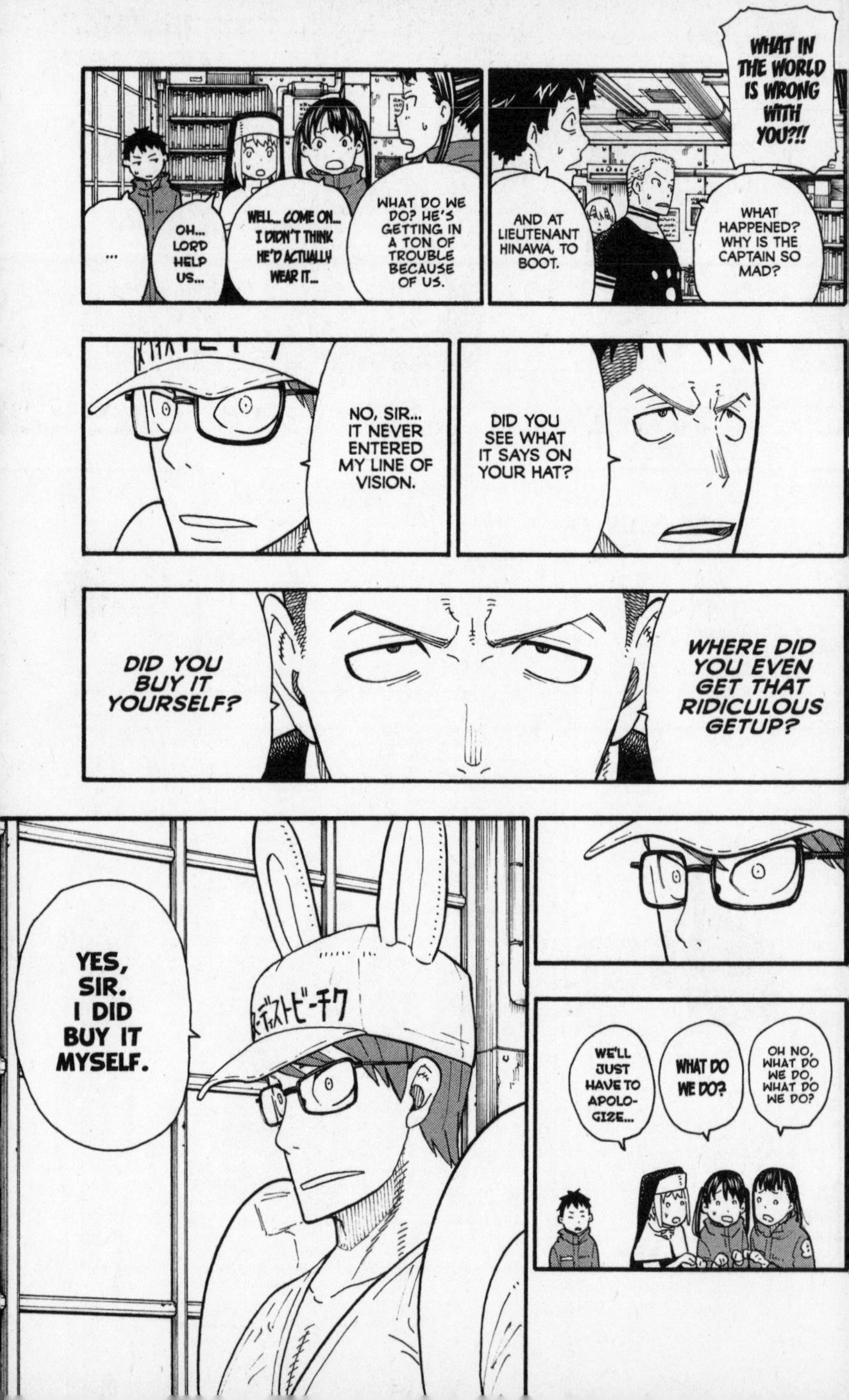
WHAT IN THE WORLD IS WRONG WITH YOU?!!
WHAT HAPPENED? WHY IS THE CAPTAIN SO MAD?
AND AT LIEUTENANT HINAWA, TO BOOT.
WHAT DO WE DO? HE'S GETTING IN A TON OF TROUBLE BECAUSE OF US.
WELL... COME ON... I DIDN'T THINK HE'D ACTUALLY WEAR IT...
OH... LORD HELP US...
...
DID YOU SEE WHAT IT SAYS ON YOUR HAT?
NO, SIR... IT NEVER ENTERED MY LINE OF VISION.
WHERE DID YOU EVEN GET THAT RIDICULOUS GETUP?
DID YOU BUY IT YOURSELF?
OH NO, WHAT DO WE DO, WHAT DO WE DO?
WHAT DO WE DO?
WE'LL JUST HAVE TO APOLO-GIZE...
YES, SIR. I DID BUY IT MYSELF.

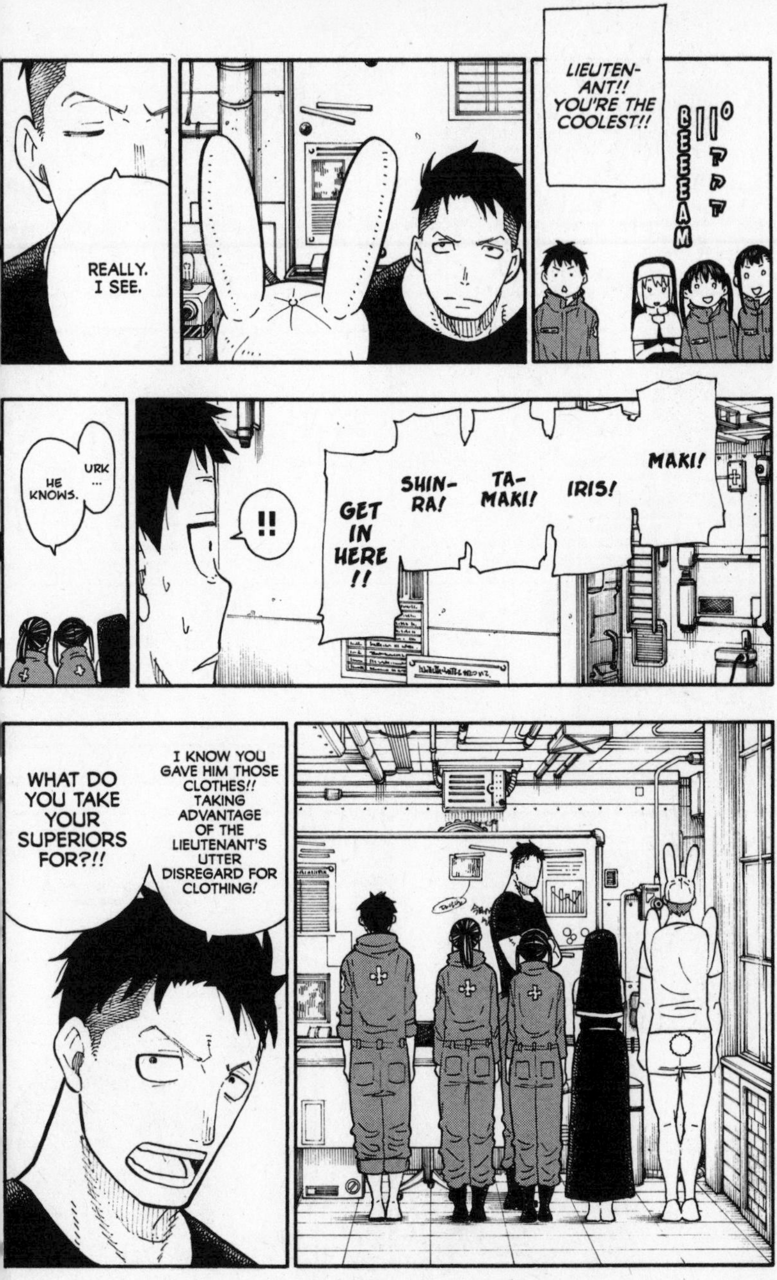
LIEUTEN-ANT!! YOU'RE THE COOLEST!!
BEEEEAM
REALLY. I SEE.
GET IN HERE!! SHIN-RA! TA-MAKI! IRIS! MAKI!
!!
URK ... HE KNOWS.
I KNOW YOU GAVE HIM THOSE CLOTHES!! TAKING ADVANTAGE OF THE LIEUTENANT'S UTTER DISREGARD FOR CLOTHING!
WHAT DO YOU TAKE YOUR SUPERIORS FOR?!!

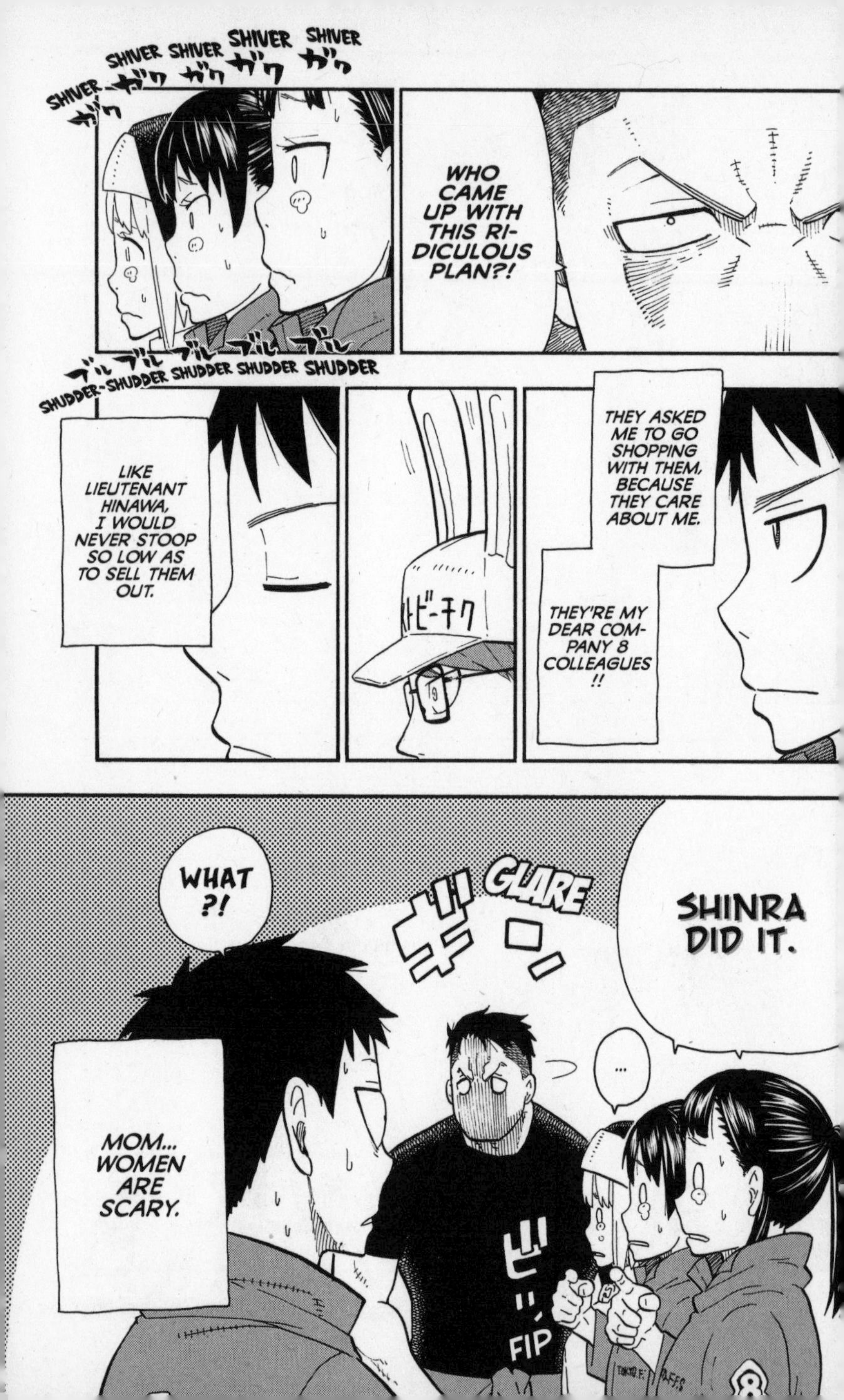
WHO CAME UP WITH THIS RIDICULOUS PLAN?!
SHIVER SHIVER SHIVER SHIVER SHIVER
SHUDDER SHUDDER SHUDDER SHUDDER SHUDDER
THEY ASKED ME TO GO SHOPPING WITH THEM, BECAUSE THEY CARE ABOUT ME.
THEY'RE MY DEAR COMPANY 8 COLLEAGUES!!
LIKE LIEUTENANT HINAWA, I WOULD NEVER STOOP SO LOW AS TO SELL THEM OUT.
SHINRA DID IT.
...
GLARE
WHAT?!
MOM... WOMEN ARE SCARY.
FIP

FIRE FORCE

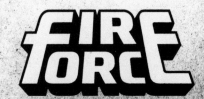

CHAPTER XCIII: SPECIAL FIRE FORCE COMPANY 4

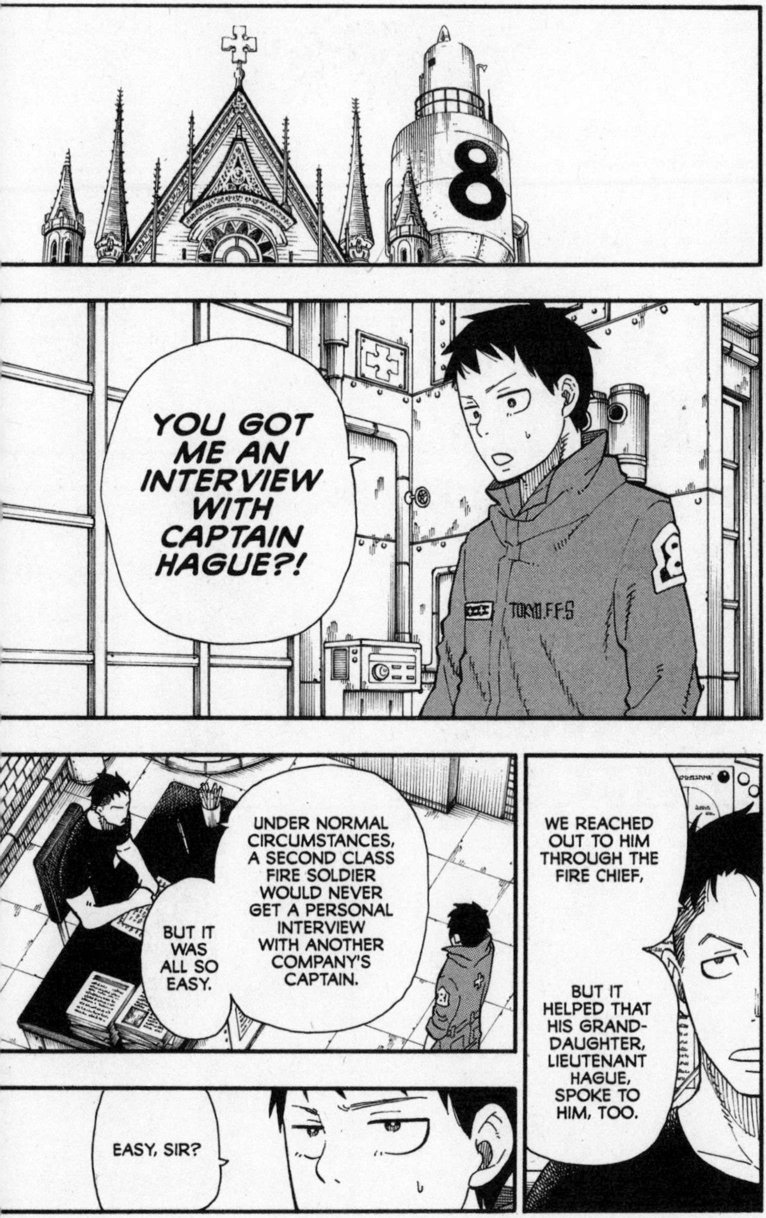
YOU GOT ME AN INTERVIEW WITH CAPTAIN HAGUE?!
WE REACHED OUT TO HIM THROUGH THE FIRE CHIEF,
BUT IT HELPED THAT HIS GRAND-DAUGHTER, LIEUTENANT HAGUE, SPOKE TO HIM, TOO.
UNDER NORMAL CIRCUMSTANCES, A SECOND CLASS FIRE SOLDIER WOULD NEVER GET A PERSONAL INTERVIEW WITH ANOTHER COMPANY'S CAPTAIN.
BUT IT WAS ALL SO EASY.
EASY, SIR?

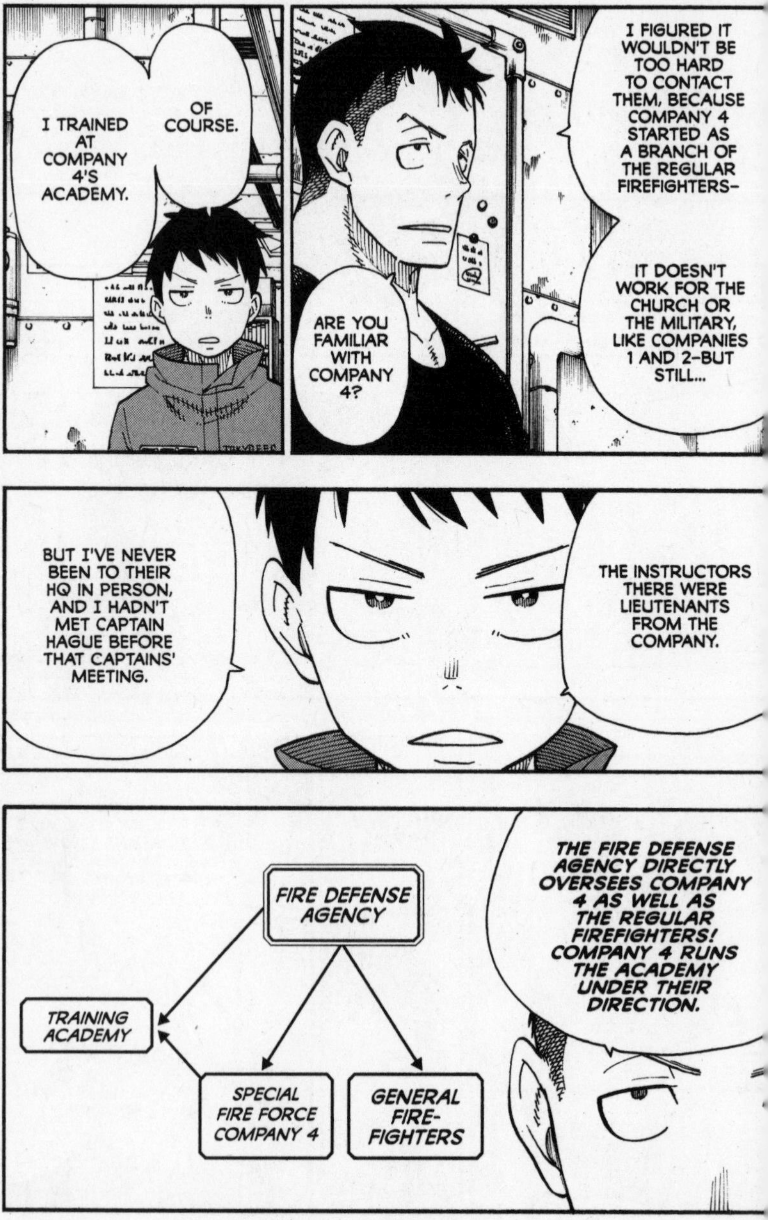
I FIGURED IT WOULDN'T BE TOO HARD TO CONTACT THEM, BECAUSE COMPANY 4 STARTED AS A BRANCH OF THE REGULAR FIREFIGHTERS–
IT DOESN'T WORK FOR THE CHURCH OR THE MILITARY, LIKE COMPANIES 1 AND 2–BUT STILL...
ARE YOU FAMILIAR WITH COMPANY 4?
OF COURSE.
I TRAINED AT COMPANY 4'S ACADEMY.
THE INSTRUCTORS THERE WERE LIEUTENANTS FROM THE COMPANY.
BUT I'VE NEVER BEEN TO THEIR HQ IN PERSON, AND I HADN'T MET CAPTAIN HAGUE BEFORE THAT CAPTAINS' MEETING.
THE FIRE DEFENSE AGENCY DIRECTLY OVERSEES COMPANY 4 AS WELL AS THE REGULAR FIREFIGHTERS! COMPANY 4 RUNS THE ACADEMY UNDER THEIR DIRECTION.
FIRE DEFENSE AGENCY
TRAINING ACADEMY
SPECIAL FIRE FORCE COMPANY 4
GENERAL FIRE-FIGHTERS

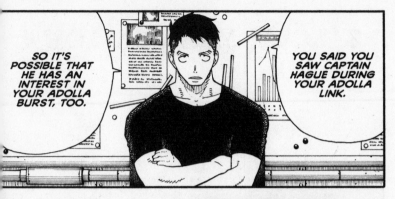

YOU SAID YOU SAW CAPTAIN HAGUE DURING YOUR ADOLLA LINK.
SO IT'S POSSIBLE THAT HE HAS AN INTEREST IN YOUR ADOLLA BURST, TOO.
...
BUT WHATEVER HIS REASON FOR SEEING YOU, IT WORKS OUT FOR US.
COMPANY 6 LIEUTENANT ASAKO HAGUE WILL BE JOINING YOU TOMORROW.
LIEUTENANT ASAKO?
MAKE IT COUNT, SHINRA!

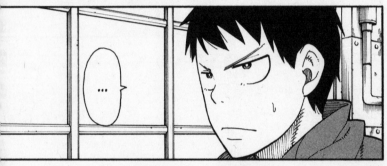

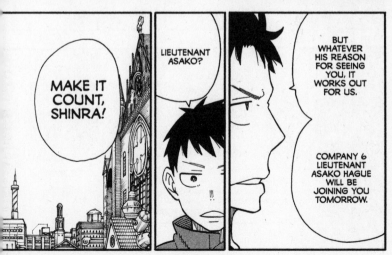

SPECIAL FIRE STATION 4

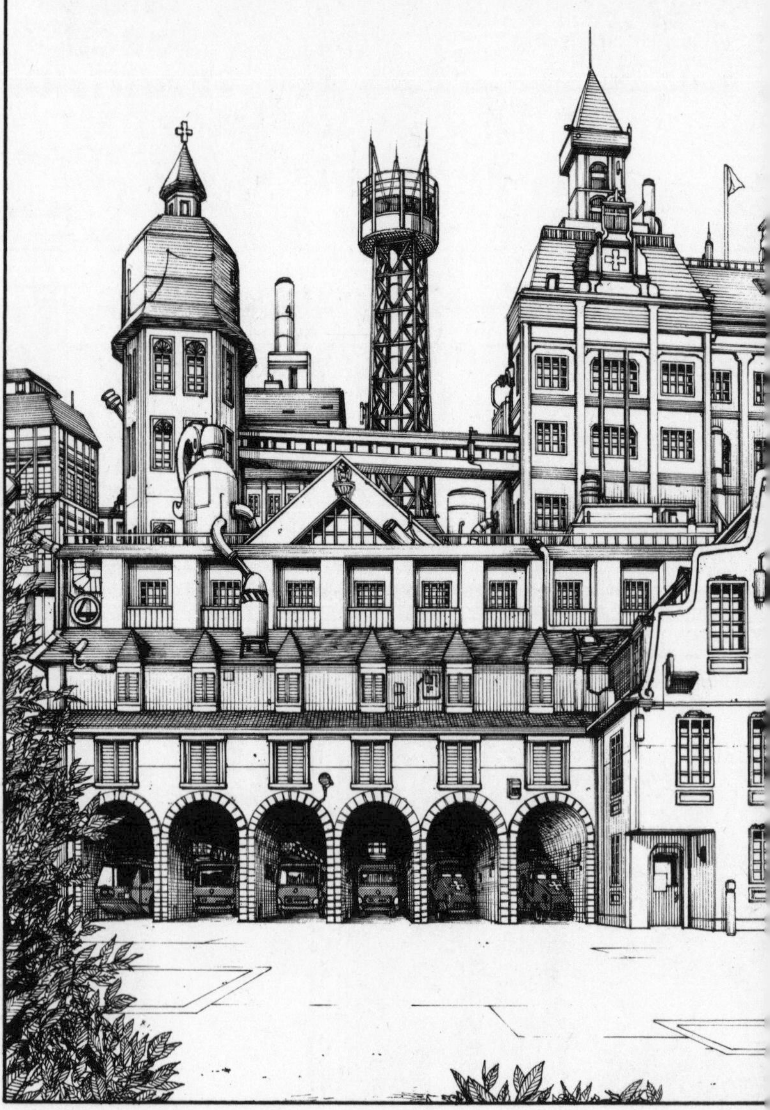

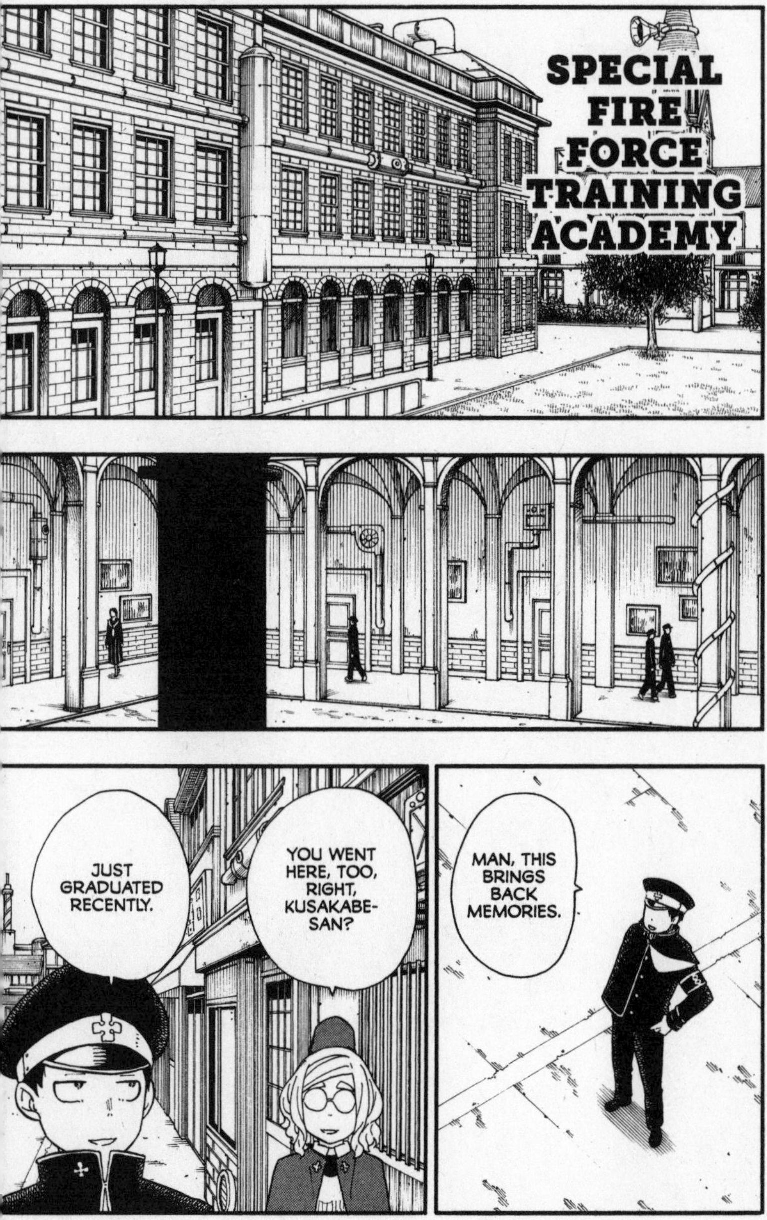
SPECIAL FIRE FORCE TRAINING ACADEMY
MAN, THIS BRINGS BACK MEMORIES.
YOU WENT HERE, TOO, RIGHT, KUSAKABE-SAN?
JUST GRADUATED RECENTLY.

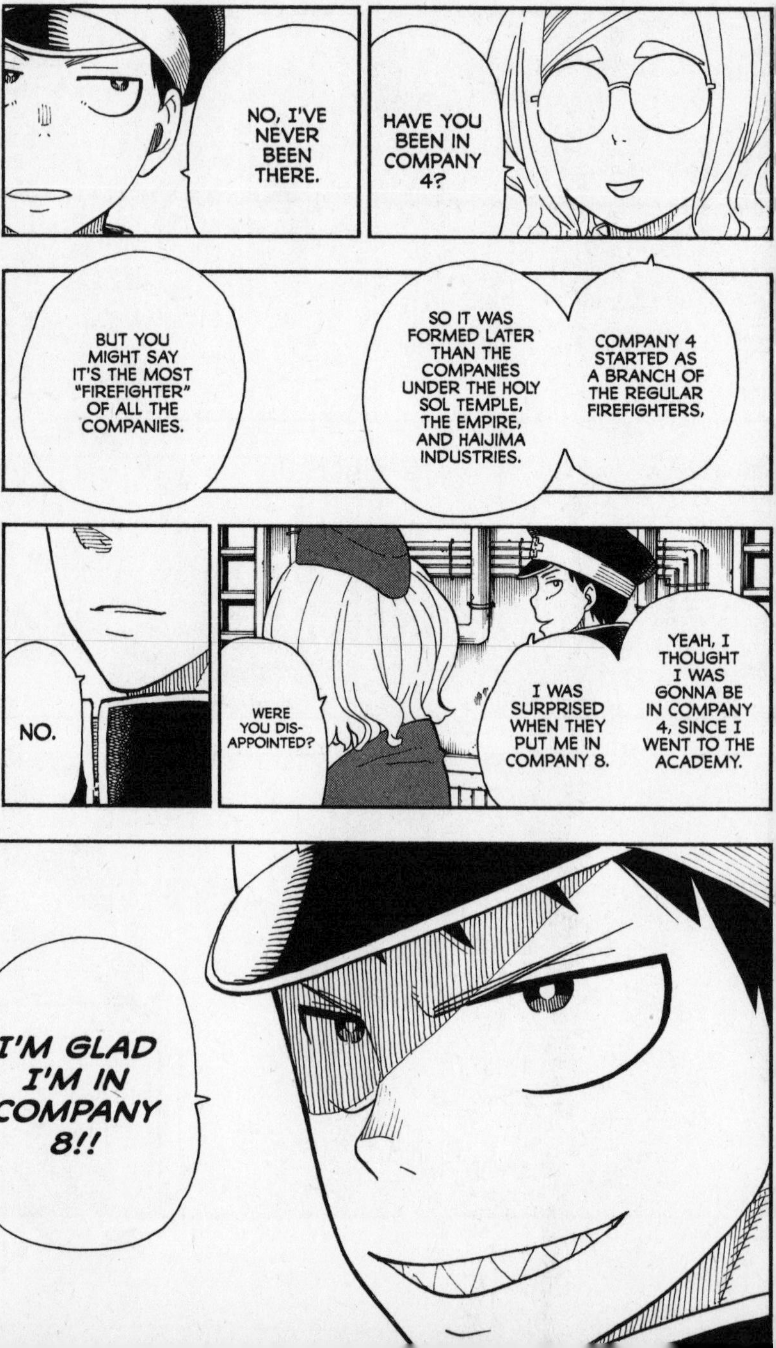
HAVE YOU BEEN IN COMPANY 4?
NO, I'VE NEVER BEEN THERE.
COMPANY 4 STARTED AS A BRANCH OF THE REGULAR FIREFIGHTERS,
SO IT WAS FORMED LATER THAN THE COMPANIES UNDER THE HOLY SOL TEMPLE, THE EMPIRE, AND HAIJIMA INDUSTRIES.
BUT YOU MIGHT SAY IT'S THE MOST "FIREFIGHTER" OF ALL THE COMPANIES.
YEAH, I THOUGHT I WAS GONNA BE IN COMPANY 4, SINCE I WENT TO THE ACADEMY.
I WAS SURPRISED WHEN THEY PUT ME IN COMPANY 8.
WERE YOU DIS-APPOINTED?
NO.
I'M GLAD I'M IN COMPANY 8!!

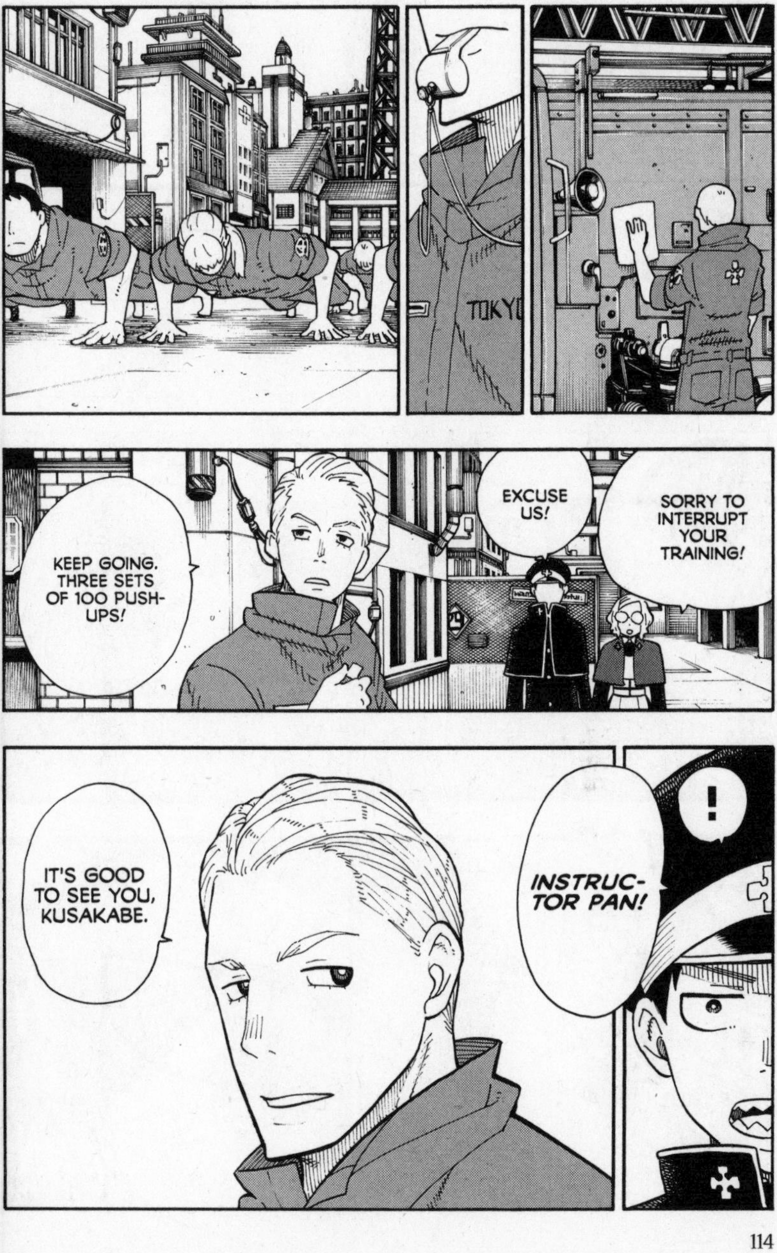
SORRY TO INTERRUPT YOUR TRAINING!
EXCUSE US!
KEEP GOING. THREE SETS OF 100 PUSH-UPS!
!
INSTRUCTOR PAN!
IT'S GOOD TO SEE YOU, KUSAKABE.

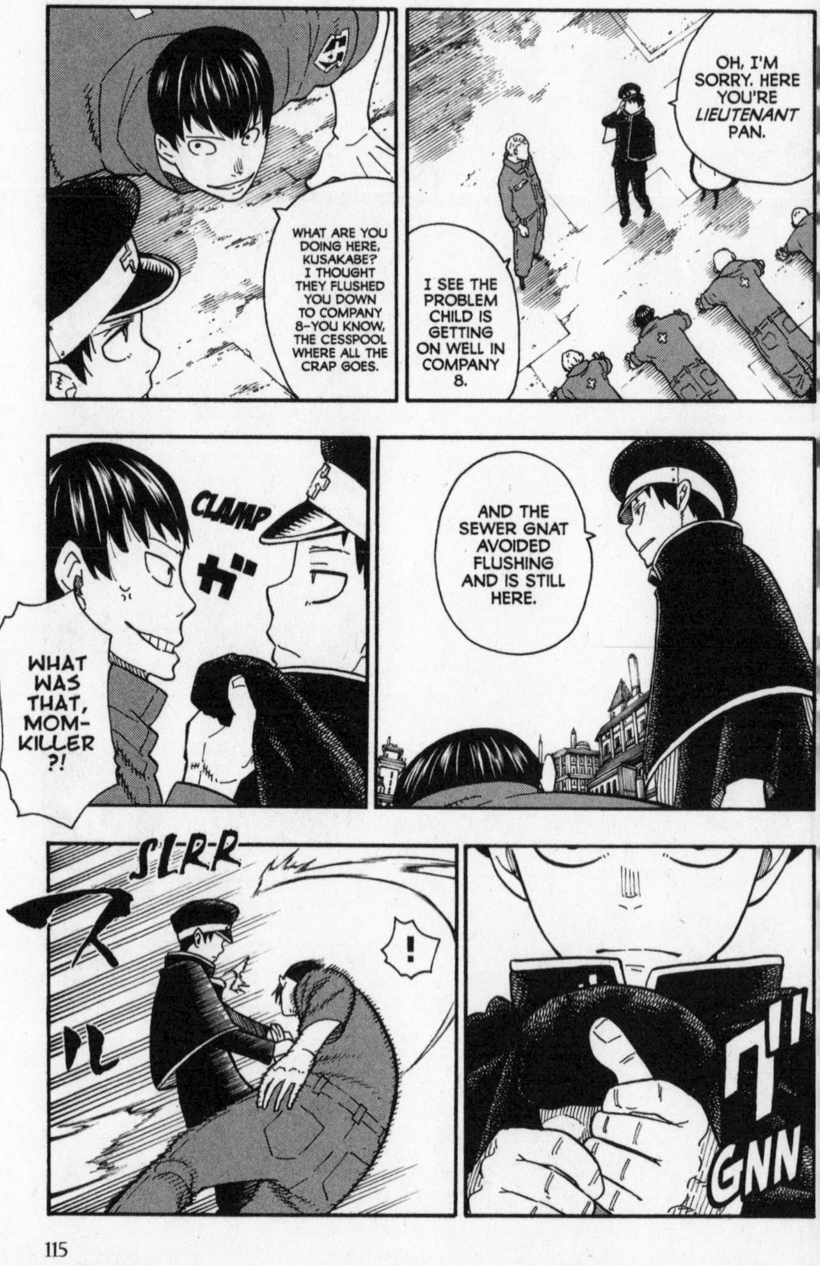

OH, I'M SORRY. HERE YOU'RE *LIEUTENANT* PAN.
I SEE THE PROBLEM CHILD IS GETTING ON WELL IN COMPANY 8.
WHAT ARE YOU DOING HERE, KUSAKABE? I THOUGHT THEY FLUSHED YOU DOWN TO COMPANY 8-YOU KNOW, THE CESSPOOL WHERE ALL THE CRAP GOES.
AND THE SEWER GNAT AVOIDED FLUSHING AND IS STILL HERE.
CLAMP
ガ
WHAT WAS THAT, MOM-KILLER?!
GNN
SLRR
!

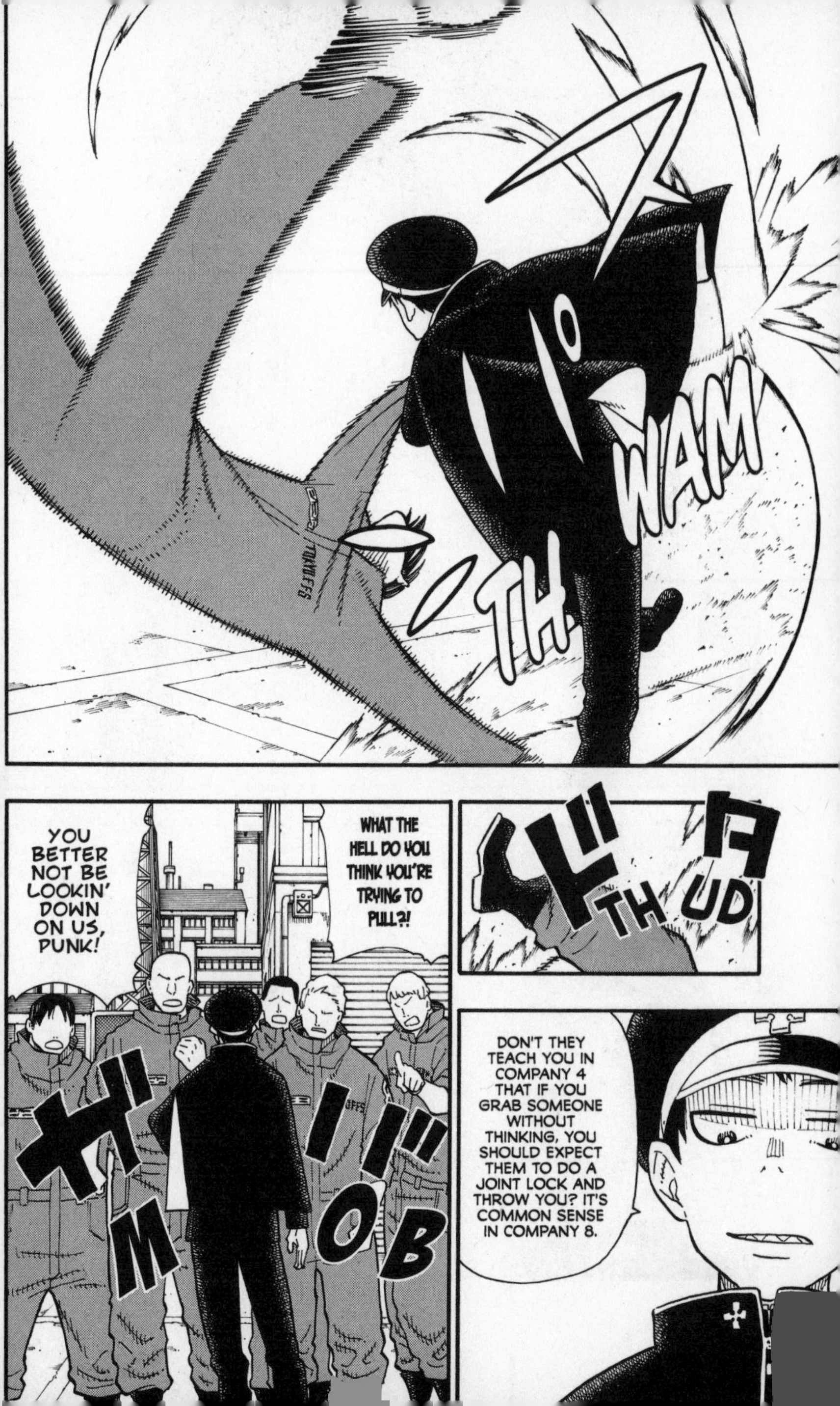
THWAM
THUD
DON'T THEY TEACH YOU IN COMPANY 4 THAT IF YOU GRAB SOMEONE WITHOUT THINKING, YOU SHOULD EXPECT THEM TO DO A JOINT LOCK AND THROW YOU? IT'S COMMON SENSE IN COMPANY 8.
WHAT THE HELL DO YOU THINK YOU'RE TRYING TO PULL?!
YOU BETTER NOT BE LOOKIN' DOWN ON US, PUNK!
MOB

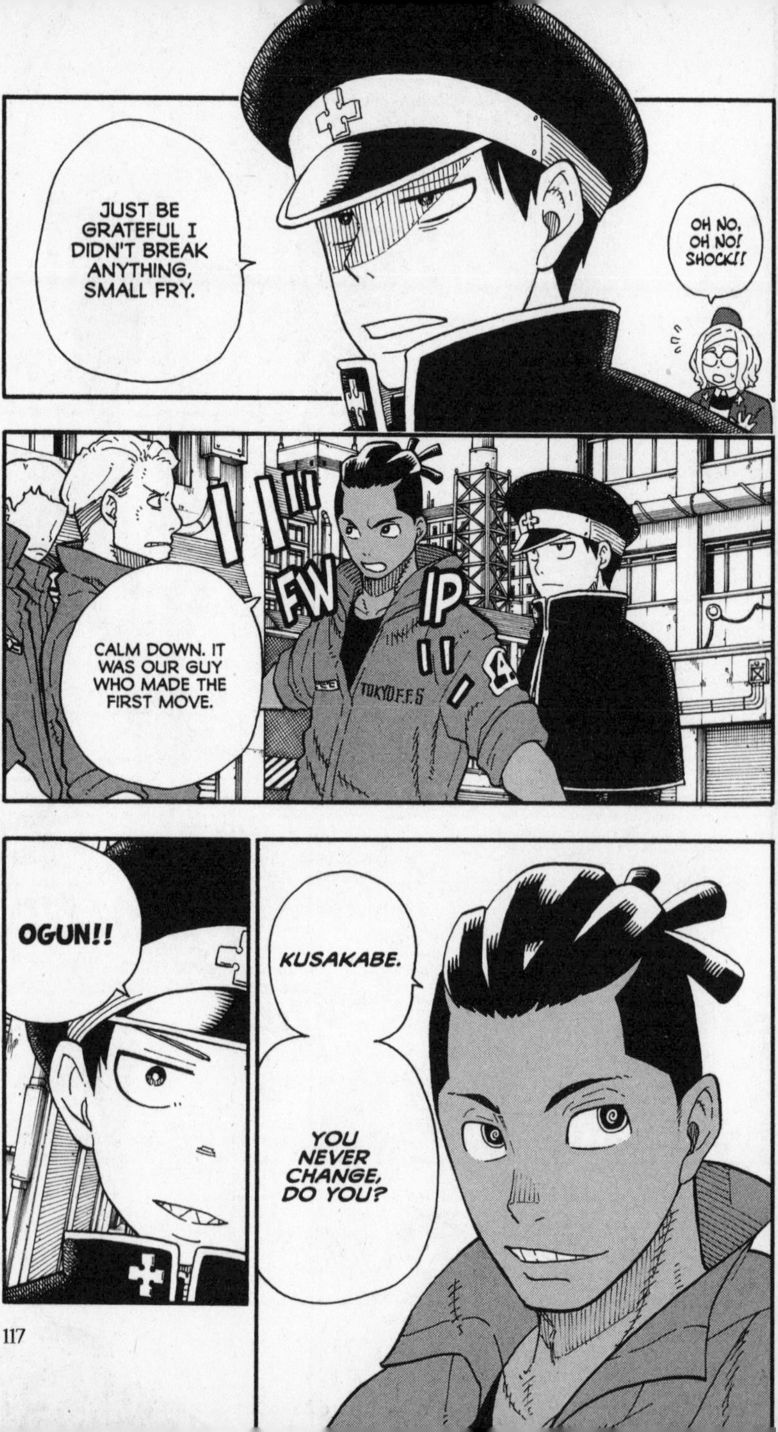
JUST BE GRATEFUL I DIDN'T BREAK ANYTHING, SMALL FRY.
OH NO, OH NO! SHOCK!!
FWIP
CALM DOWN. IT WAS OUR GUY WHO MADE THE FIRST MOVE.
KUSAKABE.
YOU NEVER CHANGE, DO YOU?
OGUN!!

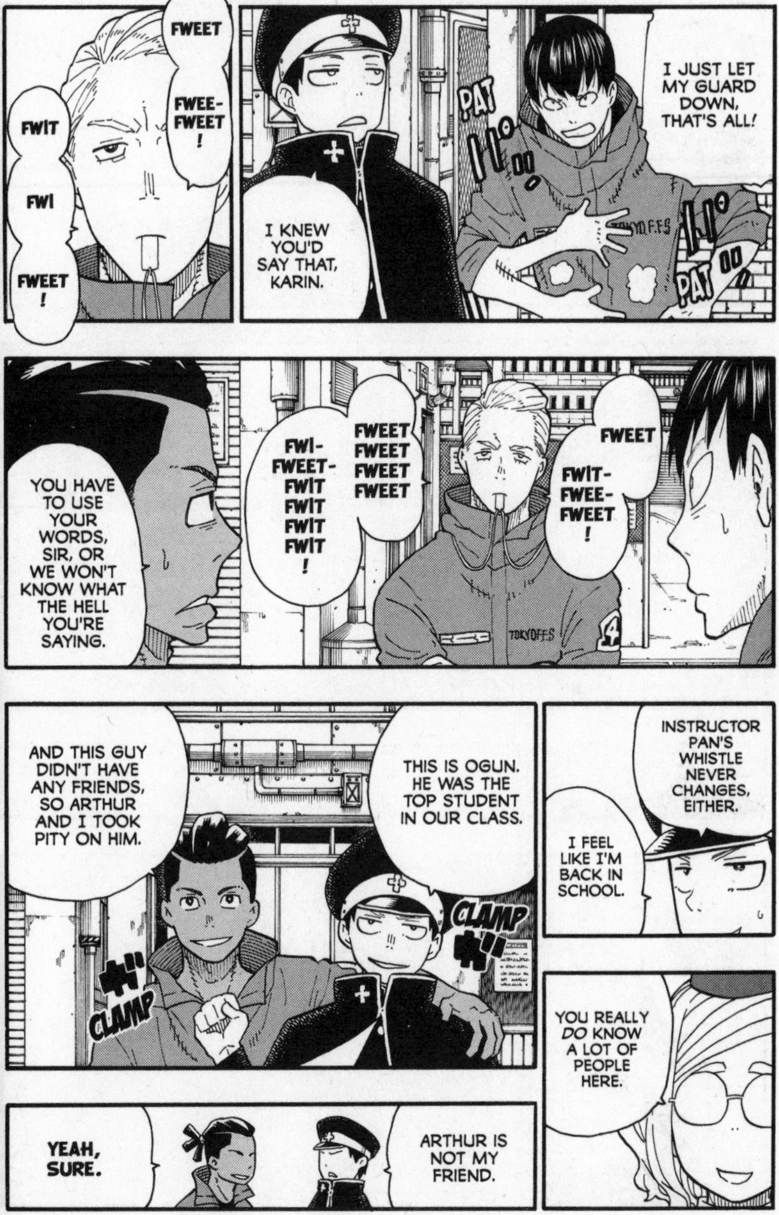

I JUST LET MY GUARD DOWN, THAT'S ALL!
PAT
PAT
I KNEW YOU'D SAY THAT, KARIN.
FWEET
FWEE-FWEET!
FWIT
FWI
FWEET!
FWEET
FWIT-FWEE-FWEET!
FWEET FWEET FWEET FWEET
FWI-FWEET-FWIT FWIT FWIT FWIT!
YOU HAVE TO USE YOUR WORDS, SIR, OR WE WON'T KNOW WHAT THE HELL YOU'RE SAYING.
INSTRUCTOR PAN'S WHISTLE NEVER CHANGES, EITHER.
I FEEL LIKE I'M BACK IN SCHOOL.
YOU REALLY *DO* KNOW A LOT OF PEOPLE HERE.
THIS IS OGUN. HE WAS THE TOP STUDENT IN OUR CLASS.
AND THIS GUY DIDN'T HAVE ANY FRIENDS, SO ARTHUR AND I TOOK PITY ON HIM.
CLAMP
CLAMP
ARTHUR IS NOT MY FRIEND.
YEAH, SURE.

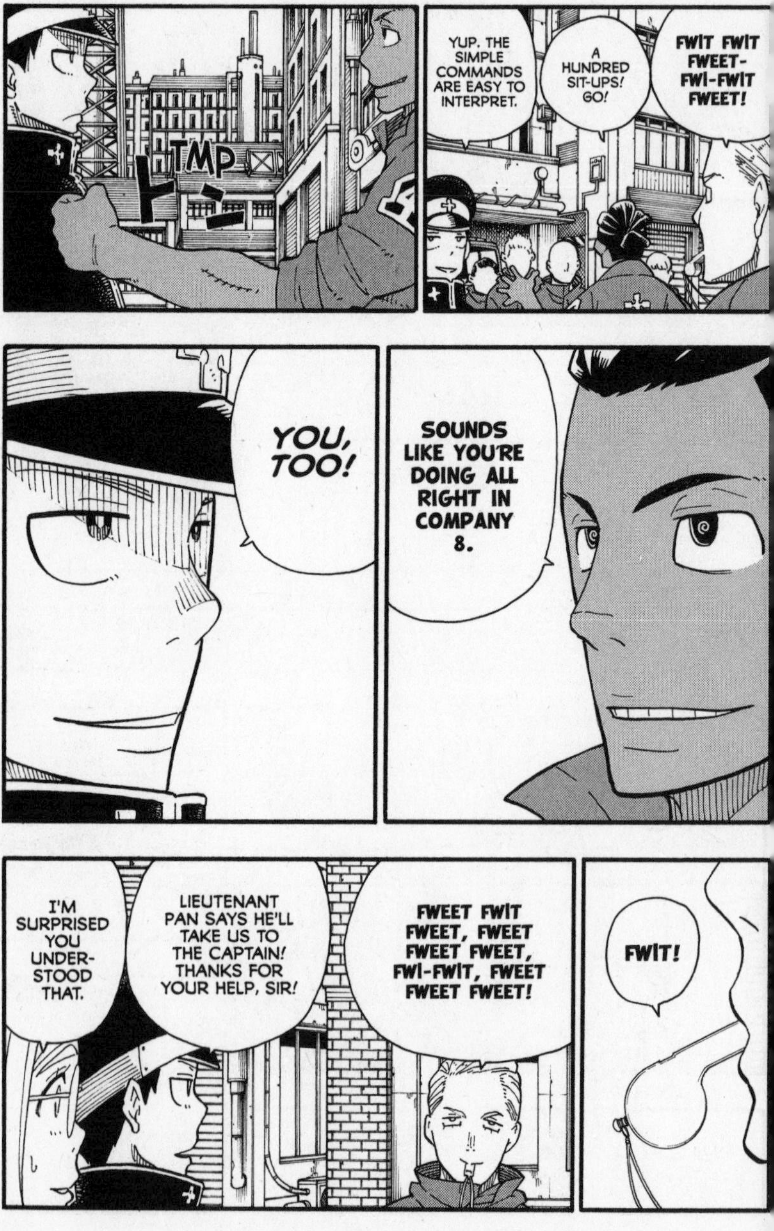
FWIT FWIT FWEET- FWI-FWIT FWEET!
A HUNDRED SIT-UPS! GO!
YUP. THE SIMPLE COMMANDS ARE EASY TO INTERPRET.
TMP
SOUNDS LIKE YOU'RE DOING ALL RIGHT IN COMPANY 8.
YOU, TOO!
FWIT!
FWEET FWIT FWEET, FWEET FWEET FWEET, FWI-FWIT, FWEET FWEET FWEET!
LIEUTENANT PAN SAYS HE'LL TAKE US TO THE CAPTAIN! THANKS FOR YOUR HELP, SIR!
I'M SURPRISED YOU UNDER-STOOD THAT.

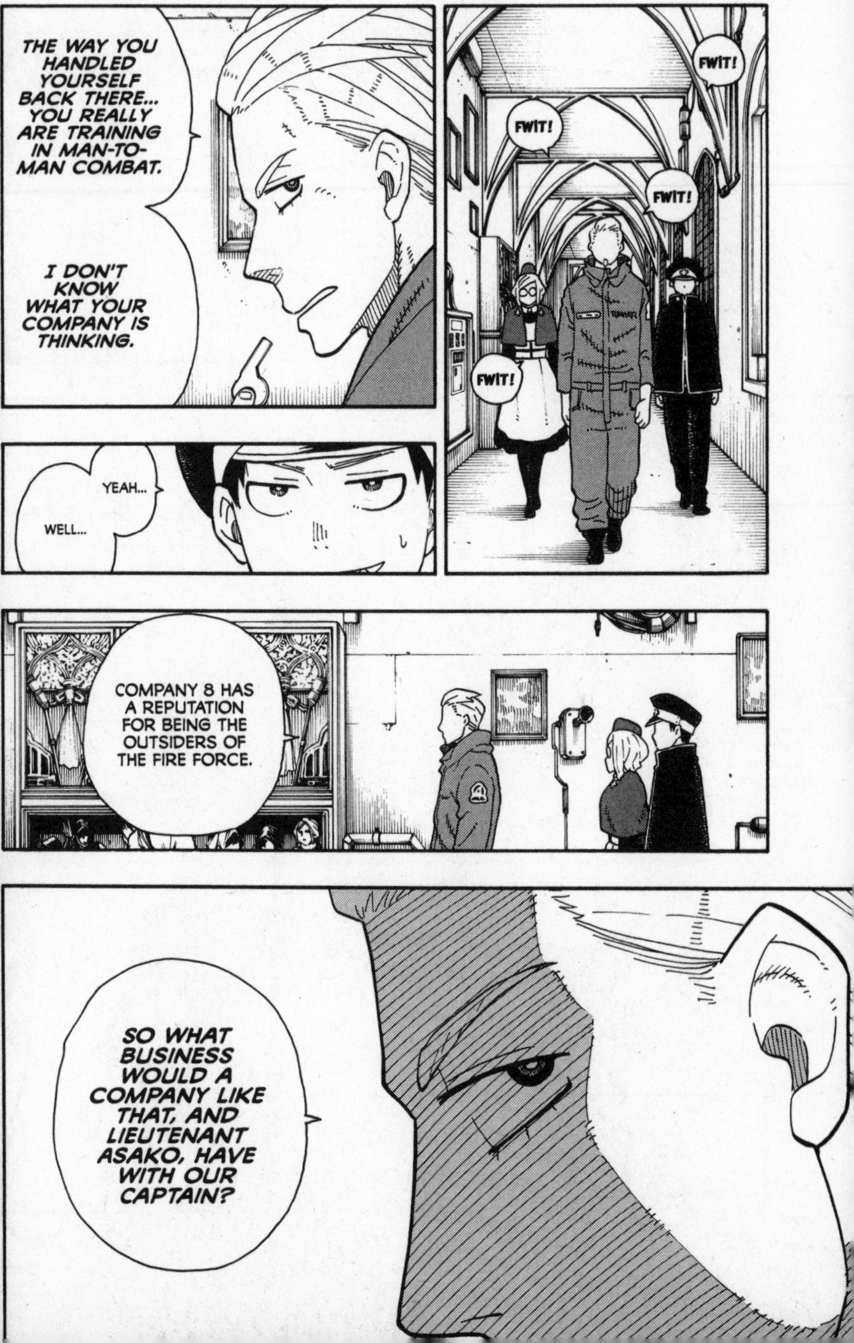
FWIT!
FWIT!
FWIT!
FWIT!
THE WAY YOU HANDLED YOURSELF BACK THERE... YOU REALLY ARE TRAINING IN MAN-TO-MAN COMBAT.
I DON'T KNOW WHAT YOUR COMPANY IS THINKING.
YEAH... WELL...
COMPANY 8 HAS A REPUTATION FOR BEING THE OUTSIDERS OF THE FIRE FORCE.
SO WHAT BUSINESS WOULD A COMPANY LIKE THAT, AND LIEUTENANT ASAKO, HAVE WITH OUR CAPTAIN?

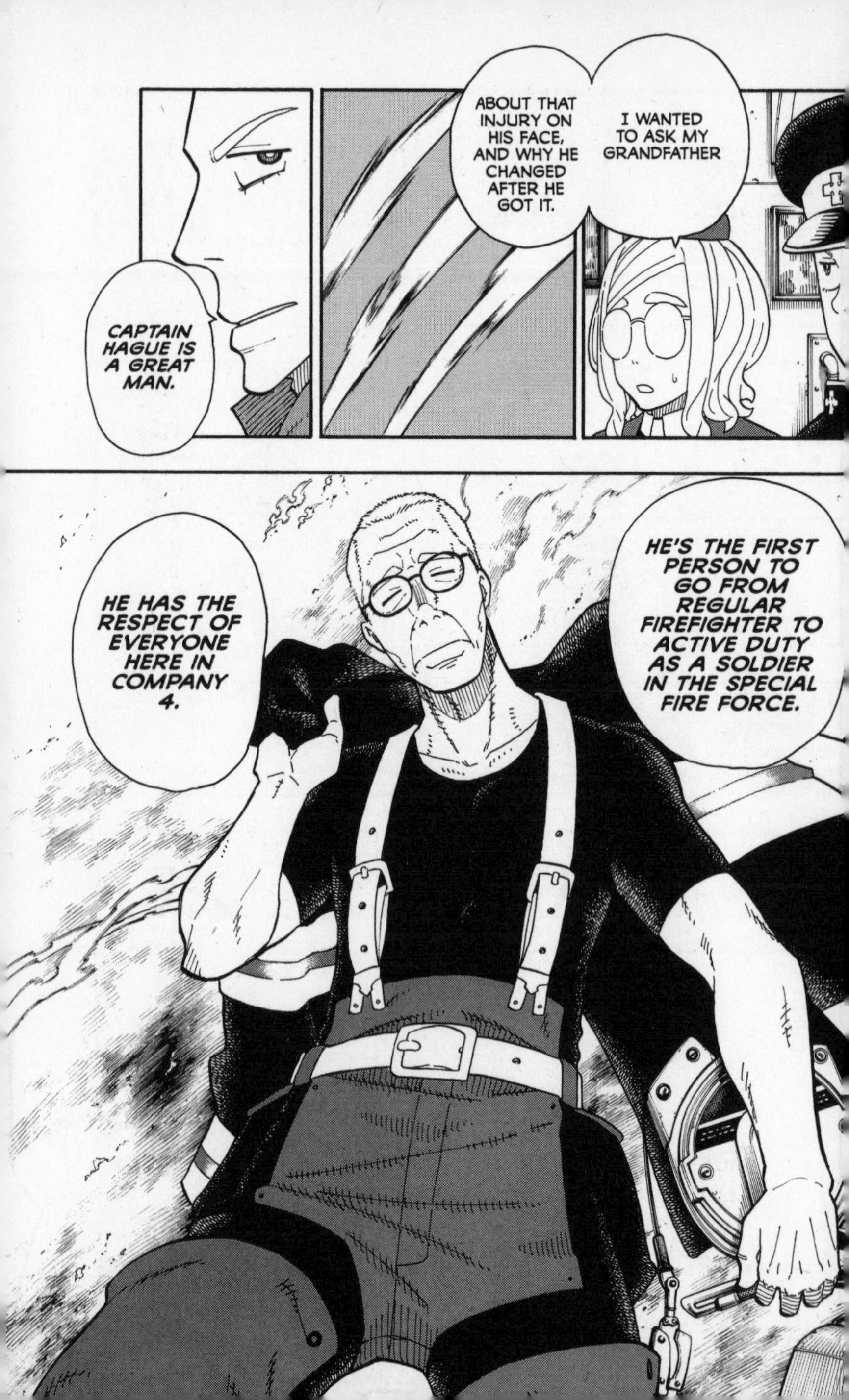
I WANTED TO ASK MY GRANDFATHER
ABOUT THAT INJURY ON HIS FACE, AND WHY HE CHANGED AFTER HE GOT IT.
CAPTAIN HAGUE IS A GREAT MAN.
HE'S THE FIRST PERSON TO GO FROM REGULAR FIREFIGHTER TO ACTIVE DUTY AS A SOLDIER IN THE SPECIAL FIRE FORCE.
HE HAS THE RESPECT OF EVERYONE HERE IN COMPANY 4.

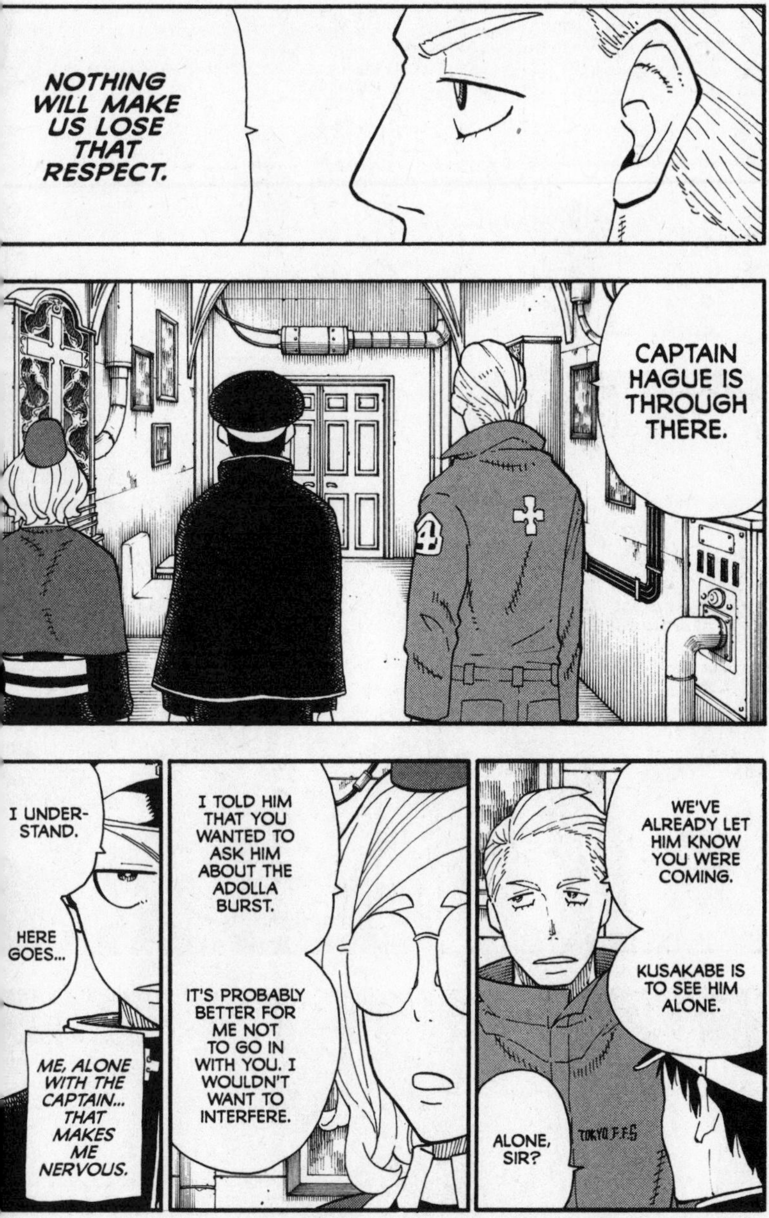
NOTHING WILL MAKE US LOSE THAT RESPECT.
CAPTAIN HAGUE IS THROUGH THERE.
WE'VE ALREADY LET HIM KNOW YOU WERE COMING.
KUSAKABE IS TO SEE HIM ALONE.
TOKYO F.F.S
ALONE, SIR?
I TOLD HIM THAT YOU WANTED TO ASK HIM ABOUT THE ADOLLA BURST.
IT'S PROBABLY BETTER FOR ME NOT TO GO IN WITH YOU. I WOULDN'T WANT TO INTERFERE.
I UNDER-STAND.
HERE GOES...
ME, ALONE WITH THE CAPTAIN... THAT MAKES ME NERVOUS.

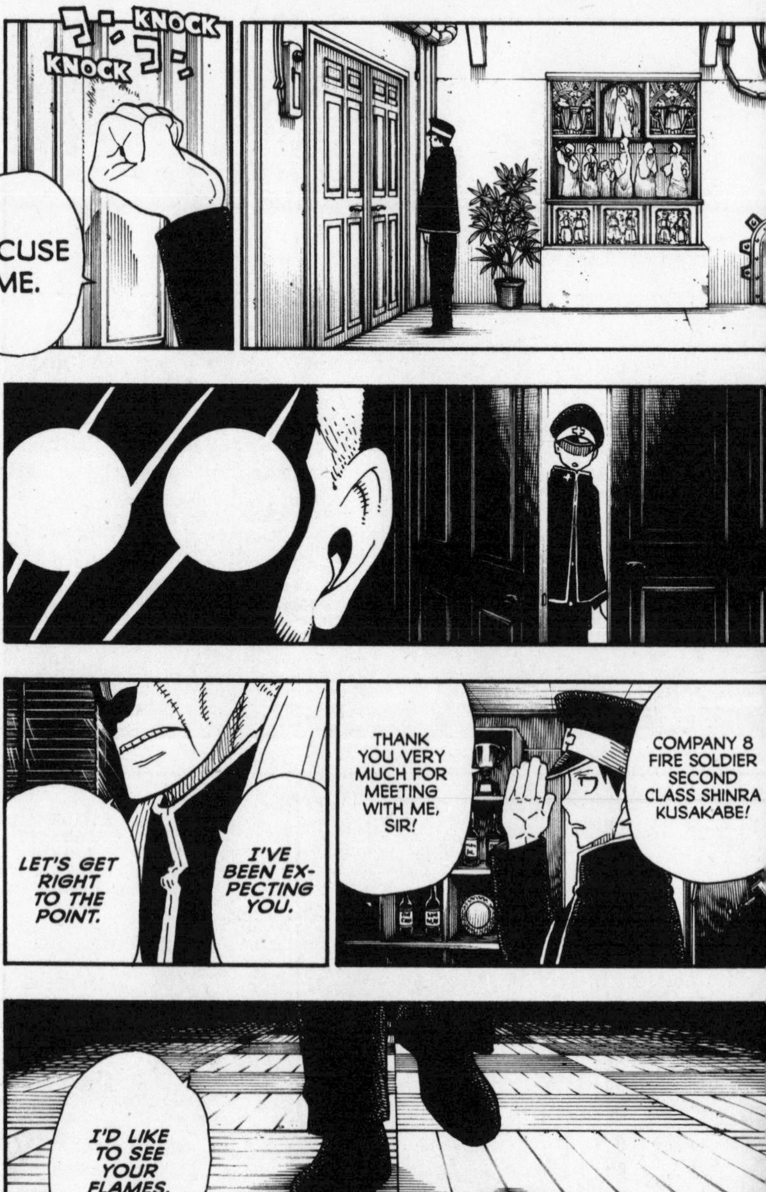
KNOCK
KNOCK
EXCUSE ME.
COMPANY 8 FIRE SOLDIER SECOND CLASS SHINRA KUSAKABE!
THANK YOU VERY MUCH FOR MEETING WITH ME, SIR!
I'VE BEEN EX-PECTING YOU.
LET'S GET RIGHT TO THE POINT.
I'D LIKE TO SEE YOUR FLAMES.

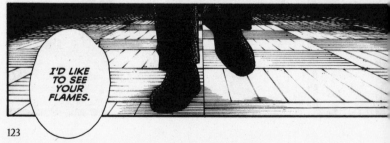

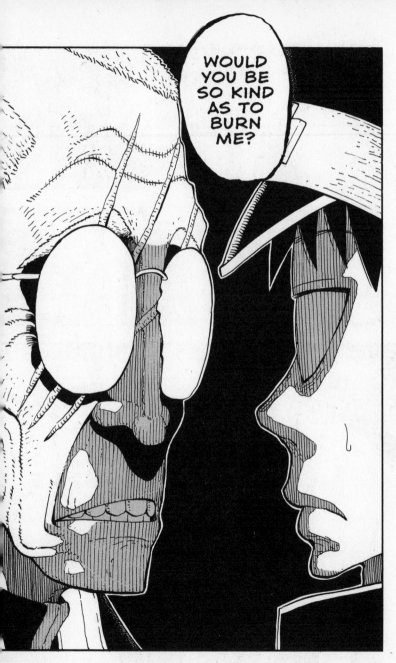

WOULD YOU BE SO KIND AS TO BURN ME?

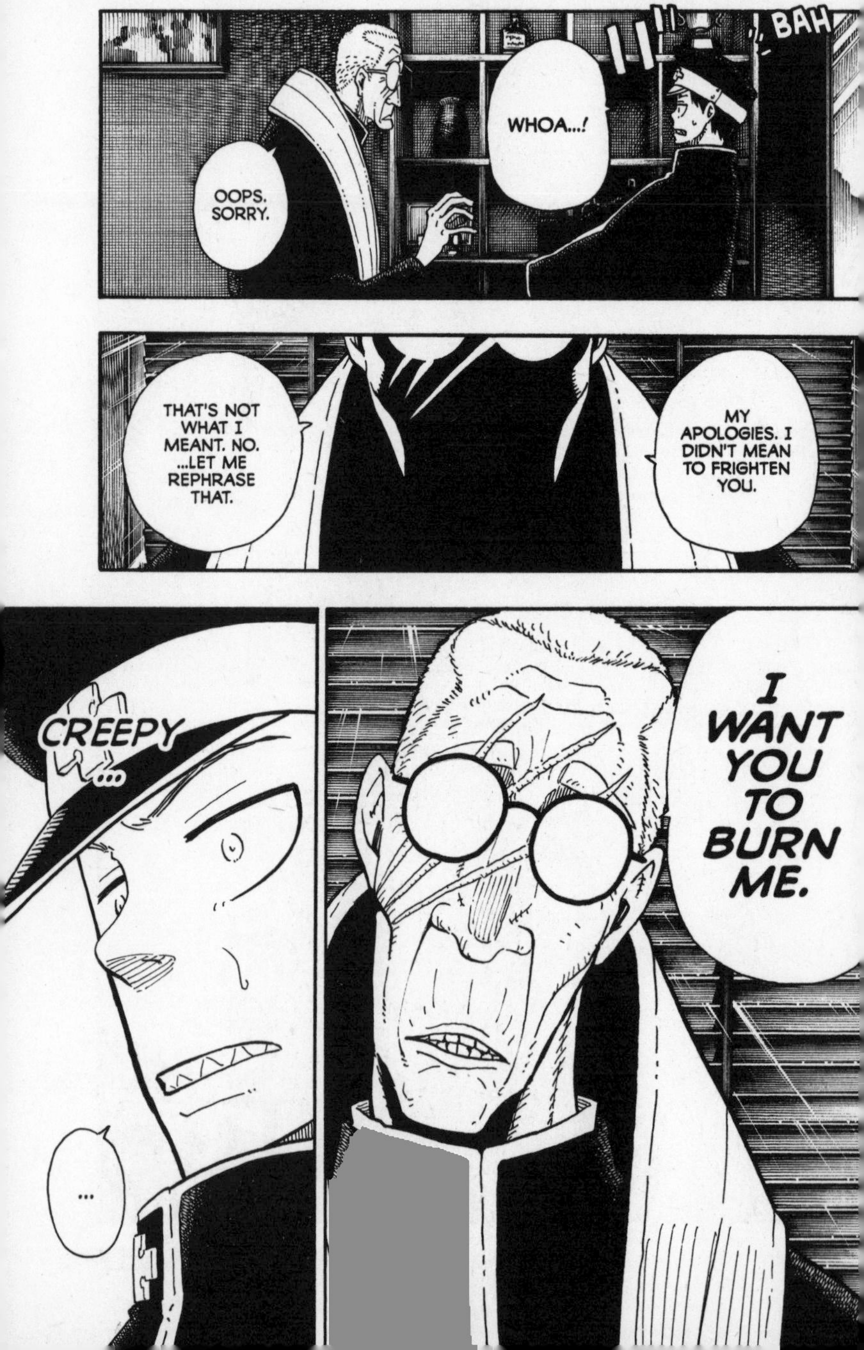
BAH
WHOA...!
OOPS. SORRY.
MY APOLOGIES. I DIDN'T MEAN TO FRIGHTEN YOU.
THAT'S NOT WHAT I MEANT. NO. ...LET ME REPHRASE THAT.
I WANT YOU TO BURN ME.
CREEPY...
...

FIRE FORCE

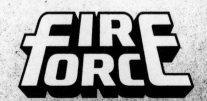

CHAPTER XCIV: SŌICHIRŌ HAGUE

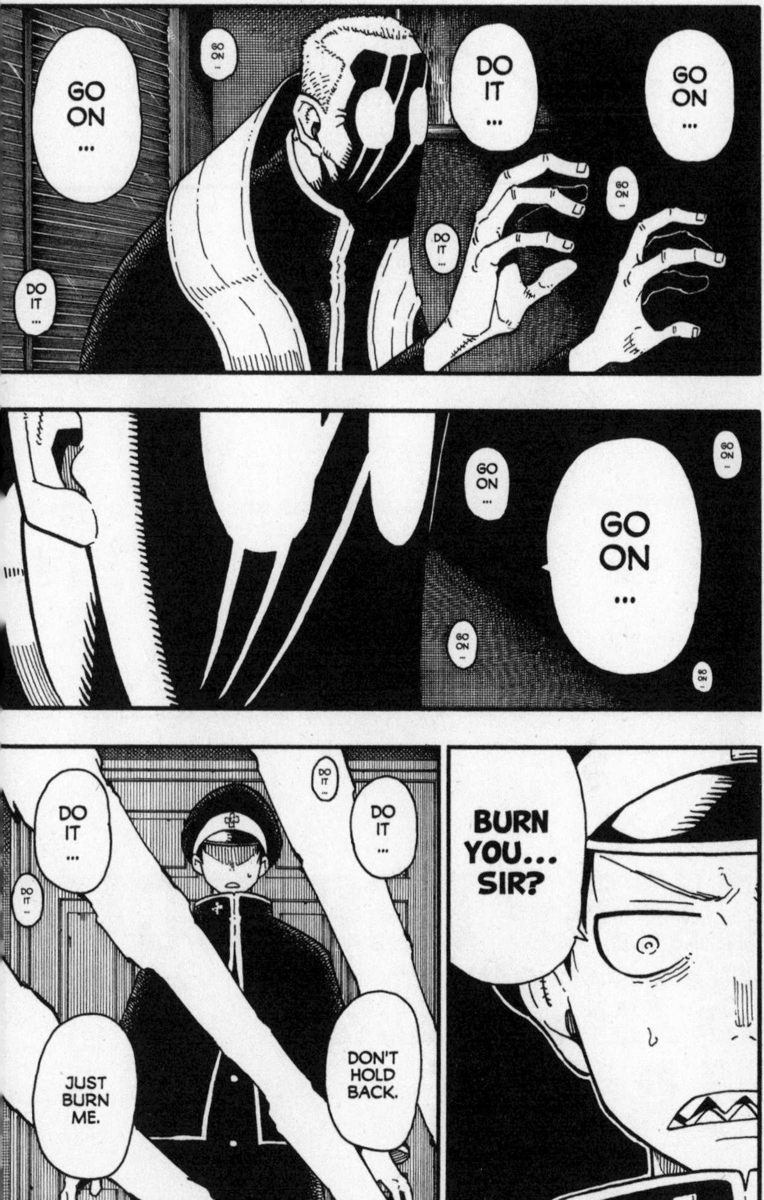
GO ON ...
DO IT ...
GO ON ...
DO IT ...
GO ON ...
GO ON ...
DO IT ...
GO ON ...
GO ON ...
GO ON ...
GO ON ...
GO ON ...
BURN YOU... SIR?
DO IT ...
DO IT ...
DO IT ...
DO IT ...
DON'T HOLD BACK.
JUST BURN ME.

YES! GIVE HIM WHAT HE WANTS. BURN HIM!

?!

BURN HIM TILL HE DIES...

BURN HIM.

BURN HIM.

BURN HIM.

I KNOW YOUR FLAMES ARE JUST BURSTING TO GET OUT.

BURN HIM.

BURN HIM!!

SO STOP HOLDING THEM BACK.

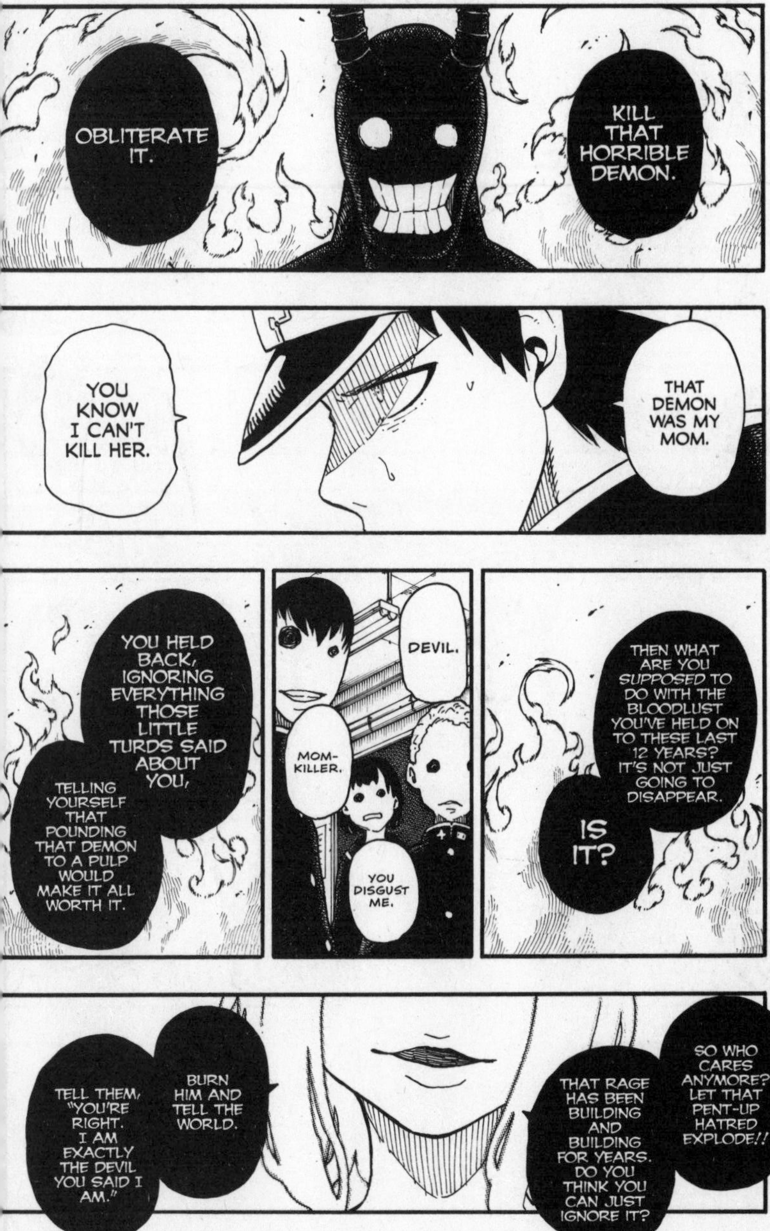
KILL THAT HORRIBLE DEMON.
OBLITERATE IT.
THAT DEMON WAS MY MOM.
YOU KNOW I CAN'T KILL HER.
THEN WHAT ARE YOU SUPPOSED TO DO WITH THE BLOODLUST YOU'VE HELD ON TO THESE LAST 12 YEARS? IT'S NOT JUST GOING TO DISAPPEAR.
IS IT?
DEVIL.
MOM-KILLER.
YOU DISGUST ME.
YOU HELD BACK, IGNORING EVERYTHING THOSE LITTLE TURDS SAID ABOUT YOU,
TELLING YOURSELF THAT POUNDING THAT DEMON TO A PULP WOULD MAKE IT ALL WORTH IT.
SO WHO CARES ANYMORE? LET THAT PENT-UP HATRED EXPLODE!!
THAT RAGE HAS BEEN BUILDING AND BUILDING FOR YEARS. DO YOU THINK YOU CAN JUST IGNORE IT?
BURN HIM AND TELL THE WORLD.
TELL THEM, "YOU'RE RIGHT. I AM EXACTLY THE DEVIL YOU SAID I AM."

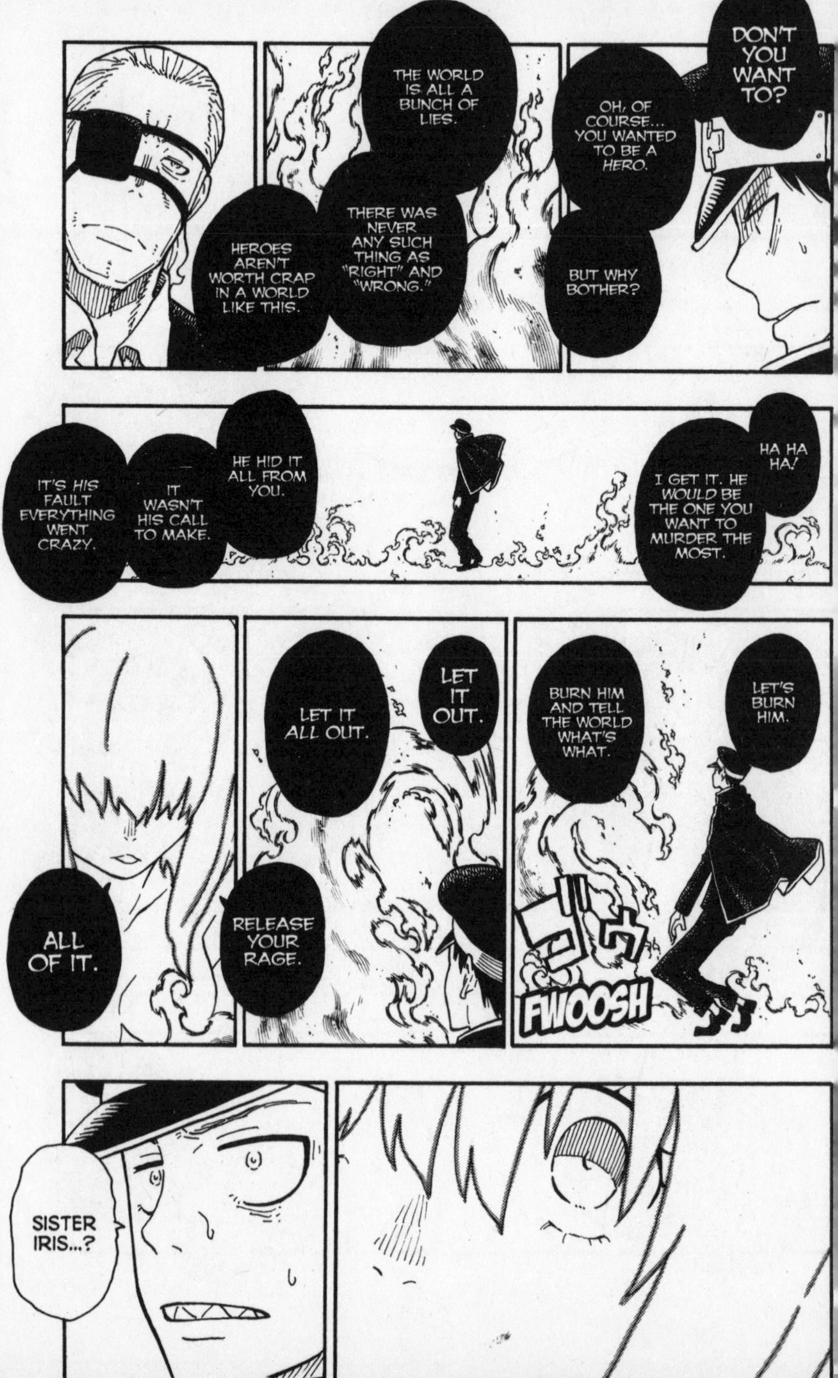
DON'T YOU WANT TO?
OH, OF COURSE... YOU WANTED TO BE A HERO.
BUT WHY BOTHER?
THE WORLD IS ALL A BUNCH OF LIES.
THERE WAS NEVER ANY SUCH THING AS "RIGHT" AND "WRONG."
HEROES AREN'T WORTH CRAP IN A WORLD LIKE THIS.
HA HA HA!
I GET IT. HE *WOULD* BE THE ONE YOU WANT TO MURDER THE MOST.
HE HID IT ALL FROM YOU.
IT WASN'T HIS CALL TO MAKE.
IT'S *HIS* FAULT EVERYTHING WENT CRAZY.
LET'S BURN HIM.
BURN HIM AND TELL THE WORLD WHAT'S WHAT.
FWOOSH
LET IT OUT.
LET IT *ALL* OUT.
RELEASE YOUR RAGE.
ALL OF IT.
SISTER IRIS...?

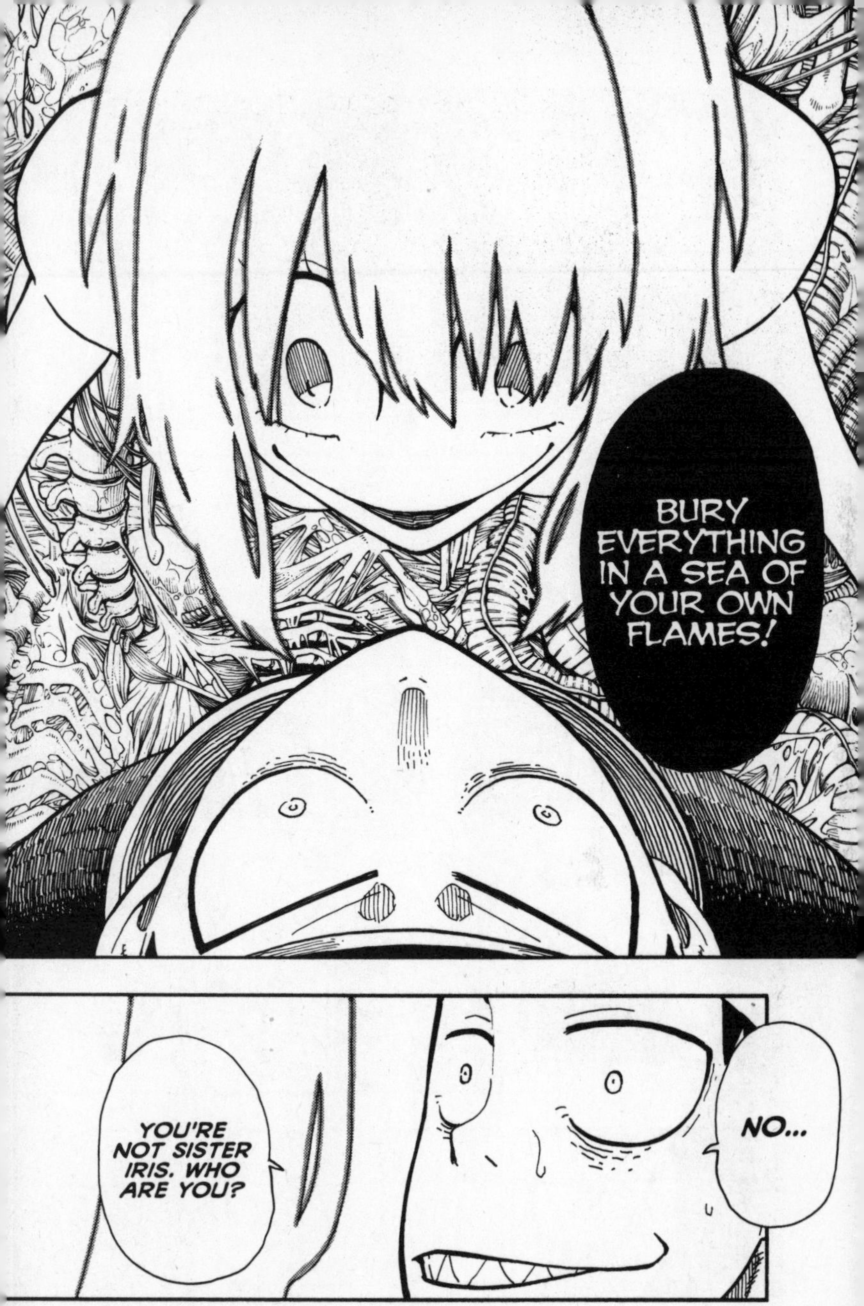
BURY EVERYTHING IN A SEA OF YOUR OWN FLAMES!
NO...
YOU'RE NOT SISTER IRIS. WHO ARE YOU?

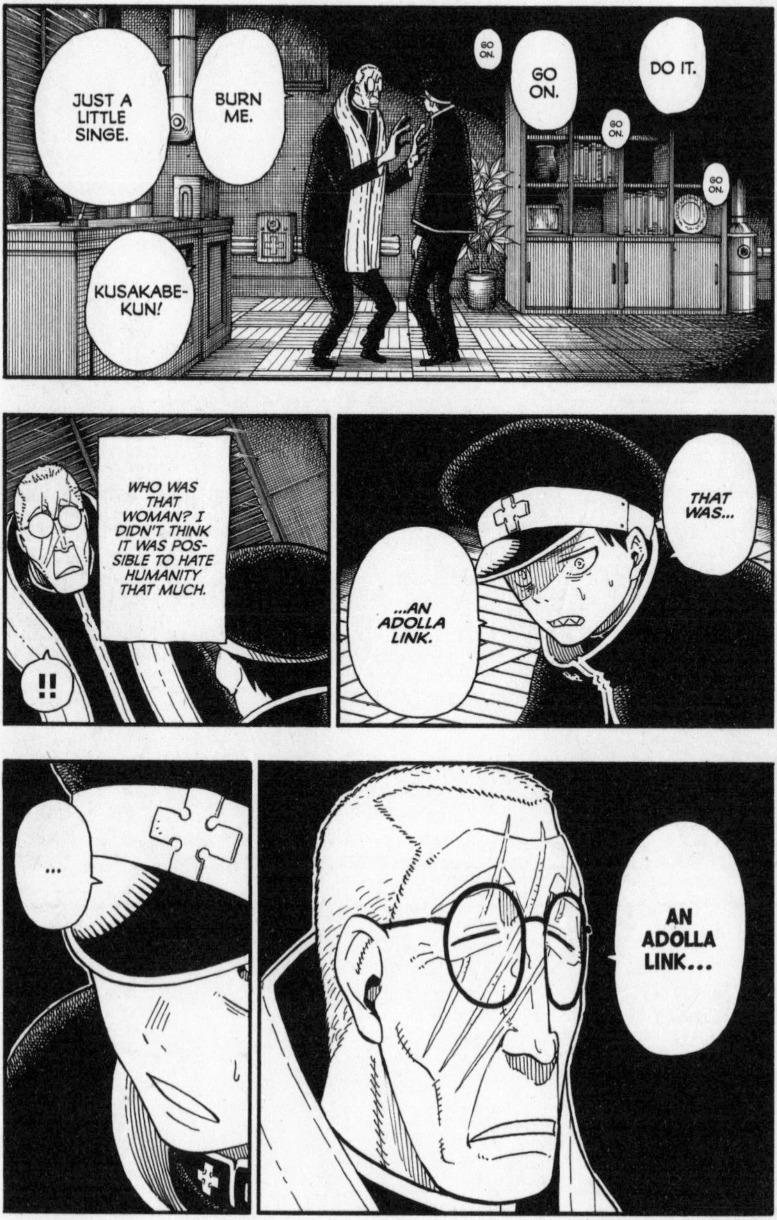
DO IT.
GO ON.
GO ON.
GO ON.
GO ON.
BURN ME.
JUST A LITTLE SINGE.
KUSAKABE-KUN!
THAT WAS...
...AN ADOLLA LINK.
WHO WAS THAT WOMAN? I DIDN'T THINK IT WAS POSSIBLE TO HATE HUMANITY THAT MUCH.
!!
AN ADOLLA LINK...
...

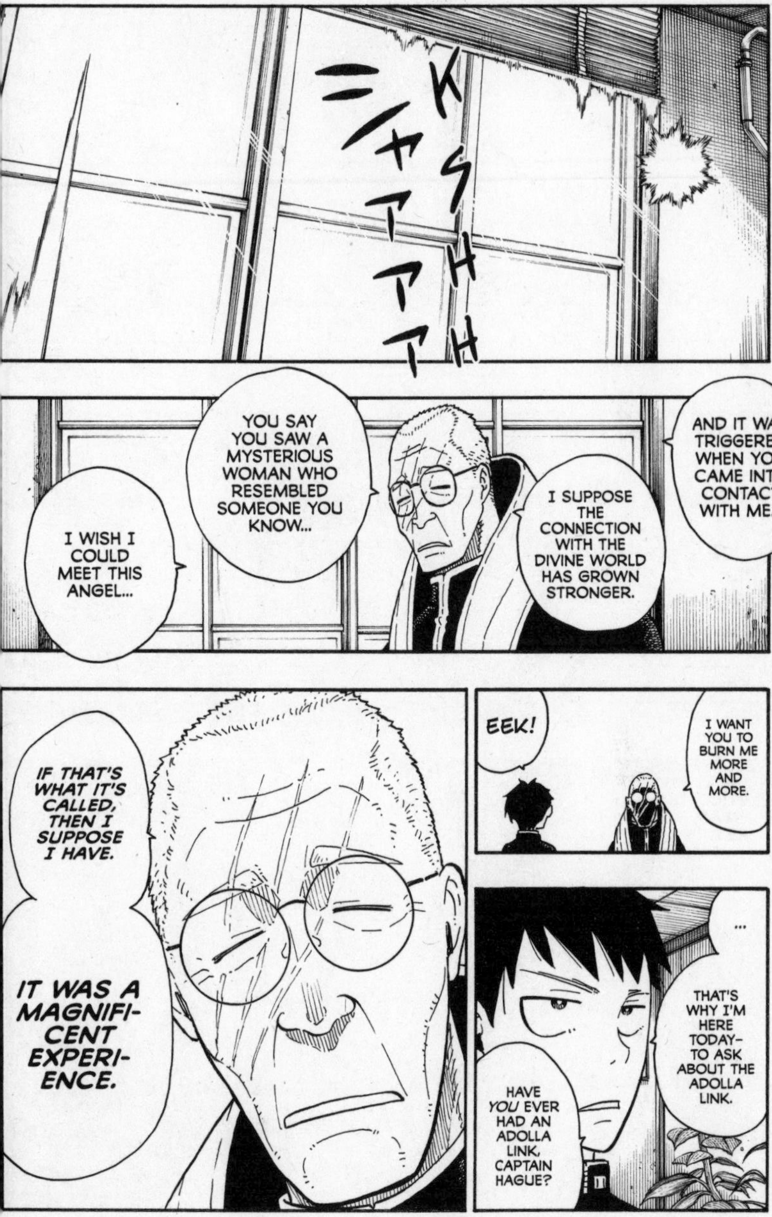
KSHH
AND IT WAS TRIGGERED WHEN YOU CAME INTO CONTACT WITH ME...
I SUPPOSE THE CONNECTION WITH THE DIVINE WORLD HAS GROWN STRONGER.
YOU SAY YOU SAW A MYSTERIOUS WOMAN WHO RESEMBLED SOMEONE YOU KNOW...
I WISH I COULD MEET THIS ANGEL...
I WANT YOU TO BURN ME MORE AND MORE.
EEK!
...
THAT'S WHY I'M HERE TODAY— TO ASK ABOUT THE ADOLLA LINK.
HAVE *YOU* EVER HAD AN ADOLLA LINK, CAPTAIN HAGUE?
IF THAT'S WHAT IT'S CALLED, THEN I SUPPOSE I HAVE.
IT WAS A MAGNIFICENT EXPERIENCE.

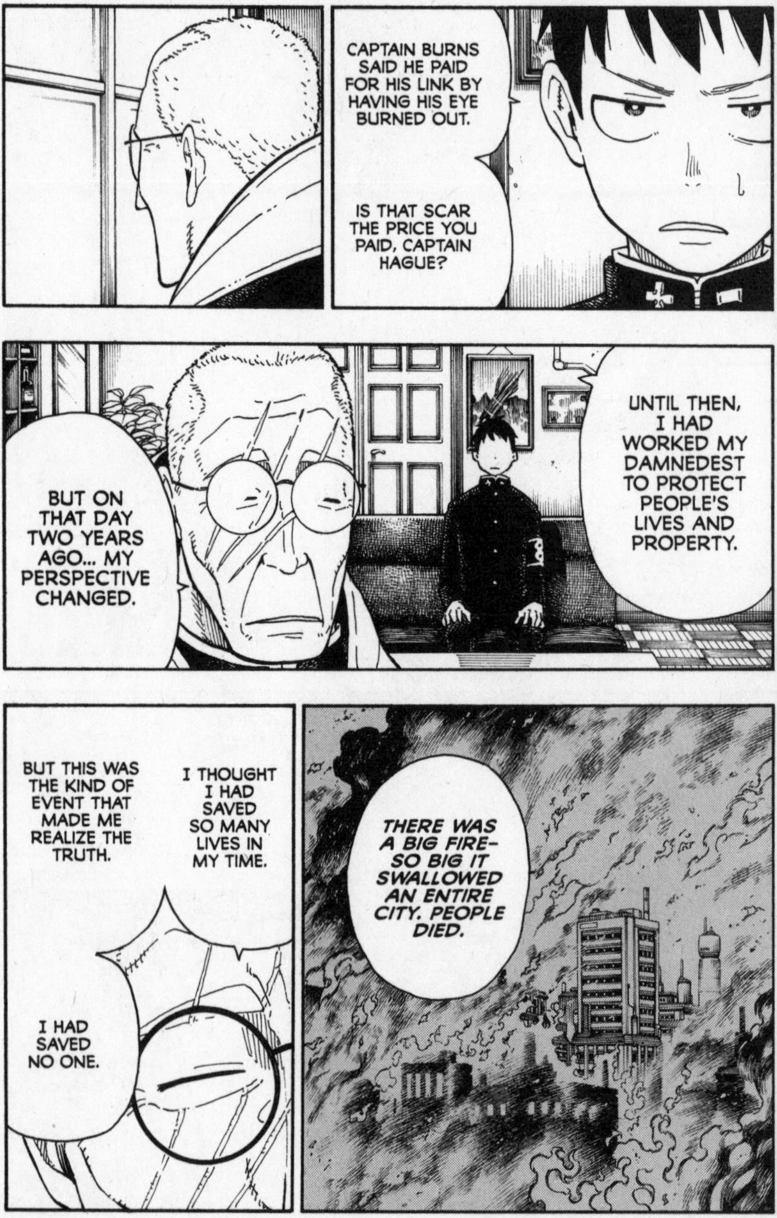
CAPTAIN BURNS SAID HE PAID FOR HIS LINK BY HAVING HIS EYE BURNED OUT.
IS THAT SCAR THE PRICE YOU PAID, CAPTAIN HAGUE?
UNTIL THEN, I HAD WORKED MY DAMNEDEST TO PROTECT PEOPLE'S LIVES AND PROPERTY.
BUT ON THAT DAY TWO YEARS AGO... MY PERSPECTIVE CHANGED.
THERE WAS A BIG FIRE-SO BIG IT SWALLOWED AN ENTIRE CITY. PEOPLE DIED.
I THOUGHT I HAD SAVED SO MANY LIVES IN MY TIME.
BUT THIS WAS THE KIND OF EVENT THAT MADE ME REALIZE THE TRUTH.
I HAD SAVED NO ONE.

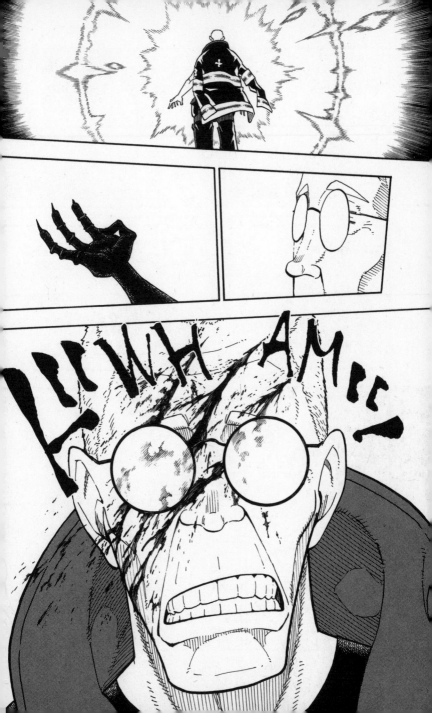

FFWHAM!!

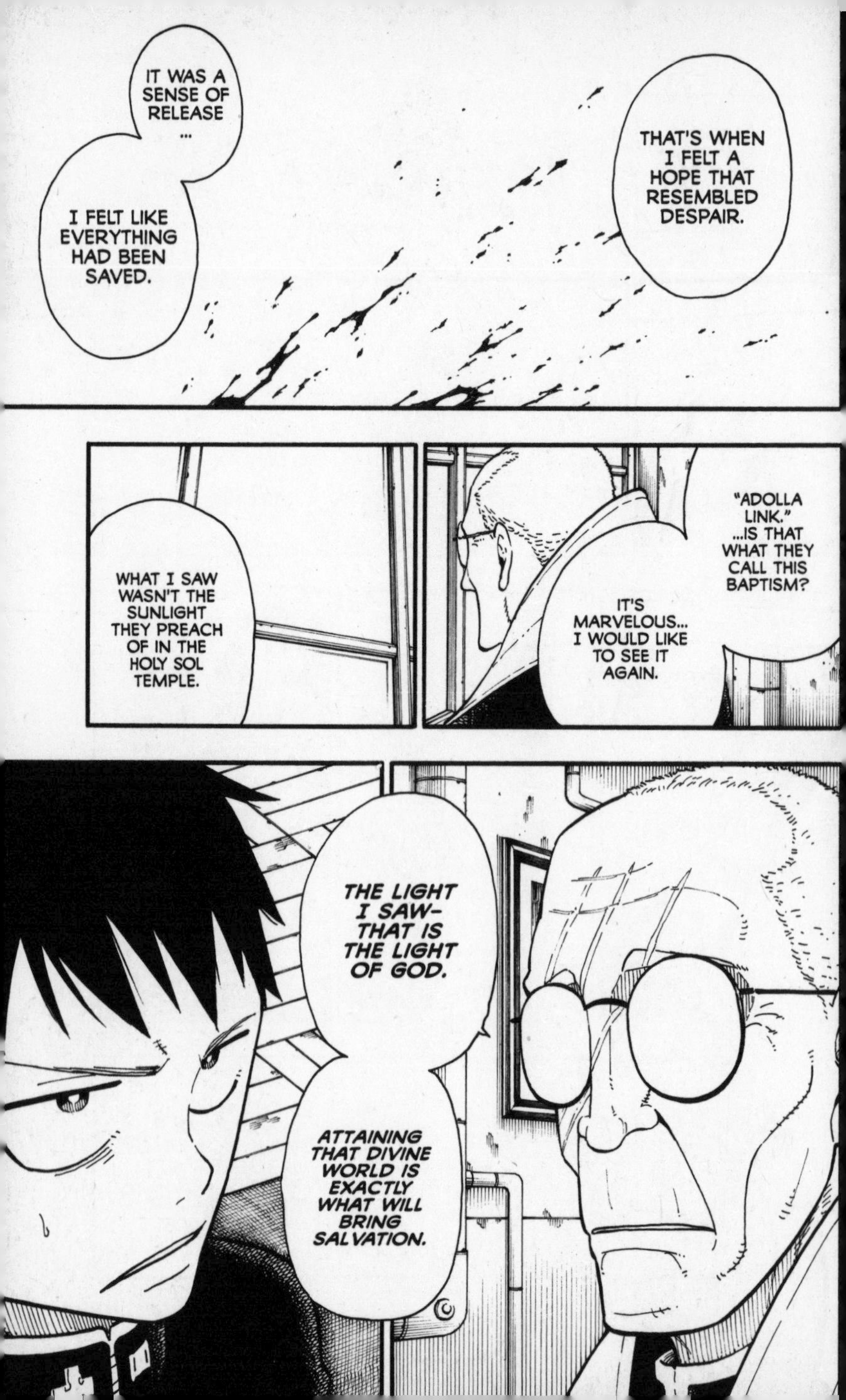
THAT'S WHEN I FELT A HOPE THAT RESEMBLED DESPAIR.
IT WAS A SENSE OF RELEASE ...
I FELT LIKE EVERYTHING HAD BEEN SAVED.
"ADOLLA LINK." ...IS THAT WHAT THEY CALL THIS BAPTISM?
IT'S MARVELOUS... I WOULD LIKE TO SEE IT AGAIN.
WHAT I SAW WASN'T THE SUNLIGHT THEY PREACH OF IN THE HOLY SOL TEMPLE.
THE LIGHT I SAW- THAT IS THE LIGHT OF GOD.
ATTAINING THAT DIVINE WORLD IS EXACTLY WHAT WILL BRING SALVATION.

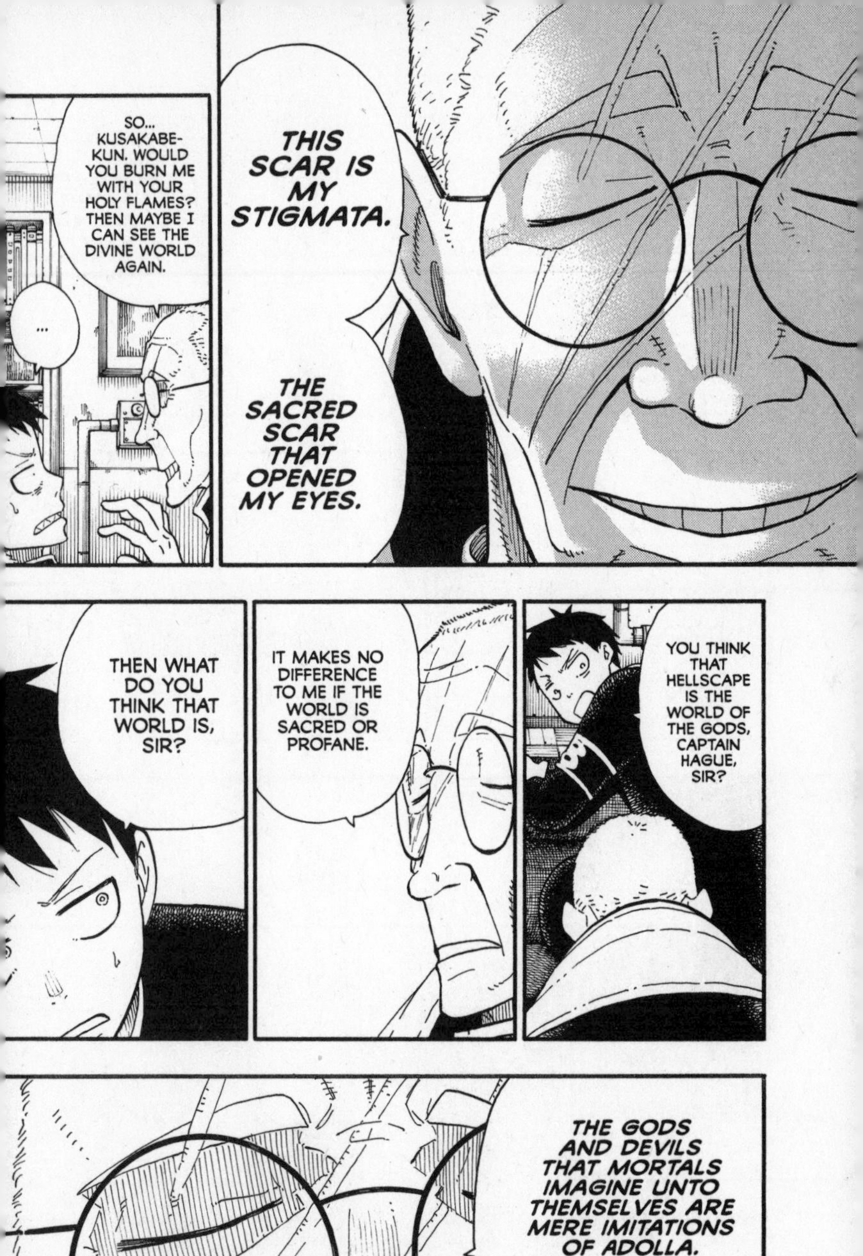
THIS SCAR IS MY STIGMATA.
THE SACRED SCAR THAT OPENED MY EYES.
SO... KUSAKABE-KUN. WOULD YOU BURN ME WITH YOUR HOLY FLAMES? THEN MAYBE I CAN SEE THE DIVINE WORLD AGAIN.
...
YOU THINK THAT HELLSCAPE IS THE WORLD OF THE GODS, CAPTAIN HAGUE, SIR?
IT MAKES NO DIFFERENCE TO ME IF THE WORLD IS SACRED OR PROFANE.
THEN WHAT DO YOU THINK THAT WORLD IS, SIR?
THE GODS AND DEVILS THAT MORTALS IMAGINE UNTO THEMSELVES ARE MERE IMITATIONS OF ADOLLA.

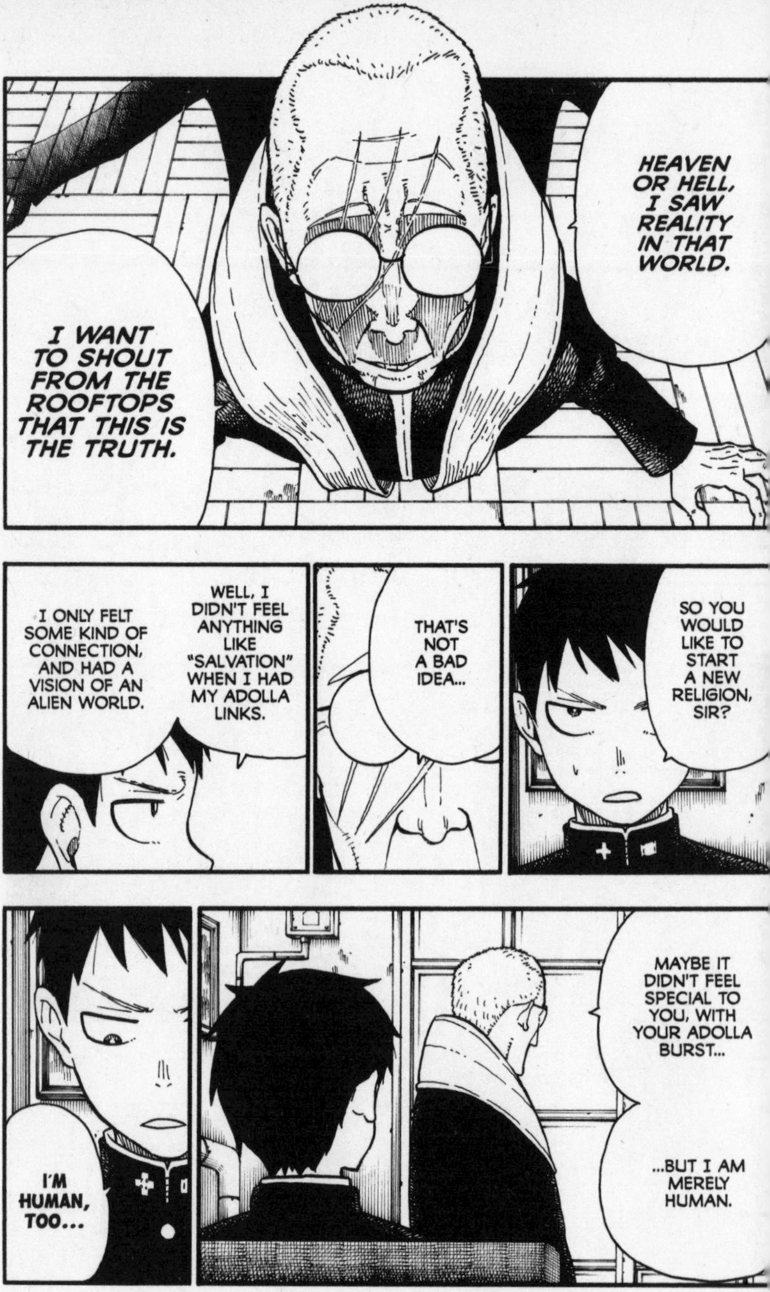
HEAVEN OR HELL, I SAW REALITY IN THAT WORLD.
I WANT TO SHOUT FROM THE ROOFTOPS THAT THIS IS THE TRUTH.
SO YOU WOULD LIKE TO START A NEW RELIGION, SIR?
THAT'S NOT A BAD IDEA...
WELL, I DIDN'T FEEL ANYTHING LIKE "SALVATION" WHEN I HAD MY ADOLLA LINKS.
I ONLY FELT SOME KIND OF CONNECTION, AND HAD A VISION OF AN ALIEN WORLD.
MAYBE IT DIDN'T FEEL SPECIAL TO YOU, WITH YOUR ADOLLA BURST...
...BUT I AM MERELY HUMAN.
I'M HUMAN, TOO...

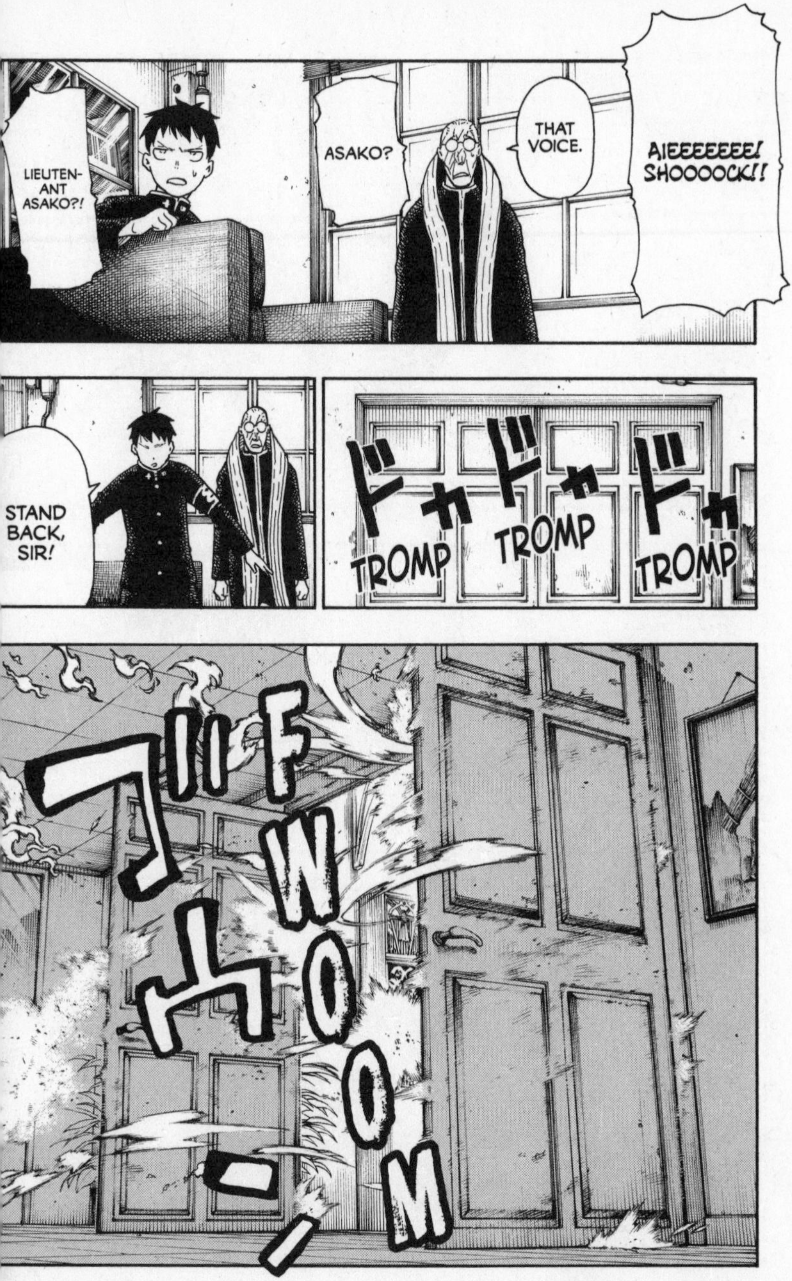
AIEEEEEEE! SHOOOOCK!!
THAT VOICE.
ASAKO?
LIEUTEN-
ANT
ASAKO?!
TROMP TROMP TROMP
STAND BACK, SIR!
FWOOOM

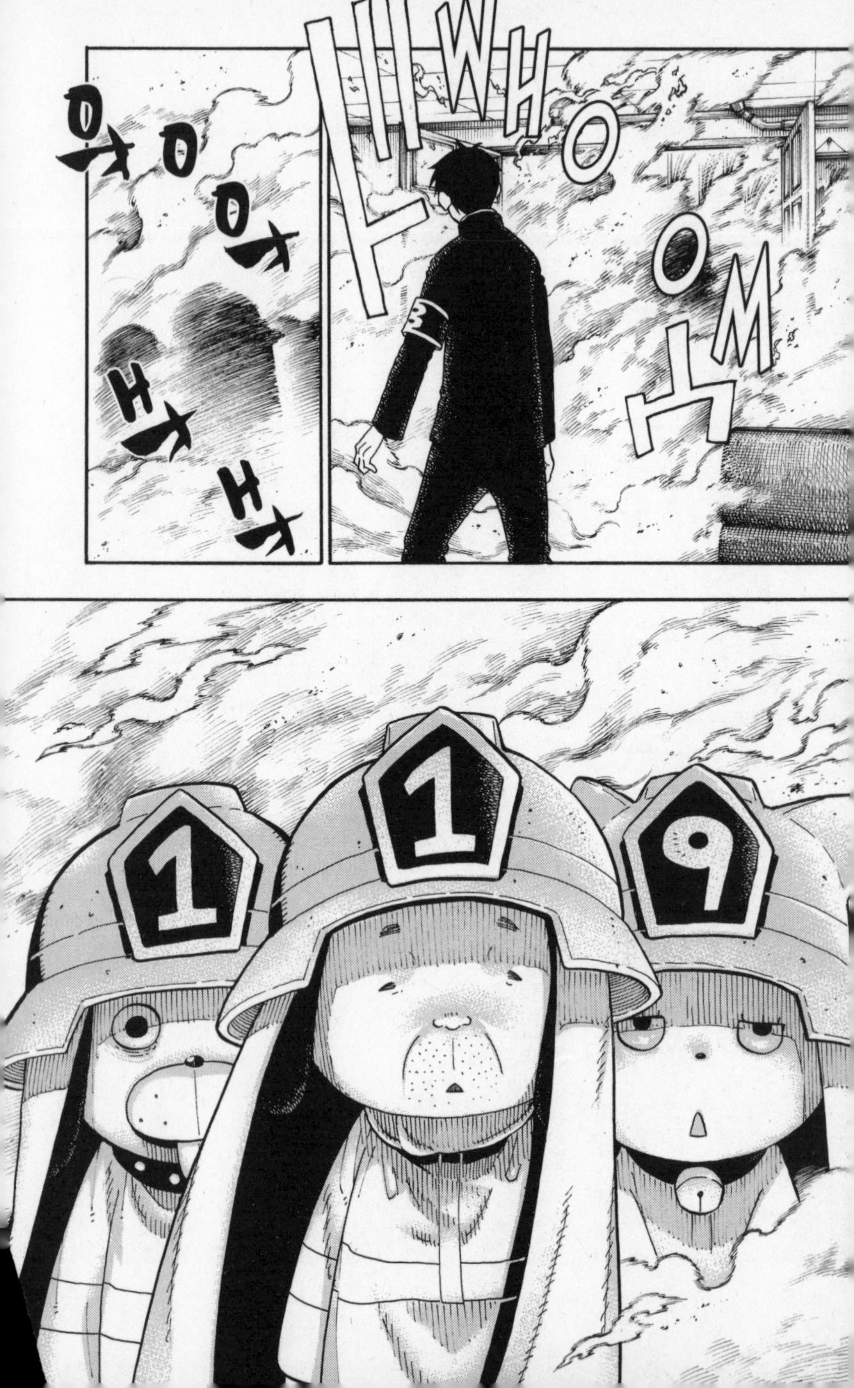
WHOOOM
OOOHH

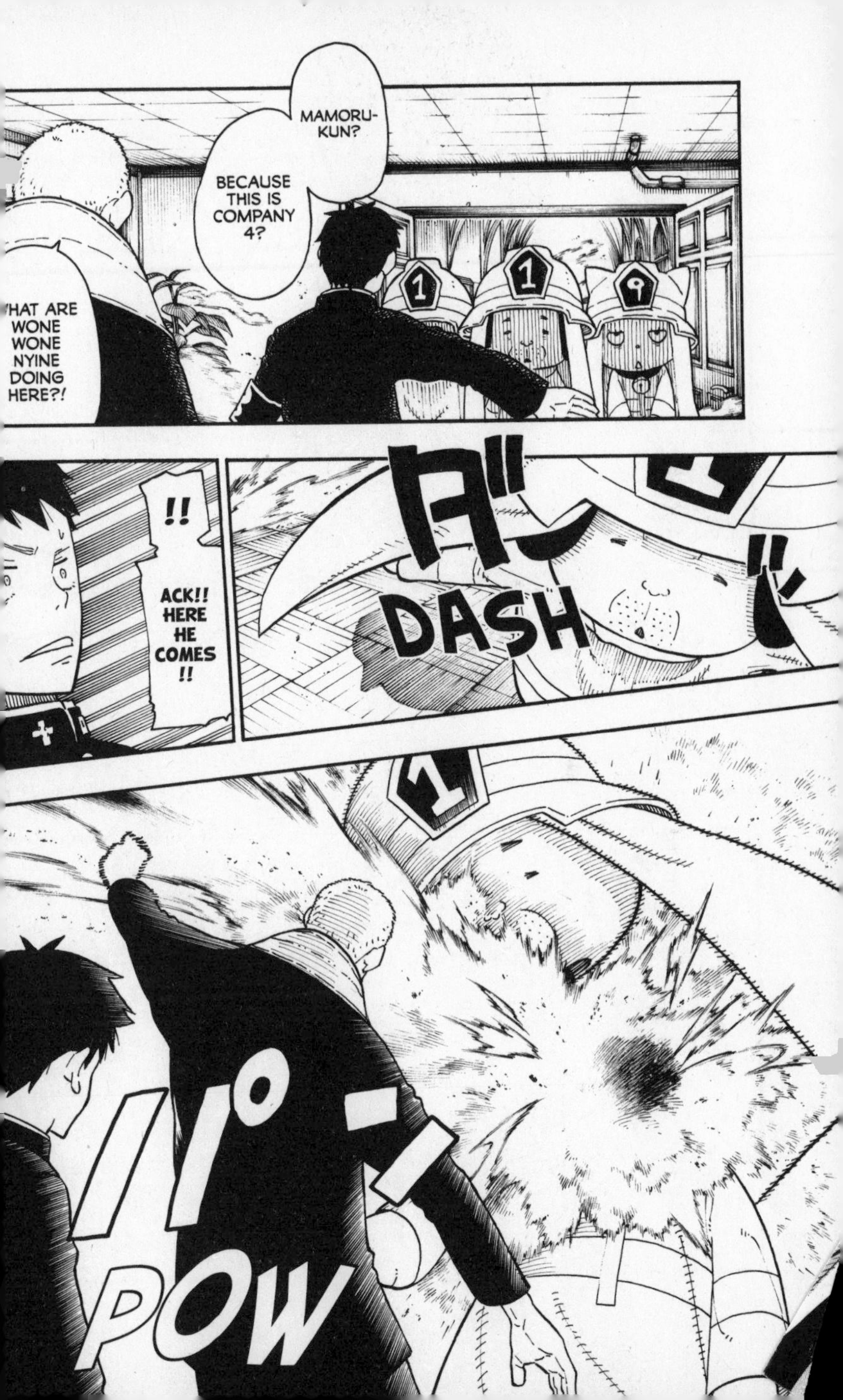
MAMORU-KUN?
BECAUSE THIS IS COMPANY 4?
WHAT ARE WONE WONE NYINE DOING HERE?!
DASH
!!
ACK!! HERE HE COMES !!
POW

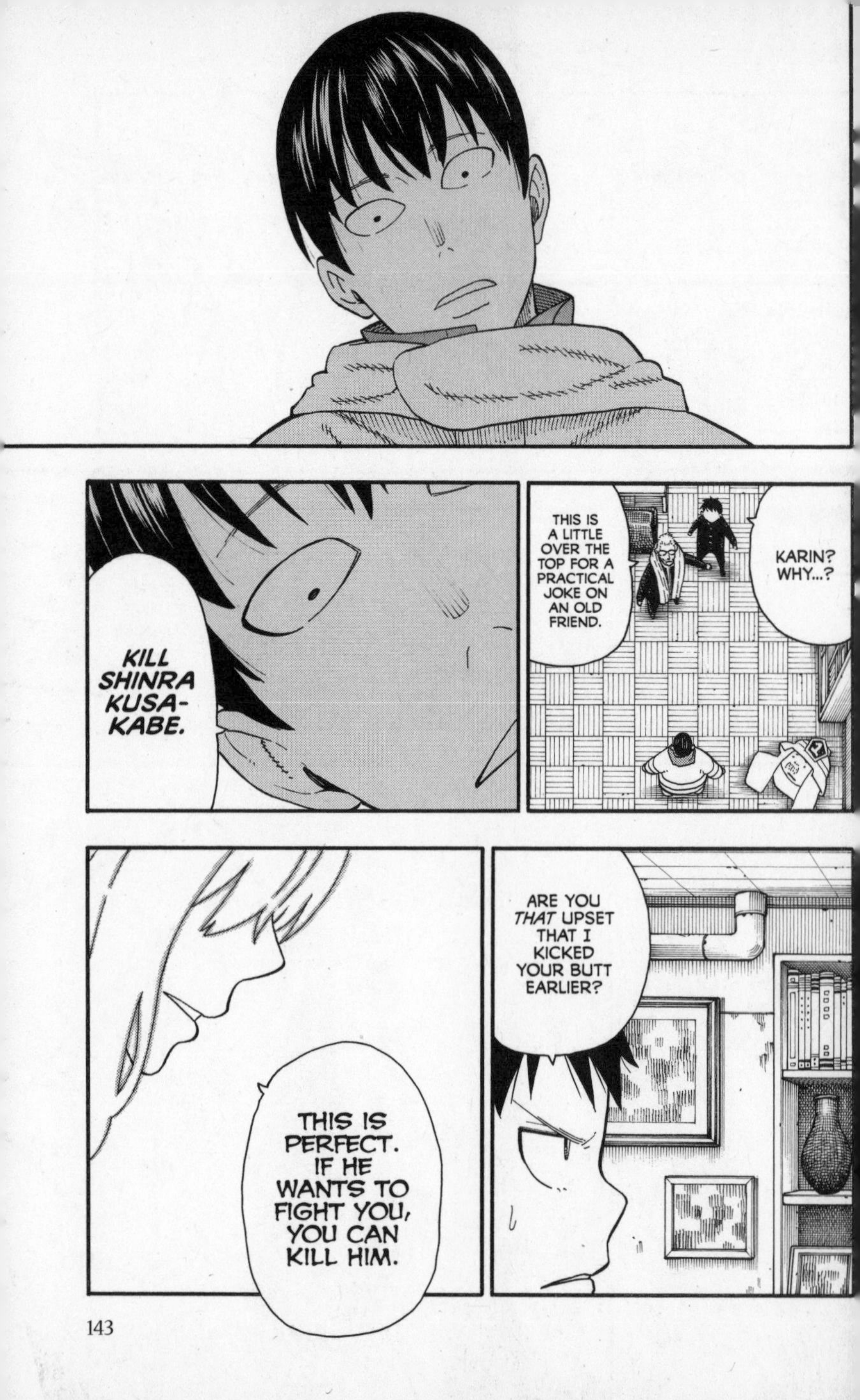
KARIN? WHY...?
THIS IS A LITTLE OVER THE TOP FOR A PRACTICAL JOKE ON AN OLD FRIEND.
KILL SHINRA KUSA-KABE.
ARE YOU *THAT* UPSET THAT I KICKED YOUR BUTT EARLIER?
THIS IS PERFECT. IF HE WANTS TO FIGHT YOU, YOU CAN KILL HIM.

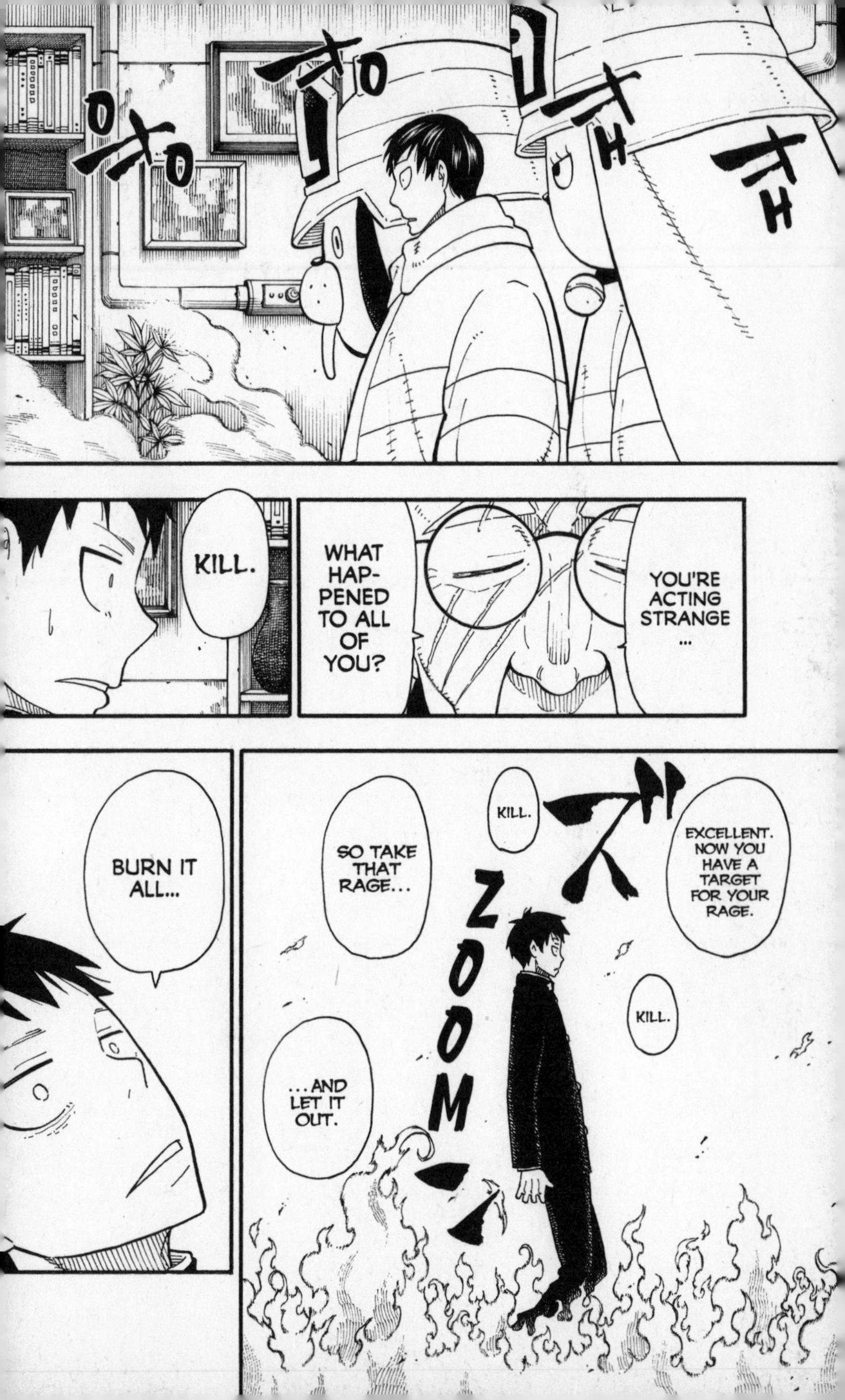
YOU'RE ACTING STRANGE ...
WHAT HAPPENED TO ALL OF YOU?
KILL.
EXCELLENT. NOW YOU HAVE A TARGET FOR YOUR RAGE.
KILL.
SO TAKE THAT RAGE...
ZOOM
KILL.
...AND LET IT OUT.
BURN IT ALL...

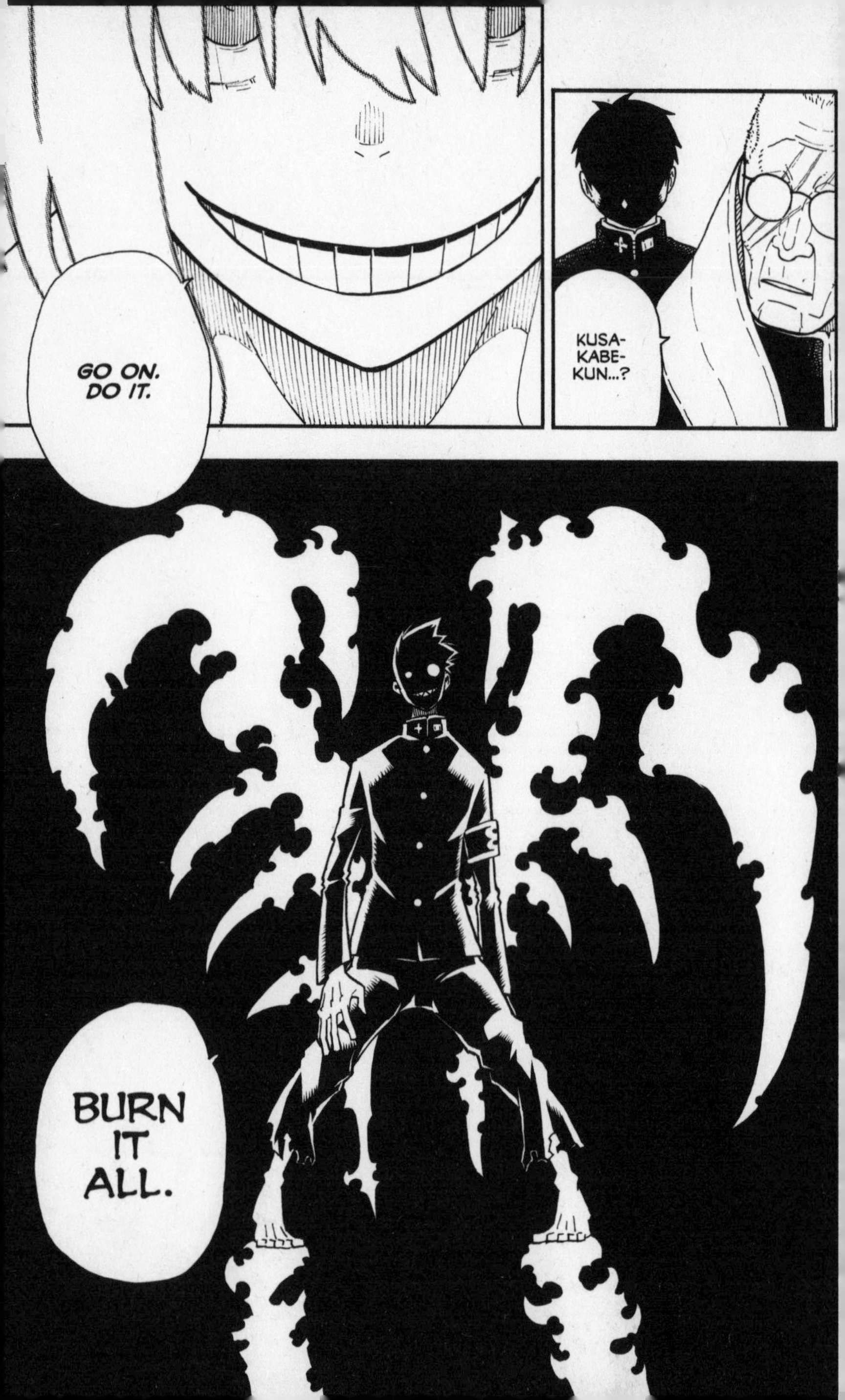
KUSA-KABE-KUN...?
GO ON. DO IT.
BURN IT ALL.

FIRE FORCE

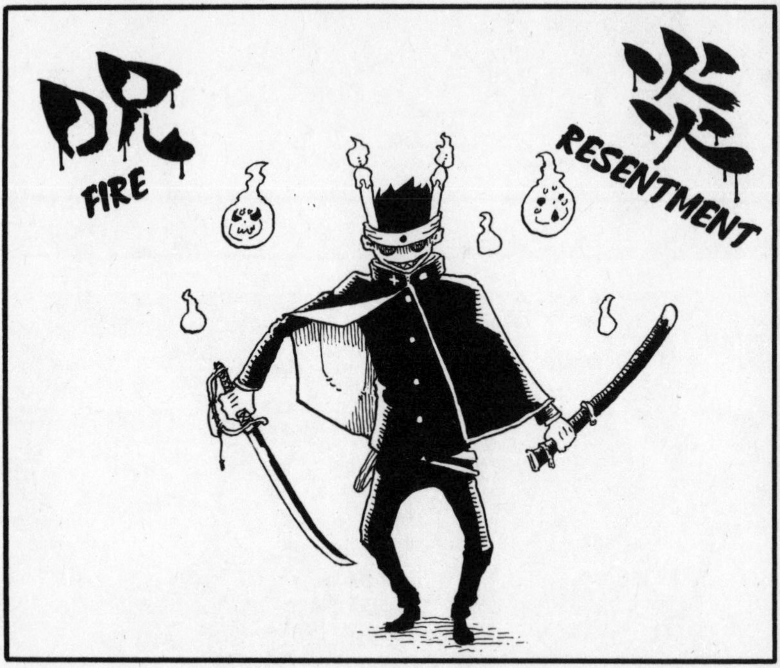
呪
FIRE
炎
RESENTMENT

CHAPTER XCV: FLAMES OF MADNESS

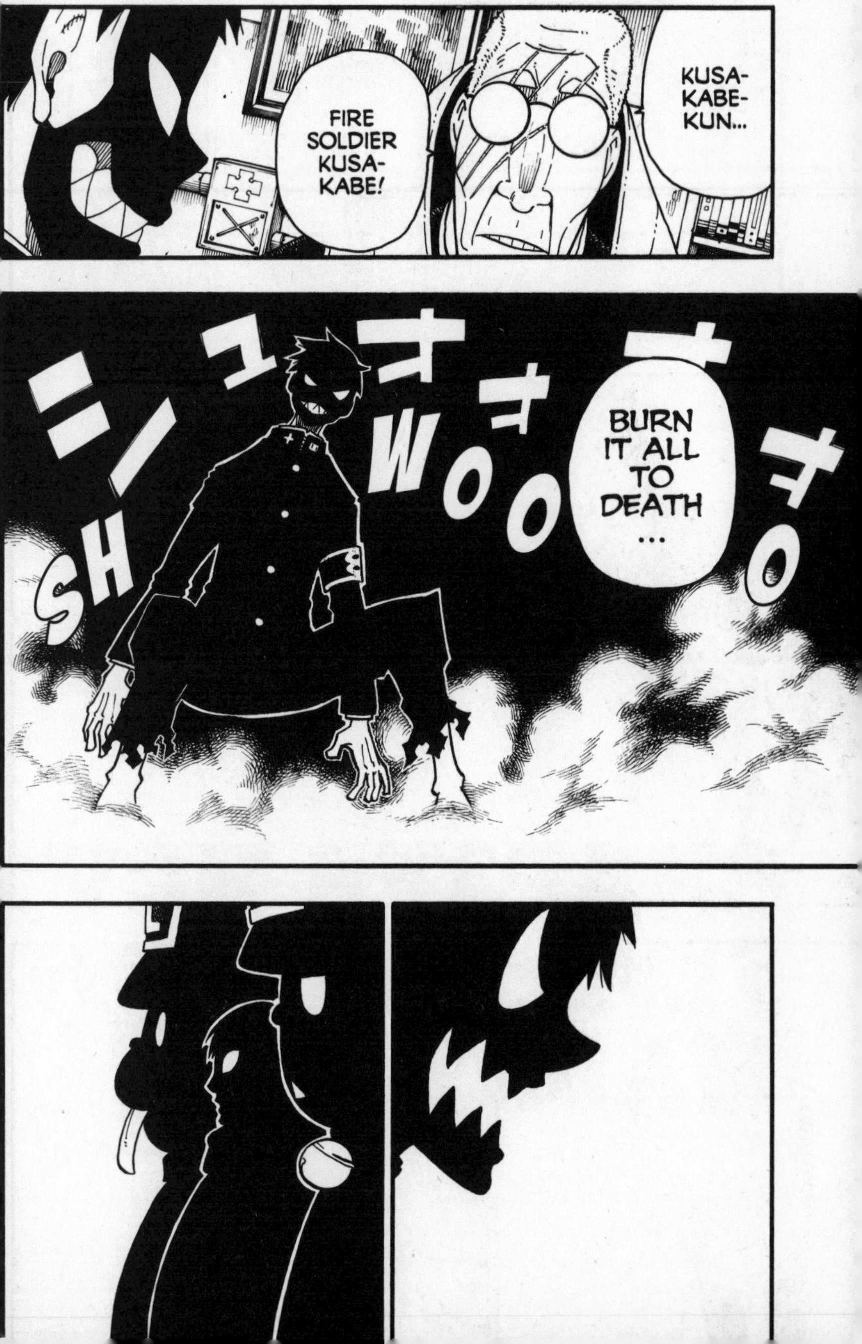
KUSA-KABE-KUN...
FIRE SOLDIER KUSA-KABE!
BURN IT ALL TO DEATH ...
SHWOOO

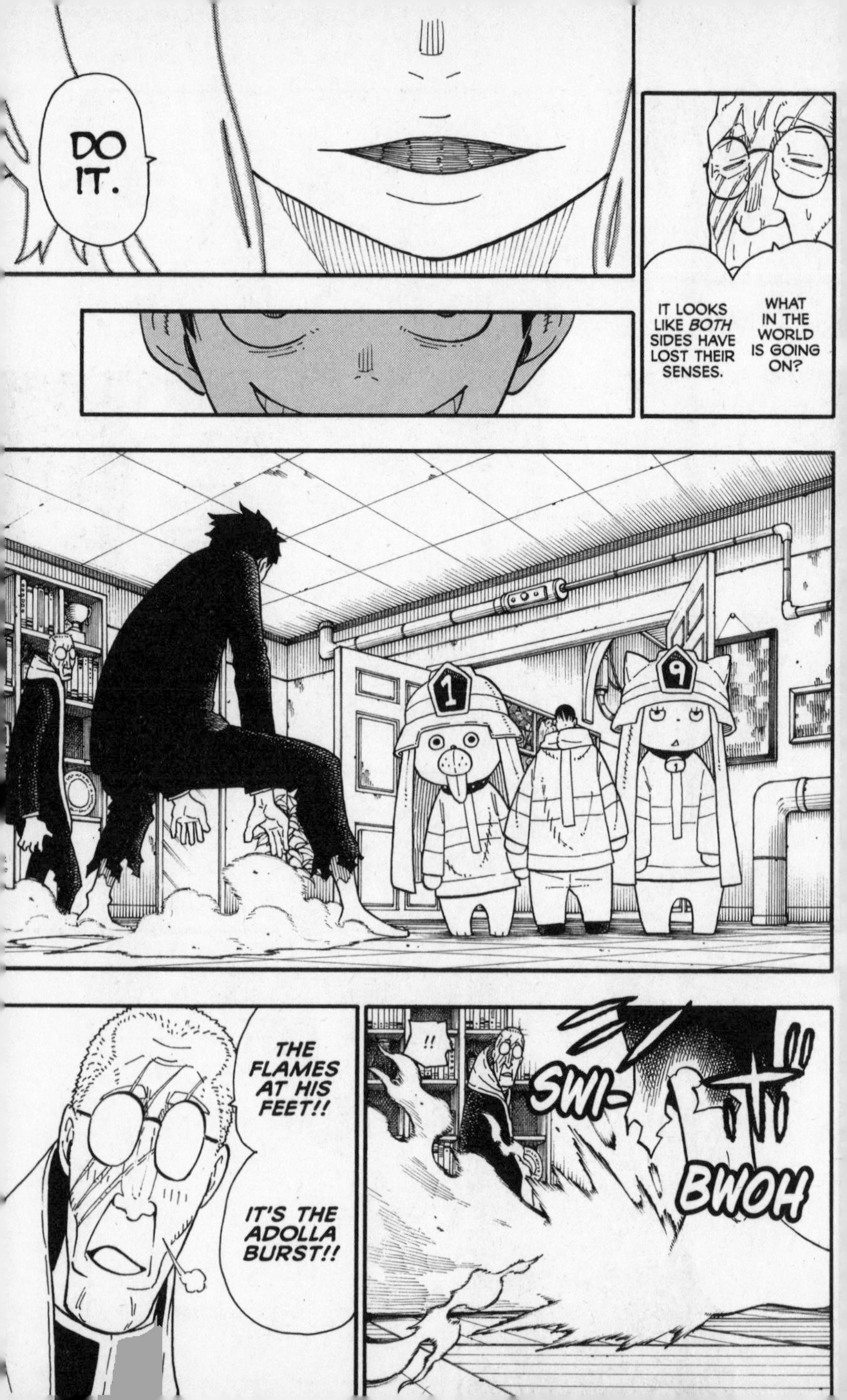
WHAT IN THE WORLD IS GOING ON?
IT LOOKS LIKE *BOTH* SIDES HAVE LOST THEIR SENSES.
DO IT.
THE FLAMES AT HIS FEET!!
IT'S THE ADOLLA BURST!!
!!
SWI-
BWOH

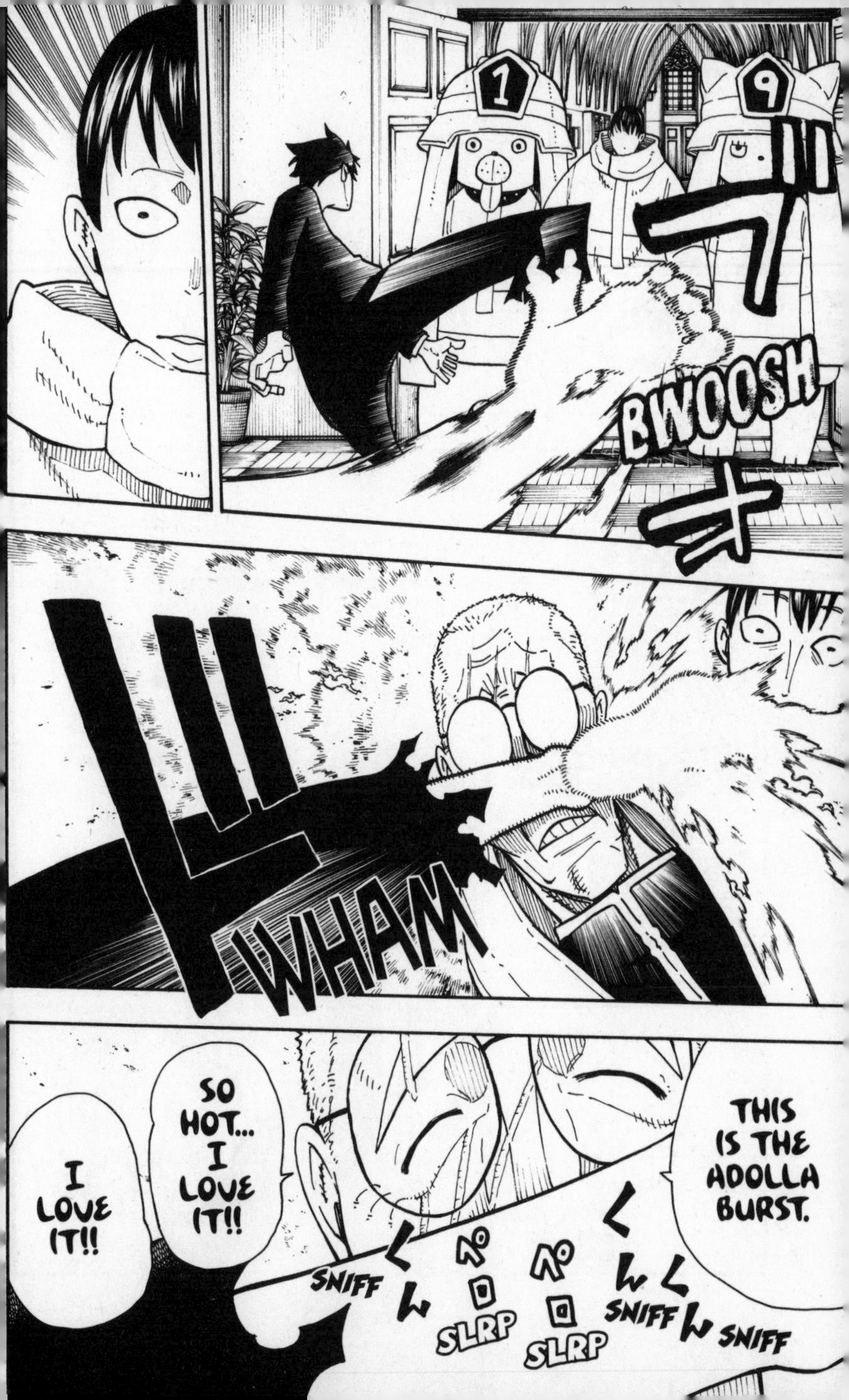
BWOOSH
WHAM
THIS IS THE ADOLLA BURST.
SNIFF
SNIFF
SLRP
SLRP
SNIFF
SO HOT... I LOVE IT!!
I LOVE IT!!

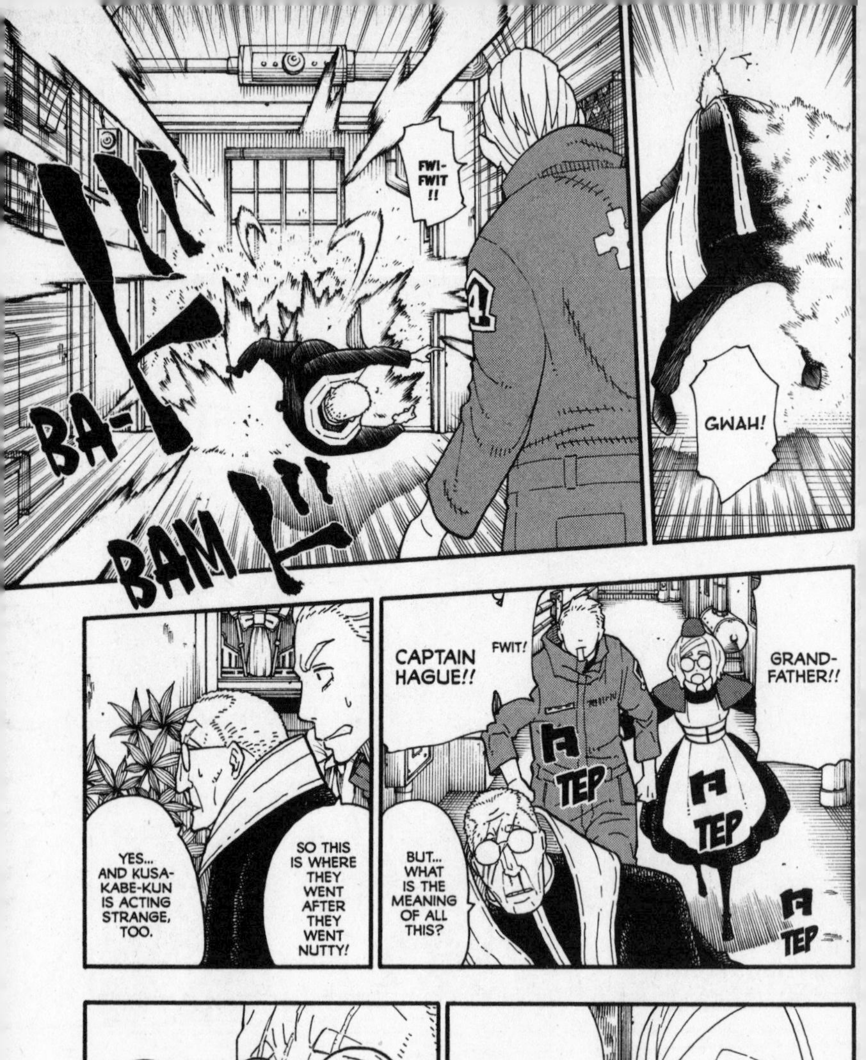
GWAH!
FWI-FWIT!!
BA-
BAM!!
GRAND-FATHER!!
FWIT!
CAPTAIN HAGUE!!
TEP
TEP
TEP
BUT... WHAT IS THE MEANING OF ALL THIS?
SO THIS IS WHERE THEY WENT AFTER THEY WENT NUTTY!
YES... AND KUSA-KABE-KUN IS ACTING STRANGE, TOO.
SHINRA-SAN, TOO? WHAT'S GOTTEN INTO ALL OF THEM?
IT'S LIKE THEY'VE BEEN POSSESSED...

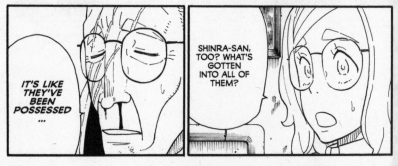

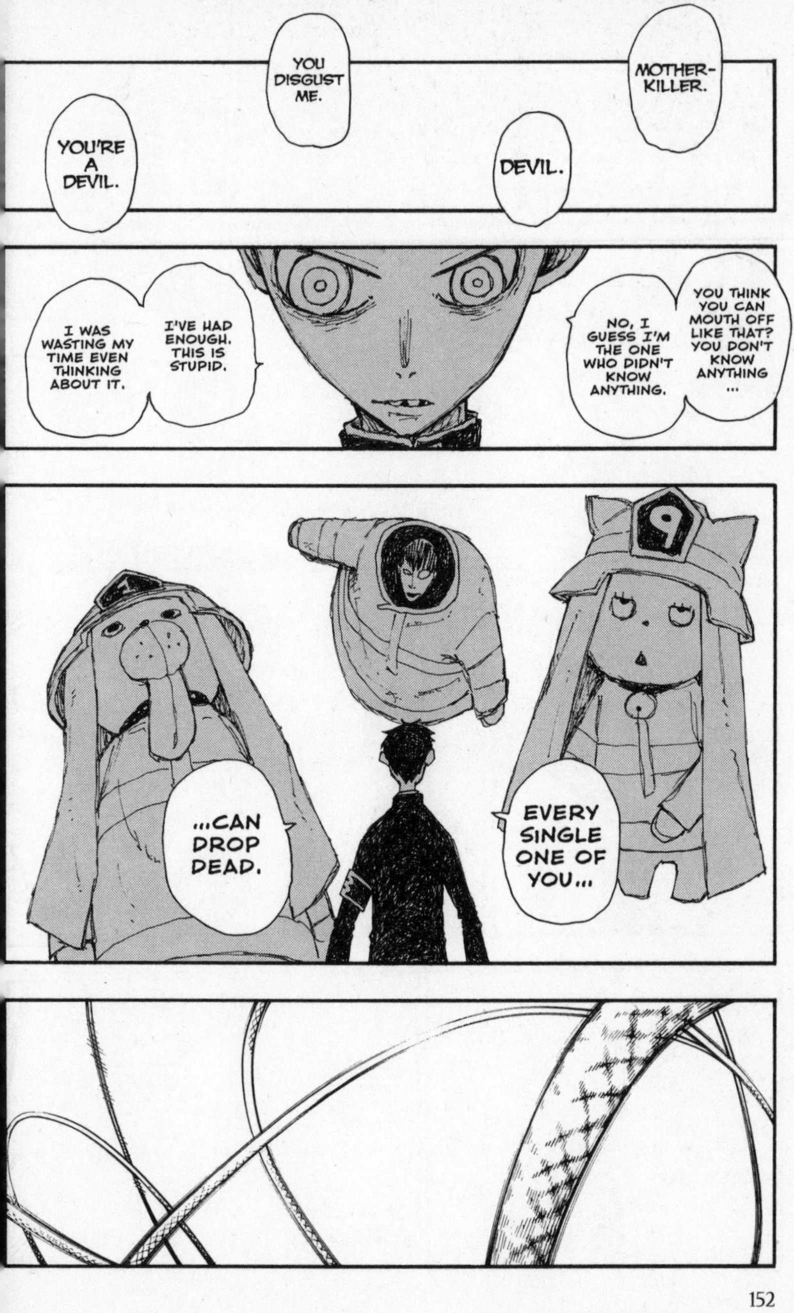
MOTHER-KILLER.
DEVIL.
YOU DISGUST ME.
YOU'RE A DEVIL.
YOU THINK YOU CAN MOUTH OFF LIKE THAT? YOU DON'T KNOW ANYTHING ...
NO, I GUESS I'M THE ONE WHO DIDN'T KNOW ANYTHING.
I'VE HAD ENOUGH. THIS IS STUPID.
I WAS WASTING MY TIME EVEN THINKING ABOUT IT.
EVERY SINGLE ONE OF YOU...
...CAN DROP DEAD.

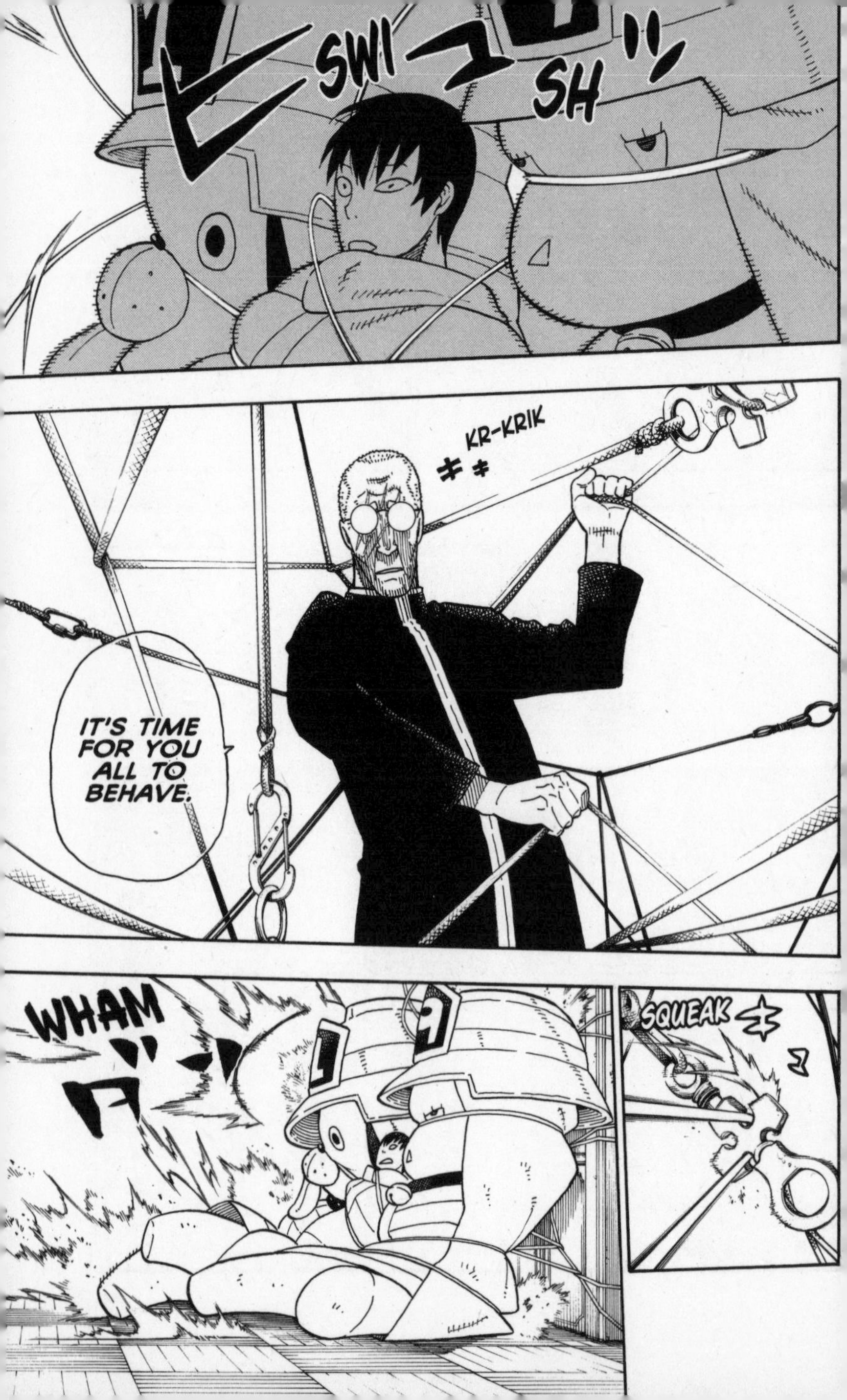

SWI
SH
KR-KRIK
IT'S TIME FOR YOU ALL TO BEHAVE.
WHAM
SQUEAK

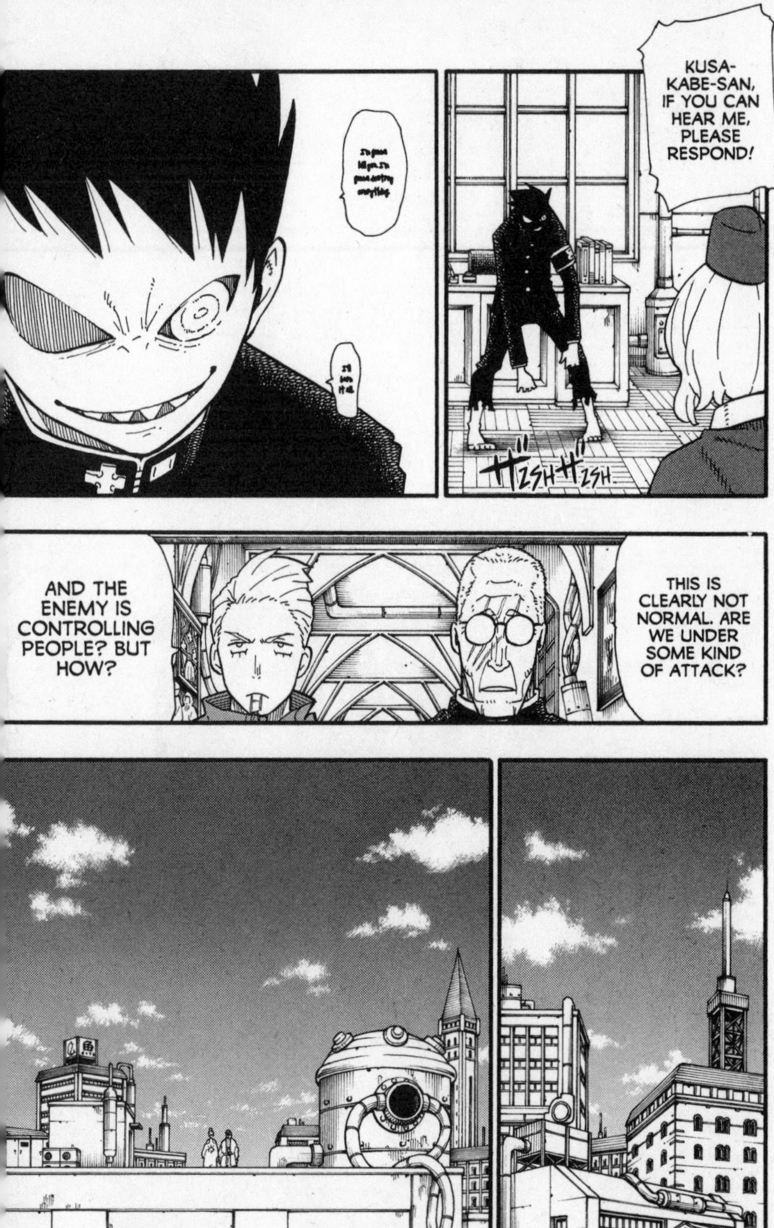
KUSA-KABE-SAN, IF YOU CAN HEAR ME, PLEASE RESPOND!
ZSH ZSH
THIS IS CLEARLY NOT NORMAL. ARE WE UNDER SOME KIND OF ATTACK?
AND THE ENEMY IS CONTROLLING PEOPLE? BUT HOW?

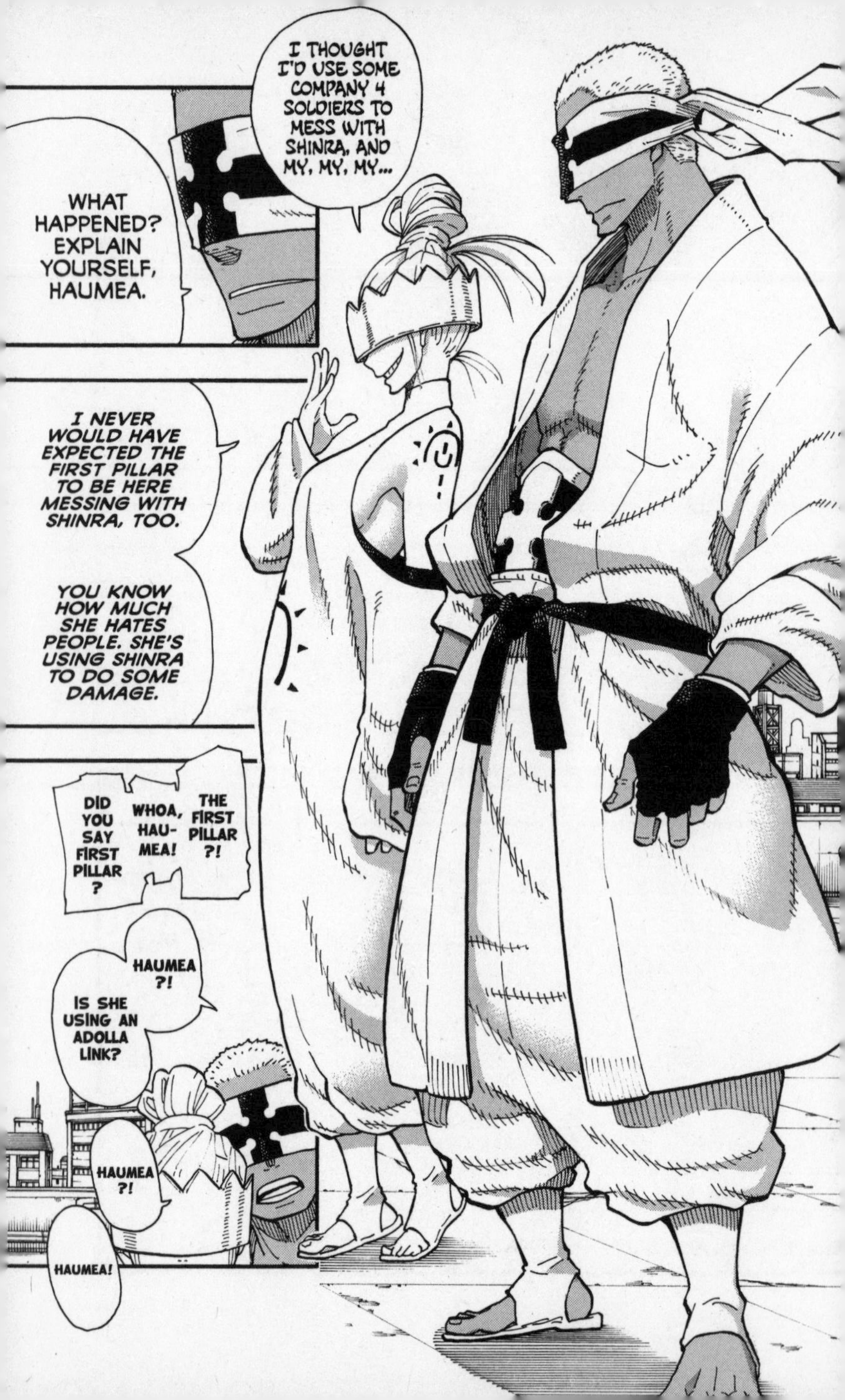
I THOUGHT I'D USE SOME COMPANY 4 SOLDIERS TO MESS WITH SHINRA, AND MY, MY, MY...
WHAT HAPPENED? EXPLAIN YOURSELF, HAUMEA.
I NEVER WOULD HAVE EXPECTED THE FIRST PILLAR TO BE HERE MESSING WITH SHINRA, TOO.
YOU KNOW HOW MUCH SHE HATES PEOPLE. SHE'S USING SHINRA TO DO SOME DAMAGE.
THE FIRST PILLAR ?!
WHOA, HAU-MEA!
DID YOU SAY FIRST PILLAR ?
HAUMEA ?!
IS SHE USING AN ADOLLA LINK?
HAUMEA ?!
HAUMEA!

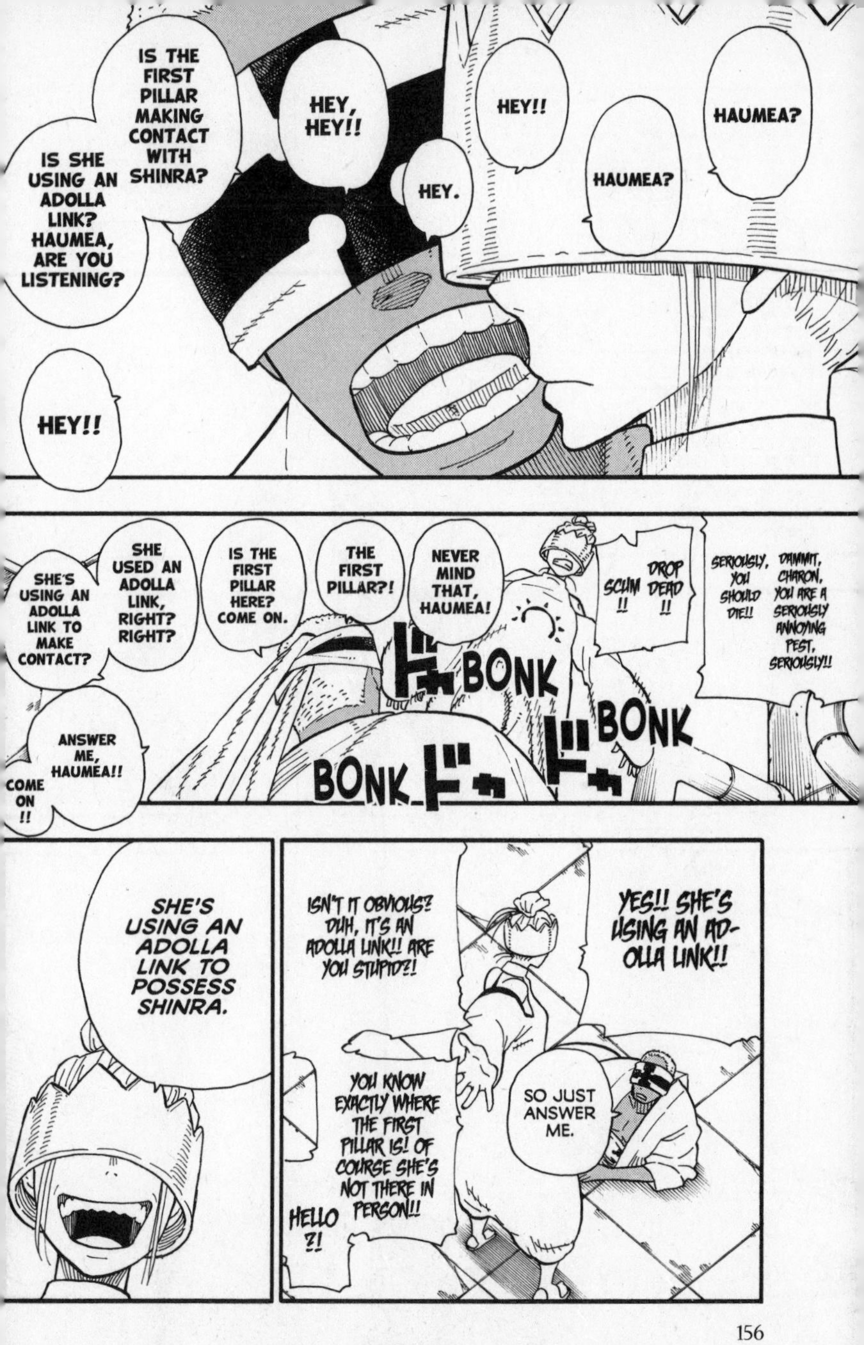
HAUMEA?
HAUMEA?
HEY!!
HEY.
HEY, HEY!!
IS THE FIRST PILLAR MAKING CONTACT WITH SHINRA?
IS SHE USING AN ADOLLA LINK? HAUMEA, ARE YOU LISTENING?
HEY!!
DAMMIT, CHARON, YOU ARE A SERIOUSLY ANNOYING PEST, SERIOUSLY!!
SERIOUSLY, YOU SHOULD DIE!!
DROP DEAD !!
SCUM !!
NEVER MIND THAT, HAUMEA!
THE FIRST PILLAR?!
IS THE FIRST PILLAR HERE? COME ON.
SHE USED AN ADOLLA LINK, RIGHT? RIGHT?
SHE'S USING AN ADOLLA LINK TO MAKE CONTACT?
ドッ BONK
ドッ BONK
BONK ドッ
ANSWER ME, HAUMEA!!
COME ON !!
YES!! SHE'S USING AN AD-OLLA LINK!!
ISN'T IT OBVIOUS? DUH, IT'S AN ADOLLA LINK!! ARE YOU STUPID?!
SO JUST ANSWER ME.
YOU KNOW EXACTLY WHERE THE FIRST PILLAR IS! OF COURSE SHE'S NOT THERE IN PERSON!!
HELLO ?!
SHE'S USING AN ADOLLA LINK TO POSSESS SHINRA.

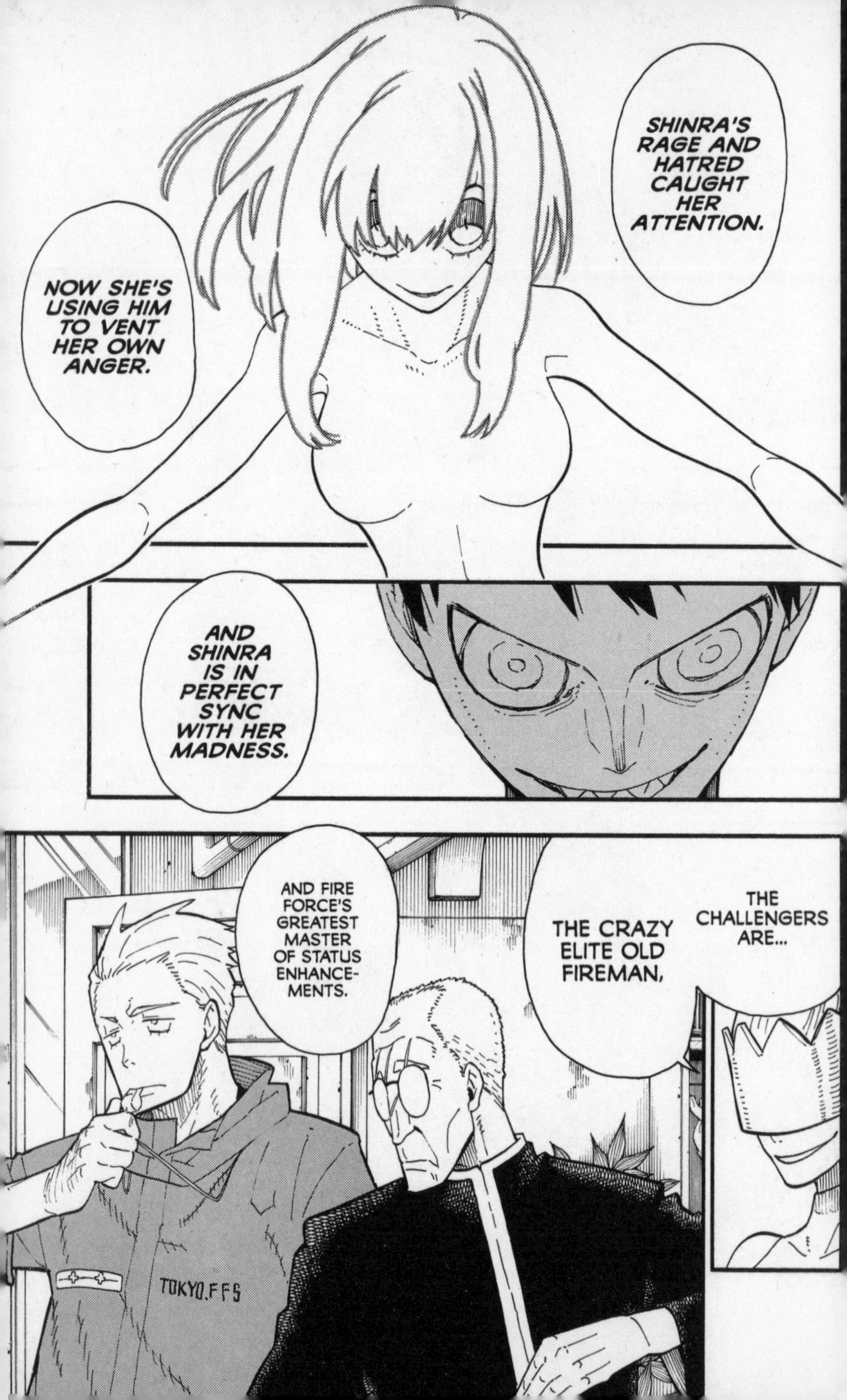
SHINRA'S RAGE AND HATRED CAUGHT HER ATTENTION.
NOW SHE'S USING HIM TO VENT HER OWN ANGER.
AND SHINRA IS IN PERFECT SYNC WITH HER MADNESS.
THE CHALLENGERS ARE...
THE CRAZY ELITE OLD FIREMAN,
AND FIRE FORCE'S GREATEST MASTER OF STATUS ENHANCE-MENTS.
TOKYO.FFS

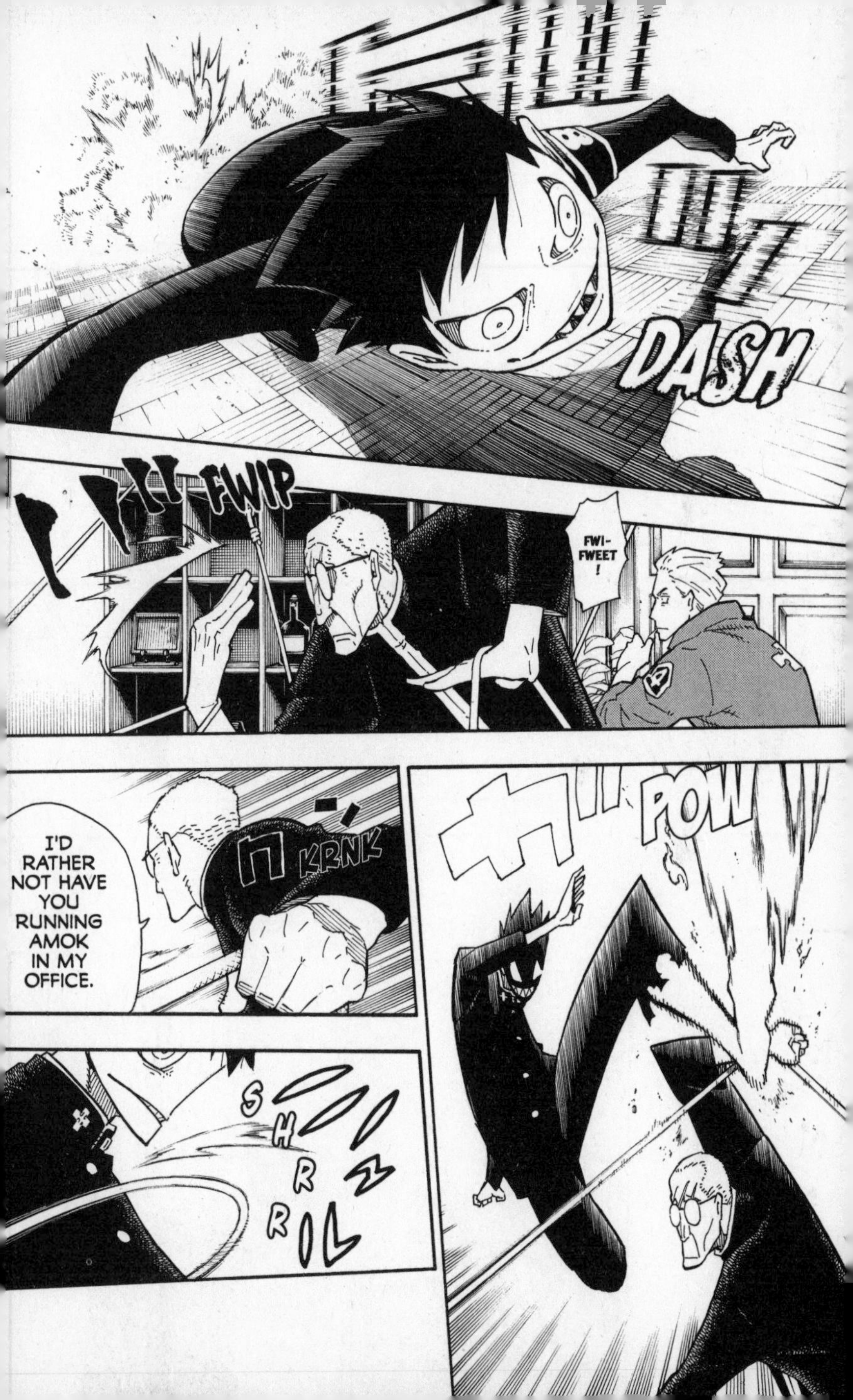
DASH
FWI-FWEET!
FWIP
POW
I'D RATHER NOT HAVE YOU RUNNING AMOK IN MY OFFICE.
KRNK
SHRRIL

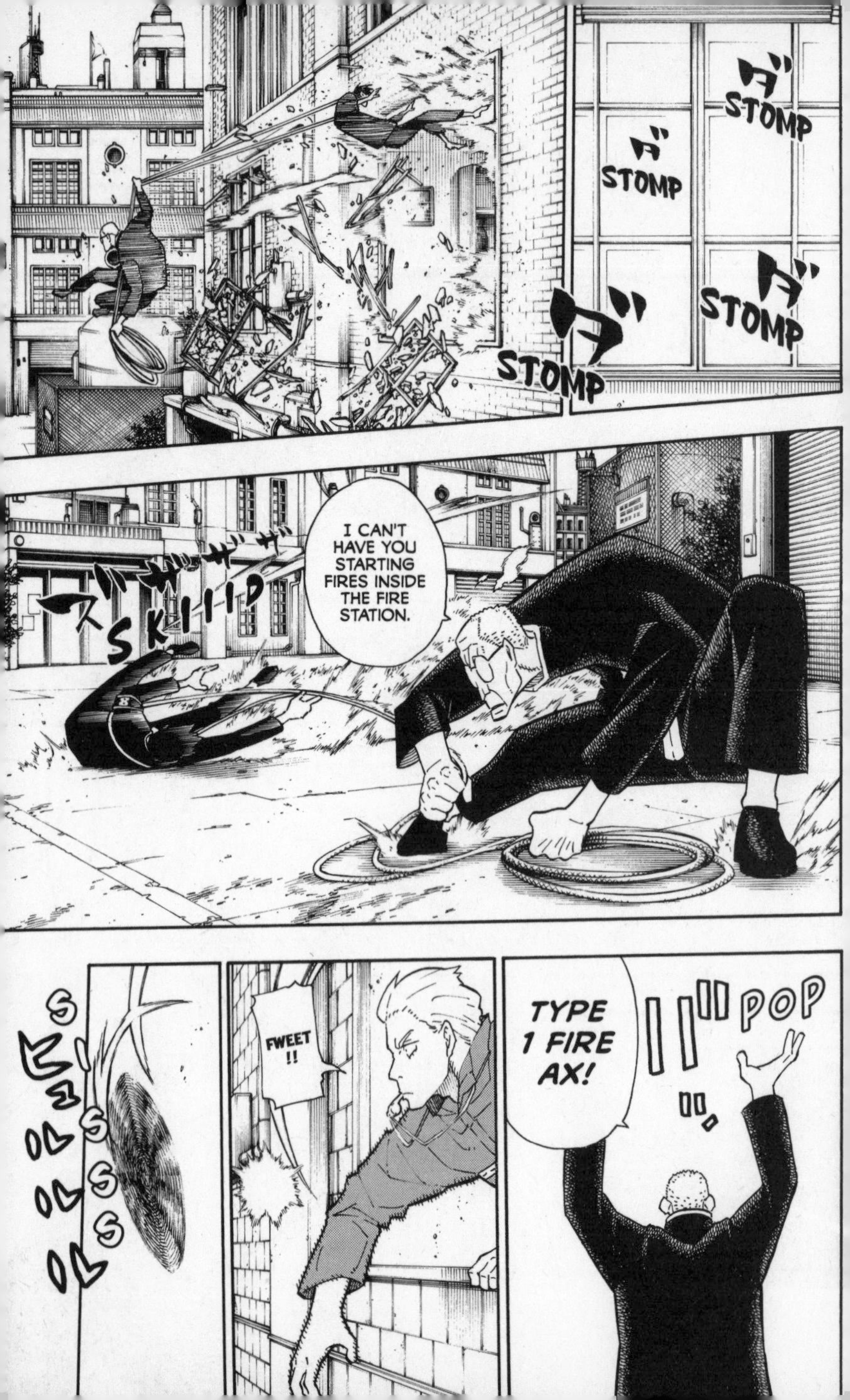
STOMP
STOMP
STOMP
STOMP
I CAN'T HAVE YOU STARTING FIRES INSIDE THE FIRE STATION.
SKIIID
TYPE 1 FIRE AX!
POP
FWEET !!
SSSS

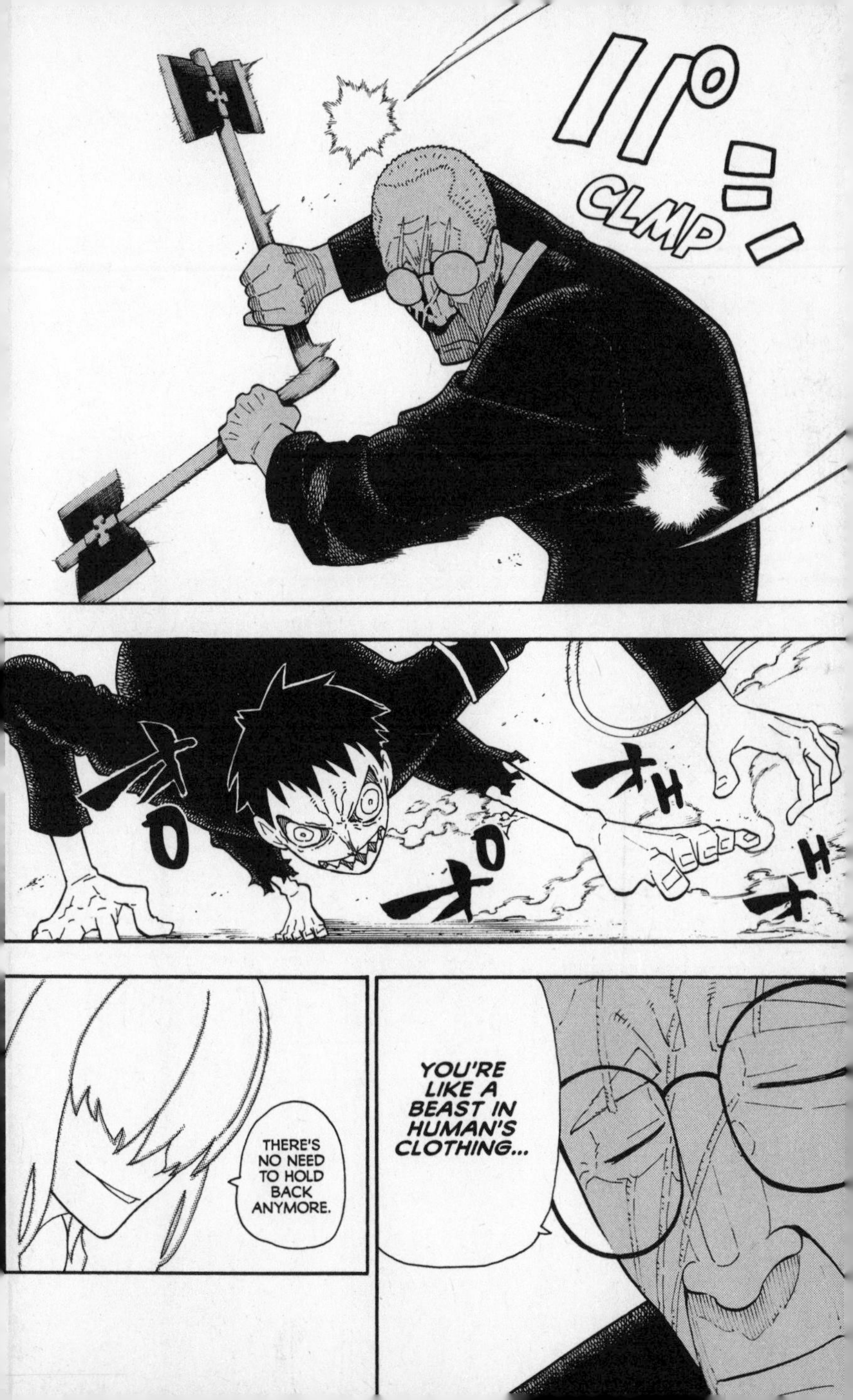
CLMP
YOU'RE LIKE A BEAST IN HUMAN'S CLOTHING...
THERE'S NO NEED TO HOLD BACK ANYMORE.

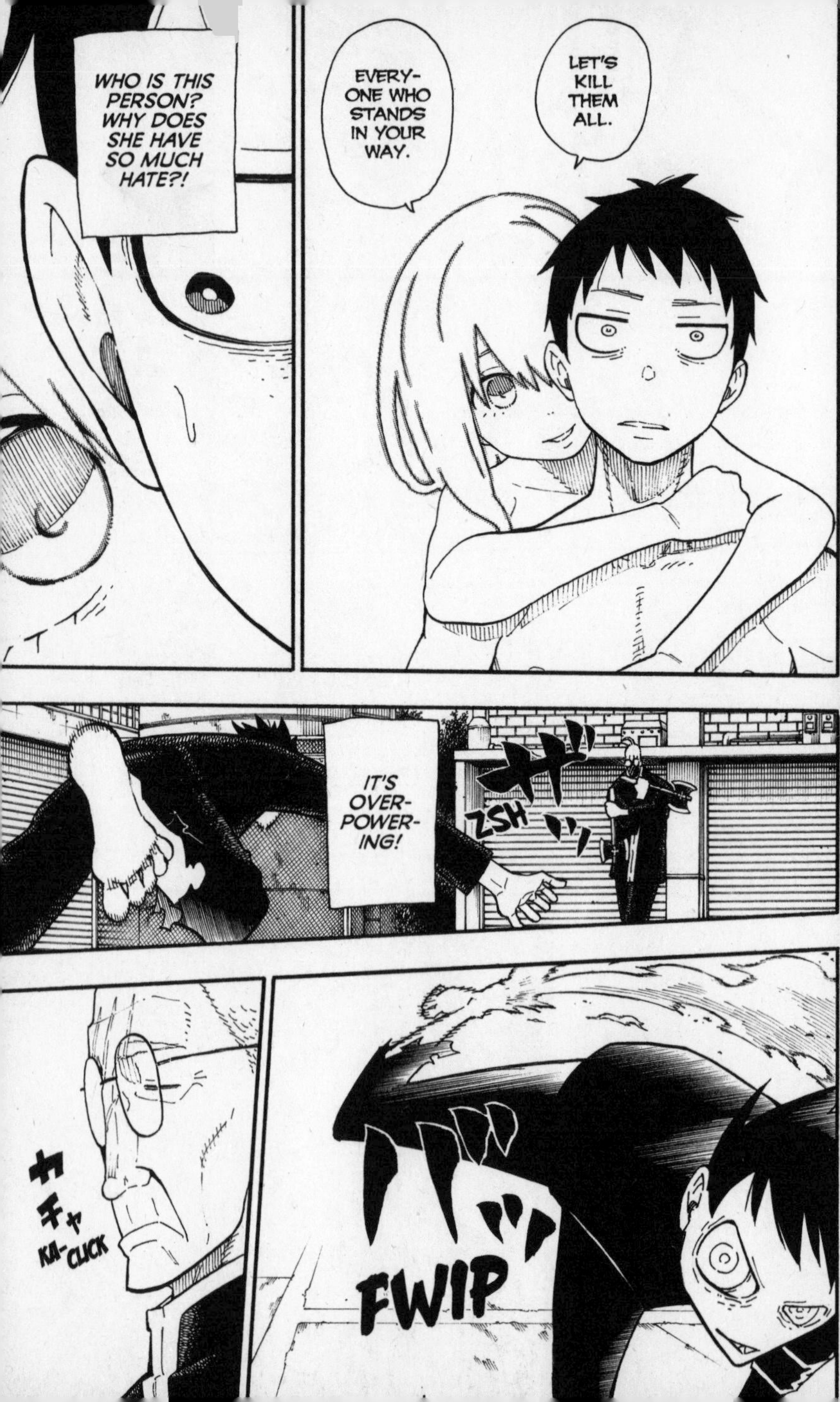
LET'S KILL THEM ALL.
EVERY-ONE WHO STANDS IN YOUR WAY.
WHO IS THIS PERSON? WHY DOES SHE HAVE SO MUCH HATE?!
ZSH
IT'S OVER-POWERING!
FWIP
カチャ
KA-CLICK

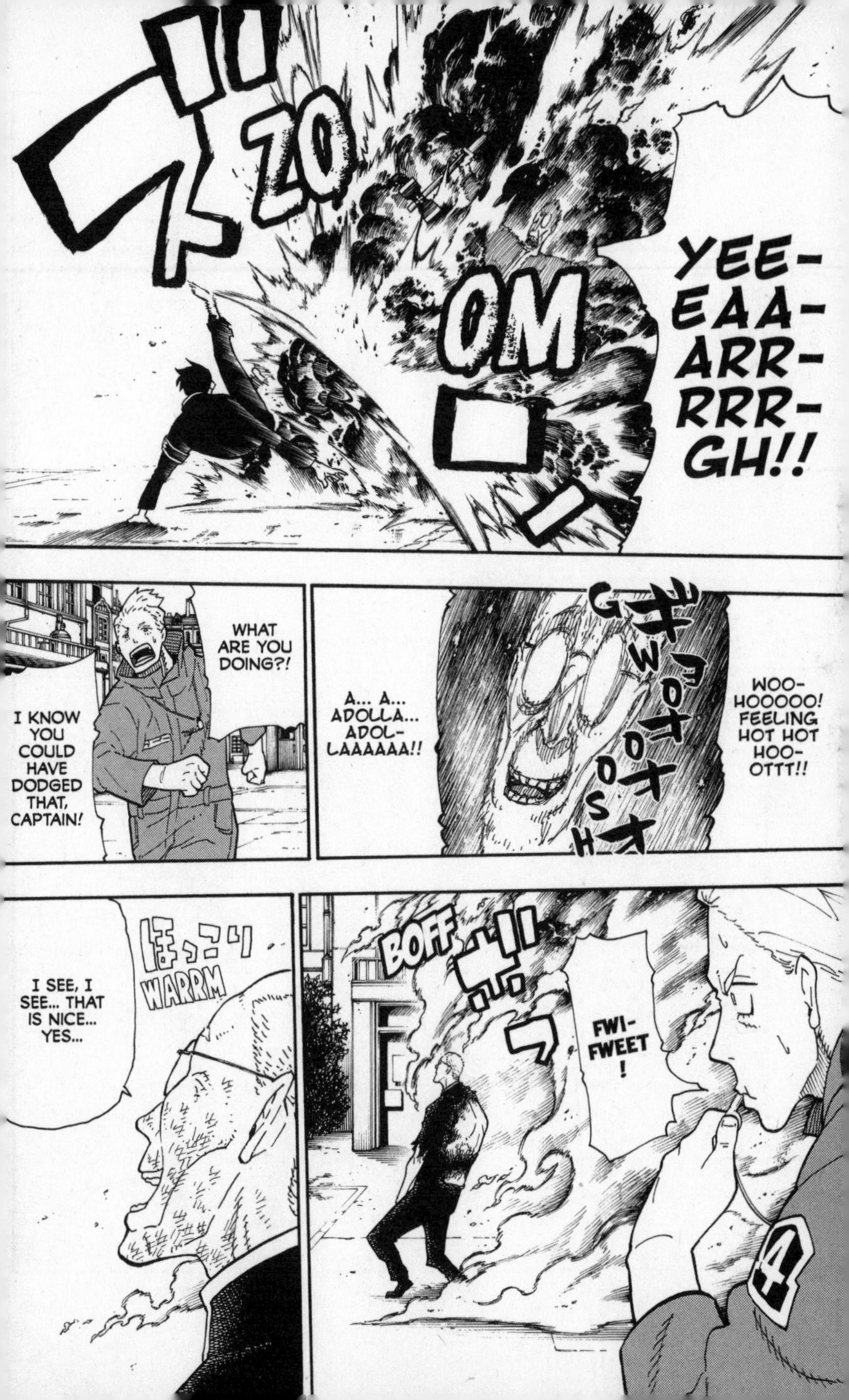
ZO
OM
YEE-EAA-ARR-RRR-GH!!
WOO-HOOOOO! FEELING HOT HOT HOO-OTTT!!
GWOOOSH
A... A... ADOLLA... ADOL-LAAAAAA!!
WHAT ARE YOU DOING?!
I KNOW YOU COULD HAVE DODGED THAT, CAPTAIN!
BOFF
FWI-FWEET!
WARRM
I SEE, I SEE... THAT IS NICE... YES...

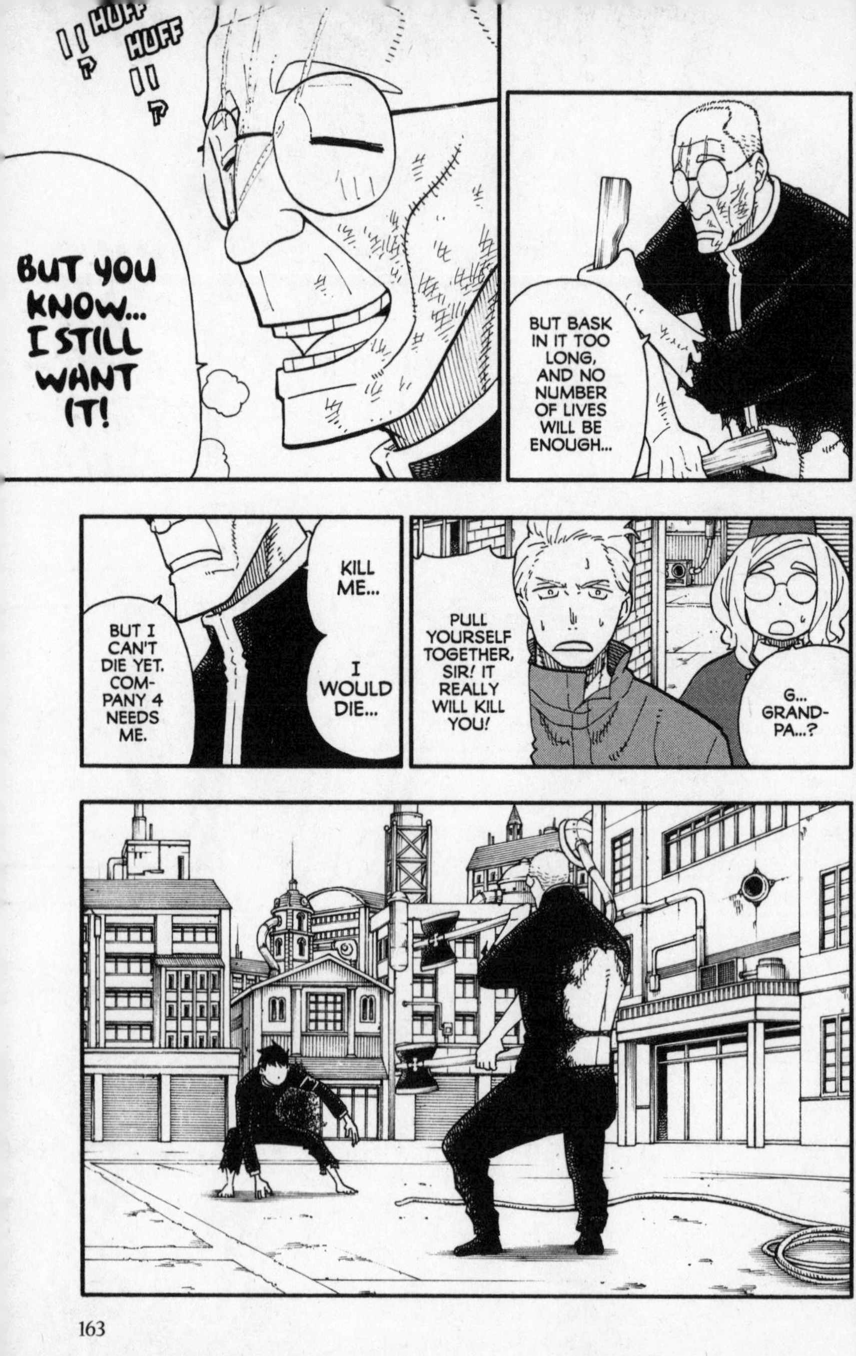

BUT BASK IN IT TOO LONG, AND NO NUMBER OF LIVES WILL BE ENOUGH...
HUFF
HUFF
BUT YOU KNOW... I STILL WANT IT!
G... GRAND-PA...?
PULL YOURSELF TOGETHER, SIR! IT REALLY WILL KILL YOU!
KILL ME... I WOULD DIE...
BUT I CAN'T DIE YET. COM-PANY 4 NEEDS ME.

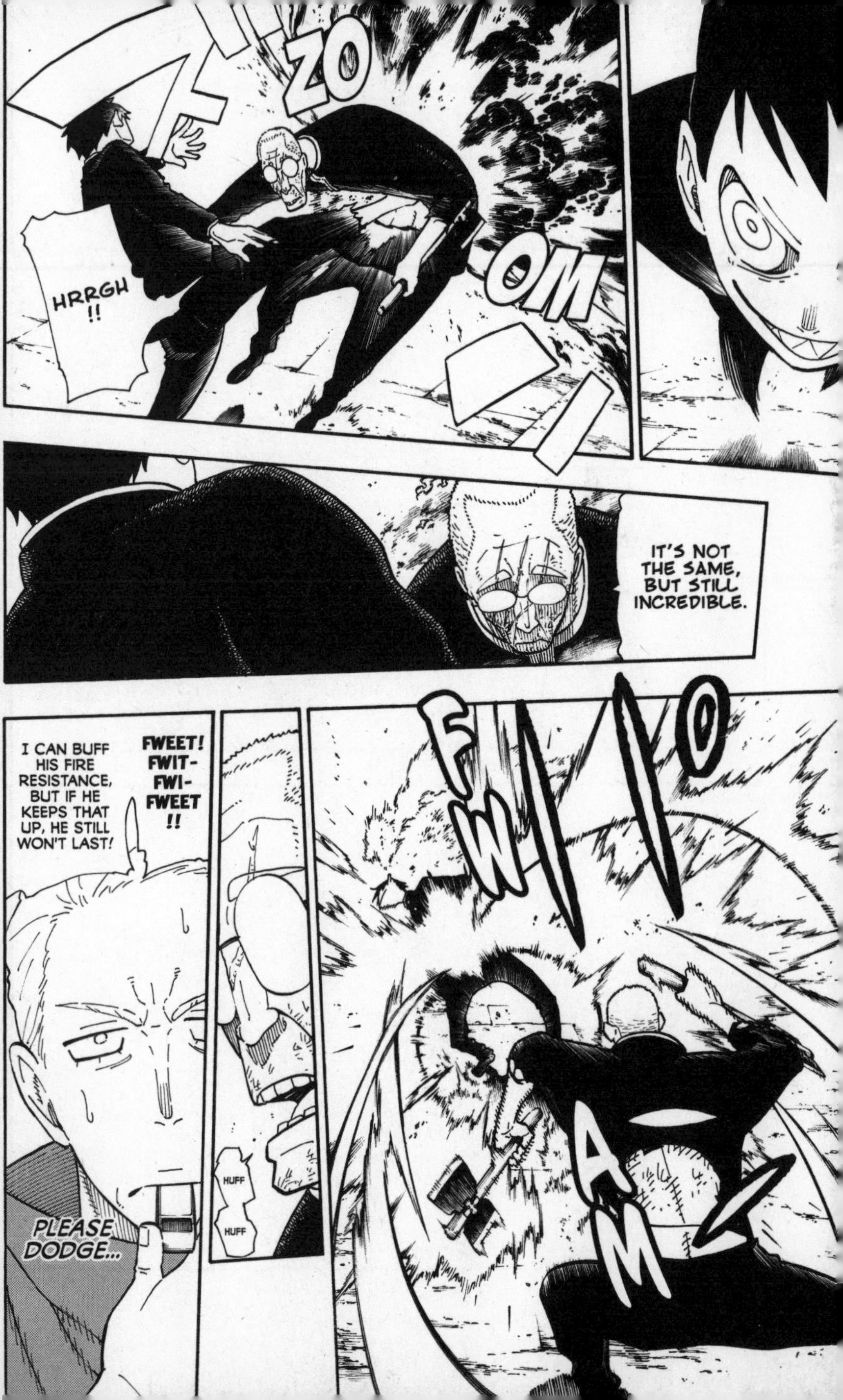
ZO
OM
HRRGH!!
IT'S NOT THE SAME, BUT STILL INCREDIBLE.
HUFF
HUFF
FWEET! FWIT-FWI-FWEET!!
I CAN BUFF HIS FIRE RESISTANCE, BUT IF HE KEEPS THAT UP, HE STILL WON'T LAST!
PLEASE DODGE...

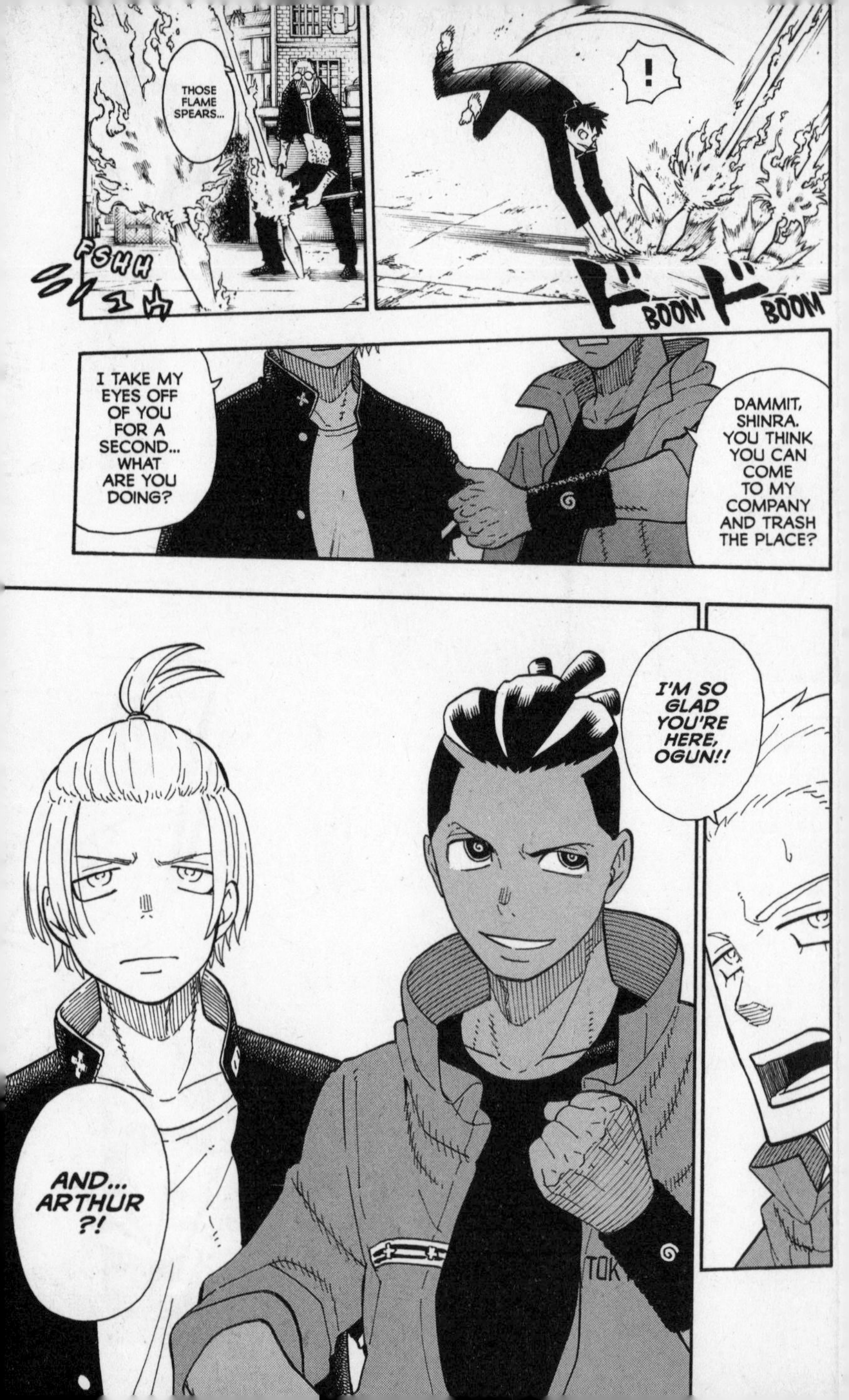
!
BOOM
BOOM
THOSE FLAME SPEARS...
FSHH
DAMMIT, SHINRA. YOU THINK YOU CAN COME TO MY COMPANY AND TRASH THE PLACE?
I TAKE MY EYES OFF OF YOU FOR A SECOND... WHAT ARE YOU DOING?
I'M SO GLAD YOU'RE HERE, OGUN!!
AND... ARTHUR?!

FIRE FORCE

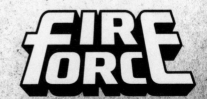

CHAPTER XCVI: OLD FRIENDS UNITED

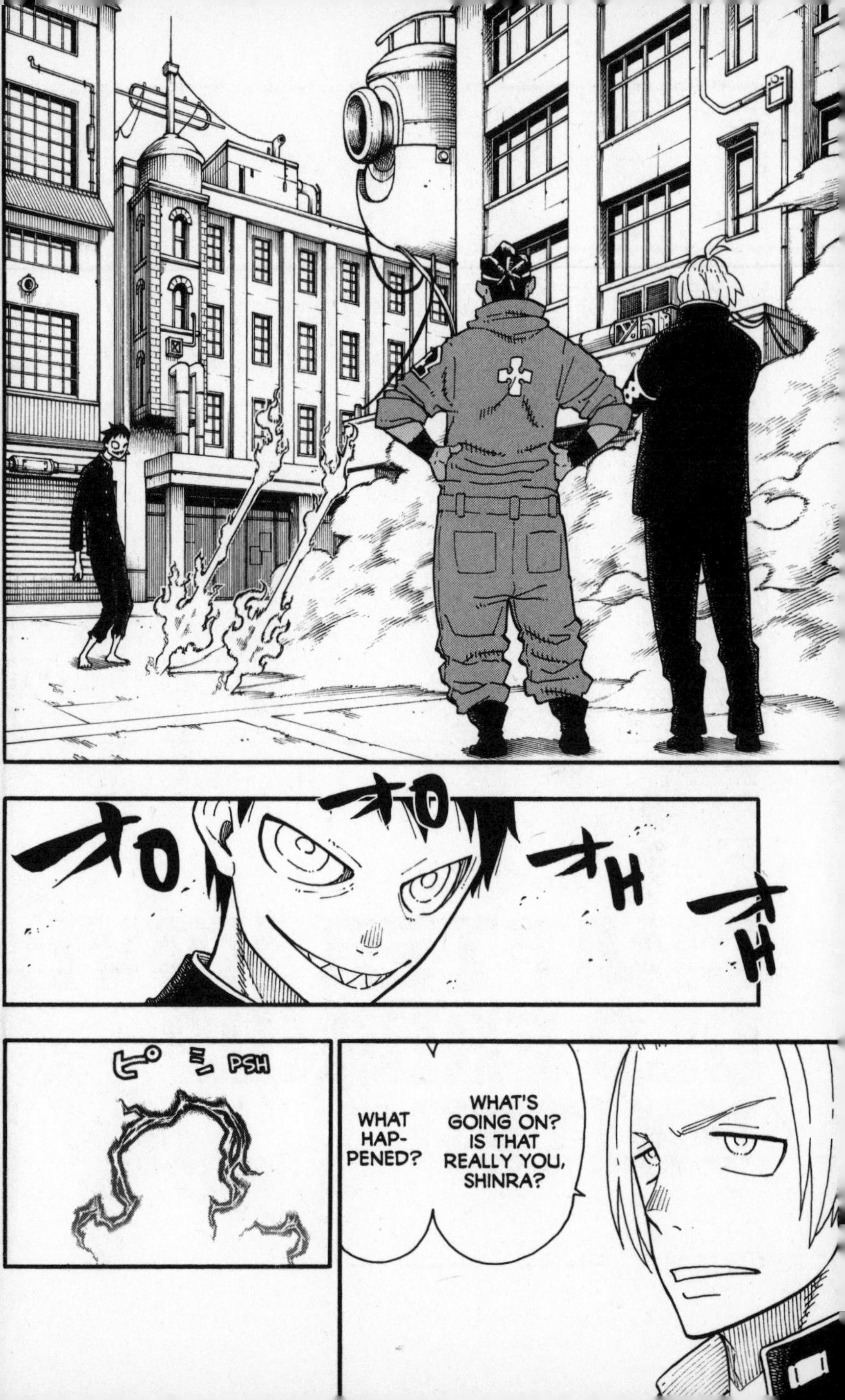
WHAT'S GOING ON? IS THAT REALLY YOU, SHINRA?
WHAT HAPPENED?
PSH

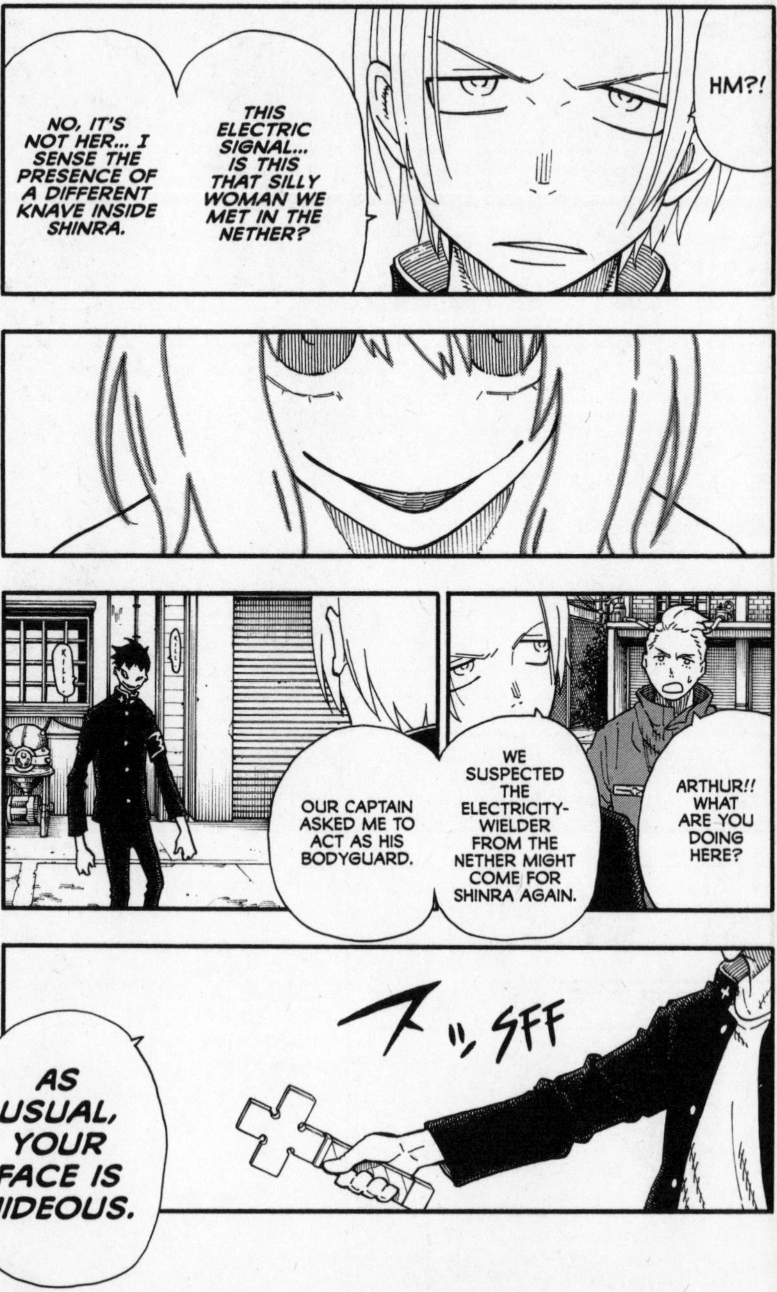
HM?!
THIS ELECTRIC SIGNAL... IS THIS THAT SILLY WOMAN WE MET IN THE NETHER?
NO, IT'S NOT HER... I SENSE THE PRESENCE OF A DIFFERENT KNAVE INSIDE SHINRA.
ARTHUR!! WHAT ARE YOU DOING HERE?
WE SUSPECTED THE ELECTRICITY-WIELDER FROM THE NETHER MIGHT COME FOR SHINRA AGAIN.
OUR CAPTAIN ASKED ME TO ACT AS HIS BODYGUARD.
KILL
KILL
SFF
AS USUAL, YOUR FACE IS HIDEOUS.

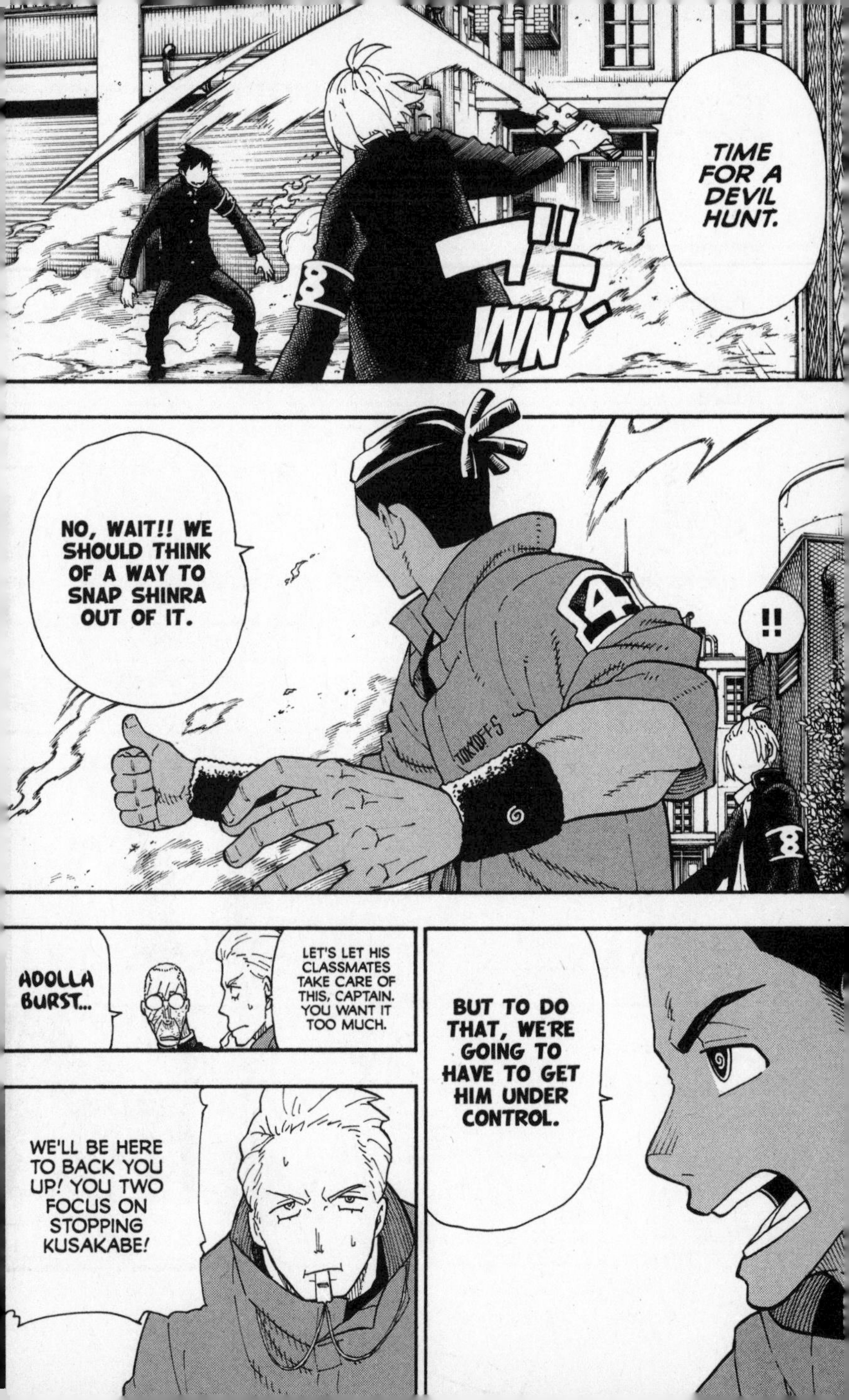
TIME FOR A DEVIL HUNT.
!!
NO, WAIT!! WE SHOULD THINK OF A WAY TO SNAP SHINRA OUT OF IT.
BUT TO DO THAT, WE'RE GOING TO HAVE TO GET HIM UNDER CONTROL.
LET'S LET HIS CLASSMATES TAKE CARE OF THIS, CAPTAIN. YOU WANT IT TOO MUCH.
ADOLLA BURST...
WE'LL BE HERE TO BACK YOU UP! YOU TWO FOCUS ON STOPPING KUSAKABE!

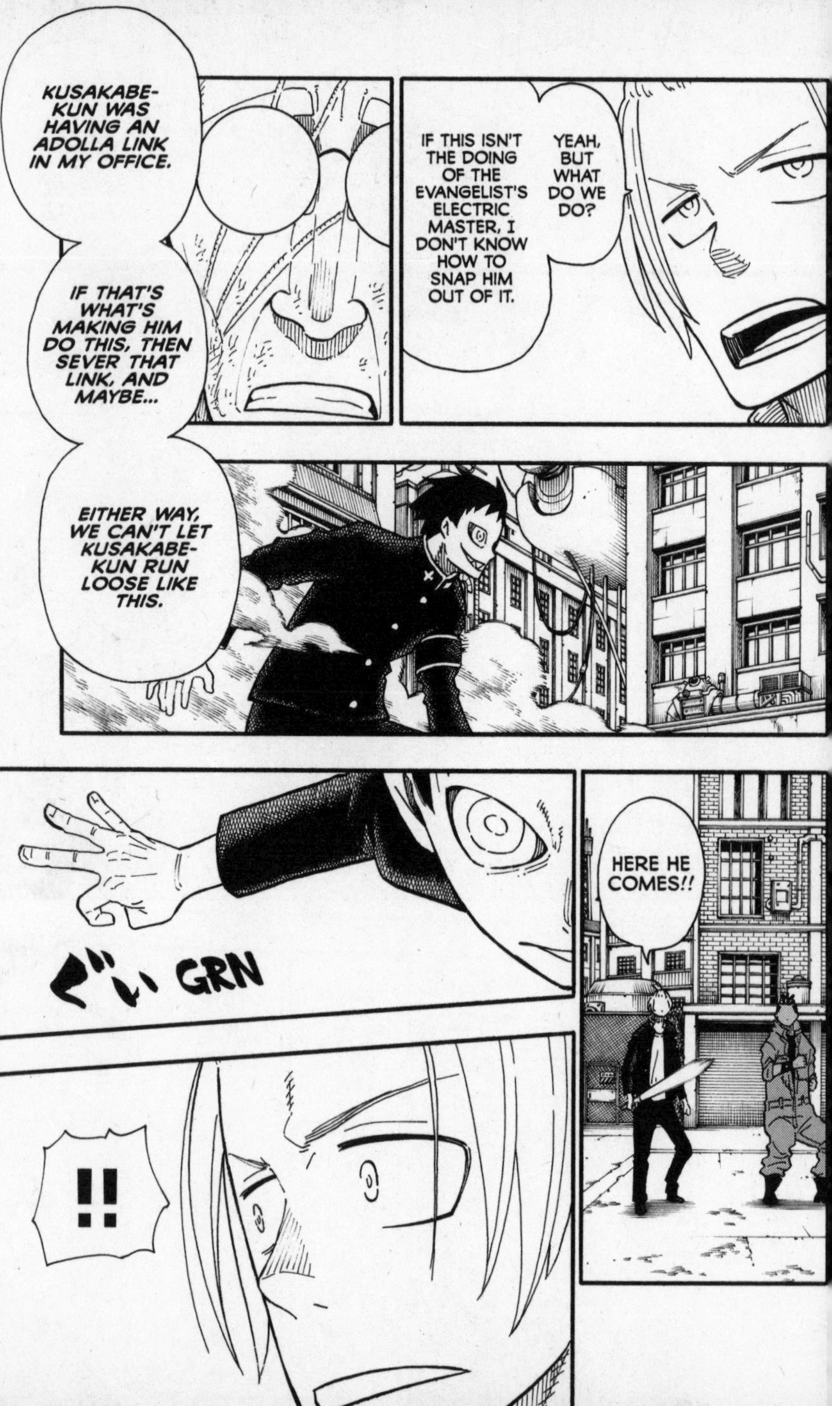
YEAH, BUT WHAT DO WE DO?
IF THIS ISN'T THE DOING OF THE EVANGELIST'S ELECTRIC MASTER, I DON'T KNOW HOW TO SNAP HIM OUT OF IT.
KUSAKABE-KUN WAS HAVING AN ADOLLA LINK IN MY OFFICE.
IF THAT'S WHAT'S MAKING HIM DO THIS, THEN SEVER THAT LINK, AND MAYBE...
EITHER WAY, WE CAN'T LET KUSAKABE-KUN RUN LOOSE LIKE THIS.
HERE HE COMES!!
GRN
!!

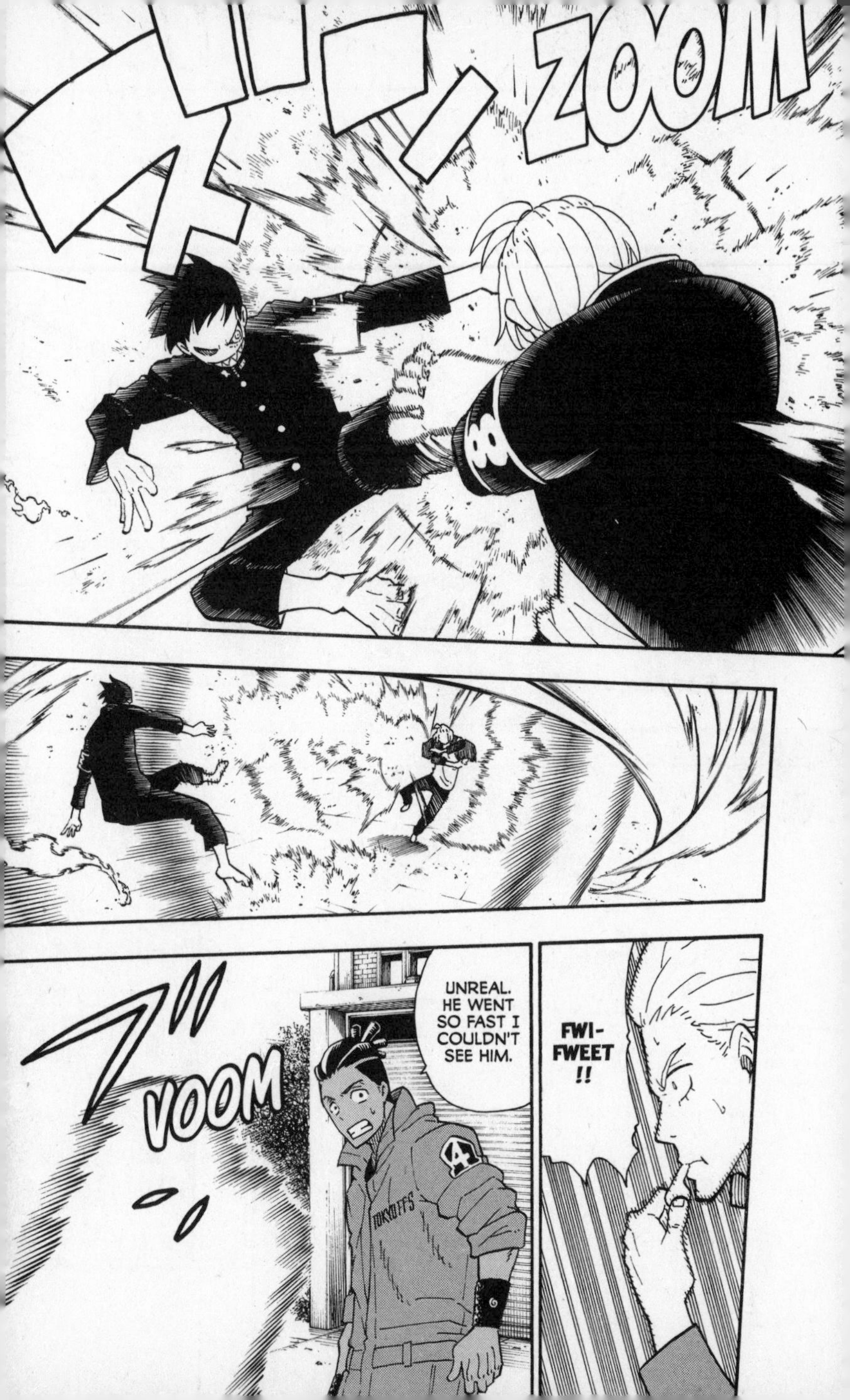
ZOOM
FWI-FWEET!!
UNREAL. HE WENT SO FAST I COULDN'T SEE HIM.
VOOM

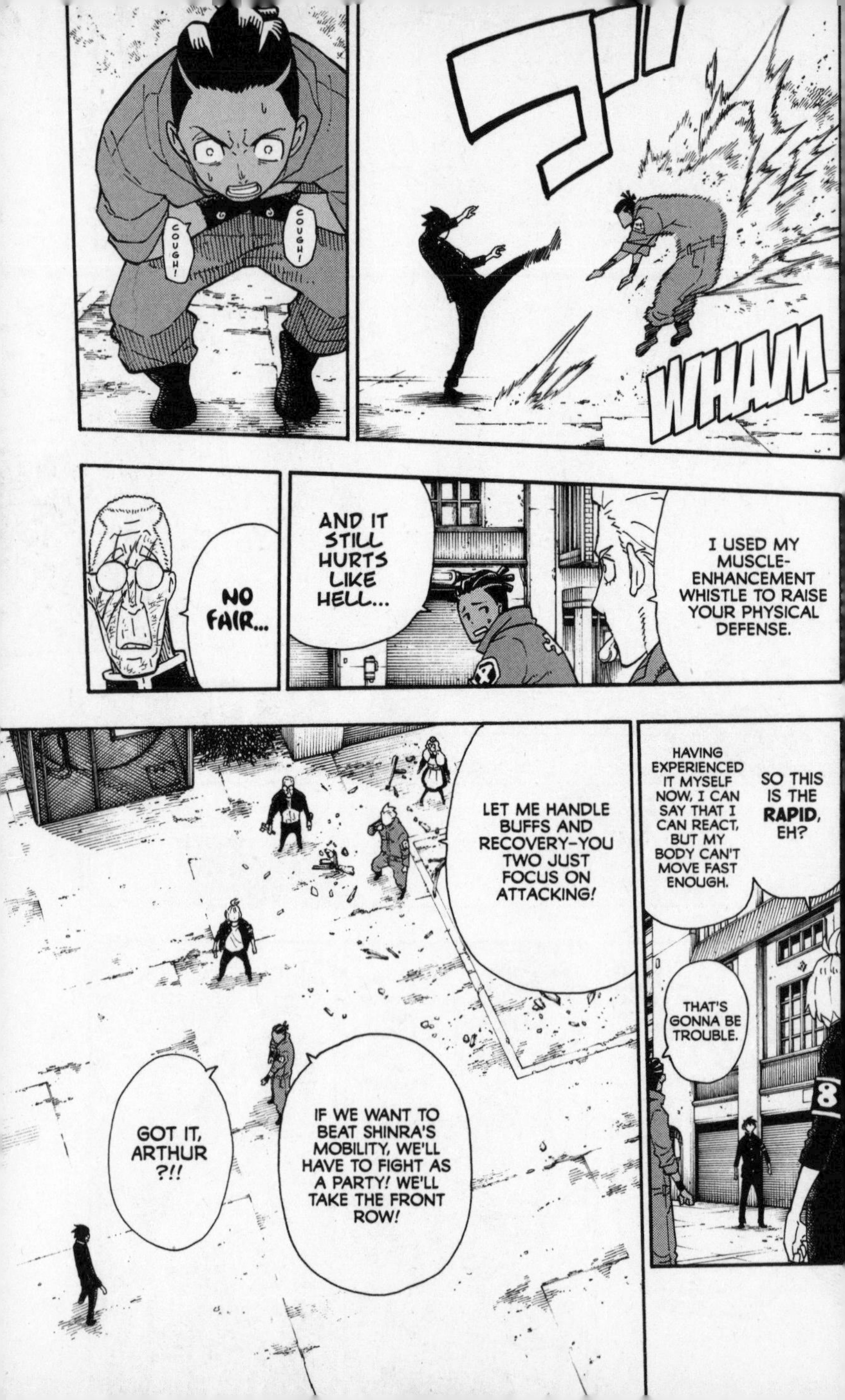
ゴ
WHAM
COUGH!
COUGH!
I USED MY MUSCLE-ENHANCEMENT WHISTLE TO RAISE YOUR PHYSICAL DEFENSE.
AND IT STILL HURTS LIKE HELL...
NO FAIR...
SO THIS IS THE **RAPID**, EH?
HAVING EXPERIENCED IT MYSELF NOW, I CAN SAY THAT I CAN REACT, BUT MY BODY CAN'T MOVE FAST ENOUGH.
THAT'S GONNA BE TROUBLE.
LET ME HANDLE BUFFS AND RECOVERY—YOU TWO JUST FOCUS ON ATTACKING!
IF WE WANT TO BEAT SHINRA'S MOBILITY, WE'LL HAVE TO FIGHT AS A PARTY! WE'LL TAKE THE FRONT ROW!
GOT IT, ARTHUR?!!

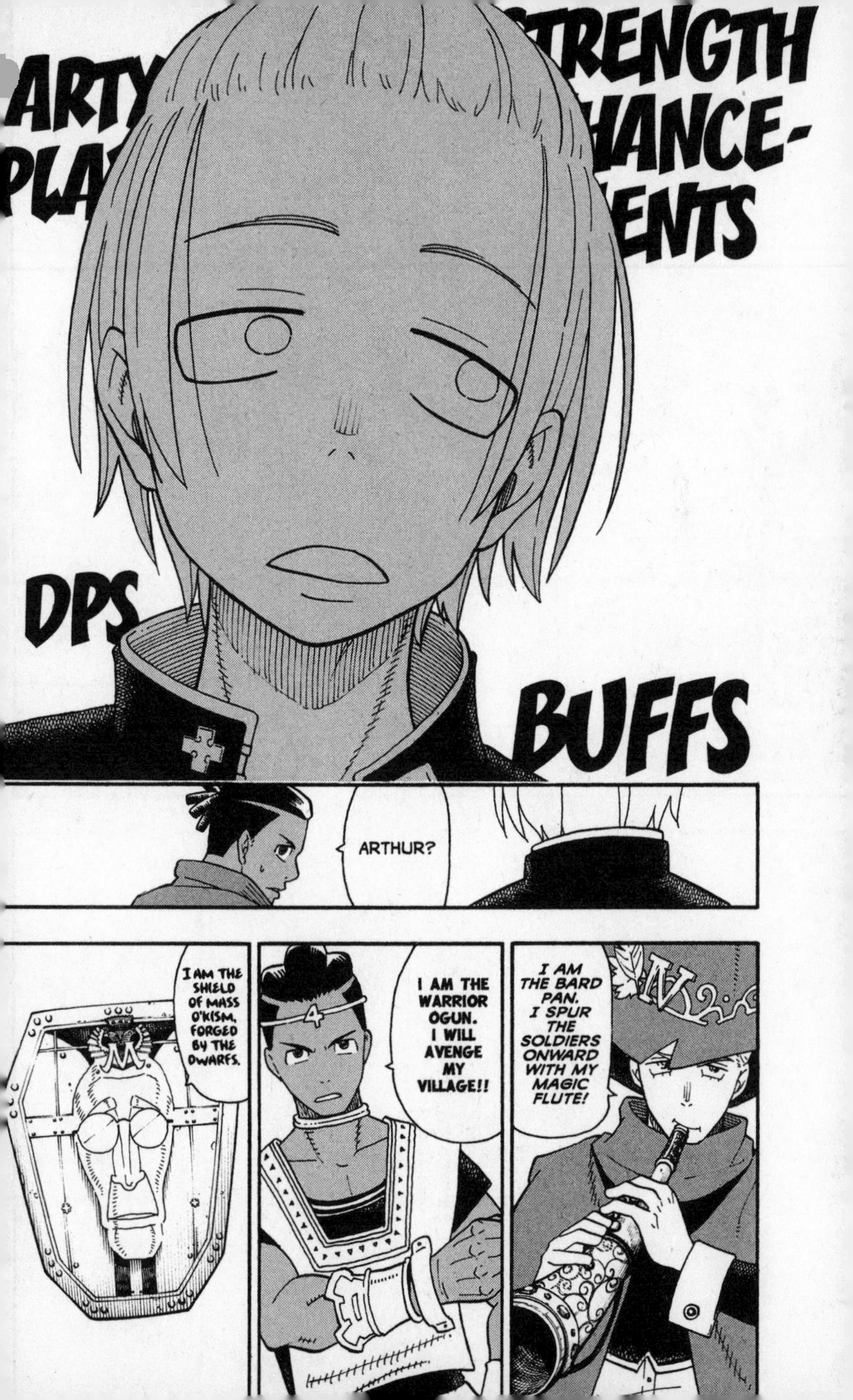
STRENGTH
BUFFS
DPS
ARTHUR?
I AM THE BARD PAN. I SPUR THE SOLDIERS ONWARD WITH MY MAGIC FLUTE!
I AM THE WARRIOR OGUN. I WILL AVENGE MY VILLAGE!!
I AM THE SHIELD OF MASS O'KISM, FORGED BY THE DWARFS.

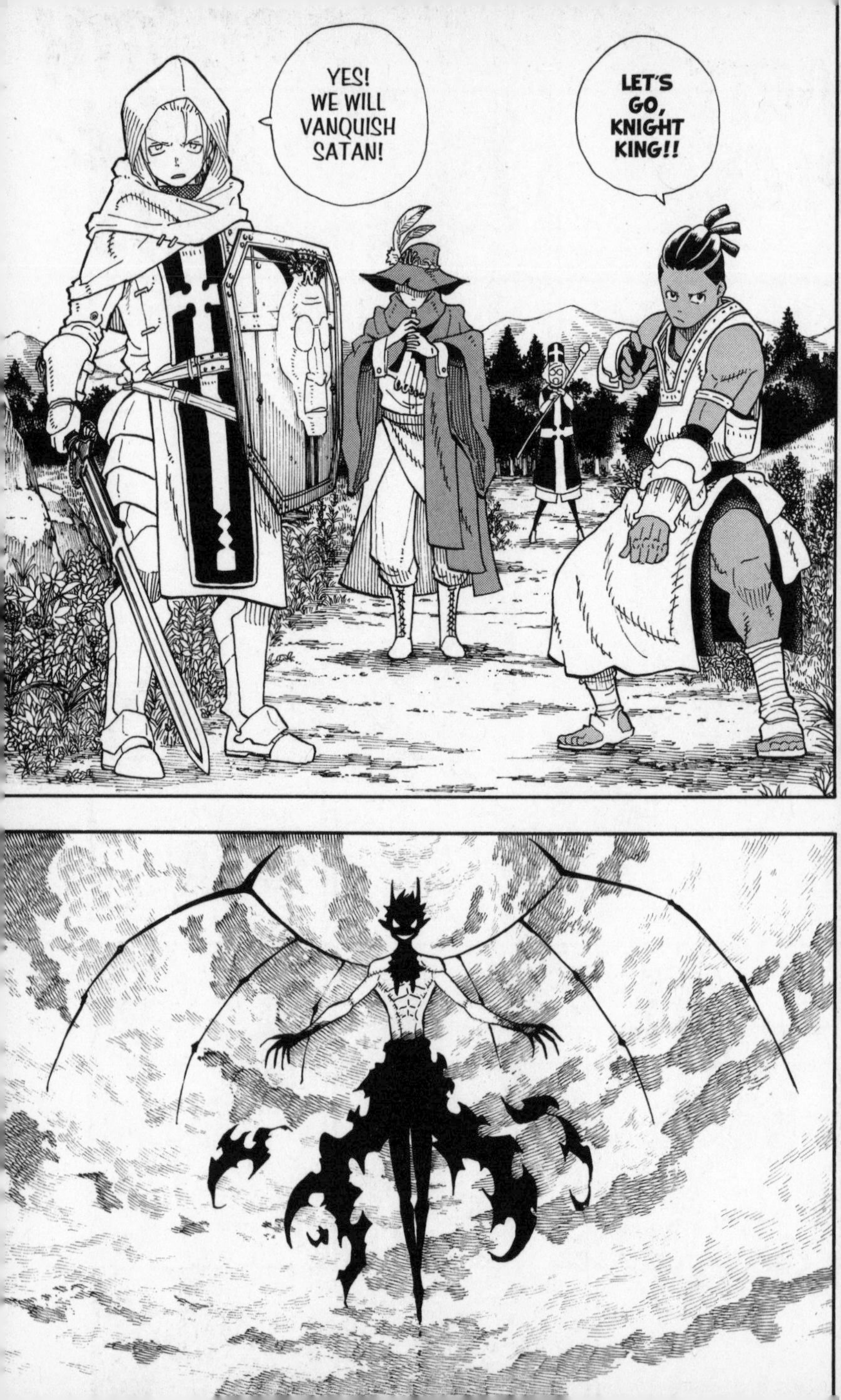
LET'S GO, KNIGHT KING!!
YES! WE WILL VANQUISH SATAN!

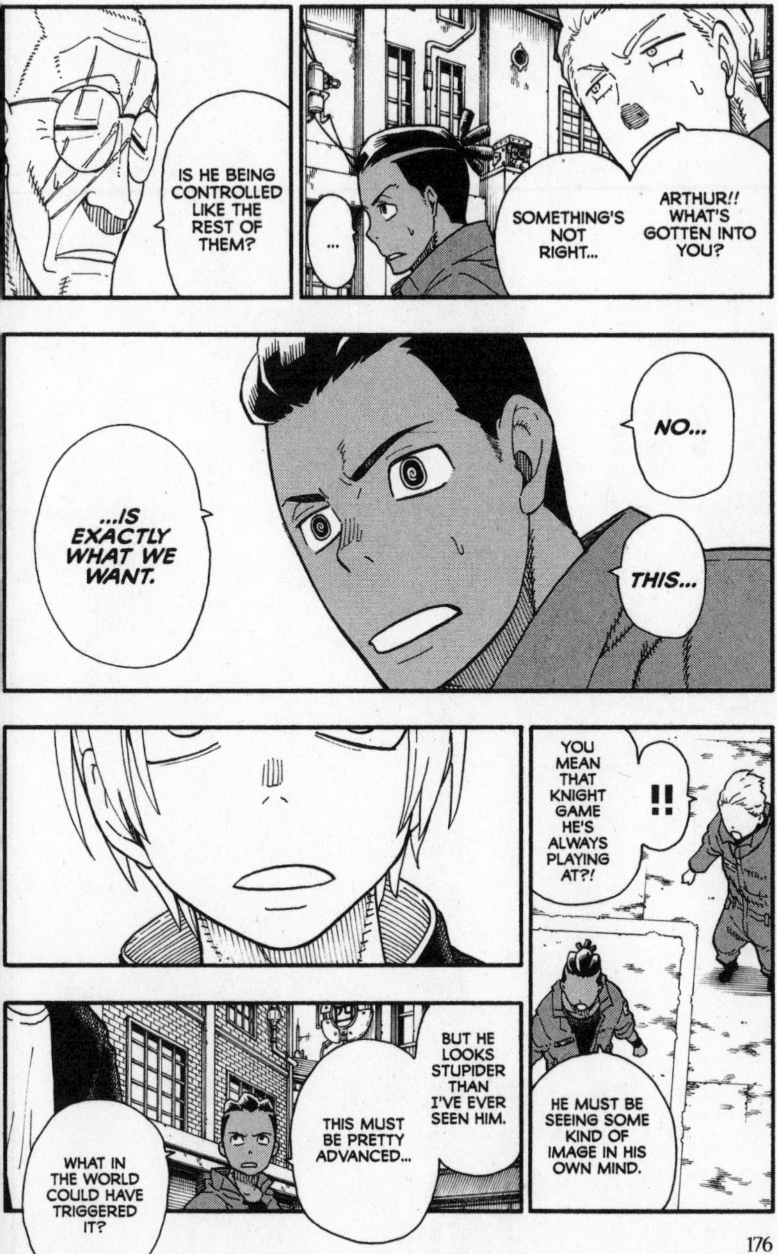
ARTHUR!! WHAT'S GOTTEN INTO YOU?
SOMETHING'S NOT RIGHT...
...
IS HE BEING CONTROLLED LIKE THE REST OF THEM?
NO...
THIS...
...IS EXACTLY WHAT WE WANT.
YOU MEAN THAT KNIGHT GAME HE'S ALWAYS PLAYING AT?!
!!
HE MUST BE SEEING SOME KIND OF IMAGE IN HIS OWN MIND.
BUT HE LOOKS STUPIDER THAN I'VE EVER SEEN HIM.
THIS MUST BE PRETTY ADVANCED...
WHAT IN THE WORLD COULD HAVE TRIGGERED IT?

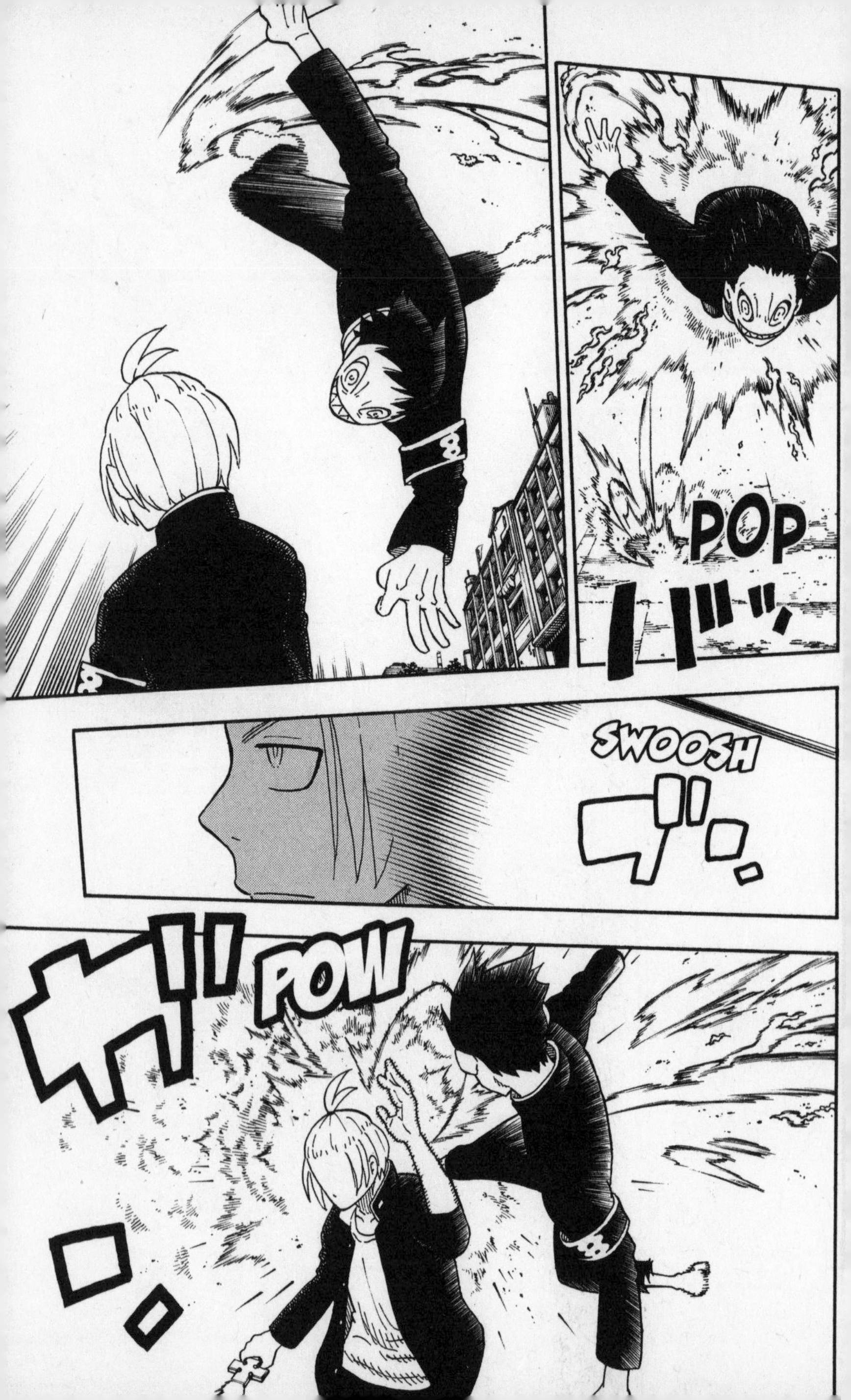
POP
SWOOSH
POW

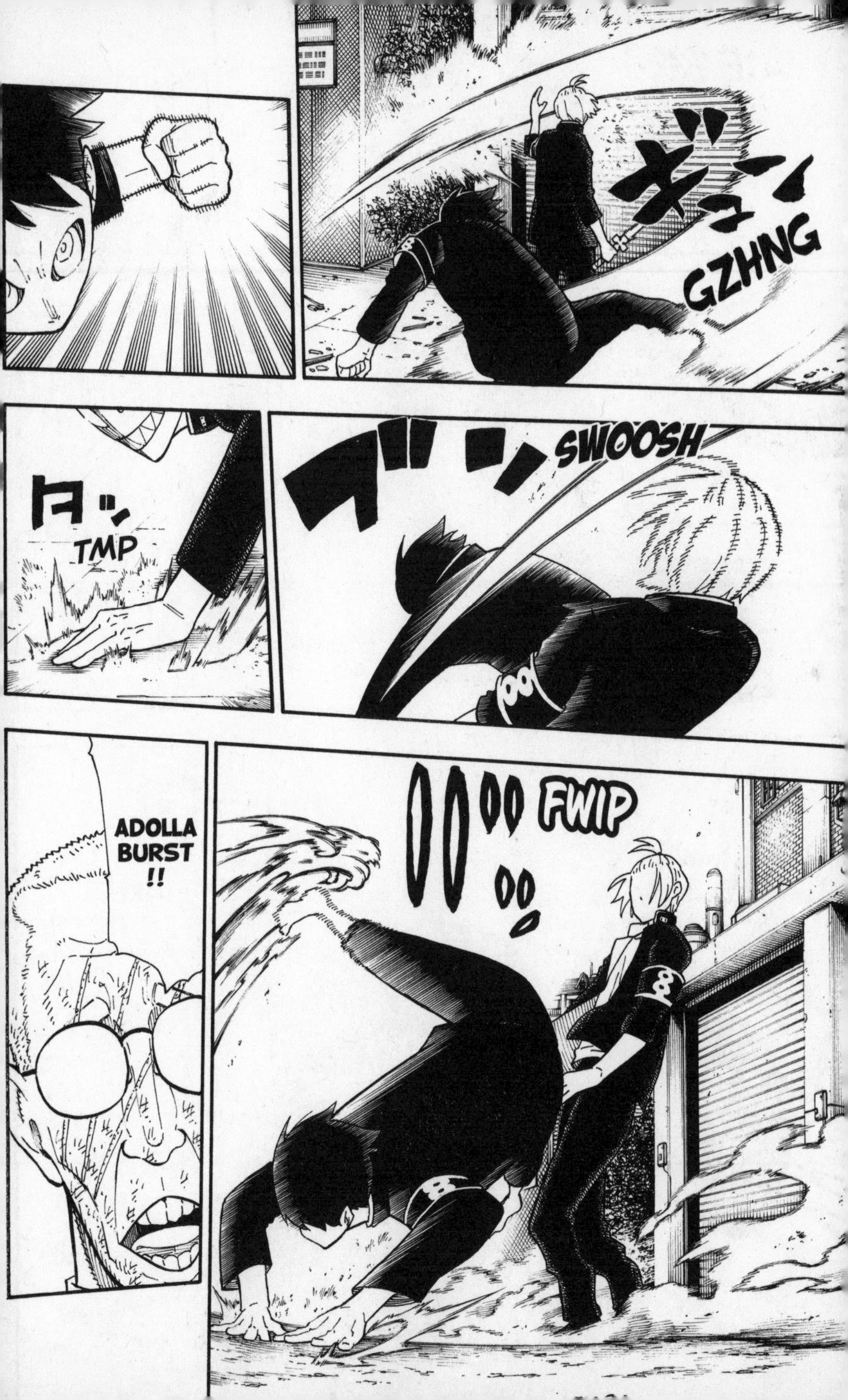
GZHNG
SWOOSH
TMP
FWIP
ADOLLA BURST !!

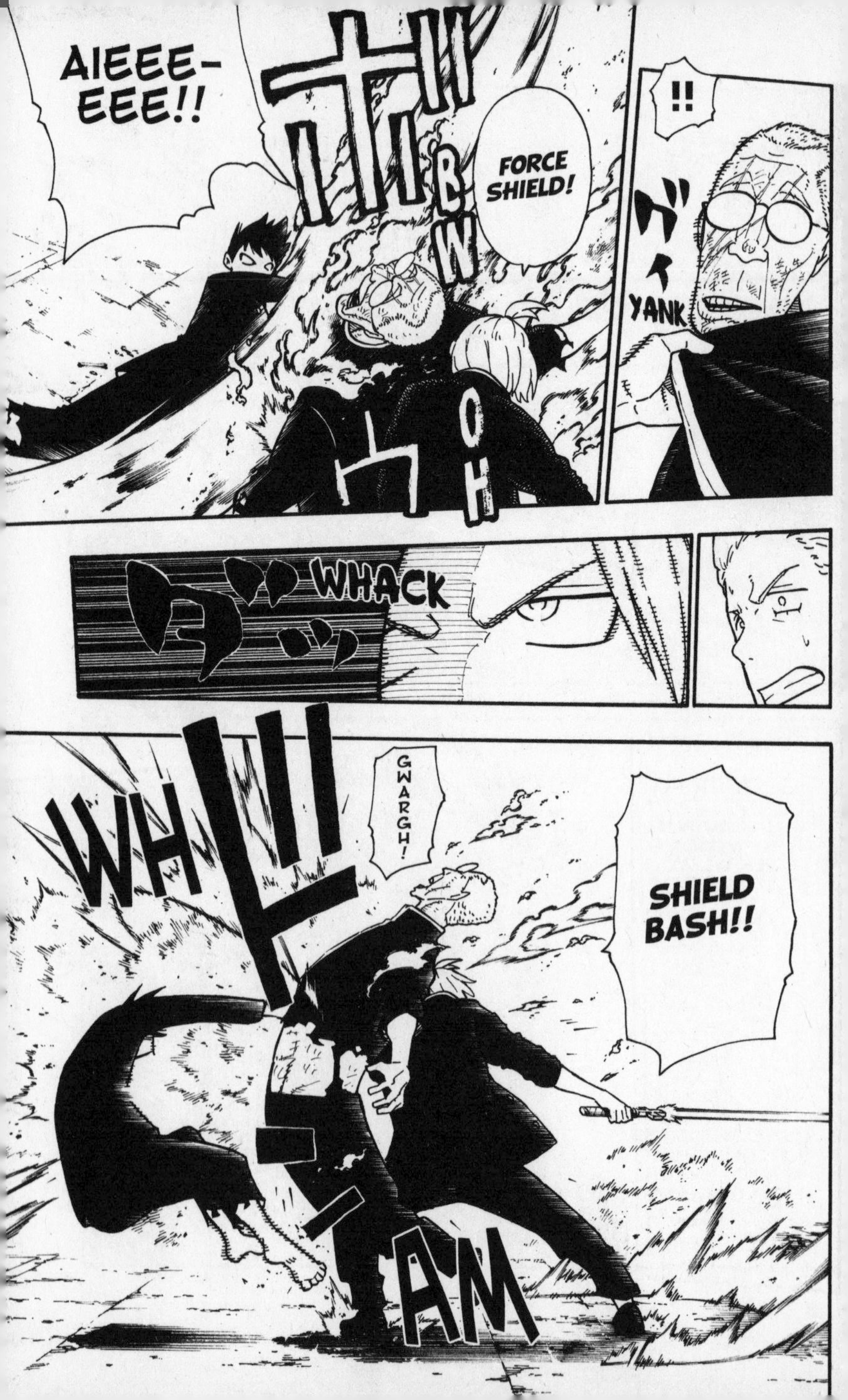
!!
YANK
FORCE SHIELD!
BWOH
AIEEE-EEE!!
WHACK
SHIELD BASH!!
GWARGH!
WHAM

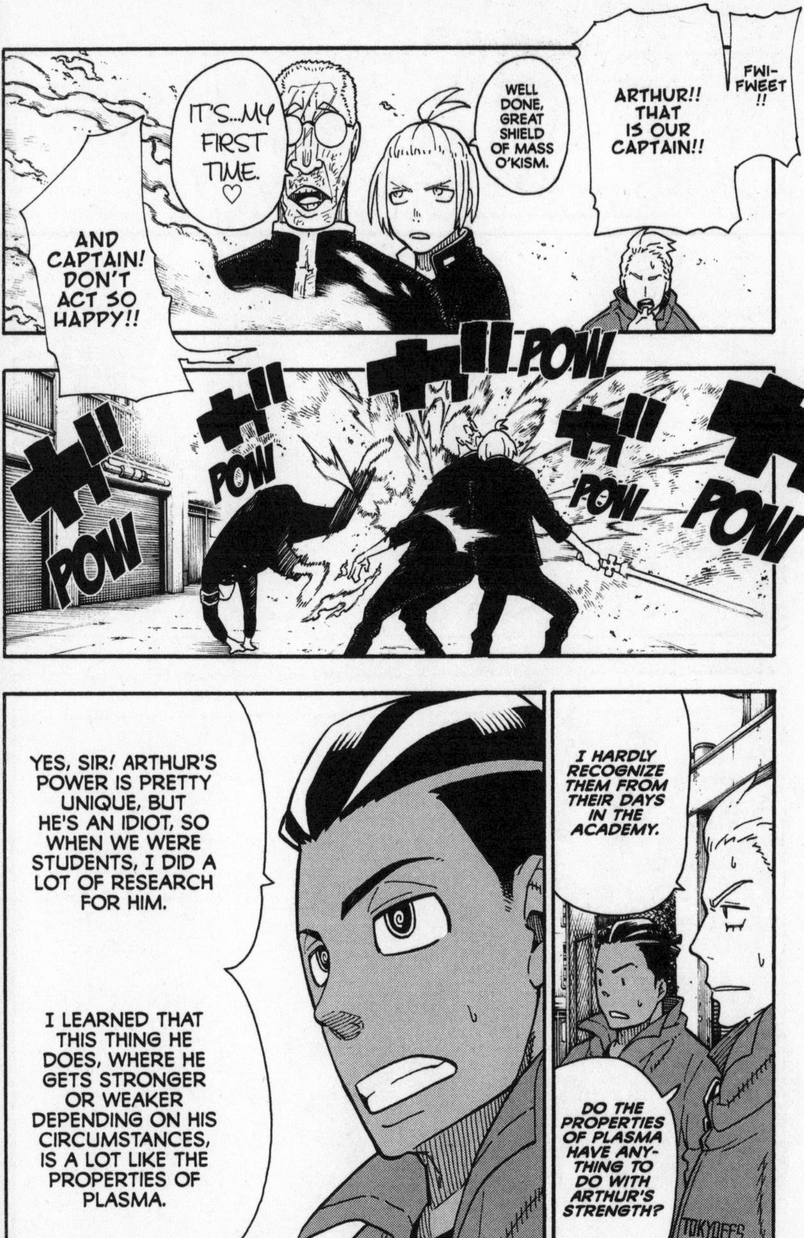
FWI-FWEET!!
ARTHUR!! THAT IS OUR CAPTAIN!!
WELL DONE, GREAT SHIELD OF MASS O'KISM.
IT'S...MY FIRST TIME. ♡
AND CAPTAIN! DON'T ACT SO HAPPY!!
POW
POW
POW
POW
POW
I HARDLY RECOGNIZE THEM FROM THEIR DAYS IN THE ACADEMY.
DO THE PROPERTIES OF PLASMA HAVE ANYTHING TO DO WITH ARTHUR'S STRENGTH?
TOKYOFFS
YES, SIR! ARTHUR'S POWER IS PRETTY UNIQUE, BUT HE'S AN IDIOT, SO WHEN WE WERE STUDENTS, I DID A LOT OF RESEARCH FOR HIM.
I LEARNED THAT THIS THING HE DOES, WHERE HE GETS STRONGER OR WEAKER DEPENDING ON HIS CIRCUMSTANCES, IS A LOT LIKE THE PROPERTIES OF PLASMA.

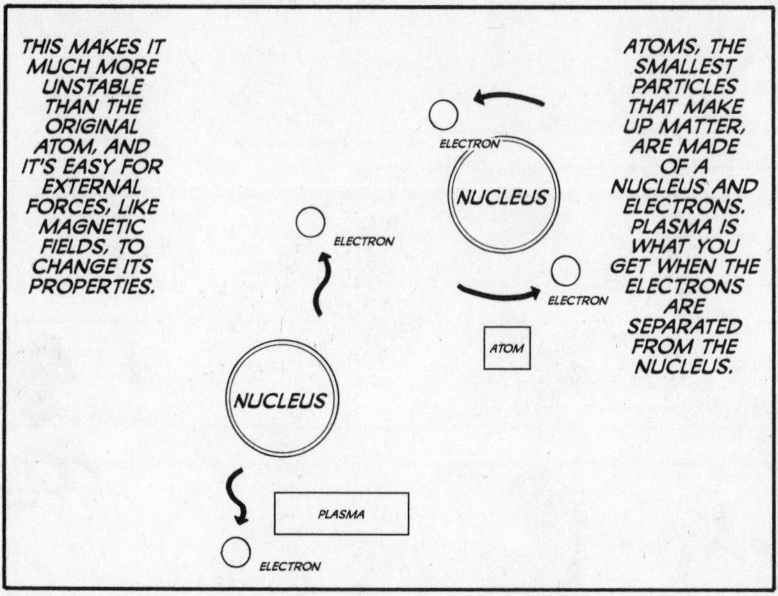
ATOMS, THE SMALLEST PARTICLES THAT MAKE UP MATTER, ARE MADE OF A NUCLEUS AND ELECTRONS. PLASMA IS WHAT YOU GET WHEN THE ELECTRONS ARE SEPARATED FROM THE NUCLEUS.
ELECTRON
NUCLEUS
ELECTRON
ATOM
ELECTRON
NUCLEUS
PLASMA
ELECTRON
THIS MAKES IT MUCH MORE UNSTABLE THAN THE ORIGINAL ATOM, AND IT'S EASY FOR EXTERNAL FORCES, LIKE MAGNETIC FIELDS, TO CHANGE ITS PROPERTIES.

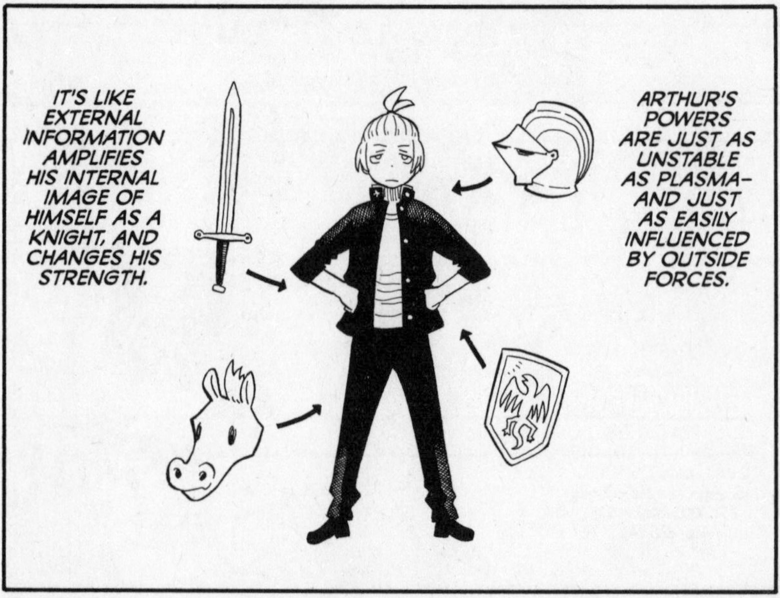
ARTHUR'S POWERS ARE JUST AS UNSTABLE AS PLASMA– AND JUST AS EASILY INFLUENCED BY OUTSIDE FORCES.
IT'S LIKE EXTERNAL INFORMATION AMPLIFIES HIS INTERNAL IMAGE OF HIMSELF AS A KNIGHT, AND CHANGES HIS STRENGTH.

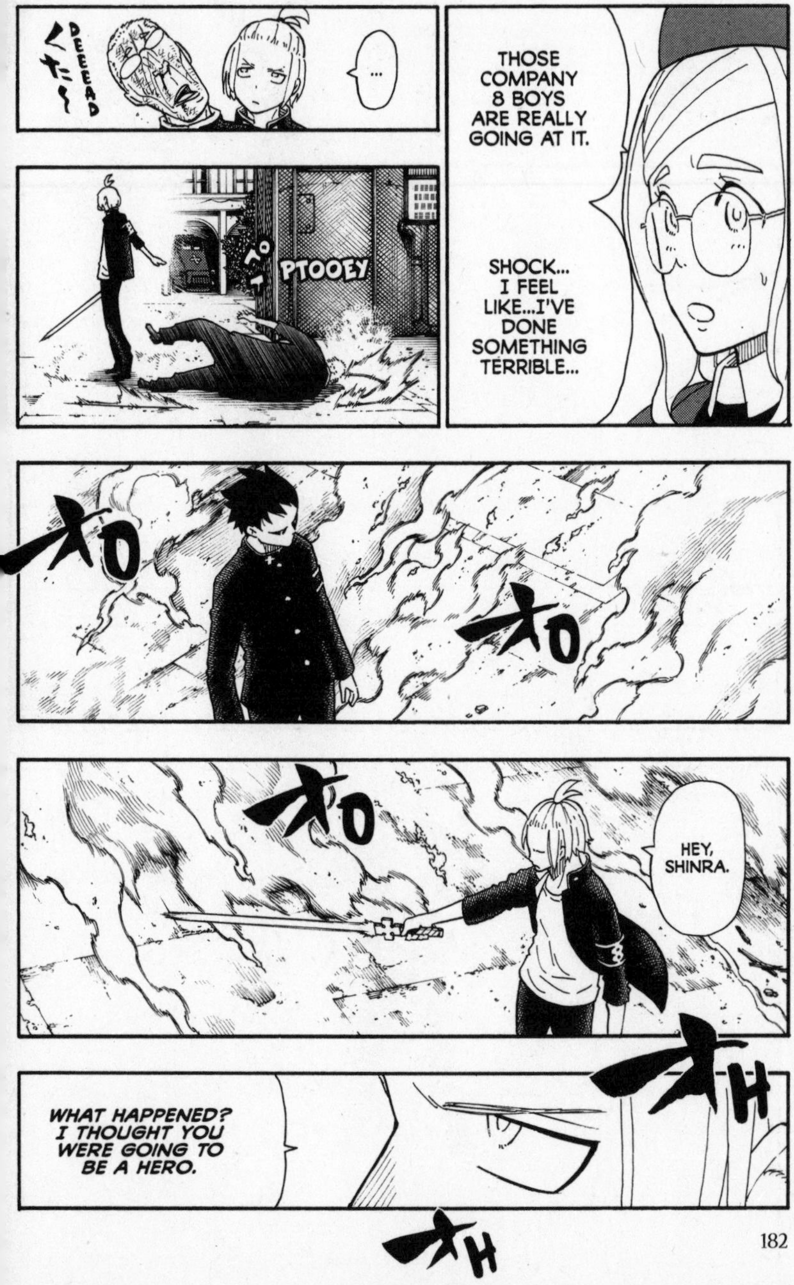
THOSE COMPANY 8 BOYS ARE REALLY GOING AT IT.
SHOCK... I FEEL LIKE...I'VE DONE SOMETHING TERRIBLE...
...
DEEEEAD
PTOOEY
HEY, SHINRA.
WHAT HAPPENED? I THOUGHT YOU WERE GOING TO BE A HERO.

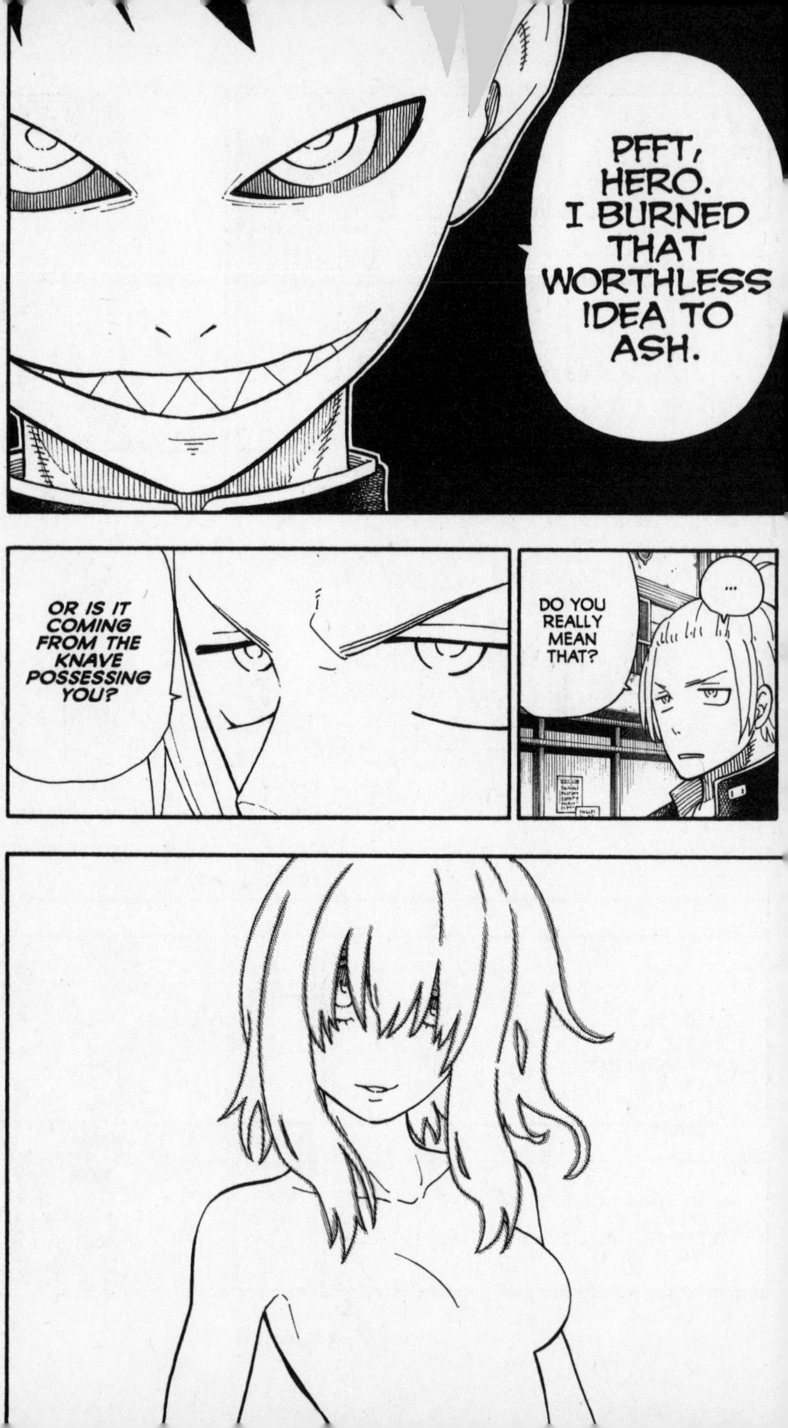
PFFT, HERO. I BURNED THAT WORTHLESS IDEA TO ASH.
...
DO YOU REALLY MEAN THAT?
OR IS IT COMING FROM THE KNAVE POSSESSING YOU?

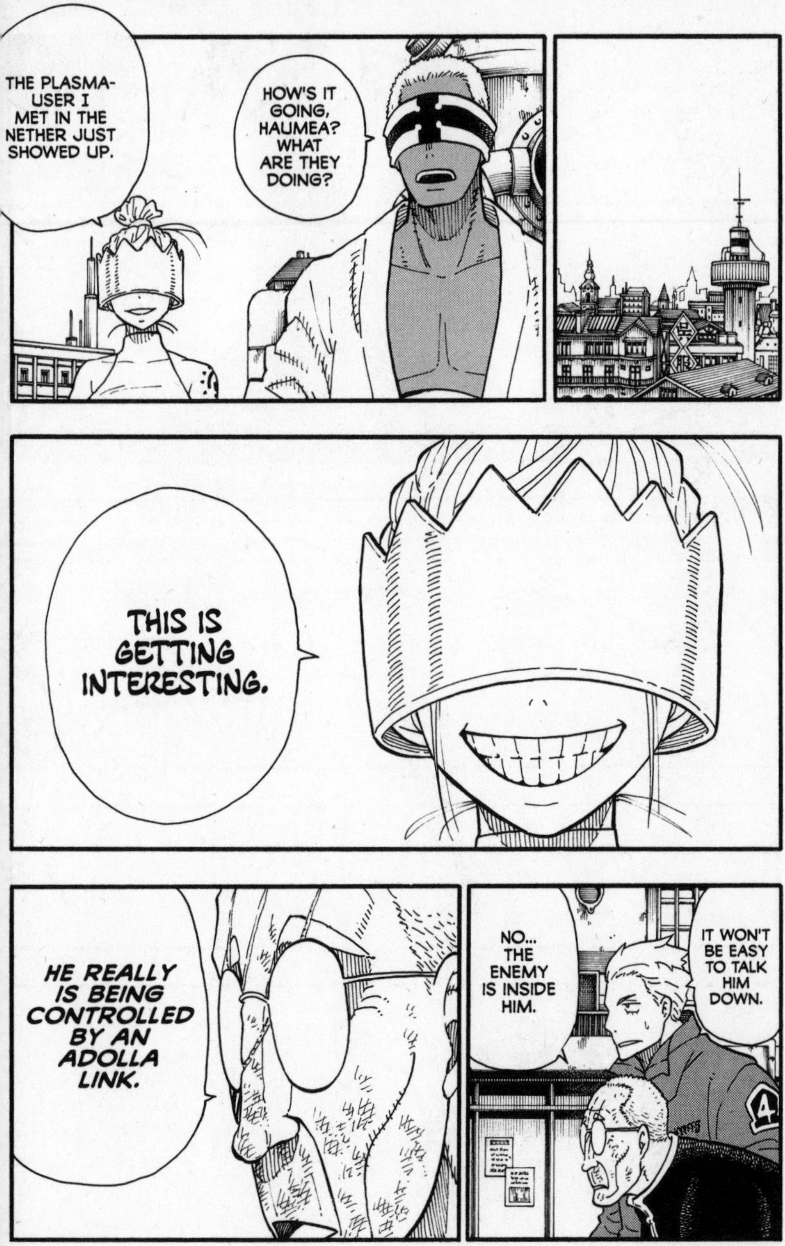
HOW'S IT GOING, HAUMEA? WHAT ARE THEY DOING?
THE PLASMA-USER I MET IN THE NETHER JUST SHOWED UP.
THIS IS GETTING INTERESTING.
IT WON'T BE EASY TO TALK HIM DOWN.
NO... THE ENEMY IS INSIDE HIM.
HE REALLY IS BEING CONTROLLED BY AN ADOLLA LINK.

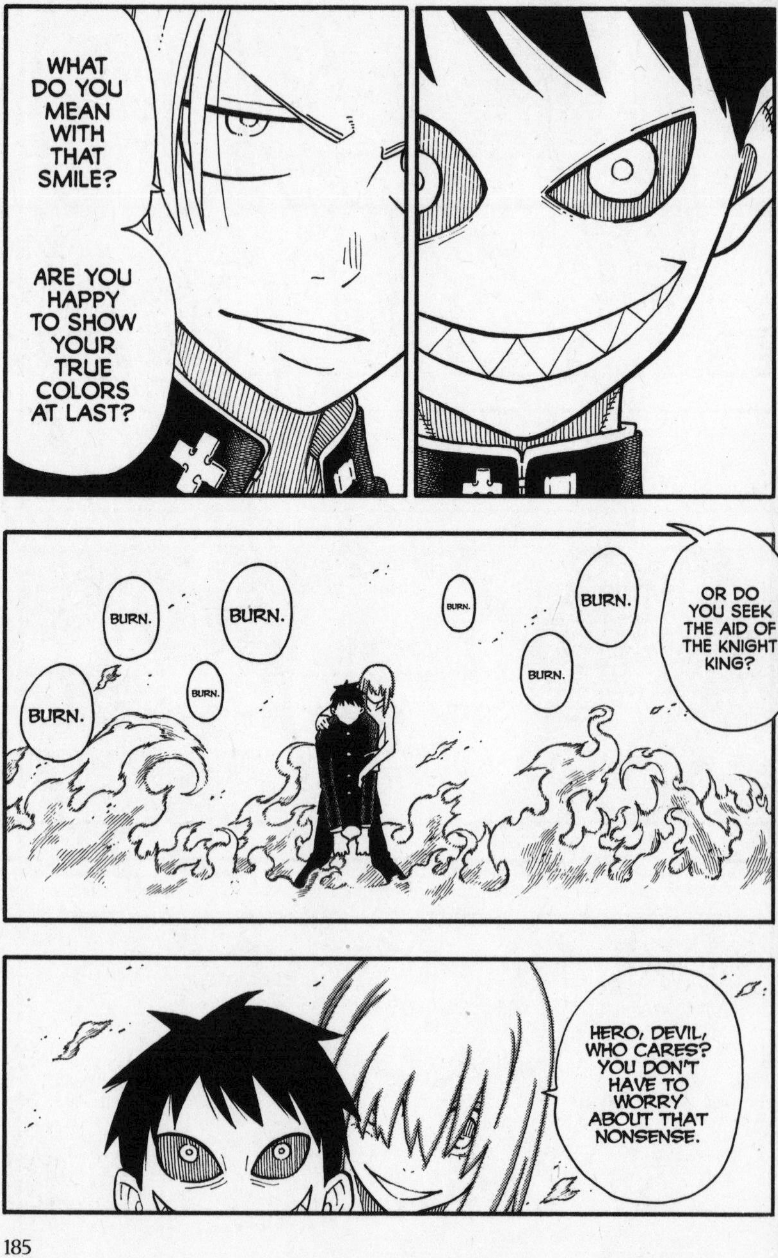
WHAT DO YOU MEAN WITH THAT SMILE?
ARE YOU HAPPY TO SHOW YOUR TRUE COLORS AT LAST?
OR DO YOU SEEK THE AID OF THE KNIGHT KING?
BURN.
BURN.
BURN.
BURN.
BURN.
BURN.
BURN.
HERO, DEVIL, WHO CARES? YOU DON'T HAVE TO WORRY ABOUT THAT NONSENSE.

I KNOW WHAT YOU WANT.

I KNOW WHERE YOUR MOTHER IS.

I KNOW HOW YOU CAN FIND HER.

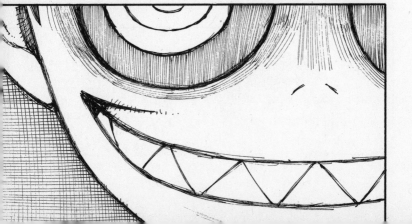

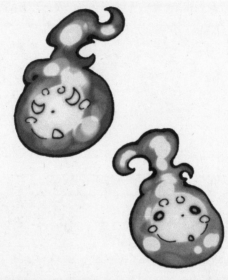

TO BE CONTINUED IN VOLUME 12!!

Translation Notes:

January and August, page 69

Before the Solar Era, many of the English names for months came from Roman gods and rulers, or just from Latin numbers. They may or may not have been changed when the Solar Era began, but in Japanese, the months are all named for the order they appear in the calendar: Ichigatsu (Month One), Nigatsu (Month Two), etc. This did not change with the new era, so there's no telling what the real English names of these months would be, but the translators have opted to use what the readers will readily recognize. Of course, naming the months after numbers makes it very easy to determine which company will adorn the calendar page of which month.

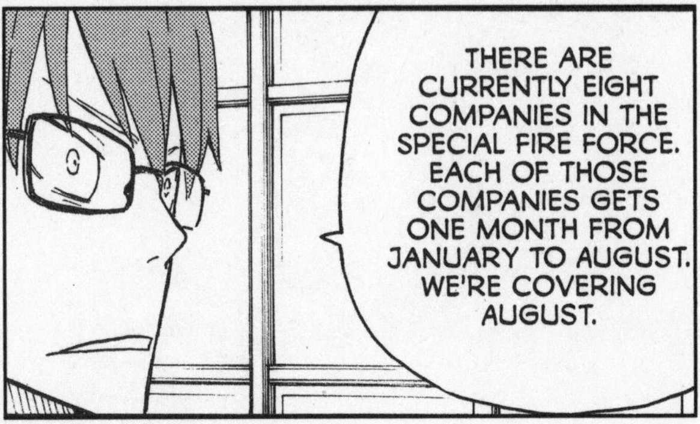
THERE ARE CURRENTLY EIGHT COMPANIES IN THE SPECIAL FIRE FORCE. EACH OF THOSE COMPANIES GETS ONE MONTH FROM JANUARY TO AUGUST. WE'RE COVERING AUGUST.

Welcome to the gun shobra, page 83

The translators would like to apologize for their very sorry attempt at recreating this pun. The Japanese word for "flexed biceps" is *chikara-kobu*, which literally means "strength lump." Captain Ōbi added a "-ra" to the end to make it *chikara-kobura*, which is now a portmanteau of "flexed bicep" and "cobra."

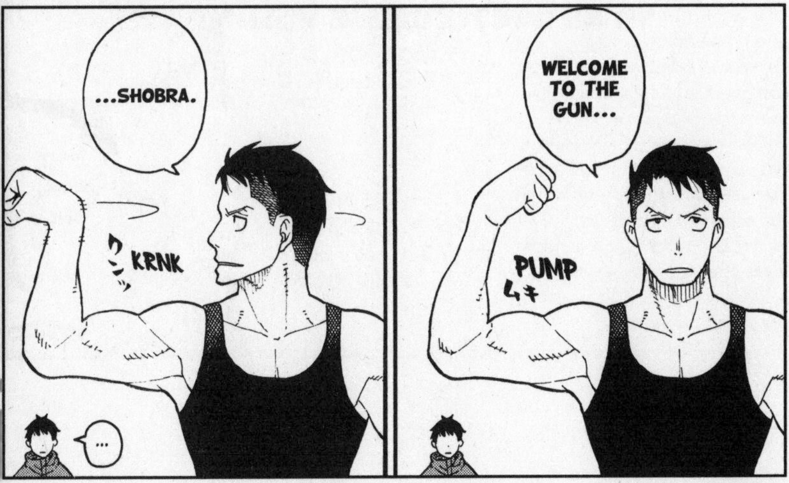
WELCOME TO THE GUN...
PUMP
...
...SHOBRA.
KRNK
...

Hat: Nudist Bitch

I'M TERRIBLY SORRY, SIR.

スーディストビーチク

Nudist Bitch, page 102

The Japanese on Hinawa's hat here is actually "*nudisto bichiku*," with "*bichiku*" being a portmanteau of the word "beach" and the swapped syllables of the word "*chikubi*," (meaning "teats.") Whether it's Nudist Bitch or Nudist Beach-Teats, Hinawa's new hat is definitely unacceptable office wear.

Where would he go for research, page 190

In Japan, chapters of manga are published in a magazine on a weekly or monthly basis, and when enough chapters have been released, they are compiled into a graphic novel. Every so often, a magazine will come out and be missing a chapter of, perhaps, a favorite manga. The editors will inform the readers that the author of said manga has taken a break for research purposes. This is a code meaning, "The artist missed the deadline."

THERE HAVEN'T BEEN ANY SUDDEN ILLNESSES OR SUDDEN DISAPPEARANCES MAKING THE READERS THINK, "WHERE IN THE HECK WOULD HE BE GOING FOR RESEARCH?"

THE SERIES HAS GONE ON WITH PERFECT ATTENDANCE.

TWO YEA WITH NC ACCIDEN AND NO VIOLATION

189

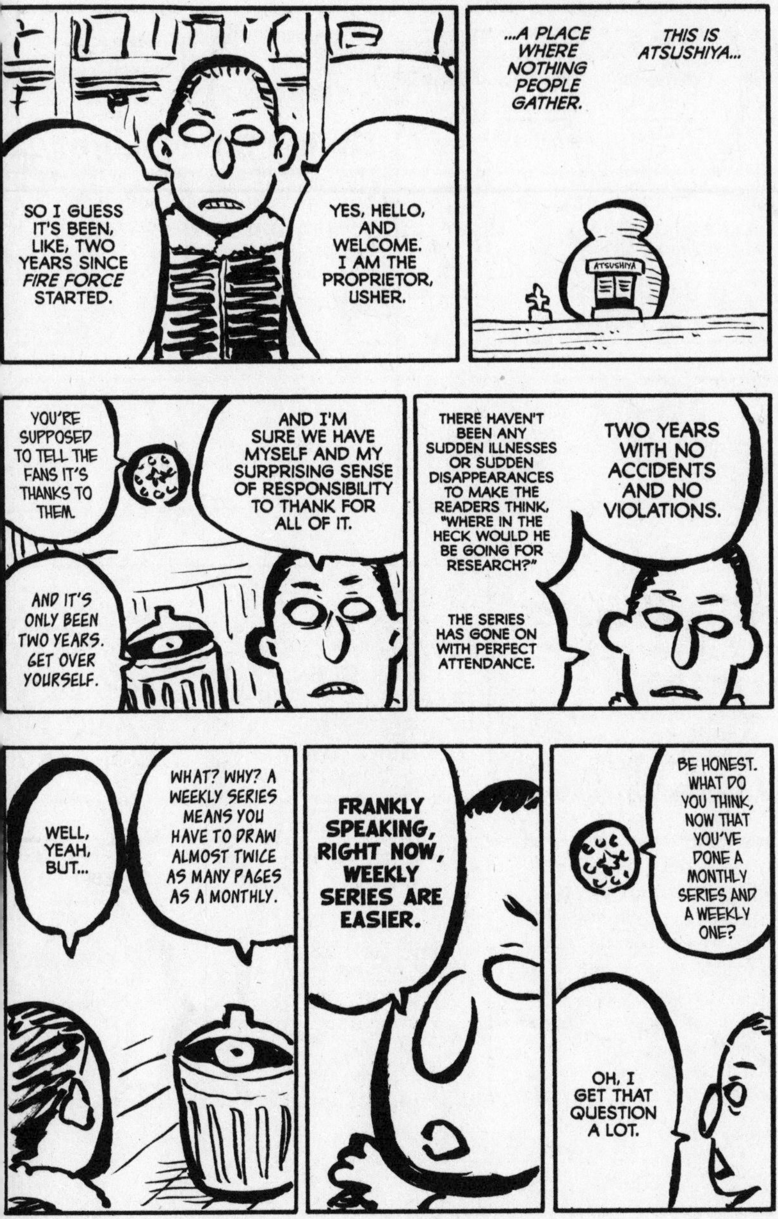
THIS IS ATSUSHIYA...
...A PLACE WHERE NOTHING PEOPLE GATHER.
ATSUSHIYA
YES, HELLO, AND WELCOME. I AM THE PROPRIETOR, USHER.
SO I GUESS IT'S BEEN, LIKE, TWO YEARS SINCE *FIRE FORCE* STARTED.
TWO YEARS WITH NO ACCIDENTS AND NO VIOLATIONS.
THERE HAVEN'T BEEN ANY SUDDEN ILLNESSES OR SUDDEN DISAPPEARANCES TO MAKE THE READERS THINK, "WHERE IN THE HECK WOULD HE BE GOING FOR RESEARCH?"
THE SERIES HAS GONE ON WITH PERFECT ATTENDANCE.
AND I'M SURE WE HAVE MYSELF AND MY SURPRISING SENSE OF RESPONSIBILITY TO THANK FOR ALL OF IT.
YOU'RE SUPPOSED TO TELL THE FANS IT'S THANKS TO THEM.
AND IT'S ONLY BEEN TWO YEARS. GET OVER YOURSELF.
BE HONEST. WHAT DO YOU THINK, NOW THAT YOU'VE DONE A MONTHLY SERIES AND A WEEKLY ONE?
OH, I GET THAT QUESTION A LOT.
FRANKLY SPEAKING, RIGHT NOW, WEEKLY SERIES ARE EASIER.
WHAT? WHY? A WEEKLY SERIES MEANS YOU HAVE TO DRAW ALMOST TWICE AS MANY PAGES AS A MONTHLY.
WELL, YEAH, BUT...

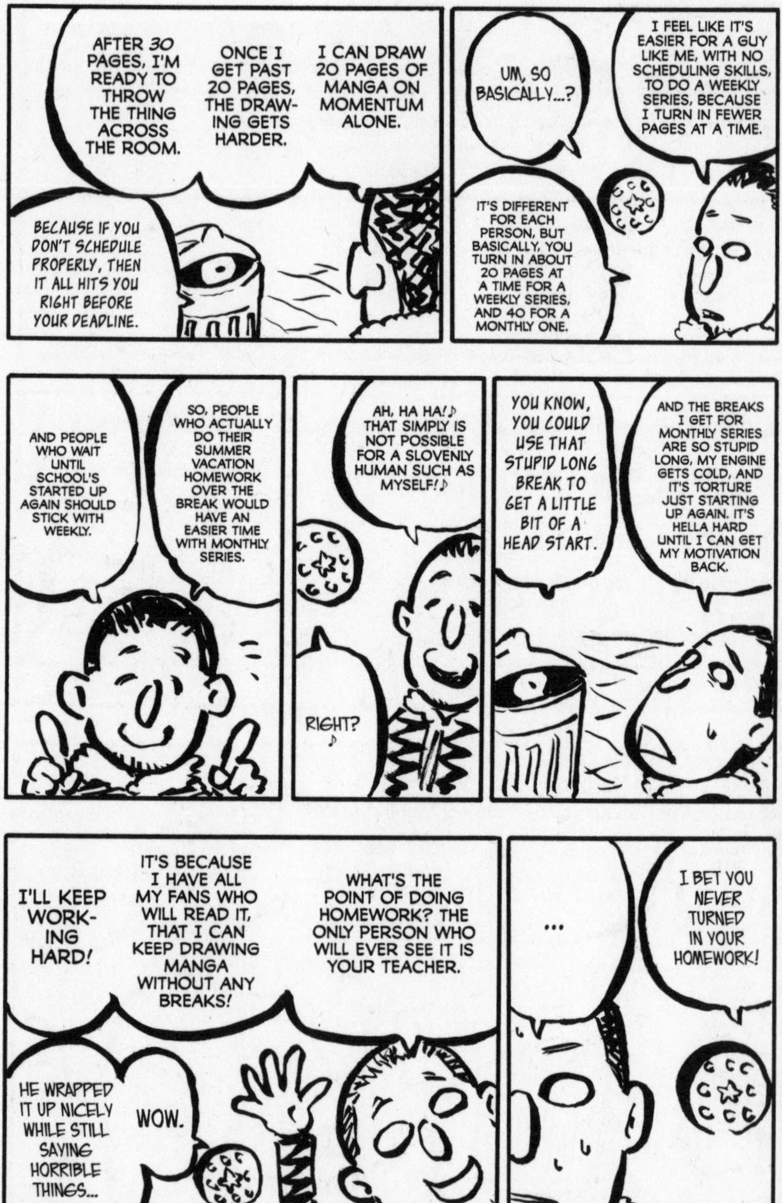
I FEEL LIKE IT'S EASIER FOR A GUY LIKE ME, WITH NO SCHEDULING SKILLS, TO DO A WEEKLY SERIES, BECAUSE I TURN IN FEWER PAGES AT A TIME.
UM, SO BASICALLY...?
IT'S DIFFERENT FOR EACH PERSON, BUT BASICALLY, YOU TURN IN ABOUT 20 PAGES AT A TIME FOR A WEEKLY SERIES, AND 40 FOR A MONTHLY ONE.
I CAN DRAW 20 PAGES OF MANGA ON MOMENTUM ALONE.
ONCE I GET PAST 20 PAGES, THE DRAW-ING GETS HARDER.
AFTER 30 PAGES, I'M READY TO THROW THE THING ACROSS THE ROOM.
BECAUSE IF YOU DON'T SCHEDULE PROPERLY, THEN IT ALL HITS YOU RIGHT BEFORE YOUR DEADLINE.
AND THE BREAKS I GET FOR MONTHLY SERIES ARE SO STUPID LONG, MY ENGINE GETS COLD, AND IT'S TORTURE JUST STARTING UP AGAIN. IT'S HELLA HARD UNTIL I CAN GET MY MOTIVATION BACK.
YOU KNOW, YOU COULD USE THAT STUPID LONG BREAK TO GET A LITTLE BIT OF A HEAD START.
AH, HA HA!♪ THAT SIMPLY IS NOT POSSIBLE FOR A SLOVENLY HUMAN SUCH AS MYSELF!♪
RIGHT? ♪
SO, PEOPLE WHO ACTUALLY DO THEIR SUMMER VACATION HOMEWORK OVER THE BREAK WOULD HAVE AN EASIER TIME WITH MONTHLY SERIES.
AND PEOPLE WHO WAIT UNTIL SCHOOL'S STARTED UP AGAIN SHOULD STICK WITH WEEKLY.
I BET YOU NEVER TURNED IN YOUR HOMEWORK!
...
WHAT'S THE POINT OF DOING HOMEWORK? THE ONLY PERSON WHO WILL EVER SEE IT IS YOUR TEACHER.
IT'S BECAUSE I HAVE ALL MY FANS WHO WILL READ IT, THAT I CAN KEEP DRAWING MANGA WITHOUT ANY BREAKS!
I'LL KEEP WORK-ING HARD!
WOW.
HE WRAPPED IT UP NICELY WHILE STILL SAYING HORRIBLE THINGS...

Fire Force volume 11 is a work of fiction. Names, characters, places, and incidents are the products of the author's imagination or are used fictitiously. Any resemblance to actual events, locales, or persons, living or dead, is entirely coincidental.

A Kodansha Comics Trade Paperback Original.

Published in the United States by Kodansha Comics, an imprint of Kodansha USA Publishing, LLC, New York.

Publication rights for this English edition arranged through Kodansha Ltd., Tokyo.

First published in Japan in 2017 by Kodansha Ltd., Tokyo.

ISBN 978-1-63236-622-1

Printed in the United States of America.

www.kodanshacomics.com

9 8 7 6 5 4 3

Translation: Alethea Nibley & Athena Nibley
Lettering: AndWorld Design
Editing: Lauren Scanlan
Kodansha Comics edition cover design: Phil Balsman